G000123712

NEVER CALL RETREAT

ALSO BY J. LEE THOMPSON

Theodore Roosevelt Abroad: Nature, Empire and the Journey of an American President (2010)

A Wider Patriotism: Alfred Milner and the British Empire (2007)

Forgotten Patriot: A Life of Alfred, Viscount Milner of St James's and Cape Town (2006)

Northcliffe: Press Baron in Politics, 1865–1922 (2000)

Politicians, the Press and Propaganda: Lord Northcliffe and the Great War, 1914–1919 (1999)

NEVER CALL RETREAT

THEODORE ROOSEVELT AND THE GREAT WAR

J. Lee Thompson

NEVER CALL RETREAT
Copyright © J. Lee Thompson, 2013

All rights reserved.

First published in 2013 by PALGRAVE MACMILLAN® in the United
States—a division of St. Martin's Press LLC, 175 Fifth Avenue, New York, NY
10010.

Where this book is distributed in the UK, Europe and the rest of the world,
this is by Palgrave Macmillan, a division of Macmillan Publishers Limited,
registered in England, company number 785998, of Houndmills, Basingstoke,
Hampshire RG21 6XS.

Palgrave Macmillan is the global academic imprint of the above companies and
has companies and representatives throughout the world.

Palgrave® and Macmillan® are registered trademarks in the United States, the
United Kingdom, Europe and other countries.

ISBN: 978-1-137-30652-4

Library of Congress Cataloging-in-Publication Data is available from the
Library of Congress.

A catalogue record of the book is available from the British Library.

Design by Scribe Inc.

First edition: December 2013

10 9 8 7 6 5 4 3 2 1

To Claudette and Jan

CONTENTS

Preface and Acknowledgments

> It is a very unjust world in which my sons and their wives and their
> mother and I have to pay for the slothful and utterly selfish ambitions of a
> cold-blooded and unprincipled demagogue. History may never discover
> it; but when this war is over I shall write a full and truthful record of why
> we went in late and so unprepared and of the incredible baseness which
> lay behind.
>
> —TR to Archibald Roosevelt, February 8, 1918

Theodore Roosevelt did not live long enough to write his promised exposé
of what he considered the many sins of Woodrow Wilson before and after the
United States entered World War I. In fact, down to the present, the only
book-length work devoted solely to TR and the Great War has been Hermann Hagedorn's 1940 *The Bugle That Woke America: The Saga of Theodore
Roosevelt's Last Battle for His Country*, a work meant to rouse America to
international dangers in the same way its subject had tried with mixed success
from 1914 until his death in January 1919.

The reasons for this neglect are many. First of all, this period in Roosevelt's life is most often seen as an aberration in an otherwise brilliant and
noteworthy career. In the war years, so the received wisdom goes, TR lost his
equilibrium out of a poisonous combination of political jealousy, his warrior's
lust for battle, and his all-consuming hatred for Woodrow Wilson—all of
which combined to drive him at least a bit mad. Consequently, this is a period
in TR's life given relatively short shrift, even in the biographical works that
cover only his postpresidential years. The most notable and recent example
of this is Edmund Morris's 2010 *Colonel Roosevelt*.

The following more in-depth work is meant to fill this 1914–18 lacuna in
Roosevelt studies. It concentrates on war-related matters such as TR's preparedness campaign while at the same time considering his plans for peace
and some sort of international league of nations, a subject Woodrow Wilson
was mostly silent on from 1914 to 1917 while the discussion was led by
Republicans such as TR, William Howard Taft, and Elihu Root. These seemingly opposed causes became intertwined with his political activities: his leadership in the Progressive Party until 1916 and his subsequent rapprochement
with the Republicans, becoming by 1918 the party's accepted leader and
presumptive 1920 candidate. Roosevelt made a good living in the war years

by his pen, and his relations with press figures like the American William Randolph Heart and Britain's Lord Northcliffe are also given their proper place.

"It would be an irony of fate if my administration has to deal chiefly with foreign problems; for all my preparation has been in domestic matters," goes one of the most oft-quoted remarks attributed to Woodrow Wilson.[1] But from TR's point of view it must have been an even more bitter "irony of fate" that when the Great War broke out it would be a completely inexperienced former college president and governor of New Jersey, and not the supremely qualified TR, who would face the world crisis as leader of the United States. Roosevelt's 1910 postpresidential visit to Europe, during which he took the measure of many later wartime leaders, including Germany's Kaiser Wilhelm II, gave him a unique insight into international relations to crown his seven years of on-the-job experience in the White House.

Roosevelt was very well aware of the German threat to world peace, and he fostered what has come to be called the "special relationship" with Britain and her Empire, several parts of which he trekked across after the presidency. In office he charted a new imperial and great power course for America, projecting his ethos of the "strenuous life" into international relations in a threatening new century. He also believed deeply in the destiny of what he called the English-speaking peoples as a positive and civilizing force in the world. He both laid the foundation for and solidified Anglo-American amity. Roosevelt's correspondence with many British friends also shaped his view of the war and he unburdened himself to figures such as Sir Cecil Spring Rice, Arthur Lee, Rudyard Kipling, and Sir Henry Rider Haggard.

Though Woodrow Wilson made sure Roosevelt did not lead troops to France, all four of his sons served, with the youngest Quentin making the ultimate sacrifice in July 1918. His daughters and daughters-in-law also had roles to play in the war. But this work concentrates on TR, the original twentieth-century multitasker, who seemed to be able to accomplish more than any other three people combined. (For example, even in the war years he actively continued his interest in and championship of conservation. In such natural pursuits TR had a long history, back to his boyhood studies of birds and other wildlife in New York, further stimulated at Harvard and in his brief, yet formative, "Cowboy" period in the Dakotas.)

Luckily for the historian and biographer, TR carried on an immense private and public correspondence. Consequently, this study reveals Roosevelt's final four and a half years largely through his words—in his letters, speeches, and articles, which remain eloquent and compelling today—and in the words of those who wrote to and about him, without overwhelming authorial prodding and embellishment. The great majority of Roosevelt's papers and diaries are in two locations: the Manuscript Division of the Library of Congress, and the Theodore Roosevelt Collection at the Houghton Library, Harvard. In addition to these, research for this work was undertaken at the Yale University Library; the British Library, London; the Parliamentary Archives, London; the Courtauld Institute, London; the Churchill Archives Centre, Churchill College, Cambridge; and the Cambridge University Library. In addition to the various Roosevelt collections, the papers of numerous contemporaries were also consulted for this work, which has been based, in part, on documents not previously published.

* * *

I must express my thanks to the following individuals and institutions who made materials available to me and gave assistance or permissions without which this study could not have been completed: Mr. Wallace Finley Dailey, Theodore Roosevelt Collection, Houghton Library, Harvard University; Jennifer Brathovde, the Library of Congress, Manuscripts Division; the Clerk of the Records of the Parliamentary Archives, on behalf of the Beaverbrook Foundation; the Churchill Archives Centre, Churchill College, Cambridge; the British Library Board; the Courtauld Institute of Art; the National Army Museum; and the Syndics of the Cambridge University Library. This work was supported by a Lamar University Research Enhancement Grant and much of the research was carried out while I was a Visiting Fellow at Wolfson College, Cambridge University.

In addition, I wish to thank Professors R. J. Q. Adams, Thomas Kennedy, and James Startt, whose gentle and insightful comments have greatly enriched the work. Special appreciation once again goes to my wife, Diane, who has with good grace for many years now shared her husband with Theodore Roosevelt and other historical figures. Finally, I wish to dedicate this book with much love to my sisters Claudette Bourque and Jan Seckbach, who helped to instill intellectual curiosity and a love of books in their often mischievous younger brother.

PROLOGUE

PEACE ENVOY, SPRING 1910

On May 4, 1910, Theodore Roosevelt and his wife Edith, daughter Ethel, and son Kermit arrived at Christiana (the future Oslo) and were greeted by Norway's King Haakon VII and Queen Maud. Once again, as they had almost everywhere in their tour across Europe, they stayed at the royal palace. The Colonel, as TR styled himself after the presidency, reported to his close friend Massachusetts Senator Henry Cabot Lodge his continuing puzzlement about the "extraordinary" receptions he received in Norway and elsewhere. Royals had vied with one another to entertain them, and the popular displays were even more remarkable. In his opinion this was largely because to them he represented the American Republic, which stood to the average European as a "queer, attractive dream"—to some a "golden utopia partially realized" and to others a "field for wild adventure of a by no means necessarily moral type—in fact a kind of mixture of Bacon's Utopia and Raleigh's Spanish Main." In addition, the former president appealed personally to their imaginations as a "leader whom they suppose to represent democracy, liberty, honesty and justice." It was all very interesting and amusing, but it was also fatiguing and irksome. As much as he dreaded getting back into the "confusion" of American politics, after 13 months abroad he longed "inexpressibly to be back at Sagamore Hill, in my own house, with my own books, and among my own friends."[1]

One more serious duty Roosevelt performed at Christiana was to deliver a four-years-belated Nobel Peace Prize Address. He was doing so, in part, as a favor to Andrew Carnegie, the world's richest man and an international peace advocate extraordinaire, who had stepped in to provide the lion's share of the financial support for the yearlong African safari that had preceded the European leg of TR's postpresidential odyssey.

World peace was prominent among the many causes Carnegie supported, and he had enlisted Roosevelt, as a kindred spirit to Germany's Kaiser Wilhelm II, to aid in this quest. Carnegie seemed to find no contradiction in turning to these two figures whose public personas often reflected the glorification of war and military virtues. One authority on the American peace movement has commented that Carnegie coupled "an extraordinarily sanguine disposition" with a "simplicity of mind that blurred the contradictory implications of specific ideas and actions."[2] In 1903 the plutocrat donated $1,500,000, a huge sum at that time, to build a "Temple of Peace" at The Hague to house the sessions of the permanent court of arbitration, the most lasting creation of the First Hague Conference called by Russia's Czar Nicholas II in 1899 to discuss disarmament. Over the rest of his life, as Carnegie followed his "Gospel of Wealth" to give away 90 percent of his fortune, he would prove a generous donor to peace organizations in the United States and abroad.

Though deeply skeptical as to his prospects of success, Roosevelt had agreed to act as Carnegie's peace envoy, not only at Christiana, but also at Berlin with Wilhelm, who was seen by Carnegie as the greatest hope for world peace, and by many others as its greatest menace.[3] Three years before, at the time of the Second Hague Peace Conference (which TR had fostered), Carnegie had told Charlemagne Tower, the American ambassador in Berlin, that Wilhelm had it "in his power to do the world the greatest service ever rendered by man." If he were to propose an international police to keep the peace, Britain, America, France, and the other powers would follow. Carnegie concluded that the Kaiser and Roosevelt "would make a team if they were only hitched up in together for the great cause of peace."[4]

Peace, the Colonel told his Nobel audience at Christiana, was "generally good in itself," but it was "never the highest good" unless it came as the "hand maiden of righteousness," and it became a "very evil thing" if it served "merely as a mask for cowardice and sloth, or as an instrument to further the ends of despotism or anarchy." Nevertheless, he believed great advances could be made in the cause of international peace along several lines. First, there should be treaties of arbitration between the "really civilized communities." The establishment of a sufficient number of these, Roosevelt argued, would go a long way toward "creating a world opinion which would finally find expression" in the provision of still-needed methods to forbid or punish transgressors.

A second line of advance could be made in the further development of The Hague Tribunal, particularly the conference and courts of The Hague. TR agreed with those who said that the First Hague Conference a decade before had framed a Magna Carta for the nations. The Second Conference in 1907 had made further progress, and he thought the next projected for 1914 should do more. The American government had more than once tentatively suggested methods for completing the Court of Arbitral Justice, and the statesmen of the world would do well to use the US Supreme Court as a model. In the third place, something should be done to check the growth of armaments, especially naval, by international agreement. In TR's opinion, granted sincerity of purpose, the Great Powers should find no insurmountable obstacle in reaching an agreement to end the present costly expenditures. Finally, it would be a master stroke if those same Great Powers honestly bent on international amity would form a League of Peace, not only to keep the peace among themselves, but to prevent—by force if necessary—its being broken by others.

The "supreme difficulty" with developing the peace work of The Hague, TR went on, lay in the lack of any executive power. And until some form of international police power to enforce the decrees of the court was developed, each nation must keep well prepared to defend itself. As things now stood, "such power to command peace throughout the world" could best be assured by some joint effort between those great nations that sincerely desired peace and had "not thought themselves of committing aggressions." At first this might only secure peace in certain definite limits and conditions, "but the ruler or statesman who should bring about such a combination would have earned his place in history for all time and his title to the gratitude of all mankind."[5] This speech constituted the strongest appeal for peace made by Roosevelt in Europe, and the final sentiment represented an obvious appeal to the German Kaiser to take the lead as Carnegie wished.

Roosevelt considered Wilhelm "an able and powerful man."[6] Besides sharing these attributes, the two were similar in several other ways. Only three months apart in age, both had overcome childhood disabilities: Roosevelt had endured asthma and poor eyesight, which had given him a mole-like perspective on the world until corrected with glasses, while the Emperor had from birth a withered left arm, which he hid in splendid uniforms. As adults they were similarly active men who dominated their surroundings physically and conversationally. Both were moralists who nevertheless had curious and wide-ranging intellects—though the Kaiser's was more limited in depth and scope by his inward-looking Prussian military upbringing and by his colossal ego, which was fed by a sycophantic entourage and dwarfed even the Colonel's own generous self-regard. The popular anecdote about TR, that he wanted to be the bride at every wedding and the corpse at every funeral, was also said in Germany of Wilhelm, with the addition of the stag at every hunt.[7] The Kaiser also shared TR's passion for building up his country's fleet, which both men saw as among their greatest national legacies.

Both men practiced a personal brand of diplomacy, and when Roosevelt had been president they had corresponded by cable and letter through crises in Venezuela, Morocco, and the Far East. TR was famous for his foreign policy creed, borrowed from a West African proverb: "Speak softly and carry a big stick; you will go far." The "big stick" was the United States Navy, which Roosevelt nurtured as president into the second most powerful in the world after Britain's Royal Navy. This policy of "protodeterrence" allowed TR the luxury of cordial relations with aggressive world powers such as Japan and Germany.[8] On the other hand, Wilhelm's motto might have been, "Speak loudly, and you will scare ancient enemies into each other's arms"—for this is exactly what he unwittingly did with England, France, and Russia in the decade before 1914.

The Kaiser considered Roosevelt to be one of the few figures on the world stage with stature great enough to be treated as an equal, and he also assumed, as did other European leaders, that he would one day again be president. After a luncheon on the first day of the Colonel's visit to Berlin, a special train took the party—which included the German Chancellor, Theobald von Bethmann Hollweg—to Potsdam, where the Kaiser proudly showed the Roosevelt family the palace. Wilhelm, whom the Colonel was surprised to find spoke perfect English, took him aside for a very rare private talk lasting an hour, in which the Emperor surpassed "even his wildest expectations and treated him with a fulsome familiarity which was as horrifying to the entourage of the 'All-Highest' as it was distasteful to T.R. himself."[9]

The Colonel was able to spend two more afternoons in conversation with the Emperor, the first on horseback for five hours while reviewing army maneuvers at Döberitz. Wilhelm was resplendent in a hussar general's uniform and helmet, while Roosevelt wore a simple khaki riding suit and black slouch hat, which from time to time he raised to acknowledge the troops. The Kaiser honored TR before his officers by making a point of addressing him as "*mein Freund*" and asked him to remember that he was the only private citizen who had ever reviewed German troops.[10] Wilhelm's mischievous nature was displayed in writing on the backs of several photos that he gave TR to commemorate the military review. On one depicting them talking seriously, the Kaiser wrote, "the Colonel of the Rough Riders instructing the German Emperor in field tactics." On another he inscribed, perhaps more seriously, "When we shake hands we shake the world." The German Foreign Office, afraid of yet another royal indiscretion among many becoming public, asked for the photos to be returned. TR refused and had them framed in glass so that both sides could be seen.[11]

The two men agreed on fundamental points of domestic and religious morality, but there was a "good deal of dogmatic theology" that meant much to Wilhelm that to Roosevelt was "entirely meaningless." They also completely disagreed on many points of international morality, which TR found understandable given that Wilhelm was brought up in the school of Frederick the Great and Bismarck, while his own heroes were champions of freedom like Timoleon, John Hampden, Washington, and Lincoln. They did concur, however, in a cordial dislike of "shams and pretense" and therefore of the "kind of washy movement for international peace" with which Carnegie's name had become so closely associated. At Döberitz, Roosevelt had mentioned Carnegie's suggestion that Wilhelm take the lead in founding a council of nations with an international police arm, and on another photo he sent TR of the mock battle staged for them, the Kaiser responded that such exertions would take care of that old "peace bore" Carnegie.[12]

Such an attitude on the part of Wilhelm, coupled with the recent death of Britain's King Edward VII, doomed any small chance their meeting might have had of furthering Carnegie's dreams of peace. Nevertheless, Roosevelt told Wilhelm that he felt the "subject was of such importance as to warrant consideration as to whether or not it was feasible to do something practical toward limiting expense and putting difficulties in the way of war." The Emperor was very courteous, but said he really had no control over the matter, which was "something which affected the German people," who would "never consent to Germany's failing to keep herself able to enforce her rights either on land or at sea." Roosevelt had especially desired to talk with Wilhelm about the alarming naval rivalry between Germany and England, and he raised the possibility of limiting the ever-increasing battleship expenditures of the two nations. The Kaiser responded there was no real use in discussing the matter, as the element he represented in Germany was determined to be powerful on the ocean.[13]

The Colonel then confessed that if he were an Englishman he would feel that "naval supremacy was a vital matter" and that under no circumstances would he "permit the fleet to sink to such a position that its mastership of the ocean" could be threatened. He was surprised that Wilhelm agreed and said that were he an Englishman he would feel the same way. Since his mother was Queen Victoria's oldest daughter, Wilhelm had spent some of his childhood in England and thought of himself as partly English. He claimed that, next to Germany, he cared for England more than any other country and added with "intense emphasis, I ADORE ENGLAND." He did not object to England's keeping up her fleet relative to all other powers, but he did complain that English statesmen, including the former Conservative prime minister Arthur Balfour, continually held up Germany as the nation against whom England specially needed to prepare. Wilhelm then earnestly asked TR to tell any British leaders he had the chance to meet all he had said, and in particular that he was not hostile to them and "on the contrary admired England and did not for a minute believe there would be war between England and Germany." Such a war, both men agreed, would be an "unspeakable calamity."[14]

This did not mean, however, that the Emperor's attitude was entirely without menace. TR reported to his English friend and "intellectual playmate" Sir George Otto Trevelyan that Germany had "the arrogance of a very strong power, as yet almost untouched by that feeble aspiration towards international equity" that the United States and England had at least begun to feel. Germany wanted a navy so strong that she could treat England as she had France over Morocco. This had shown how far Germany was willing to go in doing what she believed her own interests and destiny demanded, in total "disregard of her own engagements and of the equities of other people." If Germany had a navy as strong as England, Roosevelt did not believe "she would intend to use it for the destruction of England," but he did believe that "incidents would be very likely to occur which might make her so use it."[15]

Unlike elsewhere in Europe, and ominously for the future, TR noted that, though they behaved entirely correctly, the "Germans did not like me, and did not like my country." The "stiff, domineering and formal" upper classes, with the organized army, bureaucracy, and industry of their "great, highly civilized and admirably administered country behind them," regarded America with a dislike "all the greater because they could not make it merely contempt." Since they saw America as entirely unorganized, in their view "we had no business to be formidable rivals at all," and they were exasperated to feel that "our great territory, great natural resources, and strength of individual initiative" enabled the United States to be a "formidable" rival and, "more incredible still, that thanks to our Navy and ocean-protected position, we were in a military sense wholly independent and slightly defiant."[16]

It was with little regret, therefore, that the family left Berlin for London. While the Colonel had been in Germany, President William Howard Taft had wired a request that TR act as America's special ambassador to the state funeral of Edward VII, which brought together the grandees of Europe for a final time before the First World War swept away most of these human remnants of the old regime. Taft's military aide Archie Butt, who had also served Roosevelt, commented that with the Kaiser and TR present, it would be "a wonder if the poor corpse gets a passing thought."[17] It was with this somber duty foremost in mind that the Colonel arrived in London on May 16, 1910.

Andrew Carnegie had arrived in England a few days before. When asked by the press whether Roosevelt's reelection would further the cause of international peace, he commented that the Colonel had "a fine peace record, but we all know there's a bit of the barbarian in him." On the other hand, he declared that the Kaiser was a "true peacemaker" and "peace-lover" who would close his career "unstained by the shedding of human blood."[18] Carnegie sent TR a message of greetings from his resort hotel in Torqay: "Welcome Colonel Commanding to London." He thought it "very fine" that he was to be America's representative at Edward's funeral and planned to try to see Roosevelt's "cronie" the Kaiser afterward. He went on, "If you and he don't make a team that can drag the cart behind I am a disappointed man."[19]

Carnegie did not receive TR's report on the failure of his peace mission until the next day when he wrote again in light of it and the indefinite postponement of a conference of notable British statesmen at which TR was supposed to pass along Wilhelm's sentiments. Carnegie told the Colonel that he had not seen the Berlin papers and had not known that all had not "past [sic] off well." However, the ever-sanguine plutocrat was sure at least that "you and the Emperor *now being friends* may some day count for much." He went on that the British conference was only a way to give Roosevelt "a chance to become known to the leaders here and they to know you. It may make all the difference some day that you are friends." In his usual over-the-top style, Carnegie continued, "Your future is, recent events excepted, likely to excel your past since you are a born leader of men with the sublime audacity to perform wonders."[20]

Unfortunately for the hopes of Carnegie, the death of Edward VII scrambled all arrangements, and there would be no country-house gathering of eagles to further world peace. In June 1910 the Colonel returned home, his unmatched expertise in international affairs now augmented by personal meetings with statesmen and royals across Europe, most of whom would still be in place in August 1914. In the intervening years TR's most telling contribution to the "confusion" of American politics would be to split the Republican

Party and deny reelection to his former friend William Howard Taft. This meant, to Roosevelt's everlasting and bitter regret, that Woodrow Wilson, a former college professor and one-term governor of New Jersey with no international experience whatsoever, would be in charge of the foreign policy of the United States when the Great War exploded upon the world.

CHAPTER 1

A GREAT TRAGEDY IMPENDS

JUNE TO AUGUST 1914

The twentieth century looms before us big with the fate of many nations. If we stand idly by, if we seek merely swollen, slothful ease and ignoble peace, if we shrink from the hard contests where men must win at hazard of their lives and at the risk of all they hold dear, then the bolder and stronger people will pass us by, and will win for themselves dominion of the world. Let us . . . boldly face the life of strife, resolute to do our duty, well and manfully; resolute to uphold righteousness by deed and by word, resolute to be both honest and brave, to serve high ideals . . . Above all, let us shrink from no strife, moral or physical, within or without the Nation . . . for it is only through strife, through hard and dangerous endeavor, that we shall ultimately win the goal of true national greatness.
—"The Strenuous Life," TR speech at Chicago, April 1899

In the late spring of 1914, Roosevelt sailed again for Europe, arriving at Cherbourg on June 4 aboard the RMS *Olympic*. This trip had two main objectives: The first was to attend the wedding of his son Kermit to Belle Willard, the blonde socialite daughter of Joseph Edward Willard, the American ambassador to Spain. Besides this family obligation, this voyage also allowed the Colonel to accept an invitation to speak before the Royal Geographic Society in London to answer those who still disputed his claim to have charted earlier that year in South America an unknown "River of Doubt" as long as the Rhine.[1] It was in fact remarkable that Roosevelt was making the Atlantic voyage at all. Only a few months before he had almost died in the Amazonian jungles, at one point instructing Kermit, who came along as he had on the African safari four years before, to leave him behind and save himself and the remnants of their small party. TR's wife Edith felt herself still too ill and emotionally distraught over the death of a cousin to make the journey to Europe, so he was accompanied instead by his daughter Alice Roosevelt Longworth.[2]

Before going on to Spain, the Colonel had time for two days in Paris, where he saw a variety of friends and politicians. On June 6, after lunch with Gabriel Hanotaux, the former foreign minister, TR called on the French president, Raymond Poincaré. Roosevelt was also the dinner guest of soon-to-be-replaced American Ambassador Myron Herrick, an old Republican ally. The next day, after breakfast with the novelist Edith Wharton, a distant cousin of his wife's, the Colonel departed for Madrid, where he stayed with his new in-laws at the embassy and carried out several days of sightseeing with Alice before the June 11 civil ceremony that united Kermit and Belle. Theodore reported to Edith that he had never seen "two people more in love with one other," and he believed that the newlyweds had "as good a chance of happiness as any two lovers can have."[3] TR then went on to England, where he spent the remaining week of the European sojourn. This would be the last of his many visits to the island nation. Of course, he did not know this, nor did he, or any of his many close friends, suspect that within two months Britain and her Empire would be drawn into what came to be called the Great War, later the First World War, the most horrific conflict the globe had ever seen.[4]

For over a decade, Roosevelt had been an admirer of the British Empire and a proponent of cooperation and friendship between the two great English-speaking peoples, later dubbed the "Special Relationship."[5] Over that time, for strategic and other reasons that suited both nations, Anglo-American relations had become more cordial, in part as a consequence of the brief Spanish-American War.[6] Roosevelt had not always felt as warmly, but British support for the United States in the "Splendid Little War" reversed Roosevelt's previous opinion. The attitude of England, he told his friend Arthur Lee, whom he had first met in Cuba in 1898 when Lee was British Military Attaché, "worked a complete revolution in my feelings and the attitude on the continent at that time opened my eyes to the other side of the question." After the war, TR felt "very strongly" that the English-speaking peoples were "now closer together than for a century and a quarter, and that every effort should be made to keep them together; for their interests are really fundamentally the same, and they are far more closely akin, not merely in blood, but in feeling and in principles, than either is akin to any other people in the world . . . Our two peoples are the only two really free great peoples."[7]

On his arrival at London in June 1914, Roosevelt was welcomed by a group of dignitaries and friends, which included the Archbishop of Canterbury and American Ambassador Walter Hines Page, whose outlook in foreign policy matters had more in common with TR than the Democratic administration that had appointed him and whose advice, consequently, President Woodrow Wilson often ignored.[8] After taking lunch with Page at the embassy, the Colonel stayed at the London house of Arthur Lee, who, after being made an honorary Rough Rider in Cuba, had retired from the army and been elected to the Commons, where his constant defense of the United States got him dubbed the "MP for America." His American wife, Ruth, née

Moore, had inherited a banking fortune that allowed the pair a comfortable lifestyle including a country house, Chequers Court, which they later generously bequeathed to the nation for the use of its prime ministers.

The Colonel had told the Lees that he wanted a quiet visit with "no functions of any kind and seeing none but a few of his oldest and closest friends." But in practice the visit was "very otherwise." The Lee house at 10 Chesterfield Street was besieged by popular interest, and Arthur was soon reduced to exhaustion by his efforts to "repel boarders" in the shape of "self-invited lion-hunters, pertinacious press men and photographers, who, like Oliver Twist, were always asking for more."[9] Even though he was supposed to be an "extinct volcano," every day Roosevelt held court for twenty newspapermen. The public insisted on knowing what he did, and the reports were cabled all over the world. The press notables he saw included Lord Northcliffe, the self-made founder of the *Daily Mail*, owner of the *Times* of London, and soon to be the loudest critic of his government's war effort.

Roosevelt also met, not for the first time, with prominent politicians from both leading parties, including Liberal Prime Minister Herbert Henry Asquith, Chancellor of the Exchequer David Lloyd George, and Foreign Secretary Sir Edward Grey, the lone aristocrat in a cabinet made up mostly of lawyers. Grey shared with Roosevelt a passion for the outdoors, and when TR had visited in 1910 the two had shared a rainy daylong walk in the foreign secretary's home county, spotting birds and listening to their calls. Grey gave a luncheon for the Colonel at his house in Eccleston Square, which Asquith and Lloyd George attended. The prime minister, who was unused to being outtalked and overshadowed, recalled that Roosevelt "held the floor practically the whole time and talked to & at us as tho' we had been a public meeting or (occasionally) a Sunday school." What was it, Asquith wrote to a friend, that made "all Americans so intolerably long-winded & so prone to platitude?" He appraised TR as a "second rate man with overflowing vitality, and now & then quite a passable sense of humour—full of egotism, but *au fond* (I should think) a good fellow." Lloyd George noted that when Roosevelt "declaimed trite statements," such as "I believe in liberty, but liberty with order," Asquith "glowered at him with a look of curiosity," and he thought TR saw it. The meal, in Lloyd George's opinion, was "hardly a success."[10]

The Colonel fared somewhat better, at least in Arthur Lee's estimation, with the leaders of the Conservative opposition, who took the name Unionists in these years for their championing of a continued constitutional union with Ireland. In London, TR saw among others the former prime minister Arthur Balfour, the party leader Andrew Bonar Law, the imperial proconsul George Curzon, and the militant Ulster leader Sir Edward Carson. With the last in particular, Roosevelt had a private conversation about the Irish Home Rule crisis, which that summer dominated the attention of the country and threatened to tear apart the United Kingdom. It must have been an interesting talk, as TR had believed for some time that granting Ireland Home Rule within the British Empire was the right and proper thing to do. Lee, hardly an unbiased witness, recorded that his friend made a "complete conquest as usual of everyone" except the dour Bonar Law, who commented to Lee that that he found Roosevelt "very common-place." This, Lee went on, "must have been the first time T. R. had ever been charged with *that* particular defect." But Lee found it "irresistibly humorous" coming from Bonar Law, "the very quintessence of everything that was most bourgeois and drab."[11]

Lee also organized a lunch and talk that included Balfour—like Roosevelt, an intellectual who also happened to be a consummate politician—as well as scholars from Oxford and Cambridge. TR enjoyed the occasion greatly despite the fact that Balfour refused to talk on the intended subjects. Consequently the luncheon became, in Lee's words, a "most amusing exhibition of a gazelle eluding a bulldog." Lee found Roosevelt's versatility quite extraordinary while noting that he was sometimes accused of being an "egoist and taking the center of the stage too much." This, in Lee's opinion, was "merely a symptom of his astounding vitality," and it needed to be remembered that probably no man had "to live his daily life so much in the limelight." Taking center stage had become "almost subconscious with him."

The only way the Colonel could get even a temporary respite from the attention of the world was to "disappear in some unexplored continent," and before leaving London, he spoke before the Royal Geographical Society on his recent adventure on the River of Doubt.[12] The talk was given at the Civil Service Commission Theater on Bond Street, which that night was jammed with traffic as more than a thousand Society members tried to gain entrance to a hall built for eight hundred. Even Sir Edward Grey had a devil of a time, finally scaling a stone wall and sneaking in through a side door before taking his seat on the stage. Ruth Lee noted that the lecture, which recounted TR's four-hundred mile canoe journey, was given entirely without notes in a conversational tone and was a great success. It contained "very few technicalities and just the right sense of humour—avoiding the large 'I' with great dexterity."[13] A message from the arbiter of the society, Sir Clement Markham, acknowledged that Roosevelt had made a "very important contribution to our geographical knowledge by discovering this longitudinal valley between the Tapajós and the Madeira."[14]

The Colonel also spoke of his expedition during a country house party at Chequers Court, the Lees' country home, where he traced out the waterway's course on a huge map spread out in the Great Hall. Those invited included TR's daughter Alice, the Conservative writer and publicist F. S. Oliver, editor of the *Spectator* John St. Loe Strachey, Owen Seaman of *Punch*, the Anglo-Irish MP and agricultural reformer Horace Plunkett, and Britain's most-respected old soldier, Field Marshal Lord Roberts of Kandahar. For the previous decade, in an effort to spur a British counter to the German "nation in arms," Roberts had led a preparedness movement in England that called for the enlargement and modernization of the small British army through some form of universal service.[15] However, this found little success in the face of Britain's deeply held tradition of reliance on the Royal Navy and a small volunteer army. TR was charmed by the diminutive war hero and before

Figure 1. TR and Alice in London, June 18, 1914
Theodore Roosevelt Collection, Harvard College Library

too long would himself be called "America's Lord Roberts." At Chequers, Ruth Lee recorded that TR was "in his greatest form and perfectly dear . . . We talked upon almost every subject, history, literature, philosophy, religion, politics, natural history and human nature." At the end of dinner, it "would have required a surgical operation to remove the women from the table," so everyone stayed there and had coffee.[16]

Before he left England, TR attended a luncheon at the American embassy that included Colonel Edward M. House, Woodrow Wilson's closest advisor and confidante. In Europe on an unofficial peace mission meant to improve relations between England and Germany, Wilson's "silent partner" met with many notables in both countries, including Sir Edward Grey and Wilhelm II.[17] Wilson's personal envoy had some difficulty in Germany explaining that his rank had been bestowed by the governor of Texas for political services and that he had no military experience. The Kaiser, in House's estimation, "had all the versatility of Roosevelt with something more of charm, something less of force." During their thirty-minute conversation, Wilhelm spoke "kindly and admiringly" of England and declared that the Americans, Germans, and British were "kindred peoples and should draw closer together." When House asked why Wilhelm refused to sign the arbitration treaty offered by Secretary of State William Jennings Bryan, the Kaiser replied that Germany would never endorse such a document, which called for a "cooling off" period of up to a year. His country's strength lay in "being always prepared for war at a second's notice." Surrounded by enemies and with the "bayonets of Europe directed at her," Germany would not "resign that advantage and give our enemies time to prepare."[18] In the end, House's quest on behalf of Wilson proved as quixotic as that of Roosevelt's four years before for Andrew Carnegie.

In the intervening years Carnegie had not given up his peace crusade or the hope that the German Emperor might yet be brought to his side in the struggle. After the failure of TR's peace mission to Germany, Carnegie had put his faith in President William Howard Taft, and with Taft's blessing at the end of 1910 he had used $10,000,000 in United States Steel bonds to fund the Carnegie Endowment for Peace still at work today.[19] Elihu Root, who had been TR's secretary of state, had become the endowment's first president and would hold the position for the next 15 formative years. In 1912, for his labors in the vineyards of international arbitration, Root had joined Roosevelt as a recipient of the Nobel Peace Prize. (That same year their friendship ended when Root chaired the Republican convention that nominated Taft over TR.) The next year Carnegie had led a delegation to Germany for the celebration of the twenty-fifth anniversary of Wilhelm's reign. On his way to Berlin, Carnegie had passed through Belgium, noting its beauty and that it could never be attacked, because Germany, France, and England guaranteed its neutrality. When they met in Berlin, the boisterous Kaiser, wagging his index finger, exclaimed, "Remember Carnegie! Twenty-five years!—and twenty-five years of peace! If I am Emperor for another twenty-five years not a shot shall be fired in Europe!"[20]

When Roosevelt departed England for home from Southampton on the SS *Imperator* on June 18, 1914, Lee found the temporary valet he had assigned to TR, Fern, with "tears trickling down his cheeks." When he asked what the matter was, the man replied that in all his thirty years of service he had "never met such a gentleman as 'im." Evidently, Lee commented, Fern and Bonar Law had "different standards of human values."[21] Colonel House also returned to America that month, and before he departed, Ambassador Herrick confided "something of T. R.'s mental and physical activities." Herrick predicted that Roosevelt was "getting ready to go back home and to give the Democrats a thoroughly unhappy time." House responded that he was sure TR "could do nothing that would distress us so much at it would his fellow Republicans."[22] Prescient words, but Roosevelt would spare neither party in the following months.

On June 24, the Colonel once again returned to his sanctuary Sagamore Hill, the family home at Oyster Bay, Long Island, and was there reunited with his beloved Edith, the center of his world and the perfect complement to Theodore. More clear-eyed and wary in her outlook, Edith's composed nature moderated his exuberance in domestic and political matters. She was a combination of advisor and loving companion.[23] "Teedie" and "Edie" had grown up in the same wealthy New York circles and had been childhood sweethearts; her best friend was his sister Corinne. But while away at Harvard he had become enchanted by and married the beautiful Alice Lee, who took Edith's place, temporarily at least, in his heart. Alice's tragic death in 1884, soon after the birth of their first child, came within 12 hours of the passing of TR's beloved mother. TR would never mention his first wife's name again, not even to their daughter Alice, called "Sister" by the family, who while he recovered from the double blow in the Dakotas Badlands was put into the care of Theodore's older sister and confidant, Anna.[24]

Within two years, TR had rekindled his romance with Edith, and they married in 1886 at St George's, Hanover Square, London. At the private ceremony Theodore wore fashionable orange gloves suggested by his best man, Sir Cecil Spring Rice, a bright young British diplomat attached to the Washington embassy that he had met on the boat to Europe. Thereafter a lifelong friend, "Springy" was perhaps most famous for his only half-jesting comment about TR's youthful energy: "You must always remember that the President is about six."[25] When they returned from their honeymoon in Europe, Edith insisted that her husband's daughter Alice live with them and over the following years had five children of their own: Theodore Jr. in 1887, Kermit in 1889, Ethel in 1891, Archibald in 1894, and the youngest, Quentin, in 1897.

The boys grew up in the shadow of their father, whom they idolized and emulated in constant and strenuous competition among one another. At the same time they had the self-imposed pressure of living up to his high expectations and lofty achievements. In particular the eldest, Theodore Jr., called Ted by family and friends, had every step compared with that of his illustrious namesake.[26] By the time Roosevelt left the presidency, Ted had graduated from Harvard and begun his business career, which opened the way for Kermit, who most shared his father's love of adventure and wild places, to accompany TR to Africa and then South America. Of all the boys, Kermit also most inherited the Roosevelt predilection for deep depression, which, like his father, he endeavored mightily to stay ahead of with constant activity. The third son, Archie, was the most serious minded, censorious, and puritanical of the bunch, which cost him friends as well as a place in the elite Porcellian Club at Harvard, of which his father and brothers were alumni. Youngest brother Quentin had as a child been a miniature TR, and while his father was president he had led the adventures of the "White House Gang," often joined by the children of Washington's leading citizens, such as Charlie Taft, who on one occasion Quentin managed to nick with his father's Rough Rider saber. Later in life Quentin also displayed an unusual acumen for things mechanical. While his father was in Africa, Quentin accompanied his mother to France, where he one day gazed incredulously at a sky filled with airplanes. From this encounter grew a passion for flying that would end tragically in the Great War.

Being the oldest, "Princess" Alice—as she was dubbed by a press fascinated with the doings of the energetic First Family—developed her own highly independent spirit and idiosyncrasies, including smoking cigarettes on the roof of the White House and forming a "Race Suicide" club to lampoon what she considered one of her father's more ludicrous hobby horses. TR famously told his writer friend Owen Wister that he could run the country or control Alice, but he could not possibly do both. Her half-sister Ethel was in many ways the flamboyant and glamorous Alice's opposite. After a tomboy period spent competing with her brothers in rough and tumble games, Ethel grew up into a responsible and reserved young lady who wanted none of the limelight Alice endlessly sought out. While Alice married a dashing politician, Nicholas Longworth of Cincinnati, and had no children with him, Ethel wed a surgeon, Richard Derby, of whom TR heartily approved, and dutifully began to raise a family in line with the preaching of her father.

Four days after Roosevelt got back to Oyster Bay, on Sunday, June 28, 1914, the Austrian Archduke Franz Ferdinand was murdered by a Bosnian nationalist at Sarajevo. TR had met Franz Ferdinand during his 1910 European tour, and the archduke was in fact one of the few aristocrats he disliked. The feeling was reportedly mutual. Though newsworthy, the assassination of the heir to the throne of the Dual Monarchy was not at first considered a serious threat to world peace, but only another unfortunate incident in a series of crises since 1908 when Austria-Hungary had annexed Bosnia and its neighbor Herzegovina. The Austrian government had been appreciative when then President Roosevelt had "cordially approved" of their annexations, which he considered more a "changing of the title, although not really the substance, of the Austrian occupation." At some point he hoped the Balkan states might stand on their own, but the example of Serbia was "not sufficiently encouraging" to make him believe the two small states would make more progress alone than under Austria, whose rule was infinitely preferable to that of Turkey.[27] Neighboring Serbia, however, and her friend Russia looked on the annexations with unveiled hostility, and a fuse had been lit in 1908 that would explode with cataclysmic fury six years later. The 1914 murder gave Austria-Hungary a long-awaited excuse to take action against Serbia and the South Slav "problem" within its territories.

The day after the assassination, TR wrote to Arthur Lee from Sagamore Hill that the time at Chequers had been the "most charming" episode of the trip, if not for the memory of his lunch with Arthur Balfour and Gilbert Murray. Even events he had not thought would go well, such as his breakfast with the Bishop of London, had been successful. On the other hand, Roosevelt also reported that five minutes after Lee had left him on the tug out to his ship home, he had a debilitating attack of malarial fever originally contracted from Cuba that had lasted for days. He was still not over it and his voice was "naturally worse than ever." He had seen the noted specialist Sir St. Clair Thomson in England about his throat, and his own physician at home concurred with his advice to take four months' rest with no speeches or extended campaign tours. The Colonel complained to Lee that as soon as he got back he was "plunged into politics—and really under very disheartening conditions," for the confusion passed belief, and the "malignance" of the Old Guard Republican leaders, together with the "wild-eyed folly" of a number of his Progressive supporters, combined to make his course "anything but easy." However, he thought he had "done away" with the danger that was most threatening to him: nomination for the governorship of New York.[28]

In 1914 Roosevelt remained at the head of the Progressive Party, which had been created in 1912 to run him for the presidency after Taft's "naked theft" of the Republican nomination. Though this had only resulted in the election of Woodrow Wilson, and the party had not done well in contests since, a national organization remained in place and the coming fall elections at the state, local, and congressional level were seen by Progressives as a "supreme test" for the survival of the new party.[29] Consequently, as TR noted in his letter to Lee, Progressives flocked to Oyster Bay to consult with TR, led by the millionaire George Perkins, who with the publisher Frank Munsey had given the lion's share of the financial backing for the 1912 Progressive effort.[30] Many in the party thought Perkins—a former partner of J. P. Morgan's who still sat on the boards of the United States Steel and International Harvester companies and was much hated by unions and farmers—a poor choice to continue as chairman of the Progressive Executive Committee. But TR considered Perkins an invaluable right-hand man and ensured that he stayed in place despite the grumbling of figures like his fellow conservationist Gifford Pinchot, who also visited Oyster Bay that month, along with Robert Bass, the former progressive Republican governor of New Hampshire, and TR's old friend, Robert Bacon, a former ambassador to France and briefly secretary of state at the end of Roosevelt's administration.

On June 30, Roosevelt gave a speech at the Progressive League dinner in Pittsburgh that set the stage for the 1914 election campaign. TR noted that President Wilson had based his run two years before on the trust and tariff issues, but the administration had solved neither problem. The 1913 Underwood-Simmons Tariff had reduced some duties but, because it was arrived at via old-fashioned congressional logrolling and not by the

"scientific" commission promised, it had only led to a recession that continued to plague the country. On the trust issue, the Democrats had as yet not
delivered any legislation to carry out their pledged policy of breaking up large
combinations, rather than the regulations TR had offered in his 1912 Federal
Trade Commission proposal. The Colonel also attacked the administration
for ignoring other needed reforms like the minimum wage and the abolition
of child labor, while he renewed the Progressive pledge to support direct
democracy and women's suffrage. The same day an angry delegation of suf-
fragettes confronted Wilson in the White House.[31]

Roosevelt's most impassioned disagreements with the Wilson administration, however, came in international affairs, specifically in regard to three
areas: the political upheaval in Mexico; the "cooling off" arbitration treaties
negotiated by Secretary of State William Jennings Bryan; and most personally, the negotiations with Colombia concerning its loss of Panama when TR
was in office. He had earlier told friends in England that he was returning
to America to "rip the administration to shreds for its many sins" and mentioned in particular the "dead failure in Mexico."[32] By this time a revolution
had been bleeding the country for three years, and until the Great War overshadowed it, this was the greatest challenge to American foreign policy. In
1911 President Porfirio Díaz, who had ruled for more than three decades,
was overthrown, creating a vacuum filled by several contending generals and
politicians. The relatively moderate Francisco Madero, the first to step forward and form a government, was himself shot in a February 1913 coup carried out by one of his generals, Victoriano Huerta, who proclaimed himself
provisional president. The American ambassador on the spot, Henry Lane
Wilson, supported Huerta, whom the international community soon recognized as the legitimate head of the Mexican state, while Woodrow Wilson's
administration tried a novel policy of nonrecognition along with erratic support for Huerta's main rival, Venustiano Carranza, and his Constitutionalist
forces. All this culminated, in late April 1914, with an American occupation
of Vera Cruz.

The bloodshed and disorder in Mexico, which often spilled across the
border, nevertheless continued unabated. This threatened American ranching and mining interests, particularly in the north where the bandit general
Francisco "Pancho" Villa, nominally an ally of Carranza, promised to break
up the great estates and redistribute the land to the peasants. It was not long
before Roosevelt was delivering addresses that attacked, both with regard to
Mexico and in general, what he considered the weak and cowardly foreign
policy of Wilson and his teetotaler Secretary of State Bryan, whose "grape
juice" diplomacy made him a figure of derision in Europe. After one early
nonalcoholic diplomatic affair, a London newspaper commented that the
rumpled and rustic Bryan "not only suffers for his principles and mortifies
the flesh" but insisted that "others should suffer and be mortified."[33] However, by 1914 the pacific secretary of state had negotiated 21 "cooling off"
arbitration treaties between the United States and other nations.

The idea of limited international arbitration was not new. During Roosevelt's years in office, 24 such treaties had been negotiated by his secretary of state, Elihu Root, but these made exception for disputes relating to national honor, vital interests, or independence. Bryan's innovation was to have the signatories agree to submit all disputes, including those concerning vital national interests, to an international commission for investigation. The parties also agreed not to resort to hostilities for up to a year while the commission deliberated. Because the system had no enforcement power save international opinion, and because it covered "vital national interests," Roosevelt believed that, though it might be convenient for nations to sign them, in the real world of international politics no self-respecting country could possibly take any such agreements seriously. His contempt for the treaties, and their originators, was shared by his close friend the Boston Brahmin Henry Cabot Lodge, who filled him in on Washington affairs from his insider's position as Republican senator from Massachusetts.

Soon after Wilson had stated his "watchful waiting" policy for Mexico, TR wrote Lodge that Bryan was the "most contemptible figure we have ever had as Secretary of State," and Wilson had to accept full responsibility for him. The president, whom the Colonel regarded "with contemptuous dislike," was in his opinion a "narrow and bitter partisan" and "intellectually thoroughly dishonest." TR admitted that Wilson had "ability of a certain kind" and the "nerve" his type so often showed in civil and domestic affairs where there was "no danger of physical violence." Wilson would "jump up and down on cheap politicians, and bully and cajole men in public life" who were "anxious not to part with their political chief." But in international matters he was a "ridiculous creature."[34]

Roosevelt was especially incensed by the administration's negotiations with Colombia concerning her loss of Panama.[35] While TR had been deep in the South American jungle, on April 6, 1914, Secretary of State Bryan had signed a treaty with Colombia that expressed "sincere regret that anything should have occurred to interrupt or mar the relations of cordial friendship that had so long subsisted between the two governments." In reparation, the United States proposed to pay $25,000,000 and give Colombian citizens the same rights as Americans in the use of the Panama Canal. TR saw this as the rebuke to his support of the Panamanian rebels that it was meant to be and, in a speech at Pará, Brazil, described the treaty as "dishonorable" and the indemnity as "nothing but blackmail."[36]

The day he returned from Europe the Colonel repeated this claim, saying that as president he had declined to "allow Uncle Sam to be blackmailed" by Colombia. Wilson now desired "the black mail to be paid." If the proposed treaty was right, contended TR, then the US presence on the isthmus was wrong and the canal should be returned to Colombia and the ongoing work should stop. If the United States had been guilty of theft, then "we should restore the stolen goods." The treaty, he declared, "capped the climax" of the foreign policy of Wilson and Bryan that had made America a "figure of fun in the international world." As was his policy, Wilson declined comment on the Rooseveltian outburst.[37]

Meanwhile, in England that July the news story that dominated all others was the King's intervention in the Irish crisis and the ongoing Buckingham Palace conference meant to find a solution. Arthur Lee predicted that if the King signed the pending Home Rule Bill he would be "lighting the train that would lead to Civil War in his Realms."[38] Lee's letter to TR made no mention of the Balkan crisis on the continent following the assassination of Franz Ferdinand, in which Austria-Hungary, spurred on by Germany, was preparing to move. The Dual Monarchy drafted an ultimatum for the Serbs, whom they blamed for the murder. Delivered on July 23, it demanded among other things the right to continue the investigation of the assassination on Serbian soil as well as other conditions, including the suppression of Serbian-backed societies in Bosnia that had preached revolt. As the newspapers pointed out, Russia would never allow Serbia to be humiliated in this way, and President Poincaré and Premier Viviani of France happened to be in St. Petersburg at present for consultations.[39] When Serbia refused to comply, Austria-Hungary declared war on the nation on July 28, 1914. That day the *New York Times* opined that, as in several similar previous crises going back a decade, a general European war was "unthinkable." The continent, and the world, could not afford such a war, and "happily" the conviction was growing that "such an appalling conflict" was "altogether beyond the realm of possibility."

However, over the next few days, the long-laid mobilization plans of the continental powers came into play and led to an August 1 German declaration of war on Russia. This event activated an alliance system that had been developing in Europe for several decades: Germany, Austria-Hungary, and Italy formed a military Triple Alliance, while Russia, France, and Britain formed a looser Triple Entente. This time, for various reasons that suited most of the participants, the brewing crisis would not be contained in a corner of Europe or Africa—and so began the most terrible war the world had yet seen.

CHAPTER 2

A GREAT BLACK TORNADO

AUGUST TO NOVEMBER 1914

> The European situation is a frightful tragedy. And it is a dreadful thing that this world war should exist; but after all there is an element of splendid heroism in it, shown on both sides, and by all the nations involved. But the attitude of Wilson and Bryan is contemptible, and it reflects discredit upon us. Heaven knows, I dislike Penrose and Barnes . . . But I do not despise them quite as heartily as I despise Wilson and Bryan!
> —TR to Kermit Roosevelt, November 11, 1914

The Colonel spent the first days of August 1914 at Sagamore Hill, monitoring the war clouds in Europe as best he could while preparing to unleash a broadside against the Colombia treaty and William Jennings Bryan's peace program generally. His friend John "Cal" O'Laughlin, the Washington correspondent of the *Chicago Tribune*, advised him to hold his fire as there was little chance at present of the papers publishing anything other than the news from Europe. When the war ceased to be a "nine days wonder," the newspaperman told TR, then he hoped the Colonel would "hit and hit hard." As far as Bryan's many arbitration treaties were concerned, O'Laughlin thought the "European war would teach him that such documents were not worth the paper they were printed on." Further, he would like to put Bryan and Andrew Carnegie, "wearing their usual hypocritical smiles, between the French and German armies."[1]

The day Germany declared war on Russia, August 1, an anxious Roosevelt wrote to his English friend Arthur Lee that while "the whole question of peace and war in Europe" was in the balance and a "great black tornado" trembled on the edge of Europe, "our own prize idiot, Mr. Bryan, and his ridiculous and insincere chief, Mr. Wilson," were "prattling pleasantly about the steps they are taking to procure universal peace by little arbitration treaties which promise impossibilities." TR went on that it was not a good thing for a country to have "a professional yodeler, a human trombone" like Bryan as secretary of state, nor a "college president with an astute and shifty mind," a "hypocritical ability to deceive plain people, unscrupulousness in handling machine leaders, and no real knowledge or wisdom concerning internal and international affairs" as president. It was "dreadful to think of the frightful tragedy" that was "apparently opening for Europe," and at the moment the Colonel did not know whether or not England was "to play her part therein."[2]

Whether or not England would join in the war on the side of her Entente partners was the great question in the first days of August 1914. The British commitment to France (on which Germany declared war August 3) and Russia was, strictly speaking, not a military alliance, even though secret army and navy contingency plans had been laid with the French. However, Prime Minister Herbert Henry Asquith and Foreign Secretary Sir Edward Grey skillfully maneuvered their "wavering" Liberal party toward action against Germany if necessary, predominantly because it was in Britain's best interest to do so.[3] On the continent, the Russian mobilization had triggered the timetables of the German Schlieffen plan. According to this decades-old master strategy, France had to be knocked out quickly to avoid a war on two fronts. The naked aggression of Germany's thrust into neutral Belgium on the morning of August 4 to carry out the plan's first objective, and the plea for help from the young and dashing Belgian King Albert, healed the remaining divisions in the British cabinet and swayed public opinion away from the position of neutrality widely called for at the time.

These developments cleared the way for Grey, head of the prointervention faction, to send an ultimatum to Berlin that called for Germany to withdraw from Belgian soil by 11 p.m. that night or else face war. When the warning was ignored, in what has been called a "tragedy of miscalculation" by the Kaiser and his advisors, Britain joined the other combatants in the most horrifying war the world had yet seen.[4] The next day Woodrow Wilson proclaimed American neutrality and also made the first of many futile offers to mediate the conflict.[5] But the president was otherwise preoccupied at this time of international crisis with a more personal tragedy: his wife Ellen died of kidney disease on August 6, and Wilson left the capital for a week to mourn.

Despite Grey's oft-repeated declaration that the "lamps are going out all over Europe; we shall not see them lit again in our lifetime," the world consensus held that the European war would be brief, and this "short-war illusion" has been overlooked in subsequent analyses of Roosevelt's reaction in the early months of the conflict.[6] The intertwined national economies of 1914, it was thought, could not stand more than a few months of dislocation. On the seas, the British navy would undoubtedly make the crucial difference by defeating the enemy fleet and blockading Germany. On land, military experts predicted that the war would involve battles of movement, fought by professional armies that would be home by Christmas in the fashion of the Franco-Prussian War 44 years before. However, this time France had powerful allies, and over the following years the two sides would prove to be tragically well matched.

A few leading figures disagreed with all the contemporary assumptions, chief among them newly appointed British War Secretary Horatio Herbert Lord Kitchener of Khartoum. The hero of Omdurman and the Boer War, who had spent the previous three years as an imperial proconsul in Egypt, had only been in England to receive an earldom and would have preferred to return to Cairo rather than be trapped in the cabinet among politicians he despised. Kitchener foresaw a war of three or four years' duration and looked down on the regular army because he thought it too small for the part he believed it would inevitably have to play.[7] To build up the army, on August 7 Kitchener issued his first appeal for one-hundred-thousand volunteers, and Britain was soon papered over with his famously mustachioed image, a pointing finger emphasizing the message, "Your Country Needs You!"[8] The response overwhelmed the nation's recruitment centers.

Meanwhile, the 90,000 man British Expeditionary Force (BEF), under the command of Field Marshal Sir John French, embarked for the continent to join the armies of France and Belgium and concentrated in France near Amiens.[9] In total the French army of 2,000,000 outnumbered the Germans on the western front by 300,000 men, and the Belgian army added 100,000. A wealthy neutral nation, like America, Belgium had lagged behind its neighbors in military preparations and planning, and its army was mostly composed of reservists.[10] Though also small by continental standards, the British Expeditionary Force was well trained and its morale high. The secrecy and misinformation concerning its transport was effective; the Germans had no idea the British were in France on August 23 at the beginning of the Battle of Mons.[11] However, because of the "Great Retreat" of the French forces, the BEF was soon engaged in a hazardous tactical withdrawal to escape being outflanked by the Germans.[12]

Ten days after Britain joined the war, Arthur Lee, who as a former army officer and sitting Unionist member of Parliament was very well informed, reported to Roosevelt the part he and his country had played so far. Lee's country house, Chequers, he confided, was being turned into a convalescent home for wounded soldiers, under the command of his wife, Ruth. He was proud of the "spirit with which our Nation and all classes of society have met the first shock of this overwhelming crisis, and the cool deliberation with which everyone, from the Government downwards, is reorganizing and adapting the ordinary machinery of life without any trace of fuss or panic." On the war fronts, Lee had the highest confidence in the navy and reported that Winston Churchill, whom he knew the Colonel disliked, had "greatly distinguished himself" as civilian head of the Admiralty. He had mobilized the fleet while the cabinet "wobbled horribly up till the last moment." As a result England had "completely forestalled" the German naval mobilization and established an "almost complete command of the seas." At present the German fleet was hiding behind land fortifications, but Lee forecast, wrongly, that it would come out soon and "risk everything in one desperate attack on our concentrated fleet in the North Sea." He was sure that the British fleet's commander, Admiral John Jellicoe, was up to the challenge.

On land, Lee was also optimistic, telling TR that the Germans had "developed an increasingly swelled head" and that he had not been impressed by the maneuvers he had witnessed two years before. He also had faith that Russia would advance on Germany from the east "like a flow of lava" no matter how many millions were shot down. Consequently, Lee told the Colonel, he "did not envy the state of mind of your friend the Kaiser at this moment." For the last ten years Wilhelm II and the war party had been living in a kind of "pipe dream" that they could strike at the "most favorable moment," but they had picked a "supremely unfavorable" one. All the things they had counted on—English neutrality, the unpreparedness of France, a compliant Belgium, a revolution in Russia, the cooperation of Italy (which judged that Austria-Hungary's aggression against Serbia did not activate its responsibility under the defensive Triple Alliance), the goodwill of America, the sympathy of the rest of the world, and, lastly, the "invincibility of German arms"—were, in Lee's words, "falsified." He knew very well that TR had no illusions about the peaceful intentions of Germany and wished TR had been president rather than Wilson, the "amiable but fatuous theorist" who was, Lee understood, "offering his personal intervention when at least two million men are already locked in death grips." In Lee's view this supreme conflict had to come, and he believed that the story of the defeat of Philip II and the Spanish Armada was about to be repeated.[13] Before long, Lee would be called to the War Office and asked by Kitchener to go to France to investigate and report on military hospitals, a job that gave him over the following months a wider overview of the fighting than almost any other staff officer.

Not wanting to speak "casually and hurriedly" about the war, Roosevelt withheld comment in its first days. Lawrence Abbott of the *Outlook*, for which the Colonel had until recently been a contributing editor, assured him that whenever he did wish to make a statement his readers would be pleased to have one. He suggested that TR could write on the need to build up both the navy and a "small and able army" to protect the Panama Canal and to maintain the Monroe Doctrine without in any way weakening the "unified and patriotic spirit in the country" that Roosevelt wished to preserve.[14] In private, meanwhile, the Colonel appraised American opinion on the war to Sir Cecil Spring Rice, in the first of many wartime letters that the British ambassador shared with his Foreign Office chief, Sir Edward Grey.

Over the decades since Spring Rice had served as best man when TR and Edith were married, he had gained experience in diplomatic posts from St. Petersburg to Tehran, which made him extremely well qualified in 1913 to become ambassador to the United States. Unfortunately, Spring Rice suffered from Graves's disease, a thyroid disorder that left him irritable and prone to verbal outbursts when under stress—not an ideal combination with which to face the often delicate matters that became routine once the Great War broke out. His friendship with Roosevelt was also well known and constituted a further complication in British dealings with the Wilson administration, which often bypassed Spring Rice.[15] Nevertheless, he remained one of the English friends who would be TR's pipeline of war news over the next years. This fact, along with the barbarous course chosen by Germany in Belgium, and later on the high seas, unmistakably colored the Colonel's view of the war.

Roosevelt reassured Spring Rice that England's "consistent friendliness towards us for decades past, and Germany's attitude during the Spanish war and in South America," had combined in America to produce "a friendliness for England and a genuine apprehension of German designs."[16] In reality this appraisal reflected TR's own educated, Anglophile opinion on the urban East Coast, rather than any national feeling. Outside this wealthy pro-Ally belt, with numerous intellectual and familial bonds with England, Americans were ambivalent at best about taking sides in the struggle. Despite Roosevelt's assurances, much of the population, notably the 12 million German and Irish Americans, were either pro-German or anti-British or both. There were also substantial numbers of Jewish Americans who remembered the pogroms of czarist Russia and therefore were less than sympathetic to the Allied cause. Spring Rice was well aware of all this and reported to Grey that the "influence of the Germans" was very great and that the British "must not count on American sympathy as assured to us."[17]

Americans in general were very glad that the Atlantic once again shielded them from European entanglements and supported the tradition of neutrality that went back to George Washington's farewell address. President Wilson played to this widespread sentiment in an August 18 statement to the press that recognized the natural sympathies many groups might have but sternly warned against the great danger of partisanship. Americans, he declared, must be neutral in "fact as well as in name" and "in thought as well as action."[18] Wilson's "second personality," Colonel Edward M. House, reflected widespread opinion when he wrote to the president four days later that the "saddest feature of the situation" was that there was "no good outcome to look forward to." If the Allies won, it meant "largely the domination of Russia on the Continent of Europe." A German victory on the other hand meant the "unspeakable tyranny of militarism for generations to come."[19]

America's status as the most powerful neutral nation meant that until the country joined the war in April 1917, Britain and Germany were locked in a propaganda battle for American goodwill. Certainly the bulk of the war news had to do with these two powers, although their allies France, Russia, and Austria-Hungary also had millions of men in the field. Among the diplomats in Washington, the charming German ambassador, Count Johann von Bernstorff, proved a much more able publicist than did his British counterpart Spring Rice.[20] The low-key British propaganda efforts in America concentrated on counteracting the "sledge-hammer" appeals employed by German publicity, with the aim of ensuring continued sympathy for the Allies.[21] This was aided by the fact that the British controlled the Atlantic cable and therefore the bulk of news from Europe, although it is often overlooked that Germany had a flourishing wireless service that broadcast regular bulletins across the Atlantic.

This duel of words extended to the battlefront, where the British and French forbade correspondents, while the Germans gave the press access to their initial victorious march across Belgium and France.[22] Those allowed to follow the German army soon included neutral journalists, many of them Americans. The German General Staff even had the temerity to offer their communiqués to the *Times* of London, which the paper at first summarily refused. Soon, however, the *Times* and *Daily Mail*, both owned by the powerful gadfly and government critic Lord Northcliffe, began reporting "official" German news as better than no news.[23]

In America, one of the most important pro-German propagandists was George Sylvester Viereck, who in the 1912 election had promoted TR's cause with German Americans, among whom Roosevelt had many followers in 1914 but who were alienated during the war. In its first days, Viereck pointed out to the Colonel that even though the "channels of information in this country" were "choked and poisoned by fabrications from London and Paris," he did not doubt that Roosevelt was at least on the side of the Teuton versus Russia. TR himself, Viereck noted, had suffered in a similar way by the "perversions of the press." To "put the facts of the war fairly and squarely before the public," Viereck announced that he was starting a new weekly, *The Fatherland*, subtitled *Fair Play for Germany and Austria*, in opposition to such papers as the *New York Herald*, which was being subsidized by Russia and France.

Viereck's new publication was designed to print the official German and Austrian war accounts, review the lies told about Germany, and publish articles by other pro-German voices in America such as the Harvard professors Hugo Münsterberg and Kuno Francke. Viereck hoped at some point to publish an article from TR but realized that at present he probably could not do so due to the "political exigencies of the situation." The editor's ambitious plan was to have the paper that week on newsstands in New York and other cities and eventually to send copies of every edition to all 2,500 newspapers in America. German, Irish, and Jewish societies also agreed to help distribute the weekly. These eventually included the German-American Alliance, which had started in 1907 as an antiprohibition federation of German American societies; by 1914 it claimed two million members.[24] The first issue of *The Fatherland* hit the newsstands on August 10 and was an immediate success. Before long the publication was selling tens of thousands of copies a week, and its editor Viereck became a notorious pro-German sympathizer, in the pay of Germany.

The same day Viereck wrote to Roosevelt, Professor Münsterberg's article "Fair Play," which became the motto of the pro-German publicists, was syndicated in the leading papers.[25] It held Russia primarily responsible for the war and argued that Germany and the Kaiser were forced to fight for the cause of humanity against Slavic barbarism.[26] The Colonel was on friendly terms with Münsterberg, a German-born psychologist who sent him a copy of his article along with a letter in which he expressed the hope that TR would not be misled into a "rush against Berlin." Roosevelt assured the professor that this would not be the case and that he simply did not know as yet what the facts were and did not feel "able to pass judgment upon them." However, like every humane man, he was "very much cast down about the war." The professor knew he was "not a mere pacifist" but had always, according to his lights, "striven for Peace," although in "effective ways instead of by mere emotionalism and gush." And he had "always put even peace second to righteousness."

After reading Münsterberg's article, Roosevelt agreed that the war was inevitable and that the "several nations engaged in it" were, each from its own standpoint, "right under the existing conditions of civilization and international relations." All the present talk of international law, he went on, was "beside the mark," because there was no correspondence between it and domestic law. The power sending the ultimatum and making the attack might be doing so "merely because it is so obvious that the other side is preparing to strike first." It was the same way with the treaties guaranteeing the neutrality of Belgium and Luxembourg, "which seemingly Germany has violated even before actual fighting began." TR was not prepared to say that "in dire need" the statesmen of a nation were "not obliged to disregard any treaty, if keeping it may mean the most serious jeopardy to the nation."

Little pieces of paper like Bryan's arbitration treaties, Roosevelt continued, "with names signed to them and with no effective method of enforcement by impartial third parties" did "exceedingly little for the advancement of peace." Every now and then one of them did accomplish something, but only on the condition that the parties concerned were eager to keep the peace and had no real grave cause to demand war. In TR's view, international peace would only come "either by slow growth" as between the United States and Canada or else "by the kind of caprice" among the great powers that would "minimize the armaments of all" and "solemnly bind all the rest to take joint action against any offender." It was not necessary to discuss whether at the moment this was an "utterly hopeless idea."[27]

Hopeless or not, in the first months of the war, thirty of Bryan's arbitration treaties (which did not offer joint action against offenders) were signed and twenty ratified by the Senate. These "cooling off" treaties embodied the secretary of state's idea of delaying the use of force for a year until a commission of inquiry could investigate a dispute and suggest lines of peaceful solution. However, the recommendations of the investigating commission carried no sanction except public opinion. Bryan, who thought of himself as an apostle of peace, hosted a lavish luncheon reception at which he signed the treaties with Britain, France, Spain, and China. He personally made up the menu, which began with Neutrality Soup and ended with American Ice Cream, because "Diplomacy is the Art of Keeping Cool."[28] No treaties were signed with Germany, Austria-Hungary, or Britain's ally Japan, which declared war against Germany that August, and there was no strong opposition to the signed treaties in the Senate because they were generally considered as trivial.

Henry Cabot Lodge, who had been in England when the war broke out, told TR that he thought the treaties so "fatuous" that he had not even gone to Washington to oppose them.[29]

On August 15, 1914, while Roosevelt gave an early campaign speech at Hartford, Connecticut, the Panama Canal opened to limited commercial traffic. What should have been a triumphant culmination of ten years of colossal effort—put into motion by TR's 1904 exhortation to "make dirt fly"—was in the main lost in the news of the European war. Proposals had been put forward to have Roosevelt and William Howard Taft on hand for the occasion, but the Wilson administration was still more interested in reparation than celebration.[30] This attitude, added to the fact that work was still in progress to deepen and shore up the waterway, meant there was no grand official ceremony that day. And if he had been on hand, the Colonel certainly would not have been pleased to see that the first vessel to make the passage, the steamship *Ancon*, flew both the American flag and the banner of the American Peace Society. Because of the world war, and landslides that closed the canal completely for long periods in the following years, it was not until July 12, 1920, that the "Big Ditch" was fully opened to civilian traffic.[31] However, in 1915 the canal and its anticipated salutary effect on the Pacific coast were both celebrated at the San Francisco Panama-Pacific International Exposition, at which TR was a featured speaker.

The world war made the canal even more strategically important, but the Wilson administration, rather than building up the navy to defend the waterway in Rooseveltian fashion, hoped to get a dividend in reduced naval spending by a partition of the US fleet between the Atlantic and Pacific. The proposed division challenged a key tenet of naval strategy put down by TR's naval mentor Alfred Thayer Mahan: fleet concentration. Both TR and Mahan attacked the plan, the Colonel in the August 1914 *Outlook*. In the end the mounting criticism, the continued war in Europe, and the vexed problem of keeping the canal open to traffic at all led the secretary of the navy, the Bryanite ex–North Carolina newspaperman Josephus Daniels, to change his mind.[32] Mahan, as a retired naval officer, had his criticism afterwards muzzled by the administration for the few remaining months of his life. Roosevelt came under no such restrictions in the following years and found much to condemn.

Back at Oyster Bay after two political speeches in Maine, Roosevelt for the first time revealed in a letter the actions he would have taken had he been president when the crisis broke in Europe, confiding to Arthur Lee that he would have registered a "very emphatic protest, a protest that would mean something, against the levy of a huge war contribution on Belgium." Regarding its invasion, there was "not even room for argument." The Germans had, to suit their own purposes, "trampled on their solemn obligations," while the Belgians had fought for "their hearthstones and homes and for the elemental rights" without which it was "not worthwhile to exist." He agreed with Lee that if Germany was beaten, England would in self-defense be "obliged utterly to destroy" Germany's colonial empire and to take the "sharpest measures" in restriction of her navy. There was no alternative. For the last 43 years Germany had "spread out everywhere" and had "menaced every nation where she thought it was to her advantage to do so." Ever since unification, her "Prussianized" government had behaved in such fashion as "inevitably to make almost every nation with which it came in contact its foe," because it had convinced "everybody except Austria that it has no regard for anything except its own interest."

Roosevelt noted that Germany's other Triple Alliance partner, Italy, which had so far remained aloof from the fighting, had "really been quite as menaced by Germany as France," and confided to Lee that he would "not be a bit surprised" to see Italy "throw her forces into the scale against the two Germanic powers." He also expected at any time to hear that the Australians "had taken possession of the German islands and ports" in the South Pacific and that the "African possessions of the Germans had gone," while of course Japan would "gobble up what she has in Asia." And as it fell out, all these predictions came to pass. In Europe, even from the standpoint of "brutal self-interest," the Colonel told Lee, he believed Germany's invasion of Belgium was a mistake. He knew that they had counted on marching through Belgium before the French mobilization was complete, but three weeks had gone by and the German army was still not on French soil. If the Franco-British forces held their own, whether by victory or simply by a draw, it was in Roosevelt's judgment "all up with the Germans," who then would have to face the Russians at the same time in the east.

Because of the Russian and Japanese involvement on Britain's side, TR, like many Americans, could not agree with Lee's assertion that this was the "last war for civilization." The Colonel did not believe that Russia was any more advanced than Germany "as regards international ethics." And Japan, "with all her veneer of western civilization," was at heart "delighted to attack any and every western nation" whenever the chance came to gain what she desired "with reasonable safety." TR closed by admonishing his friend that all these opinions were only for himself and his wife, Ruth. As an ex-president, the Colonel felt his public attitude "must be one of entire impartiality—and above all no verbal or paper 'on to Berlin' business."[33]

Roosevelt did not at first publicly apportion blame for the war, but Germany's invasion of neutral Belgium had made this sorely difficult. After the assault on Liège in the first week of the conflict, an emissary of the Kaiser, a German count (whose name the Colonel later claimed he could not remember but was likely Franz von Papen) called on him at Progressive Headquarters in New York, at Forty-Second Street and Madison Avenue. The count carried a message from His Imperial Majesty that he wished TR to know that he always kept in mind the great pleasure it had given him in May 1910 to entertain the Colonel as a guest in Berlin and at the palace at Potsdam, and that he "felt assured he could count on my sympathetic understanding of Germany's position and action." Roosevelt bowed, looked the emissary straight in the eye, and answered, "Pray thank His Imperial Majesty from me for his very courteous words; and assure him I am very deeply conscious of the honors done me in Germany" and that he would never forget the way in which the Kaiser received him in Berlin—"*nor the way in which His Majesty King Albert received me in Brussels.*" The Count then looked TR in the eye without changing expression, clicked his heels, bowed, and left the room without speaking another word.[34] When the war had broken out, Roosevelt did not really believe the Kaiser was to blame and thought him simply a tool. But gradually he was forced to realize that Wilhelm was "one of the leading conspirators, plotters and wrongdoers."[35]

A month into the war the German army approached the outskirts of Paris and the French government prepared to evacuate to Bordeaux. Spring Rice reported to TR from Washington that "Poor Jusserand," their mutual friend the French ambassador, was "a good deal shattered and nervous" but was "quite determined that the only thing is to go on." And, Spring Rice imagined, "his people will say and think the same thing." His impression was that the Germans calculated on a short war with a striking and overwhelming victory and planned to "propose peace terms that would look moderate, but really leave the western nations paralyzed and helpless." The aim was that only two empires would remain: the German and the Russian.[36] In the face of this grave crisis, the Entente partners, France, Britain, and Russia, officially became the Allied powers by signing the Pact of London, in which they pledged not to negotiate or make peace separately.[37]

On September 5, TR departed for a brief speaking tour in Louisiana, where he officially opened the fall Progressive campaign with speeches at New Orleans, Franklin, Jeanerette, and New Iberia. His host was the New Orleans cotton broker John M. Parker, the chief Progressive organizer in the South and a former reform Democrat whom Roosevelt had brought into the Progressive Party fold in 1912. The Colonel's Labor Day address in New Orleans was delivered to 5,000 at the French Opera House. On the occasion TR received the greatest ovation when he turned to foreign policy and asserted that the United States must "always be able to demand justice as a right instead of begging it as a favor." At New Iberia, 400 mounted "Rough Riders" met the caravan of automobiles that had toured the Teche backcountry from Franklin. Roosevelt joined them to lead the procession, including Parker and other Progressives, into town, where he delighted a crowd estimated at 15,000 by concluding his speech in French.[38]

Over the next two months before Election Day, the Colonel thrilled similar audiences across the country, giving 110 formal addresses in 15 states supporting the party and its candidates. To conserve resources, and as a matter of political expediency, the party did not offer candidates in most southern and border states. For the 32 Senate seats that faced popular election for the first time as a result of the recently ratified Seventeenth Amendment, Progressives supported 23 candidates against Republican and Democratic opponents. In 21 of the 32 states that elected governors in 1914, the Progressives put forward many distinguished and well-qualified men.[39] Prospects for the party in these early days appeared bright, and the political stakes, everyone knew, were high.

At the same time, Spring Rice reported from Washington that he was impressed by the members of the Belgian special mission to the United States. They were "modest but very determined people." The Socialist member, Emile Vandervelde, told him, "When I saw the German ultimatum in the papers, I didn't need to look to see what the answer would be. I knew at once." That, in Spring Rice's opinion, was "some talking." Though it might seem odd coming from a gloomy fellow like himself, Spring Rice advised Roosevelt not to be "down about politics." The time was "not ripe and other things are doing." He was sure the best thing to do was to "collect your reserves and train them upon peace." His chief Sir Edward Grey, Spring Rice told TR, longed for peace, but "it must be a peace which gives satisfaction to Belgium for all she has suffered, and a sure guarantee for the future."[40]

The foreign secretary had given letters of introduction to two writers, J. M. Barrie and A. E. W. Mason, whose books he had no doubt TR had read. They were coming to America, said Grey, not to make speeches or give lectures, but to "meet people, particularly those connected with Universities, and explain the British case as regards this war and our view of the issues involved."[41] Barrie, the creator of *Peter Pan*, and the now less-remembered Mason, whose most famous novel was *The Four Feathers*, joined TR for lunch in New York and made up only the first ripple of what would become a river of British propaganda aimed at the United States for the rest of the war.

Much the most effective anti-German propaganda grew out of the pitiless occupation and exploitation of Belgium. Newspaper howls of righteous indignation over German atrocities began in the first weeks of war. The London *Daily Mail* printed stories of "German Brutality" including the murder of five civilians corroborated by sworn statements.[42] An August 21 article chronicled the "sins against civilization" and "barbarity" of the Germans. A week later in a story based on accounts by wounded British troops, the paper continued to report incidents of Germans cutting off the hands of Red Cross workers and using women and children as shields in battle.[43] At the end of August the Belgian Legation in London began releasing official reports of German "excesses."[44] The next month the *Daily Mail* reported the "Horror of Louvain," where the university library and its priceless collection of manuscripts had been burned, and continued with subsequent revelations of outrages at Maline, Rheims, and elsewhere.

Papers in the United States repeated many of these stories but also contradicted and debunked them. The most effective of these was a September 7 wireless report from Berlin signed by five noted American war correspondents—Roger Lewis, Irwin S. Cobb, Harry Hansen, James O'Donnell Bennett, and John T. McCutcheon—in which all denied seeing any evidence of such atrocities.[45] Whatever the truth of the stories, Roosevelt's friend Rudyard Kipling wrote to him that he wished TR could spend half a day with the Belgian refugees as they came into Folkstone and witness the look on their faces, which was "enough without having to hear their stories," which were like "tales from Hell." He went on, "When people congratulate each other that so and so's womenfolk were shot outright one realizes a bit about German culture." It appeared the "rapings &c" were "put through as part of a set plan to 'strike terror into the world.'" It was extraordinary to see the "frank methods by which the Teuton sets out to destroy, and, to do him justice, his leaders and philosophers for the last generation never took the trouble to disguise what their methods would be. But we didn't heed." The English, Kipling told TR, were frankly "aghast" that the United States had not even made a protest. It was "almost incredible" to the author that America, which had always stood out against such horrors, should maintain her silence.[46]

The Colonel replied that he personally "utterly and completely" rejected the foreign policy of Wilson and Bryan, but that an ex-president must be "exceedingly careful, in a crisis like this, how he hampers his successor who has to deal with the situation." It would be "not merely useless but mischievous" for him to give his views about what ought to have been done, when as a matter of fact it had not been done, and when he was "personally powerless" to see that it was.[47]

In September, the early battlefield misfortunes of the Allies were reversed when their armies successfully rallied and counterattacked in what came to be called the First Battle of the Marne. This halted the German advance, saved Paris, and spelled the end of any remaining illusions of swift victory and the premature settlement that Spring Rice feared. "The war would begin next spring," Kitchener announced in London, and Walter Hines Page confided to Colonel House that this was "probably true." The perceived wisdom of the moment held that France would hold on in the west through the winter while in the east Russia crushed Austria. And then in the spring the British would "go in with a million and a half fresh men and get the fox's tail," as did Wellington at Waterloo. In the American ambassador's view, the war was really between England and Germany, but Britain had made sure Russia and France were in before she entered. He went on that the "blindest force in this world to-day" was the "Prussian war party—blind and stupid."[48] However, when it came to forecasting the course of the war, the Prussians would not be alone in their blindness and stupidity.

In its September 23 issue, the *Outlook* published "The World War: Its Tragedies and Its Lessons," TR's first lengthy pronouncement on the conflict. He began by stating his profound gratitude that the United States, "alone among the great civilized Powers," was "unshaken by the present worldwide war." Though it was outside the conflict, he nevertheless proclaimed that America had "a twofold duty." First the country "must profit by reading aright the lesson writ in fire and steel before our eyes" and "safeguard our own future against the onfall of any similar disaster." Second, the United States "must not only stand ready to act as an instrument for the achievement of a just peace if or when an opportunity arises" but also do "whatever we can to formulate and secure adhesion to some kind of efficient international agreement whereby the chances of the recurrence of such a world-wide disaster shall at least be minimized." To serve these ends, Roosevelt called for unanimous, nonpartisan, and loyal support of the Wilson administration, asking only that the policy be one that "in truth and in fact" upheld the "honor and interest of our Nation" and was "helpful to the cause of permanent and righteous world peace."

If there was "any meaning to the words 'right' and 'wrong' in international matters," Roosevelt declared, the invasion of Belgium was wrong. But he admitted that in the past other great powers, including the United States, had carried out similar outrages when they thought national self-preservation was at stake. He also pointed out, ominously for the future, that the German system in no way limited "its disregard of conventions to disregard of neutrality treaties." For an example he used German General Friedrich von Bernhardi's assertion that even in peacetime, if there was no other means of defending one's self against a superior force, it was advisable to attack the enemy by submarine with torpedoes. Von Bernhardi also advised that war against enemy trade must be "conducted as ruthlessly as possible" so that, in addition to the material damage, the "necessary terror" was "spread among the merchant marine," making "peaceful tradesmen stay in safe harbors." Belgium, TR went on, had "felt the full effect of the practical application of these principles," and Germany had "profited by them exactly as her statesmen and soldiers believed she would profit." At the same time, Roosevelt emphasized that he was "not now criticizing" or "passing judgment one way or the other upon Germany's action." He admired and respected the German people and was "proud of the German blood in my veins."

In view of what had happened in the war, argued Roosevelt, "surely the time ought to be ripe for the nations to consider a great world agreement among all the civilized world powers *to back righteousness by force.*" Such an agreement would establish an "efficient World League for the Peace of Righteousness." It would limit the amount to be spent on armaments, and after "defining carefully the inalienable rights of each nation which were not to be transgressed by any other," it could also provide that any cause of difference among them should be submitted to an international court. To "supplement and make this effectual it should be solemnly covenanted that if any nation refused to abide by the decision of such a court the others would draw the sword on behalf of peace and justice and would unitedly coerce the recalcitrant nation." But all this lay in a possible future. At present each nation "must in the last resort look to its own strength." This state of things could only be abolished "when we put force, when we put the collective armed power of civilization, behind some body which shall with reasonable justice and equity represent the collective determination of civilization to do what is right."[49]

Roosevelt commented to Sir Edward Grey about the *Outlook* article, and a syndicated series on the war that he was preparing, that he had done his best not to be offensive to Germany but had at the same time "emphatically backed the position that England, and specifically you, have taken." TR confided that he was in a difficult position. Since he was in opposition to the Wilson administration, it would do "harm and not good" if he declared he would have taken a reverse position. This was particularly true because the bulk of the people did not understand foreign affairs and had no notion about "any impending military danger." Roosevelt believed that when he had been president he had "really succeeded in educating them to a fairly good understanding of these matters," and if he had been in office at the beginning of the war, Americans would have supported "my taking the stand I most assuredly would have taken as the head of a signatory nation of the Hague treaties in reference to the violation of Belgium's neutrality." But he of course would not have taken such action unless he was prepared to "back it up to the end, no matter what course it necessitated."[50]

The idea that the United States might have "come forward on the eve of the outbreak of the war to uphold Treaty rights," Grey replied, made him "glow at the thought of what might have been achieved." At the same time, the foreign secretary saw the difficulty there would have been with American public opinion and understood that the line the Wilson administration had taken was, "of course, the natural and expected one." If the United States had taken action, he went on, this might "possibly" have stopped the war, but "the accumulated evidence of the enormous preparation of Germany, her confidence, and her intention" made Grey doubt whether "anything could have stopped her at the last moment." And now the foreign secretary could see "nothing for it but to fight on till we can get a peace that will secure us against Prussian militarism." He still thought it possible that the United States government might "play a great part in the making of the peace at the end of the war" and in "securing permanent peace afterwards." But it had become a point of honor for Britain that there should be "reasonable redress" to Belgium for what she had suffered. Germany would not consider this until she was beaten, and the British could not "give up contending for it while we are unbeaten." Roosevelt entirely agreed that Britain must fight on and Belgium's grievances must be redressed.[51]

In Cleveland four days after the *Outlook* article was published, TR met at the Hollenden Hotel with members of the Belgian Royal Commission on Atrocities that was touring America presenting their claims and soliciting aid. After their long interview in French, all the parties declined to comment to reporters on their discussion, but Paul Hymans, the Belgian minister of state, did reveal that the commission had thanked the Colonel for "the tone of his recent war articles," which the members considered "favorable to the Belgian cause."[52] Though sympathetic with the Belgian commissioners, after meeting them Roosevelt confided to Kipling that he suspected their atrocity reports were exaggerated. He also pointed out that the British in Ireland, and the Americans during their Indian wars, had been guilty of similar offences.[53] A month later, TR wrote again to Kipling that personal friends of his who had followed the German armies had never been able to get statements from men who had "actually seen the outrages committed, nor to speak to the women and children." What was needed, he went on, were "authoritative statements, backed by official authority." He suggested to Kipling (and others) that the way to reach world opinion was to have Kipling's government investigate, get statements with places and dates, and photographs if possible, "and publish them in an official document."[54]

Just such an investigative commission had already been convened under TR's friend Lord Bryce, known as the "British Tocqueville" for his acclaimed book *American Commonwealth*. An accomplished man of affairs as well, Bryce had preceded Spring Rice as British ambassador to the United States. The Bryce commission's sensational findings would be published in the United States in May 1915 as the *Report of the Committee on Alleged German Outrages*.[55] This work exposed a variety of German brutalities and included reports of the impaling of babies on bayonets and the amputations of women's breasts. Besides the domestic audience, these broadsides also were aimed at world and, most importantly, American opinion.

Whatever the truth of the atrocity charges, Roosevelt argued in the first of a series of four war articles for the Wheeler press syndicate, "What America Should Learn from the War," that so long as a "power with the defective morality of Germany" was at large, the primary lesson to be drawn was the uselessness of relying on treaties alone.[56] This first installment, dealing with preparedness, reached an audience of 15 million, and it increased the circulation of the *New York Times* alone by thousands of copies. The London *Daily Mail* agreed with TR's assessment of Germany while at the same time praising the arbitration treaty between the United States and Great Britain just ratified by the Senate. Americans, the paper went on, were only slightly "less concerned than ourselves in seeing that the Prussian system of international brigandage" was "broken forever."[57]

The German side, as might be expected, took a much different view. In the *Tages Zeitung*, government spokesman Count Ernst zu Reventlow accused Roosevelt of "deliberate bad faith" in ignoring that Germany was fighting a "defensive war that was forced upon her in the most just of all possible causes." The *Frankfurter Zeitung* asked what sort of neutrality Roosevelt would exercise in the name of America if he should again become president. Germany must consider what would happen as must the "German-American electors" in the United States.[58] The Cologne *Gazette* personally attacked TR as a man "never gifted with modesty" who "never had a full insight into European affairs." The paper went on that he had been treated with "special respect" in his 1910 visit to Germany because he had been president, but at the "last Presidential election he lost all his prestige."[59]

Roosevelt was pleased with the attack of the Cologne *Gazette*, he told Spring Rice, because he wished to be "scrupulously fair and not in the least bitter towards Germany" but at the same time to make his position "as clear as a bell." As a matter of fact, he went on, it had been very hard "to keep myself in." The Colonel also intended to remind those Americans "clamoring for peace now" that there were "in the northern United States in 1864 several hundred thousand men who in the loudest terms declared their extreme devotion to peace and that to a man voted against Abraham Lincoln." If England and France had joined, "as certain of their public men wished them to join, in offering mediation so as to bring about 'peace,' we should have treated it as an unfriendly act." TR was glad that opinion in America was on England's side and also believed that the British would "put the war through." At any rate, there was "no question as to where the interests of civilization lie at this moment."

If he had been president, TR told Spring Rice, he would have "acted on the thirtieth or thirty-first of July, as head of a signatory power of the Hague treaties, calling attention to the guarantee of Belgium's neutrality" and that he accepted the treaties as "imposing a serious obligation" that he expected not only the United States but all other neutral nations to join in enforcing. Of course, Roosevelt went on, "I would not have made such a statement unless I was willing to back it up." He also believed that if he had been president, "the American people would have followed me." Whether or not he was mistaken about that, he did believe that a majority were now so following Wilson in neutrality. In his view, "only a limited number could or ought to be expected to make up their minds for themselves in a crisis like this, and they tend, and ought to tend, to support the President." It would therefore be "worse than folly" for Roosevelt "to clamor now about what to be done or ought to have been done, when it would be mere clamor and nothing else." He told Spring Rice that this was only "for yourself" and that it was a "freer expression of opinion than I have permitted myself in any letter hitherto."[60]

For public consumption, on October 4, 1914, the *New York Times* and other papers carried the second in TR's syndicated war series. In this he discussed the "difficult task of securing peace without the sacrifice of righteousness." His first point was the "extreme unwisdom and impropriety" of making promises that could not be kept. And second, the "utter futility" of expecting that in any but exceptional cases a "strong power" would keep a promise it found to its disadvantage. In his view there were "certain respects" in which the United States could "fairly claim to stand ahead of most nations in its regard for international morality." For example, the previous spring when the country took Vera Cruz in Mexico, individuals in the city fired on its troops in the same fashion alleged to have been taken place in Louvain, but it "never for one moment entered the heads of our people to destroy Vera Cruz." In the same way the promise was kept to leave Cuba independent after "an orderly Government" was established, performing an act that, as far as TR knew, was "without parallel in the dealings of stronger with weaker nations." The same could be said for the treatment of Santo Domingo and Panama under his administration.

Roosevelt recognized that some "good and well-meaning people" thought him "not zealous in the cause of Peace." To the contrary, he professed to "abhor war" and that he was "inexpressibly saddened by the dreadful contest now waging in Europe." He put peace "very high as an agent for bringing about Righteousness." But if he must choose between the two, he would "choose Righteousness." Therefore, TR held himself "in honor bound" to do anything in his power to "advance the cause of the Peace of Righteousness throughout the world."

In the last month before the 1914 election, the Colonel concentrated his campaign efforts on New York, with brief side trips to Illinois, Pennsylvania, and New Jersey. This punishing itinerary began October 5 with speeches at Yonkers, Cold Spring, Beacon, Wappingers Falls, and Poughkeepsie. That night was spent at Hyde Park with his Democratic Roosevelt cousins, despite Theodore's warning to his cousin Sara that this might reflect badly on her son, Franklin, the assistant secretary of the navy in the Wilson administration.[61] Theodore's daughter Alice once commented that her fifth-cousin Franklin, married to TR's favorite niece Eleanor, was overprotected by his mother, "Cousin Sally," who was in her opinion "a domineering tartar." Alice illustrated the difference between Franklin and his Sagamore Hill cousins by noting that FDR "used to sail a boat instead of sweatingly rowing it in the hottest weather as Father would insist on our doing." Nevertheless, she recalled, the Colonel liked Franklin very much and was very helpful to him.[62]

Though the slim and handsome Franklin looked nothing like him, Alice's stocky and toothsome father was certainly a political inspiration and model for Franklin, who, though in the opposition party, from an early age followed a calculated path to the presidency in "Cousin Ted's" footsteps.[63] Both men graduated from Harvard and attended Columbia Law School, but unlike TR, FDR went on to pass the New York bar exam and practiced for a time. Both served in the state legislature, and in 1913 FDR, age thirty, was rewarded for his support of Wilson with the navy post, previously held by TR. (Unlike the Colonel, however, he would stay in his job once war was declared.) Both men were also followers of the navalist theories of Mahan. After FDR took the navy job, TR sent congratulations and soon after advice on Mahanian lines, likely not needed, to keep the fleet intact and not to divide it because of the slim possibility of a Japanese attack, which, if it came, would "come suddenly."[64] One authority on TR described FDR as a "mole" in the Wilson administration who passed along clandestine and alarming information to the Colonel, such as the fact that 13 second-line battleships were out of service because the navy did not have the men to crew them.[65] Another has called Franklin a "Rooseveltian in the Wilson camp."[66]

Back on the campaign trail the next day after his night at Hyde Park, TR gave speeches at Kingston, Saugerties, Catskill, Athens, Hudson, and Troy. Everywhere there were enthusiastic crowds, but as in 1912, many came out simply to see their "Teddy." At Troy the Music Hall was packed, and a crowd surrounded the hall hoping for a glimpse of the Colonel, but the local newspaper reported that as soon as he spoke, and then departed, few stayed to hear Bainbridge Colby and other New York Progressive candidates. It was not a hopeful sign for the party.[67] The problem for Progressives was that TR was not on the ballot. That month William Randolph Hearst's *American Magazine* revealed that Roosevelt had come out on top in its poll to find "the Greatest Man in the United States." Thomas Edison finished second, followed by Wilson, with Secretary of State Bryan fifth behind "Mr. Ordinary Citizen."[68]

Shortly before Roosevelt launched his last push of the 1914 campaign, the Wilson administration, not unaware of the Progressive threat, was able to counter their charges of a failure to act on the trust issue with two pieces of legislation. On September 26, Wilson signed an act creating the Federal Trade Commission, a regulatory agency strikingly like the one TR had been calling for since 1912. To help draw up the bill, Wilson had even called in George Rublee, a New York attorney who had worked on the 1912 Progressive platform. Further, on October 15, Wilson signed the Clayton Anti-Trust Act, which, among other things, contained provisions that could be interpreted as prounion and, consequently, was praised to heaven by the American Federation of Labor's chief, Samuel Gompers, as "labor's Magna Carta."[69] This undoubtedly cost the Progressives labor votes, as did the party's support in some places for prohibition of alcohol, despite TR's objections.

Nevertheless, Roosevelt pressed on to the finish. On October 23, at Monticello, New York, TR underlined the theme of the last weeks of the campaign: "Be sovereigns of your own souls." He told the people of Monticello to be "true to yourselves." He wished, fundamentally, to make his appeal "not in the interest of the candidates, but in your own interest." In public the Colonel kept up his enthusiasm and predicted victory, "if only we can get the rubbish off the souls of the weary plain citizens." But in private, by the end of the campaign Roosevelt feared the party would make "such a pitiful showing" that by "common consent its existence as a separate political party" would be "at once ended."[70] The election had become for TR a test for not only the party but the American people.

The last also would be true for the national campaign for preparedness Roosevelt undertook after the political season was over. The first shot in this new battle that before long consumed him was fired that month in Congress. With one eye on the war in Europe and another on the military inadequacies revealed by the Mexican border mobilization, Republican representative Augustus P. "Gussie" Gardner of Massachusetts, Senator Lodge's son-in-law, introduced a resolution calling for a formal investigation into the state of the nation's defenses by a national security commission. Gardner had been in Europe at the start of the war and witnessed both the German military machine and Britain's unprepared condition. Once home, the congressman declared that he had sat like a coward in the House for 12 years while the country remained defenseless and felt he had to speak out.

In this "new and hostile world" of huge armies and super-dreadnought battleships, both "past victories and present treaties" were useless. He wanted his commission to "throw a public searchlight" on America's weakness as represented by its undermanned navy (which had slipped at best to third most powerful in the world), tiny regular army, and not much larger militia, 60 percent of which could not use the army rifle.[71] Alice would later recall a bit of doggerel about Gardner by their common friend Spring Rice:

> What does Gussie Gardner say,
> In his nest at break of day?

'Wake up, every mother's son,
Buy a double-barreled gun,
Shoot a Dutchman or a Jap,
Or some other foreign chap.[72]

Woodrow Wilson, on the other hand, saw nothing humorous in the call for preparedness. To the president, the war was an opportunity for America to demonstrate her moral leadership and to mediate the crisis—a position that would, he believed, be imperiled by arming. Any inquiry into defense, the president told Gardner, would create "very unfavorable international impressions." He dismissed Gardner's clamor for a defense investigation as a "good mental exercise" and only the same sort of partisan "scare tactic" that had been going on since he was a boy. The president was not interested in military matters, he was uncomfortable as commander-in-chief, and supported by a pacifist secretary of state and a Bryanite navy secretary, Josephus Daniels, he was more interested in moral power than sea power. In addition, frugal and antimilitarist Southern Democrats dominated Congress.[73] But at least one figure within the administration agreed with Gardner regarding the state of naval preparedness and had advised the congressman on his resolution. It was obvious to Franklin Roosevelt that his chief, Daniels, a North Carolina newspaperman with no naval credentials whatsoever, was bewildered by the events in Europe.[74]

In an October 31 address to students at Princeton, TR also rallied to Gardner's cause. He spoke of the war, and for the first time he publicly revealed that he had seen plans made by "two of the empires now at war" (obviously Germany and Japan) dealing with the capture of the ports of New York and San Francisco. These were to be held for ransoms "that would cripple our country and give funds to the enemy for carrying on the war." After the speech, he refused to elaborate, saying only that he thought it the country's duty "to put itself in such shape" that it would be able to "defend its rights if they are invaded." Roosevelt hoped that the time would come when the United States would provide that every man would "have to practice marksmanship and have some military training." A fight, he went on, "never was won by parrying; you've got to hit and not hit softly." The American people owed it "to themselves to make their hands safeguard their head."[75]

At the same time on the western front in Europe, after the Battle of the Marne the so-called race to the sea unfolded in which the opposing armies attempted to outflank each other all the way to the English Channel. The triumph of modern defense over attack was demonstrated in the defeat of the German attempt to break through at the First Battle of Ypres.[76] Crucially, the German failure to take Calais, Dunkirk, and Boulogne left these ports open for the British to transport troops and material assistance to France. The stalemated front soon extended hundreds of miles from the English Channel to the Swiss border, marking the end of the war of movement and the beginning of three-and-a-half years of almost stationary trench warfare. By the end of 1914 the French already had suffered 528,000 casualties, the British had lost 90,000, and the Belgians had lost half their combat strength. On the eastern front, to advance into German and Austrian territory—most of which they would not be able to hold for long—the Russian "steam roller" suffered massive losses of 1.8 million men, including casualties and captured. Fighting against Russia, Austria-Hungary had lost 1.25 million, and Germany, fighting on two fronts, counted 800,000 casualties.[77]

On the ground in the west, Germany held most of Belgium, with its strategic coastline and great cities such as Antwerp and Lille, as well as the northern provinces of France that held three-quarters of its coal output and had accounted for almost two-thirds of its steel production. As a result, while the French provided most of the Allied troops on the western front, they were now dependent on British coal and manufactures, as well as the Royal Navy, British shipping, and treasury loans. Over the following years the French, British, and Belgians fought to regain the lost territory and were therefore forced into bloody and futile offensives that they would continue despite horrific losses.[78] The German failure to knock out France meant a two-front war, and in 1915 the German army turned its main attention to the Russian front, from which its two greatest figures of the war, Paul von Hindenburg and Erich Ludendorff, would emerge, leaving the Kaiser, in his own words, "only a shadow."[79]

Many of TR's English friends, and their sons, had already gone off into this maelstrom. He wrote to Kipling that he had heard that his son John, after a struggle with the authorities on account of his poor eyesight, had been at last accepted into the army. Roosevelt heartily congratulated his friend; he had told his own sons that "if there was any war in their lifetime," he wanted them to be able to explain to their children "why they did go to it, and not why they did not go to it."[80] Of course, for TR's sons this would need to be a war in which the United States was a belligerent, though some Americans did volunteer to fight on the ground and in the air with the British and French, perhaps most famously with the Lafayette Escadrille flying squadron. Many others also undertook other noncombat duties such as driving ambulances or working in hospitals.

Ironically enough, the first of the warlike Roosevelt clan to give service in Europe was perhaps the most unlikely: his demure daughter Ethel, who a month after the war began left her six-month-old son behind at Sagamore Hill to accompany her surgeon husband Richard Derby to France. She reported to her parents from the American Ambulance Hospital at Neuilly that while Richard operated she had taken charge of the dispensary, where minor wounds were dressed. Ethel found the mostly English patients to be "wonderfully brave & very cheerful." She did not often go into the wards, because she could not bear to see the appalling damage from shell fire, which carried clothing and everything into the wounds so there was always infection present. She could not believe that "men should do such things to each other." Ethel also passed along tales of atrocities she heard from Ambassador Herrick and went on that if the American people had seen and heard what she had they would not be able to stay neutral.[81] Though he was made anxious by his daughter's proximity to the fighting, Roosevelt wrote to Ethel that he was "*very* proud of you both" and that "two of my family, should have worthily met the call of high privilege to do their part in the great world tragedy."[82]

In the first months of the conflict, the war at sea had also taken an unexpected turn. After his early success in mobilizing the fleet, Winston Churchill's actions at the Admiralty came under increasing press and public criticism.[83] The British nation expected great things of the Royal Navy and had been disappointed by the escape of the German battle-cruiser *Goeben* to Turkey (which subsequently joined the Central Powers to take the place of Italy), the sinking of three outdated British cruisers in one day by a German submarine, and the capture and internment at Antwerp of the Royal Navy Division. The failed defense of Antwerp personally involved Churchill.[84] At the end of October, in response to widespread public and press demands led by Northcliffe, Lord Fisher, the father of the first *Dreadnought*, was recalled from retirement to right the Admiralty's course.

On November 1, the *New York Times* carried the next of TR's Wheeler syndicate war series, "The Peace of Righteousness," which at length restated many of the same comments the Colonel had for months been making in his private correspondence, in particular noting the "disaster terrible beyond belief" that had befallen innocent Belgium and the "loquacious impotence" of the Bryan-Wilson arbitration treaties and the ultrapacifist "gospel of national abjectness." Roosevelt agreed with a recent article by Lord Bryce that the United States must "insist on righteousness first and foremost" and "strive for peace always; but we must never hesitate to put righteousness above peace." In order to do this, in the world as it now was, the country must put "force back of righteousness." A policy of blood and iron, said TR, was "sometimes very wicked," but it rarely did as much harm, and never excited "as much derision," as a policy of "milk and water." And it came "dangerously near flattery" to call the present foreign policy of the United States "merely one of milk and water."

There was just one way, in the Colonel's view, "to meet the upholders of the doctrine that might makes right," and that was to prove that "right will make right, by backing right with might." A letter to the editor of the *New York Times* from Alfonso Villegas Restrepo, the wealthy founder of the Colombian newspaper *El Tiempo*, reminded readers that it was exactly 11 years since TR "failed to practice what he preaches" when he treated the Treaty of 1846 between the United States and Colombia as a "scrap of paper" and deprived the writer's country of the Panama Canal, its "most valuable and cherished possession." November the Third was "still taught in the schools of Colombia as the anniversary of the rape of the Isthmus."[85]

In the United States, November 3 was Election Day, and by then, if not before, Roosevelt must have realized the futility of his campaign efforts. When the votes were tallied in what has been dubbed the "stand pat" election of 1914, the Democrats retained control of congress while the Republicans made up some ground. For the Progressives, the election was a disaster.

In every state save California, where Governor Hiram Johnson's popularity carried the day, the Progressive Party was soundly defeated. Their attacks on Democrats too often translated into votes for the Republicans, the traditional alternative, and in uncertain economic times the people responded to the tried and true GOP promise of a "full dinner pail."

In TR's view the "pressure of want was the controlling cause" in the defeat. Businessmen, farmers and laborers alike all wanted "some little prosperity . . . some chance to earn their living." They did not care about "civic morality or industrial justice or anything else" against the chance to get a job. This was natural. The voters were "sick and tired of hearing us exhort them to be virtuous and they wished to relieve their feelings by voting for every corrupt scoundrel in sight. Accordingly they did so!"[86] Many Old Guard Republican enemies of TR, like former Speaker "Uncle Joe" Cannon, either regained their seats or were reelected, as was Senator Boies Penrose in Pennsylvania. As for his old party, the Colonel commented to William Allen White, "At the moment the dog has returned to its vomit."[87]

Roosevelt refused to comment on the election to reporters, telling them instead to read II Timothy 4:3–4. The November 5 papers dutifully printed the verses:

> For the time will come when they will not endure sound doctrine; but after their own lusts shall they heap to themselves teachers, having itching ears;
>   And they shall turn away their ears from the truth, and shall be turned into fables.[88]

Privately, Roosevelt shared his view of the election debacle with several family members including Kermit and his bride Belle, both of whom to TR's great relief had made it safely to South America so that Kermit could take up his new job at the Buenos Aires office of the National City Bank of New York. The Colonel confided that the election had gone substantially as he had forecast to Kermit in the jungles of South America that spring. The party in New York had "practically come to an end," but it had been his duty to "raise the black flag and go down with the rest of my associates."[89]

Among the followers with which a temporarily downcast Colonel met in New York at Progressive Headquarters that month were Walter Lippmann and Herbert Croly, who days after the election published the first weekly issue of the *New Republic*.[90] Croly's 1909 *The Promise of American Life* had influenced, if not inspired, Roosevelt's 1912 New Nationalism Progressive party campaign and had catapulted Croly into prominence. The new journal was intended to promote TR's brand of progressivism against the Wilsonian New Freedom preached by magazines such as *Harper's Weekly*. The Colonel's friend Willard Straight (with the support of his socialite wife Dorothy Whitney) provided the financial backing. But it would not be long before the independent and reasonable views displayed in the *New Republic* brought a breach with its inspiration.

Figure 2. "Interned" *New York World*, November 18, 1914
Theodore Roosevelt Collection, Harvard College Library

Meanwhile, the London *Daily News*, a Liberal paper that generally supported the Asquith government, commented that the "collapse of the Progressive party" would be read throughout the United States as the "political passing" of Roosevelt and a failure from which he could "hardly recover." The editorial went on that TR had not "worn well out of office" and that the hold he once had on the "imagination of his countrymen struck many observers as evidence of unripeness." Over the past few years the political education of the American people had moved forward and they now realized that a man of Roosevelt's "temperament and trend" was not the leader needed "in this very critical hour of the world's fortunes." On the other hand, there was "no statesman throughout the world" whose reputation had risen as steadily or stood higher than President Wilson's. He had "created the conviction" that his conduct of foreign affairs was "determined by justice" and he had an "iron will" to pursue the course he thought right "in the teeth of clamor and passion." He hated jingoism and loved peace and his understanding was "as clear as his principles are high."[91] And it would be exactly those "principles" that Roosevelt would deride over the next years as he took off his gloves in more and more heated criticism of Wilson and everything for which he stood at home and in foreign affairs.

Very near the end of the campaign that fall, TR had told the progressive publicist O. K. Davis that he had "paid all his debts" and done everything "everybody has wanted. This election makes me an absolutely free man. Thereafter I am going to say and do just what I damned please."[92] Because he knew it was not popular and his friends had feared it would hurt them in the November elections, Roosevelt had tempered his criticism of Wilson's foreign policy. But now, he told Lodge, he meant to "smite the administration with a heavy hand."[93]

CHAPTER 3

TO SERVE RIGHTEOUSNESS

NOVEMBER 1914 TO APRIL 1915

> More and more I come to the view that in a really tremendous world struggle, with a great moral issue involved, neutrality does not serve righteousness; for to be neutral between right and wrong is to serve wrong. The neutrality our government now boasts . . . serves ease and selfishness at the moment; but it does not serve morality, nor in the long run real national interest.
> —TR to John St. Loe Strachey, February 22, 1915

With the cataclysm in Europe showing no signs of ending in the three months widely forecast, and "utterly sick of the spiritless neutrality" of the Wilson administration, Roosevelt unfurled his fourth syndicated war series article, "An International Posse Comitatus," which in "emphatic language" publicly recounted several themes he had already rehearsed in private conversations.[1] Up to this time, the Colonel declared in his article, he had been "reluctant in any way to criticize" the actions of Woodrow Wilson and William Jennings Bryan in foreign affairs. He had "faithfully," and in some cases against his own "deep-rooted personal convictions," sought to justify what had been done in Mexico and regarding the present world war. But the time had come when loyalty to the administration in foreign affairs meant "disloyalty to our own national self-interest and to our obligations toward humanity at large."

Regarding Belgium, the administration had "clearly taken the ground that our own selfish ease forbids us to fulfill our explicit obligations to small neutral nations when they are deeply wronged." And there would never be a "clearer breach of international morality" than that committed by Germany in this case. Roosevelt felt this particularly deeply because as president he had ordered the signature of the United States to the Hague conventions and he "most emphatically" would not have "permitted such a farce to have gone through" if it had entered his head that "this government would not consider itself bound" to do all it could to see the articles to which it became a party were observed. Further, as the "most disinterested and strongest" of the present neutral powers, he felt the United States "should therefore bear the main burden of responsibility in this matter." If his statements appeared "hostile to Germany," TR was careful to point out, he would have taken the same view and put the United States on the side of Germany if it had been similarly attacked.

The Colonel likened the present international situation to the lawless days of the Old West. And in light of the "stupendous and discreditable failure" of existing treaties to stop the outbreak of war, he proposed a new method to deal with wrongdoing in the absence of any "central police power." "We must recognize clearly," TR argued, that measures must be taken to "put force back of good faith in the observance of treaties." This meant putting the "collective and efficient strength of all the great powers of civilization back of any well-behaved power that is wronged by another." To this end Roosevelt again proposed the establishment of "some great international tribunal" and securing the enforcement of its decrees "through the action of a posse comitatus of powerful and civilized nations."

Until a new international system could be put in place, however, TR called for renewed and heightened naval and army preparedness to keep disaster from striking the United States. He urged the nation to follow the examples of democracies such as Switzerland and Australia and "require military training for all our young men" to build a capable reserve force for the army (rather than the improvised and untrained "make-believe" soldiers of the "Wilson-Bryan theory"). It was only the efficient Swiss army, in his view, that had protected her neutrality in the present war. And England was only saved from the fate of Belgium by her navy. On the other hand, the small size of Britain's army and lack of preparations, said TR, without doubt afforded "the chief reason why this war has occurred at all at this time." If England had followed the advice "so often urged upon her" by Lord Roberts (who had died that month at the age of 82 while visiting his beloved Indian soldiers at the front) and had been able to put an army as large as that of France in the field, there "probably" would have "been no war."

Unfortunately, as in England before 1914, similar warnings about America's unpreparedness had now also gone unheeded. Augustus P. Gardner's calls for a national security commission had been answered by President Wilson with a "cheap sneer" and "unworthy levity." The repeated warnings of America's most respected soldier, TR's old commander General Leonard Wood, were "treated with the same indifference." Nevertheless, Roosevelt did not believe "this attitude on the part of our public servants" represented the "real convictions of the average American." He continued to believe that American society was "sound at core" and accepted "as the basis of sound morality not slothful ease and soft selfishness and the loud timidity that fears every species of risk and hardship, but the virile strength of manliness which clings to the idea of stern, unflinching performance of duty, and which follows withersoever that ideal may lead."[2]

Roosevelt's call for action and preparedness garnered little popular support. And even though he used "Posse Comitatus" in the Latin legalist sense, his explicit comparison to the lawless Old West revived the old charges that he was once again running amuck in "cowboy" fashion. National sentiment for neutrality remained strong. The November *Literary Digest* published a poll of 367 American editors and writers that very likely mirrored the population at large. Only 20 favored the Central Powers, while 105 favored the Allies. The vast majority, 242, favored neutrality.[3] Newspaper reaction to Roosevelt's latest article, as might be expected, divided along partisan lines. The *New York World* opined that if the United States followed such an unprecedented policy of protest concerning Belgium, "we should become the common scold among the nations of the earth." The *New York Evening Post* found the idea of policing the world "absurd," while the New York *Mail* thought Roosevelt's ideas proper but that a "noble opportunity had been lost" because it was too late to take action, an early use of the "spilt milk" argument often thereafter used to counter Roosevelt's criticisms.[4]

The preparedness campaign continued with a November 15 article in the *New York Times*, "Self-Defense without Militarism," which repeated TR's call for the country to adopt the Swiss system of universal military training. Further, that month he invited Colonel William Sanger, a leading figure in the New York National Guard, to Sagamore Hill to discuss "starting some kind of propaganda" to institute something like the Swiss system in the United States.[5] Theodore Jr., who had embarked on a lucrative career in investment banking, and Archie, still at Harvard, also involved themselves in the military training and preparedness movement.[6] Sanger, TR reported to Archie, had been "very interested in your proposals." Sanger's son was also at Harvard, and Sanger planned to visit them both and "talk the whole thing over." Roosevelt went on that he doubted much could be done at present "except agitate among our people," for the effort needed a "prolonged course of preliminary agitation before we can get them to see any sense."[7] Before long Archie's "disruptive" on-campus efforts led Harvard's antipreparedness President Lawrence Lowell to warn TR that his son might be suspended.[8] TR also looked with favor on a new preparedness group organized at this time: the National Security League. This avowedly nonpartisan organization supported Congressman Gardner and promoted universal military training. Within a year the league grew to seventy branches with thirty thousand members. Roosevelt's friend Robert Bacon was the first president.[9]

However, TR's most important ally in this campaign, and the real leader of the preparedness movement in the United States, was General Leonard Wood, commander of the army's eastern district, with headquarters at Governor's Island in New York harbor.[10] Wood, Roosevelt's old Rough Rider commander, had also made his name and career in the Spanish-American War. He had risen in a decade from President McKinley's physician to army chief of staff and had come to Governor's Island the previous year. The crisis in Mexico had forced Woodrow Wilson to reluctantly give him "supreme command" of a hypothetical army with which to intervene if necessary—a contingency that never occurred. Over the previous years, Wood had traveled the country in uniform making speeches calling for preparedness in opposition to the policies, and to the annoyance, of both William Howard Taft and Wilson.

Taking a lead from Cornell professor Henry Bull, Wood had also instituted what proved to be a popular system of summer army-training camps for college students, the first two on opposite coasts at Monterey and Gettysburg in 1913, in an attempt to build a cadre of reserve officers for the future. Wood assured Roosevelt that his articles had done good for the movement and asked for further help in the form of a letter to be used in his own publicity. He went on that he had "been doing all I can here to interest people and have the papers call attention to the necessity of preparedness." But as a serving soldier under a president hostile to any military buildup, he could not "proceed beyond a certain point." Orders had been issued that officers were not to comment for publication, so at present it had come down to "speaking where there were no reporters" and giving the best advice he could to those who were writing on the subject. To Wood, the nation's unpreparedness was "so alarming" that no thoughtful American could view the situation "otherwise than with great apprehension." And the moment now seemed to be a favorable one to take "intelligent action."[11] In answer to those who called for preparedness and a larger army William Jennings Bryan declared in December that "if this country needed a million men, and needed them in a day, the call would go out at sunrise and the sun would go down on a million men in arms." Wood, who knew full well how long it would take to train one million civilians, dismissed the secretary of state as "an ass of the first class."[12]

That same month Roosevelt's naval mentor and ally, retired Admiral Alfred Thayer Mahan, passed away.[13] Like Wood, Mahan had been muzzled by the Wilson administration when he openly supported Britain's course after the war broke out. TR commented that Mahan, like so many other "patriots," had been "treated despicably" by the administration.[14] The Colonel wrote to Mahan's wife, Ellen, that he wished her to know "how deeply Mrs. Roosevelt and I feel for and with you." He had not only "immensely admired the Admiral but regarded him as one of the greatest and most useful influences in American life." Mahan was a not only a "great man" but a "very good man and a good citizen."[15] Along with numerous similarly laudatory obituaries, the death of Mahan also brought sympathetic newspaper articles reprising his theories of sea power and sparked a renewed support for naval preparedness, including the creation of a naval general staff like that of the Royal Navy.[16]

Interestingly enough, that month the New York *Sun* published a little noticed interview with Mahan's German counterpart, Minister of Marine Admiral Alfred von Tirpitz. TR had gotten to know von Tirpitz four years before in Berlin when they had discussed, among other things, the voyage of the Great White Fleet that Roosevelt had dispatched on an epic circumnavigation of the globe. In his 1914 interview, the German admiral noted that America had "not raised her voice in protest" or taken any real action in response to Britain's "closing of the North Sea to neutral shipping" with mines and wondered what the response would be if Germany declared "submarine war on all enemy merchant ships." England wanted to starve his country, said von Tirpitz, but Germany could play the same game and "bottle her up" by torpedoing all ships that neared any British harbor, thereby "cutting off large food supplies."[17] In December, Germany in fact escalated the conflict, not with submarines, but instead with a campaign of zeppelin raids and naval bombardments on civilian targets along the British coast, which brought home to the population for the first time the bitter reality of twentieth-century warfare. The German shelling of Scarborough and other coastal towns killed many women and children, and the London *Daily Mail* howled over the "inhuman and malignant action."[18]

Though Roosevelt admired England's sacrifices, and particularly her rallying to the aid of Belgium, he refused to sign a more general "hands across the sea" appeal for the British cause. The Colonel explained to one of the promoters of the appeal that he did not approve of asking Americans to "proclaim themselves Anglo-Americans" on the ground that England was the "motherland." This was not, in his opinion, the "right attitude for Americans to take." England was not his motherland any more than Germany was his fatherland. "My motherland and fatherland," he went on, "and my own land are all three of them the United States."

In perhaps his first wartime use of a term forever after associated with him, TR went on that he did "not believe in hyphenated Americans . . . in German-Americans or Irish-Americans," and he believed "just as little in English-Americans." He did not approve of Americans of German descent "forming organizations to force the United States into practical alliance with Germany" any more than he did English-descended Americans doing the same. Americans were a separate people, "although akin to many European peoples." The country had a right to ask all these immigrants, and their sons, "that they become Americans and nothing else; but we have no right to ask that they become transplanted or second-rate Englishmen." "Most emphatically," declared the Colonel, he was "not an Englishman once-removed! I am straight United States!"[19] The pro-German organization referred to in this letter was obviously the powerful German-American Alliance, which carried out a loud campaign for strict neutrality and railed against the Wilsonian policy of allowing arms sales and loans to the Allies. The Alliance would soon add Roosevelt to the list of its political foes, while his name was struck off the rolls of many German-American societies that had elected him to honorary memberships in friendlier times.[20] Georges Sylvester Viereck's *The Fatherland* also began a running anti-Roosevelt campaign that would end their friendship.

In his annual address to Congress, on December 8, 1914, Wilson responded to TR and others who called for heightened preparedness. The president praised the student training camps while at the same time declaring that the defense of the country would not rely on a standing army, or even a reserve army, but "upon a citizenry trained and accustomed to arms," maintaining an American military tradition that reached back to the Revolution. "More than this," said Wilson, carried with it a "reversal of the whole history and character of our polity." It would mean that "we had lost our self-possession, that we had been thrown off balance by a war with which we have nothing to do, whose causes cannot touch us, whose very existence affords us opportunities of friendship and disinterested service which should make us ashamed of any thought of hostility or fearful preparation for trouble."[21]

Roosevelt countered that in his message to Congress the president had "announced that we are in no danger and will not be in any danger." Even ex-president Taft had "stated that an awakening of interest in our defenses indicated 'mild hysteria.'" To TR such utterances showed a "fatuous indifference to the teachings of history." They represented precisely the kind of thinking that a century before had led to the "burning of Washington by a small expeditionary hostile force, and to such paralyzing disaster in war as almost to bring about the break of the Union." In his message Wilson had also justified a refusal to build up the navy "by asking—as though we were discussing a question of pure metaphysics—when will the experts tell us what kind of ships we should construct—and when will they be right for ten years altogether?" Wilson turned away from the subject. It was not new. There was "no need to discuss it." TR noted that if England had taken the same attitude toward naval preparedness in the previous decade, "the island would now be trampled into bloody mire, as Belgium has been trampled."[22]

Only a few days after Wilson's message was delivered, Secretary of War Lindley Garrison published a report that called it "absolutely imperative" for the nation to build up the chronically undermanned regular army to full strength and to train more men for the reserve. The report, sounding decidedly more Rooseveltian than Wilsonian, noted that those who were thoughtful and had courage faced the facts of life and took lessons from experience. In Garrison's view the advocates of antipreparedness disregarded all known facts and flew in the face of all known experience, and "must rest upon faith in that which has not yet been made manifest." He ridiculed pacifists who cried "militarism" in response to "any preparation or organization of the military resources of the nation."[23] Henry Cabot Lodge took some heart from Garrison's report, observing to TR that he had "seldom seen a better or stronger argument than he has made in regard to all the humbug talk about militarism."[24] The obvious disagreement between Garrison and the president, to whom he tried to be loyal, led the secretary to offer his resignation. This Wilson refused, telling him that it would cost the Democrats two million votes in the next election.[25]

The president's subsequent reaffirmation that he was against any investigation into "our unpreparedness" and his continued policy of neutrality led an exasperated Roosevelt to declare to Lodge that Wilson and Bryan were "the very worst men we have ever had in their positions" and that it would "not hurt them to say publicly" what was in his view "historically true" that they were "worse than Jefferson and Madison," who also had submitted in cowardly fashion to multiple insults from foreign powers without going to war. He also told Lodge that he had accepted an offer from a new venue for his articles on these questions, *Metropolitan* magazine, a rather literary monthly with gorgeously illustrated covers that that January began to bill itself as "The Magazine Col. Roosevelt Writes For." The first would be on the "Panama-Colombia business."[26] At present, TR confided to Kermit, what he had to say was "not of much consequence to the larger audience," because the American people and himself were not currently interested in the same things. But the *Metropolitan* connection did give him a chance to make certain social and political arguments that he thought ought to be made. And he took a "certain grim satisfaction" in having the American people "pay me heavily to hear from me what they won't listen to if I give it to them for free."[27]

Roosevelt spent a "delightful" Christmas at Sagamore Hill with three grandchildren in the house and Ethel and Dick newly returned from France. Ethel had been badly worn down, mentally and physically, by the work, and her concerned father believed she ought never to have been taken abroad. He told Kermit that he was "no friend to having women trapsing [sic] abroad to take part in what ought to be men's jobs." It was too rough on them, and "heaven knows they have a lot that is hard in life to face anyhow." Of course he was proud of the work Ethel and Dick had done in Paris, but the big countries could take care of themselves, and the only real way to have aided the Belgians would have been to help them keep the Germans out, as he wished the United States had done. After five months, he went on, the "absolutely unscrupulous" Germans were "clearly ahead," and the Austrians "stronger than they were immediately after the beginning of the war."[28]

That December a little noted agreement was made under which J. P. Morgan and Company became the American commercial agents of the British government.[29] They had already been given permission to organize loans, and by the time America joined the war two years later, the Allies had borrowed billions of dollars and purchased further billions worth of war-related materials from the United States, where thousands of foreigners worked in a powerful and legally neutral sovereign nation, overloading the country's factories with orders and ending its economic slump with the enormous amount of trade and loans generated by the colossal needs of the Allied war effort. The British apparatus in place was "officially unofficial" in order to circumvent the strictures of international law concerning the construction of a supply base in a neutral country.[30] This ostensibly very unneutral policy did not go unchallenged. One strong voice of opposition came from the Hearst press, which railed against the bankers who supported the proprietor's old enemy Britain, whose ally Japan was a favorite target of Hearst's "yellow peril" jeremiads.[31] Unlike TR, who was converted by the British position during the Spanish-American War, William Randolph Hearst remained an unrepentant Anglophobe, which in the end cost his papers the use of the Atlantic cables controlled from London.

Across the Atlantic the British population became ever more personally acquainted with the realities of total war. The zeppelin and naval bombardments that had begun on coastal cities at the end of 1914 continued, and the mounting battlefield casualties directly affected more and more "Home Front" families. In 1915 it also became apparent that England would have to contribute more than monetary and naval aid to her allies while Lord Kitchener's new armies prepared for battle. A toll of British blood more substantial than that already shed would be necessary to ensure that France and Russia stayed the course and did not fall prey to German peace overtures. The debate shifted from whether a large British army would be dispatched to where a morale-boosting victory might best be obtained for the Allies.[32]

On the seas, at the beginning of the war it had been assumed that the British fleet would soon defeat its enemy counterpart and blockade the German coast.[33] When the German navy rested at anchor and refused to engage, the British had erected a blockade to intercept trade and waited for the foe to emerge. A set of wartime blockade rules had been drawn up and agreed to by most of the international community in the 1909 Declaration of London. Britain, however, never ratified the agreement to which the United States tried to hold her. A British Order in Council of August 20, 1914, unilaterally added food to the absolute contraband list drawn up before the war and made other revisions.[34] In the following months reports began to appear in the American press concerning the detention of US merchant ships taken into port for extremely thorough and time-consuming searches. On November 3 the British proclaimed the North Sea a "military area" into which no neutral vessel could travel without stopping at a British port first for inspection.

These actions drew protests from the Wilson administration. A December 26 note declared that British seizures of ships and cargoes exceeded the "manifest necessity of a belligerent" and constituted "restrictions upon the rights of American citizens on the high seas" that were "not justified by the rules of international law or required under the principle of self-preservation."[35] In the official British view, neutral hardships were unfortunate but unavoidable when balanced against the vital interests of the Empire. The British also did not hesitate to point out a policy similar to theirs had been carried out during the American Civil War by the Union navy against British shipping.

Germany countered the British blockade, not with the dreadnoughts she had been busy building for a decade, but, as Admiral Tirpitz had foreshadowed, with submarines. Submarines were expected (by the Allied and neutral nations at least) to follow cruiser rules of engagement designed for surface ships, which mandated that a warning shot be fired and passengers allowed to evacuate the targeted ship before its sinking. However, their small size made it impossible for the U-boats to remove passengers and made them vulnerable, if they surfaced to fire the required warning shot, to armed merchantmen, whose guns were often concealed. When the Germans bent the rules in retaliation to the British blockade with their submarine campaign, their vital interests were not recognized by the British or American governments.[36] Roosevelt, the first American president to cruise in a submarine, fully expected trouble in the North Atlantic, where, he wrote to Ted, neutrality would "not count for anything in the end, no matter how many white flags a coward might care to fly."[37]

In 1915, the flagship venue in which the Colonel published his preparedness (and other) pleas was the *Metropolitan*. The addition of TR to an eclectic group of contributors, from the popular novelist Booth Tarkington to the firebrand antiwar socialist John Reed, boomed its circulation.[38] And on the two days a week the Colonel spent at the *Metropolitan* offices on Fourth Avenue, the premises of "The Livest Magazine in America" were made even livelier by his dynamic energy and by the host of famous and colorful visitors he attracted. The magazine was owned by the wealthy horse-racing enthusiast Harry Payne Whitney and edited by Henry James Whigham, an Englishman of rather radical politics who had been a correspondent in the Spanish-American War. Roosevelt's first piece was, from his point of view at any rate, aptly titled "The Panama Blackmail Treaty." The proposed Thomson-Urrutia Treaty with Colombia pending in the Senate, the article declared, was a "crime against the United States which, if justified, would convict the United States of infamy." It was a "menace to the future well-being of our people," and the payment of $25,000,000 could be justified "only on the grounds that this nation has played the part of a thief."[39]

German General Friedrich von Bernhardi and former Austrian Ambassador to the United States Baron von Hengelmuller both took advantage of this controversy to answer Roosevelt's many criticisms of the Central Powers. They declared that the United States had seized Panama on the principle that the interests of the American people were "higher and greater than abstract principles of international law," just as Germany had seized Belgium. TR replied that to "talk of Colombia as a responsible power to be dealt with as we would deal with Holland or Belgium or Switzerland" was a "mere absurdity." The analogy was more with a "group of Sicilian or Calabrian bandits; with Villa and Carranza." The United States could no more make an agreement with the Colombian rulers than "you could nail currant jelly to a wall." The *New York World*, enjoying its old enemy's discomfiture immensely, commented that the "hair shirt thus presented to Colonel Roosevelt seems to us to be a very snug fit, and we trust that he is having a bully time wearing it."[40]

At the same time, the publisher George Putnam asked Roosevelt if he would be interested in the suggestion made by the London branch of his firm to publish a collection of his 1914 articles and letters on the war.[41] The Colonel had already decided to do this, and in January 1915 Scribner's released just such a book: *America and the World War*. This was applauded by TR's preparedness allies and pilloried by the supporters of Wilson. The *Nation*, for example, found the book in "execrable taste and offensive to all fair-minded readers," as was "his openly contemptuous abuse of the President and his administration."[42] On the other hand, TR's novelist friend and cousin-in-law Edith Wharton, who had lived in Paris for years and wholeheartedly supported the cause of France and the Allies against the "Boche," was heartened by the book's appearance. It was said of Wharton and Roosevelt that they were "both self-made men," a witticism that pleased the writer, who repeated it among her circle.[43] In these years Wharton threw herself into relief work and became a sort of "general officer in the war on tuberculosis and homelessness," for which she was awarded the French Legion of Honor.[44] The copy the Colonel sent her of *America and the World War* was inscribed, "From an American—American."[45]

On February 4, 1915, while the Colonel was temporarily incapacitated at Sagamore Hill with a recurrence of what the newspapers called an "African fever," Germany proclaimed a U-boat "war zone" around the British Isles to take effect two weeks later. In response Wilson warned the Germans they would be held to "strict accountability" should their submarines "destroy on the high seas an American vessel or the lives of American citizens." He also warned Great Britain of the "inherent peril in the unauthorized use of the American flag" to mask its vessels.[46] Off the Irish coast five days before, Wilson's peace envoy, Colonel Edward M. House, had noted the shipboard "excitement, and comment and speculation" aroused when his vessel, the British Cunard liner *Lusitania*, followed what had become standard antisubmarine practice by raising the Stars and Stripes.[47]

Meanwhile, the administration, led by the ambitious and able Treasury Secretary William Gibbs McAdoo, who had married Wilson's daughter Eleanor the previous year and was dubbed the "Crown Prince," went forward with a proposal to create a government-owned merchant fleet by purchasing 31 German-flagged ships interned in American ports. This was seen by the British as negating the power of the Royal Navy—which had forced the vessels off the sea—while also representing a financial windfall for cash-strapped Germany.[48] TR felt the British had a right to protest against the American purchase of the ships and told his friend Sir Cecil Spring Rice that he had done all he could to prevent the passage of the bill, "which is pushed by the German interests here and by the Jewish bankers who are doing Germany's business." Further, the U-boat proclamation had given him an "uneasy feeling" lest what he had also hinted at in a letter to Sir Edward Grey might "come to pass and the submarines may make effective war against the merchant vessels going into England." This would be a "very serious business" and might mean that England's "whole chance of going on with the war at all" depended on American merchantmen bringing in food. This was obviously something the British needed to consider when they made protests about neutrality rights or confiscated cargoes. However, he assumed they knew "their own interests and their own capabilities."

Roosevelt went on to say to Spring Rice, as strongly as he knew how, that he hoped "at all costs your people will avoid a clash with us, where we are right." On grounds of expediency, he also hoped that the British would avoid a clash "even though we were wrong—just as it was expedient for the United States to avoid a clash with Great Britain or France during the Civil War, even although they were wrong." The Colonel concluded by adding that if the Allies had to "act against us on some point, where they are clearly right and we are clearly wrong," he wished it could be "a French ship that took the action."[49] Spring Rice passed this advice on to Grey. And in fact when the *Dacia*, a German ship that had been transferred to private American ownership, was seized on February 27, it was done by the French cruiser *Europe*, avoiding a direct confrontation with Britain.[50]

Ten days before this, Henry Cabot Lodge had brought TR up to date on developments in Washington. The Ship Purchase Bill, the senator reported, had been "jammed through the House in six hours," but the administration could not get it through the senate "except by mob law." The Democrats, Lodge feared, were ready to "resort to almost anything" to "gratify one man's determination to have his own way." In view of the German war zone decree, the situation was "extremely serious," and Lodge found it unbelievable that the president wanted to "complicate it by purchasing these German ships."[51] Two days later the senator was relieved to be able to report that the bill was dead.

Nevertheless, the more Lodge thought of it, "the more positively criminal" it seemed for Wilson to try to jam it thorough. "Here we are," he told TR, "with the German war zone order, which may at any moment bring us to war with Germany if she blows up one of our ships or an English ship with two or three hundred American passengers on board," while the president tried to get through a bill that would "create a situation in which we would have been on the verge of war . . . with every one of the Allies." Wilson was, in short, "arranging a situation where we were likely to go to war with both sides, which required no slight ingenuity."[52] Lodge soon after confessed to Roosevelt that he had "never expected to hate anyone in politics with the hatred I feel towards Wilson."[53] The successful fight against the Ship Purchase Bill, and their shared hatred of Wilson, brought TR back into closer touch with many Republicans besides Lodge, who spent a weekend at Sagamore Hill for the first time in almost four years. Before long the newspapers were printing stories that Roosevelt, because of Wilson's weak foreign policy, was showing signs of returning to the Republican camp and would support the party candidate in 1916.[54]

The Colonel's criticisms coincided with complaints from Taft about the administration of the Philippines. This drew a comment from Wilson at one of his press conferences, when he said that he hoped after he left office that his successors would not express any opinion about what he said about them, just as he kept silent regarding Taft and Roosevelt. Wilson noted how unusual it was for there to be two ex-presidents living and that they were all "trying to invent an etiquette." When pressed about TR's recent attacks concerning the Ship Purchase Bill and foreign affairs, however, Wilson broke his own rule to remark that he supposed the Colonel would be "willing to make it only a committee of one on this etiquette business."[55]

No such niceties were apparent in the comments of New York Special Sessions Chief Justice Isaac Russell, who branded TR "a hellhound of war." The *New York Times* came to the Colonel's defense in an editorial that chided Russell, "that model of the woolsack," for departing from the "sagacity and wisdom" that characterized his judicial utterances. The paper pointed out that, while in office, Roosevelt often "bared his teeth" but was in fact "the most peaceful President it would be possible to imagine." And it was "easily possible" to think that a lover of peace, to whom warfare was abhorrent—"even a man who had been in charge of a university before he became President"— might, with all good intentions, "endanger the peace of a country more than a ferocious President who knew how the business of nations was conducted."

In seven years, the editorial went on, Roosevelt "did not embark our nation in any bloody adventure." Once he had been asked to tell what was in his estimation the "greatest service he had rendered in the cause of peace." Instead of the expected response of ending the Russo-Japanese war, TR smiled and replied, "The sending of the American fleet to the Pacific in 1907" to intimidate the Japanese. In the paper's opinion, Roosevelt may have been mistaken in this judgment, but it declared that there could be no question that "the man who does the most for peace may be the man who knows best the meaning of war." At any rate, "well-meaning Administrations with a theoretical and academic love of peace" were not always "the surest guarantees against strife."[56]

On the preparedness front, in February 1915 Roosevelt lent his name to the establishment of an organization called the American Legion (unconnected with the post-1918 veterans organization that Theodore Jr. helped to found), a volunteer civilian group associated with the Army League and enjoying the unofficial support of the US army and General Leonard Wood. The Legion's goal was to establish a paper reserve of between 250,000 and 500,000 trained and experienced men, including many formerly in the army, navy, and guards, who would be ready for "instant response to any call in an emergency." Its creation was announced to the press at the end of the month by the secretary of the New York headquarters, Dr. John E. Hausmann, a former medical officer of the volunteers, and an army adviser, Captain Gordon Johnston, a former Rough Rider who was aide-de-camp to Wood. Hausmann explained, first of all, that the Legion did not "believe in militarism" but did believe in "being able to defend ourselves if attacked" and that there was "a vast difference" between the two. Second that, while all who were loyal and patriotic were wanted to join, there would be "small place in its ranks for hyphenated Americans."[57]

As the most notable sponsor of the Legion, TR's endorsement letter was released to the press. In this he declared himself "in most cordial sympathy with your purpose" and added that he and his four sons would all join. Further, he had agreed to serve as Chairmen of the Board of Honorary Advisers. He hoped and prayed that there would be no war, but in his view the "surest way to avert war" was to be "prepared for it." And the only way to avoid "disaster and disgrace" was by preparation "in advance." Roosevelt also announced that if the United States entered the European war, he would ask the permission of Congress to raise a nine-regiment volunteer division of cavalry such as he had served with in Cuba. He did not doubt that these regiments would be filled by the men of the Legion, or men like them, for in the event of war there would be no time to train those "first called upon in such duties as shooting, riding and taking care of themselves in the open."

The nation, Roosevelt went on, should have begun to prepare "the minute this war broke out seven months ago." In his opinion it was "'absolutely impossible" to be sure, when there was "such a tremendous war," that the United States would not be "drawn into it against our will." The people were only beginning to realize the extent of the country's unpreparedness, and the Legion would help to accomplish "one of the important things needed for defense": the formation of a first reserve, now entirely lacking. This scheme would need coordination with the army, and TR was happy to learn that it was "heartily backed by our leading regular officers." Even the "most extreme advocate of peace at any price" could hardly raise an objection, since the Legion would only "unify, classify and co-ordinate defensive factors already in existence."[58]

Despite its denials of any connection to "militarism," the Legion was immediately denounced on just such grounds, and as yet another example of the jingoism indivisible from Roosevelt.[59] Bishop David Greer, the head of the American League to Limit Armaments, complained to Wilson that Wood was sponsoring an un-American and unconstitutional organization. All this drew a letter of inquiry from Secretary of War Garrison. Despite Wood's attempt to explain that Roosevelt was only a volunteer and that the Legion was simply compiling a card index and not carrying out any propaganda, the secretary warned off the general. He recognized the potential value of locating, classifying, and keeping track of available men and was looking into creating such a scheme for the army, but he told Wood that he thought it "undesirable for officers of the army to have any connections with organizations outside the War Department." Garrison ordered the Legion offices out of the Army Building on Governor's Island and instructed Wood in future not to involve himself, however unofficially, in any such enterprise.[60] Three weeks before this Garrison had issued a general order for officers, aimed at Wood, that they should not give out for publication "any interview, statement, discussion or article on the military situation in the United States or abroad."[61]

In late February the *Metropolitan* printed TR's latest broadside, "Uncle Sam and the Rest of the World," on the Wilson administration's confusing Mexican policy, which had taken sides against Victoriano Huerta to support Pancho Villa and then abandoned Villa for Venustiano Carranza. There was no reason, said Roosevelt, for any American to uphold Huerta, but to antagonize him on moral grounds and then "endeavor to replace him with a polygamous bandit" was incompatible with "any intelligent system of international ethics." It might be "entirely proper" to take the view that the United States should have no concern with the "morality of any chief who is for the time being the ruler of Mexico," but to do as the president had done and "actively take sides," condemning Huerta for misdeeds while "ignoring the far worse misdeeds" of Villa, and then to abandon him to support Carranza, "who was responsible for exactly the same kind of hideous outrages," was an "affront

to all" who believed in "straightforward sincerity in American public life."
In point of public morality, declared Roosevelt, Wilson's policy was "fundamentally as evil a declaration as has ever been put forth by an American
President in treating foreign affairs." From Deadwood, South Dakota, TR's
old cowboy friend Marshall Seth Bullock wrote him that the *Metropolitan*
article was "a corker." How long, asked Bullock, would the people stand for
this "jack rabbit administration?" Rather than the American eagle, it seemed
to him more appropriate at present for the "Mephistis Mephitica" (skunk) to
be the "national emblem." Ending on a personal note, Bullock added that if
TR would let him know when he planned to have the "spring round-up of
grandchildren," he would try to be there and "help you ride circle."[62]

In the British House of Commons on March 1, Prime Minister Herbert
Henry Asquith read out a note sent to neutrals that stated that in retaliation
against the German submarine campaign the Royal Navy would "detain and
take into port ships carrying goods of presumed enemy destination, ownership or origin." This would, the prime minister went on, unlike the German
campaign, pose no risk to the safety of American ships or lives. In dealing
with an opponent who had "openly repudiated all the restraints, both of law
and humanity," the British would "not allow our efforts to be strangled in
a network of juridical niceties." Outraged American newspapers compared
the "juridical niceties" phrase to German Chancellor Bethmann-Hollweg's
"mere scrap of paper" reference to Britain's treaty obligations to Belgium at
the beginning of the war.[63] Some suggested a wait-and-see attitude, which the
British answered on March 11 by tightening their surface blockade with an
Order in Council that enlarged the campaign to include all German trade.[64]

That day Wilson's private envoy, Colonel House, who had been in Britain for a month working for peace with figures from Sir Edward Grey to
George V, left London to continue his mission in Paris and Berlin. He would
find there the same polite lack of cooperation and enthusiasm that he had
in the drawing rooms and ministries of England.[65] The confident Germans
told House they would not pull out of France or Belgium without reparations, while by this time the French government had publicly vowed not to
end the war until it regained Alsace-Lorraine, which had been taken by the
then newly created German state as part of the humiliating settlement of
the Franco-Prussian War.[66] Britain and Germany were equally at loggerheads
over Belgium and the German colonies, as were Russia and the Central Powers over control of Poland, parts of which before the war had been ruled
by Germany, Austria-Hungary, and Russia.[67] Both sides already had paid a
previously unimaginable toll in blood and treasure that could not simply be
forgiven and forgotten, and neither was likely to agree to negotiations unless
it felt it had the upper hand and could call the settlement. Nevertheless, while
the war ground grimly on, Wilson and House would continue to try. The
whole prospect of mediation, TR wrote Kermit, was "simply vaporous."[68]

Roosevelt received several firsthand reports on the new trench warfare
that had developed over the previous months from Arthur Lee, whose job
inspecting army medical services for Kitchener allowed him to motor all along

the British line. The struggle, Lee told TR, had become a "gas-engine war on land, in the air and under the sea." The transport and ambulance services were all mechanical, and the "odour of petrol" was "abroad in the land." Unlike his time in Cuba with Roosevelt, Lee had not been on a horse and seldom even seen one except with the light artillery, while the heavy guns "puff about behind tractor engines." It was not "romantic or picturesque," but it was "most assuredly war!" For the last six months it had been "a very dull war" and an "extraordinarily uncomfortable one," but the men had shown a "tenacity and a spirit to 'stick it' that has never been surpassed." They had "practically been living underground in a swamp—when the water comes into the trenches always a little faster than you can bail or pump it out."

British casualties, Lee admitted, had been heavy: not less than 150,000 with 2,000 officers killed. And yet they were "only at the end of the beginning instead of the beginning of the end." The British army now had 500,000 men at the front, including many from India and other parts of the Empire, and soon would have 1,000,000. Then, with the "advent of fine weather, the war ought to begin." The conflict kept "slipping backwards into savagery," and by the time it ended Lee did not think that a single one of The Hague or Geneva conventions would remain unbroken. "I only hope," he went on, "that the Germans would have sufficient sense of humour to put the finishing touch" by bombing Carnegie's Peace Palace in The Hague, preferably while Carnegie was "in it & presiding" at one of the British pacifist Norman Angell's lectures.[69]

That month the *Metropolitan* published TR's article "The Need of Preparedness," which argued that "Uncle Sam's only friend" was Uncle Sam, and therefore he should be able to defend himself. The Colonel had come to this conclusion after speaking with knowledgeable men who had traveled to Europe, where they found "a growing feeling of dislike, and even of contempt," for the United States. One of Roosevelt's informants had spoken with the Swiss ex-president who had declared that the only reason Germany had attacked Belgium and not Switzerland was because the Swiss had an army of four hundred thousand while the Belgians had only eighty. Swiss independence was "based on a foundation of steel," not "parchment." Tiny Switzerland was able to field such an army because of their system of universal service in which all young men at age 19 took six months of military training. This taught them how to live under canvas, how to march and shoot, and how to take care of themselves in the open and prepare food and find shelter. In TR's view the United States should immediately institute a similar system, which would "not in the least" tend to "militarism" but would "make us efficient to defend ourselves in time of need." It would also be of immense benefit to both the men and the nation in civilian life by increasing "their efficiency in industry" as had occurred in Switzerland, where civic order had also been strengthened and violent crime decreased.

The United States, Roosevelt went on, was also shirking its duty in Mexico, and at any moment the "attitude of foreign nations" might challenge the Monroe Doctrine and make intervention "imperative." Such an intervention would be "really a war against banditti" and ought to be handled by the regular army, not volunteers subject to the same deficiencies that had cost many needless deaths in the Spanish-American War. To this end he called for an army of 200,000, which would allow adequate garrisoning of coastal fortifications, the Panama Canal, other insular possessions, and still leave a mobile force of 120,000 to be kept at the highest state of efficiency by annual maneuvers. On the seas, the submarine war had shown that perhaps the day of the battleship would soon be over and that undersea vessels, possibly in combination with aircraft, were the wave of the future, and consequently the United States needed to develop these arms. Nevertheless, the continuing usefulness of surface ships was clearly demonstrated by the British battle fleet, which had played as important a part in the present war as it had against Napoleon a century before. The German counterpart and her merchantmen had been driven from the seas, and British Empire troops were brought safely to the war fronts.

The Colonel also raised the specter of two other present dangers to the country: professional pacifism and hyphenated Americanism. The first he dismissed as worthless in dealing with international affairs "from the standpoint of the betterment of humanity." To approve the Wilson-Bryan "universal peace treaties" while not daring to demand the enforcement of the Hague conventions was "either cowardice or odious hypocrisy." The only advocate for peace "entitled to respectful consideration" was the man who put "force back of the demand for right." The second "equally ominous movement," which had developed over the last seven months, was "the effort on the part of certain American citizens of German birth or origin" to bring about a "political system of unadulterated mischief and evil" in which America would be split up into "groups of warring nationalities." It was impossible in Roosevelt's opinion "too strongly to condemn these so-called German-Americans" who acted as the instruments of the policy of "our foreign detractors and opponents." In the end TR believed the American public would "wake up to the national menace contained in such a propaganda."[70] French Ambassador Jean Jules Jusserand congratulated the Colonel for his *Metropolitan* article, telling him "what a fine bugle you sounded . . . It will be heard all over the country and will waken those who sleep when they should not."[71] There were rumors that month that TR might visit Europe. Grey sent Spring Rice a telegram: "Hope that Roosevelt will find time for another walk with me if he comes."[72]

At the same time in England parallels were being drawn between the "watchful waiting" policy of Wilson in Mexico and the "wait and see" course followed by Asquith's Liberal government in the war. By March 1915 revelations of a critical lack of high explosive shells for the British army came to exemplify the shortcomings of the administration. The great danger on the western front, Arthur Lee wrote TR, was that the stalemate of siege works would continue because of the shell shortage. It was "abundantly clear" that neither side could break through the fortified barrier or make any advance, "except with the help of such a gigantic expenditure" of ammunition that "no manufacturing resources seem able to cope with it." Consequently, France had become "one vast shell factory," and England was beginning to follow suit, though "criminally late in the day." The Allies could make good use, said Lee, of any amount of ammunition America could provide. It had in fact become "more a war of ammunition than of men," and this was why it was worthwhile for the British at any cost to "prevent copper or any other necessary ingredients from entering Germany" even if neutral countries were "seriously inconvenienced." Lee went on that this was not an "ordinary war." To the British it was a "case of victory or absolute ruin; black and irretrievable." And as Germany had openly abandoned the "rules of the ring we must punch her, anywhere and all over, regardless of murmurs from neutral spectators." So far it appeared the United States seemed to understand this and was taking a reasonable view toward the British blockade.

Like most officers in the British army, Lee believed the only way to win the war was to concentrate on the western front and was against diverting ammunition, supplies, or men anywhere else. It was only by "killing off the Germans," he told TR, that the war could be brought to an end. The Russians were also doing their part, and Lee estimated that total German "wastage" on both fronts must be 300,000 a month, or 3,500,000 a year. And it was "*that* which must finish them at the long last." But, Lee complained, the stalemate in France had led "amateur strategists" in the British government to "embark on subsidiary and wild-cat enterprises with our New Armies in other theatres of war" as a "way round."[73]

The prime example of this was Winston Churchill's Admiralty plan to use the British fleet to run the Dardanelles straits and capture Constantinople. This operation, Churchill argued, would both take Turkey out of the war and open a warm water supply line that would bolster Russia.[74] The great danger in this strategy, Lee prophesied—correctly, as is turned out— was that even if the British took Constantinople (which they did not), another army would have to be sent to extricate the "inferior" one sent there. In Lee's view, Kitchener, who was attracted to Churchill's plan, was a great organizer but not a great strategist, and "none of our best soldiers have confidence in him as such."[75] Russian pleas for assistance in early 1915 made Kitchener open to Churchill's scheme, especially if, as the First Lord of the Admiralty insisted, minimal numbers of troops would be required.[76] As Lee and others had feared, the naval bombardment failed, and rather than face a humiliating withdrawal, Kitchener was forced to divert more troops and ammunition to the Dardanelles from the western front. This infuriated the British commander there, Sir John French, who continued to plead for resources.

The lack of ammunition, particularly high explosive shells, came to a head after the Battle of Neuve Chappelle once again demonstrated the futility of using shrapnel shells against heavily entrenched German positions. Though small by the standards of later engagements, Neuve Chappelle involved more troops than Waterloo and confirmed the theory that a breakthrough could be accomplished with enough artillery support. But, Lee confided to TR, the expenditure required was "colossal and very seldom practicable." In an hour's bombardment, five hundred guns trained at a short segment of the German line "literally blew all the defenders, all their defences, to bits." This allowed the infantry to move in to take the position with light casualties. However, in a pattern that would be sadly and tragically repeated many times in the following years, over the next few days a stout German counterattack cost 15,000 British and 20,000 German men. Lee reported that 3,000 still lay in the no man's land between the armies. If America wanted to help, Lee again told TR, they should send ammunition as quickly as possible. The British did not want Wilson's help or interference in negotiations. Lee also reported to Roosevelt that his letter to Grey requesting that American correspondents be allowed to tell the story of the British army "had the desired effect." Frederick Palmer and others had arrived at the British general headquarters (GHQ) "unofficially," and the provost marshal had "winked at" their presence. He hoped now the British effort would get a "fair shake" in the American press.[77]

In this period, at least one other intrepid American writer made it to the front, when the novelist Mary Roberts Rinehart, a preparedness ally of Roosevelt on assignment for the *Saturday Evening Post*, became the war's first female correspondent. In London, Lord Northcliffe gave her letters of introduction to the Belgian premier and army commander, as well as Sir John French. Despite the press lord's skepticism as to her chances of actually reaching the front, Rinehart used her nursing credentials to cross the channel on a fabricated mission to report on war hospitals. Once across, she managed a tour of the Allied armies that included a visit to British GHQ and an interview with the Belgian King Albert.[78] Unfortunately, Rinehart later wrote, by the time her war articles were "emasculated for a country still rigidly neutral they sounded to me like the piping of a small bird in a hurricane" and were not at all what she wanted them to be.[79]

Roosevelt himself turned down more than one lucrative newspaper offer to go to Europe. In April 1915, the *Detroit News* proposed that he go as an "Ambassador of the American people." In this scheme, TR would be backed by the largest newspaper in each state and parlay with the "contending governments."[80] The Colonel had about as much interest in this offer as he did in attending the International Congress of Women set to convene that month in The Hague, with peace high on its agenda. An American delegation gathered in Chicago before departing for Europe and was made up largely of members of the Woman's Peace Party, which had been formed four months before by Jane Addams, the renowned social reformer who had seconded TR's nomination at the 1912 Progressive Convention.[81] The Colonel wrote to Spring Rice about the "Jane Addams inspired idiots" going to The Hague to "bleat about peace." He felt the "keenest indignation as an American" that American women should make "such an unworthy exhibition of themselves" when the English, French, and Belgian women "within a stone's throw were in the black abyss of woe and suffering." And in spite of this, they were "leading lives and doing deeds of uncomplaining heroism." It was painful for Roosevelt to think that "while these women were giving up life and what was far dearer than life" and "toiling and suffering for the loftiest ideals," any American women like Jane Addams "and her foolish, foolish associates," should, "whether from mere folly or from thirst for self-advertisement, do their feeble and futile best on the side of wrong."[82]

Remarkably, given his attitude, Roosevelt was nevertheless invited to join the welcoming committee for the peace delegation on its return, which he of course refused. He commented about "poor foolish Jane Addams on her return from her noxious mission abroad" that there could be "nothing more absurd" than the statement that she and her colleagues had given Europe "an exhibition of finer courage than that displayed on the battlefields." Quite to the contrary, they had not shown the "smallest particle of courage," and all their work had been done to "advance the cause of international cowardice." In his view, anyone who greeted or applauded them was "actively advancing that cause."[83] One of the leaders of the Woman's Peace Party, Catharine Waugh McCullough, responded that Roosevelt did not realize that the "day of the big stick" was past and that people were now seeking to solve problems by the "application of intellect" and not "brute force." His was the "cry of a barbarian out of his element." It was half a century out of date, and the longer the Colonel lived the more out of date he would become. In her view the women who went to Europe to "spread the plea for peace" were doing a "greater deed than the Colonel ever accomplished"; they were "marking an epochal advance of civilization."[84]

The minor muckraker and Wilson-admirer George Creel joined the chorus against TR in a *Harper's Weekly* article, "Red Blood." Convinced that Wilson would be able to hold back America from the "abyss that has engulfed Europe," Creel said Roosevelt had chosen "Red Blood" in answer as his campaign cry. After berating peace-seeking American women as "base," TR had warmed to his campaign "in ancient fashion" by branding Wilson's policy of neutrality as "wicked" and "craven." Many quiet months spent with his "ear pressed right against the ground," said Creel, had convinced the Colonel that "Preparedness for War and Ignoble Peace" were phrases "well suited to the public temper and admirably calculated to restore his former influence." After listing the many inconsistencies and changes of course in TR's "fliberty-gibbet career," from his stand on socialism to his treatment of Colombia in the Panama Canal affair, Creel insisted that he did not mean to charge Roosevelt with "premeditated insincerity." It was simply the case that he lacked "deep-seated convictions" and ran his race "without regard to other than purely personal goals."

More than any other man in public life, Creel went on, TR had the "gift of making people *thrill* rather than *think*." Since Wilson became president, the people had been thinking, but two years was "not long enough to have formed the habit firmly." It took "time and patience to make people *think*. The boom of a gun, the roar of fustian, a piece of claptrap sentiment" made them instead "*feel*." The Colonel, argued Creel, was to statesmanship what the movies were to the drama. He gave a "picture but never a thought." Like a kaleidoscope, TR's "incessant display of color" forced "forgetfulness of form." He blazed across the "mediocrity of everyday existence like a meteor," and his strength was that he made his rivals "seem colorless and shabby."

Such a man, said Creel, was "always dangerous, and doubly so when he appeals to primitive instincts and ancient wanton lusts." It would be interesting, Creel concluded, "to watch the progress of the Red Blood issue." Would the "Roosevelt color retain its ancient sorcery," or had the people "decided to think?"[85] Ironically enough, two years later when Creel's sycophantic support of Wilson would be rewarded with his being made head of the government's Committee on Public Information, "thinking" would have no place in the propaganda his agency broadcast across the United States. In millions of "red, white and blue" books and the speeches of thousands of "four minute men," a kaleidoscope of "claptrap sentiment" would form a successful campaign to replace three years of pacific neutrality with "Red Blood" and total war.

Creel's attack on his convictions and career led the Colonel to label him an "absolute liar." He had seen evidence of this "again and again in deliberate and willful falsehoods" about himself and Hiram Johnson. Roosevelt was willing to bet, he wrote a friend, that Creel could not find "anything to my discredit in anything I have said or written or testified to under any conditions." He could only find "inconsistencies," just as he could find them in the writings of Washington and Lincoln, which reflected "an occasional honest and necessary change of mind" and, more often, "a change of circumstances which necessitated a change on my part," precisely as Lincoln had changed on emancipation. In his view, a man who took sentences out of context and twisted them to "mean something which they obviously do not mean" was "guilty of the meanest form of mendacity" and "unfit to associate with decent people." And the editors who employed him were "not much better."[86]

In mid-April, Edith, who had been unwell for some time, underwent an unspecified "serious operation" (most likely a hysterectomy) at Roosevelt Hospital, endowed by a great-uncle and one of the finest in New York. TR reported to Kermit's wife Belle that Edith was recovering from the "great weakness and depression which naturally followed." He hoped she would be completely recovered in six weeks and would be "better than she has been for the last year."[87] Leonard Wood, just back from an inspection trip to Panama, sent his best wishes for a speedy recovery. He also complimented TR's *Metropolitan* article on preparedness as "right to the point" and wrote that he wanted to talk about his "alarm & disgust" with the situation.[88] Another preparedness ally, Vitagraph President J. Stuart Blackton, offered the services of his motion picture company, which he told TR was the country's and probably the world's largest, to make a film for use in the Colonel's campaign.[89] In the end this was based on a popular book, *Defenseless America*, written by Hudson Maxim, whose more famous brother Hiram was one of the inventors of the machine gun.[90] Hudson was himself an inventor, specializing in high explosives, to which he had lost a hand in an accident three years before.

On April 18, Roosevelt was forced temporarily to put preparedness aside, and while Edith recuperated at Sagamore Hill, he traveled to Syracuse for the beginning of the $50,000 libel suit brought by the New York Republican boss William Barnes over TR's statement in the heat of the 1914 gubernatorial primary that had linked Barnes to "bi-partisan" corruption in alliance with the Democratic boss Charles Murphy.[91] TR had already won one victory in getting the trial moved from Albany, where no jury would have found against Barnes, and the Colonel's courtroom strategy (and that of his lawyer John M. Bowers) was to turn the tables and prove his accuser guilty of corruption.[92] On the other hand, Barnes's attorney, William M. Ivins, believed he could show that while TR had been Republican governor of New York he had also entered into deals with the Tammany machine, and he had assembled a mass of evidence to that effect, including a multitude of letters the Colonel had written to various political figures. After the attorney told Elihu Root he was going to Syracuse to "nail Roosevelt's hide to the fence," Root advised Ivins that he knew TR and that "you want to be very sure that it is Roosevelt's hide that you get on the fence."[93]

For his defense, the Colonel had to rely in the main on his own testimony, as the politicians who had been so outspoken privately concerning Barnes, including United States Supreme Court Justice and former New York Governor Charles Evans Hughes, refused to repeat their charges in open court, a betrayal the Colonel would not forget.[94] One witness who stayed true to TR was a Democrat and a member of the Wilson administration: cousin Franklin. Despite the possible political consequences of consorting with his Republican relation, FDR traveled to Syracuse from Washington to testify ably on his behalf.[95] The trial dragged on for more than a month while both sides presented their evidence, Roosevelt first. Meanwhile, newspapers of all political colors reveled in the circuslike atmosphere, and front-page courtroom drama temporarily displaced the European war in the headlines.

Before the libel trial opened, TR's friend Cal O'Laughlin had passed on to him a report from an unnamed "high official" who had just returned from Germany. The letter noted the hostility to Americans and the remark of the newly minted hero of the Eastern Front, Field Marshal Paul von Hindenburg: "How can I feel kindly towards a people, with whom we have no quarrel and whose ammunition is daily killing my soldiers?" The Germans were also upset that the United States did not protest the British war zone and mines in the North Sea but did oppose the submarine counterblockade. In their view the war would already have been over if not for American ammunition, and Germany looked "with extreme tranquility upon a possible conflict" with the United States, as it would "hardly alter the present situation." Noting the huge German and Irish American populations, the letter hinted at divisions that would "put the union to a serious test" if America joined the war.

To the German official the shipping question was "extremely simple." Should a German submarine come upon the British liner *Lusitania*, whether under English or American flag, O'Laughlin's source promised to sink her "without a moment's hesitation." The British had "loudly proclaimed their intention to starve our peaceful people, women and children, so we need not bother about theirs being drowned incidentally." O'Laughlin's fear

Figure 3. TR and FDR in Albany, May 1915
Franklin D. Roosevelt Presidential Library

that two or three hundred Americans might also be drowned was "quite justified, but nothing in the least would happen." The guilt would be on the British and their cowardly policy of flying US flags, which the *Lusitania* was well known to do in the Irish Sea.[96] The reality of this menace was underlined by the May 1 torpedoing of an American oil tanker out of Port Arthur, Texas, the *Gulflight*—an act that Roosevelt labeled "piracy pure and simple."[97]

This attack, and the "insolent" official's letter, TR wrote to O'Laughlin from Syracuse, made his "blood boil to see how we are regarded." All the European nations looked down on the United States, but the Germans were the worst. He went on, "Lord, how he would like to be President," in view of what was said about the German and Irish Americans and the *Lusitania*. The Colonel would warn the German official that "we would hang any man," including him, who "raised his little finger" to, as he said, "put the union to a serious test." And "if any of our people were sunk on the *Lusitania* I would confiscate all the German interned ships." This was the kind of letter that, said Roosevelt, "if I did not keep a grip on myself, would make me favor instant war with Germany."[98] On the following day the *Lusitania* was sunk by a German U-boat off the Irish coast.

CHAPTER 4

A Course of National Infamy

May to August 1915

Our people . . . have been misled by the screaming and shrieking and bleating of the peace people until really good men and women have gotten so puzzle-headed that they advocate a course of national infamy. I have spoken out as strongly and as clearly as possible; and I do not think it has had any effect beyond making people think I am a truculent and bloodthirsty person, endeavoring futilely to thwart able, dignified, humane Mr. Wilson in his noble plan to bring peace everywhere by excellently written letters sent to persons who care nothing whatever for any letter that is not backed up by force!

—TR to Arthur Lee, June 17, 1915

On May 7, 1915, the German submarine campaign galvanized the world when, 11 miles off the Irish coast, a torpedo from the U-20 sank the British Cunard ocean liner RMS *Lusitania*, the "Queen of the Atlantic" and the fastest ship on the seas. The liner, which had made four safe wartime round trips between New York and Europe, exploded and went down in 18 minutes, killing 1,198 of the 1,959 passengers and crew, including 128 American men, women, and children.[1] The next day's London *Daily Mail* labeled the action "Premeditated Murder" and two days later published photographs of dead women and children lined up at the Queenstown "charnel house." In America the papers also recounted the tragedy, noting that a "stunned" President Woodrow Wilson was "in seclusion" and that official Washington believed a "grave crisis" was at hand.[2] The *New York Evening Post* called the sinking a deed "for which a Hun would blush, a Turk be ashamed, and a Barbary pirate apologize."[3] "WHAT A PITY," declared the New York *Herald*'s banner headline the day after the sinking, that "THEODORE ROOSEVELT IS NOT PRESIDENT!"[4]

The shocking news was passed to the Colonel while he was sitting with his lawyer at his table in the courtroom at Syracuse, still embroiled in the Barnes libel trial. Since there were two German Americans on the jury, TR's attorney implored him to hold his tongue on the matter until after the trial was completed. Nevertheless, once he heard the details that night, the Colonel dictated a statement that the sinking represented "not merely piracy, but piracy on a vaster scale of murder than any old-time pirate ever practiced before being hung for his misdeeds." It seemed to him inconceivable that the United States could "refrain from taking action in this matter, for we owe it not only to humanity, but to our own national self-respect."[5] Cal O'Laughlin cabled TR that he hoped he would continue to "take the lead" in denouncing the *Lusitania* crime.[6] The Colonel, however, held his fire for a few days, hoping, if not expecting, that even Woodrow Wilson would have to take strong action in the face of this event.

Though almost no newspaper headlines called for war, many in Europe and America expected the United States to follow the president's stated rule of "strict accountability."[7] TR's friend Sir Cecil Spring Rice was among those who correctly assessed American public opinion as outraged against Germany, but not out for blood. The British ambassador, who until the *Lusitania* took center stage had been worried about an Anglo-American rift over the commercial blockade, now reported to Sir Edward Grey that the German embassy was "openly provocative," and it was probable that war would not be unwelcome to Germany, as it would cut off American arms supplies to the Allies. He also did not like the challenging tone of the British press calling for American action, cabling London, "As our main interest is to preserve U.S. as a base of supplies I hope language of our press will be very guarded."[8]

From London, both Colonel Edward M. House and Ambassador Walter Hines Page, who had undergone an anti-German conversion not unlike Roosevelt's over the previous months, exhorted Wilson to declare war. House sent a cable, which Wilson read to the cabinet: "America has come to a parting of the ways, when she must determine whether she stands for civilized or uncivilized warfare. We can no longer remain neutral spectators." It would "not be a new war, but an endeavor to end more speedily an old one," and American intervention would "save, rather than increase, the loss of life." Further, what the country did now would "determine the part we will play when peace is made" and how far America might "influence a settlement for the lasting good of humanity."[9] But all these arguments, cogent though they might be, were to no avail, as the president remained unwavering in his desire to keep the United States neutral. This was reflected in his May 10 Philadelphia speech, in which he declared that a man may be "too proud to fight" and a nation "so right that it does not need to convince others by force that it is right."[10] This "delightful statement," Roosevelt wrote to Arthur Lee, seemed to him "to reach the nadir of cowardly infamy."[11]

On May 11, TR told reporters that in view of Germany's "murderous offenses against the rights of neutrals," he would forbid all commerce with her while ensuring that trade of every kind be "permitted and encouraged with France, England and the rest of the civilized world." He did not believe that a "firm assertion of our rights" would mean war, but pointed out that it was well to remember that there were things "worse than war."

Roosevelt had seen in the press that Germany had offered to stop her unlawful practices on the high seas if the United States would "abandon further neutral rights, which by her treaty she has solemnly pledged to see we exercise without molestation." Such a proposal in his view was "not even entitled to an answer." The manufacture and shipment of arms and ammunition to belligerents, TR went on, was moral or immoral according to the use to which the weapons were to be put. If they were to be used "to prevent the redress of the hideous wrongs inflicted on Belgium," then it was "immoral to ship them." If they were to be used "for the redress of those wrongs and the restoration of Belgium to her deeply wronged and unoffending people," then it was "imminently moral" to send them.[12]

"That interview of yours this morning," Cal O'Laughlin congratulated Roosevelt, "was a peach" and precisely along the lines he had wanted. The words had drawn praise even from old enemies and had "forced strong action."[13] The impresario David Belasco, who had lost his dear friend and fellow producer Charles Frohman on the *Lusitania* and was heartbroken, wrote to TR that it "did me good to read your statement this morning. You are a man and I wish to God we had more like you."[14] Sir George Trevelyan had also lost loved ones in the tragedy and wrote Roosevelt on May 13 that he had read that morning "the sentence in which you set forth the *moral* side of the munitions of war question—whether they were to be employed for the rescue of Belgium or her continued enslavement." For Trevelyan, reading this had "kindled into a flame the smoldering consciousness" that there was a man in the world who was "never wanting chivalry, humanity, and the dictates of high moral duty." TR knew, he went on, that "you are my hero, and always will be," and there was "no need to enlarge on that topic."[15]

Another English friend, Sir Henry Rider Haggard, offered his condolences for the losses of the Colonel's countrymen, telling Roosevelt that "of course we all hope the states will take some vigorous line—not [to] help but to show their own honor, though I do not think this is generally expected."[16] The writer, most famous as the creator of Allan Quartermain, the hero of *King Solomon's Mines* and many other adventure stories, had first met TR a decade before when he was president, and the two men had been instantly drawn to each other. Roosevelt himself had more than a little in common with his friend Rider Haggard's fictional hero. A recent biographer has commented that TR was "the living antidote to the dawning twentieth century's problems: small like Allan Quartermain; energetic, virile, an attractive and boisterous personality; an explorer of wildernesses; a hunter, both of grizzlies in the American west and of lions in Africa; a fighter (when needed) both of men and the powers of darkness in high places; and, not least, a prolific writer."[17]

From her country house Chequers, which had been transformed into a military hospital that she oversaw, Ruth Lee also sent a letter. The *Lusitania* horror, in her mind, was only one more example, with the gas attacks and other atrocities, of the fact that the war was getting "more overwhelming in its horror every day." She remembered their all sitting together two years before on the terrace, little realizing the house would be a hospital in the Great War, a war she never thought would come, "in spite of all Arthur's teaching." On a more cheery note, she told TR that she had given the scarf Quentin had knitted to a wounded British officer who was "much interested" to hear of its origin. The man then "took to knitting himself on the spot."[18] Her husband Arthur was away, continuing his service as a liaison between War Secretary Lord Kitchener and Britain's last Liberal government, which had nearly come to the end of its days.

This development was driven by events on the war front in Europe, where, soon after the Battle of Festubert in France began on May 9, Kitchener notified the British commander, Field Marshal Sir John French, that 20,000 rounds (20 percent of his reserve ammunition) were to be earmarked for a separate campaign in the Dardanelles.[19] A few days later, frustrated by failure on the battlefield, French shared the War Office correspondence over the shells with the military correspondent of the *Times* of London, Charles à Court Repington.[20] The "Shells Scandal" that followed was the culmination of months of newspaper demands for more shells on the front and a reorganization of the country's munitions production.[21] Repington's account, published on May 14, of the failed attack on Aubers Ridge five days before charged that "the want of an unlimited supply of high explosives was a fatal bar to our success."[22] The article has also been viewed as the final straw that prompted David Lloyd George to inform Herbert Henry Asquith he could not go on.[23] To further complicate matters, on May 15 Lord Fisher, unable to contain his bitter disagreement with Winston Churchill over the Dardanelles campaign, tendered his resignation from the Admiralty.

Over the next week a coalition government, in which Asquith remained prime minister, was formed.[24] To straighten out the muddled shells situation, Lloyd George accepted the new post of minister for munitions. As one of the Welshman's "admirers and sympathizers," Roosevelt sent congratulations on the "action that had been taken in getting a Coalition Cabinet, and especially upon your part therein." He also congratulated Lloyd George on what he had already accomplished during the war. After the war he could return to domestic reform questions such as labor and Ireland, but "the prime business at present" for him to do was to "save your country," and TR expressed his admiration for the "single-hearted manner with which you have devoted yourself to this great duty."[25] Elsewhere in the new arrangement, Fisher's resignation was accepted and Churchill also left the Admiralty to be replaced by Arthur Balfour. The new First Lord of the Admiralty replied to TR's note of congratulations, writing that "it had given me great pleasure. My personal regard for yourself, and my respect for all you stand for, make this expression of your good will specially valuable." Balfour did not "venture to say anything about the course of events upon your side of the Atlantic," as the subject was "too delicate; but it was a great pleasure to think that, on all the great ethical issues raised by this world war, you and I think alike."[26]

While these events played out in Britain, the United States and Germany exchanged what proved to be only the opening round of diplomatic messages over the *Lusitania*. German Ambassador Count Johann von Bernstorff had submitted a note to the neutral nations that expressed regret for the loss of life but placed all blame in the matter on the British "hunger blockade," which forced Germany to extreme measures in retaliation. British merchant ships that attempted to ram submarines, the note explained, prevented "visit and search" procedures that would have shown that the *Lusitania* was carrying contraband. The German government regretted that the American passengers had relied on British promises rather than the German warnings that had been prominently posted in the New York papers before the *Lusitania* sailed.[27]

On May 13 the Wilson administration sent a first *Lusitania* message, cabled under William Jennings Bryan's signature, to Germany. This began as a draft by Robert Lansing, the counselor to the State Department, and was revised by Wilson himself. In the cabinet debate, Bryan, who thought it possible the *Lusitania* had been carrying munitions (and was in fact), had argued for a simultaneous warning to be sent to England about her blockade of Germany and revived his previous suggestion that the American government should warn its citizens of the dangers of sailing on the vessels of belligerent nations. Wilson rejected both ideas. The note finally sent, which was meant to be tough, but not strong enough to precipitate an immediate break in relations, reminded Germany of the principle of "strict accountability" and that Germany had been warned not to kill Americans on the high seas. The note made it clear that "no warning that an unlawful inhumane act will be committed" could possibly be "accepted as an excuse" for that act or abate "the responsibility for its commission." The United States looked forward to the German government's disavowal of the action, offer of reparation, and declaration of immediate steps to prevent a reoccurrence. An angry reply arrived in Washington on May 31, which stated that Germany had already expressed "deep regret" for the deaths of neutral citizens and suggested the United States carry out a "careful examination" of the events. It repeated previous German claims that the *Lusitania* was an armed auxiliary cruiser carrying Canadian troops and munitions of war that led to the explosion that had caused the swift sinking; that the British hid their ships behind neutral flags; and that British merchantmen had orders to ram submarines.[28]

The day after Wilson dispatched his first note, Roosevelt confided to his sister Anna that he was "sick at heart" at the way Wilson and Bryan had acted toward Germany and "above all the way the country, as a whole, evidently approves of them and backs them up."[29] He nevertheless attempted to keep up pressure for action on the administration in a signed *Metropolitan* editorial, "Murder on the High Seas," written two days after the *Lusitania* sinking. It had been centuries, wrote TR, "since any war vessel of a civilized power had shown such ruthless brutality towards non-combatants, and especially towards children," as in the *Lusitania* affair. "In the teeth of these things," Roosevelt went on, the United States earned "measureless scorn and contempt" as a nation if it followed the lead of those who "exalt peace above righteousness"—if it heeded the voices of "those feeble folk who bleat to high heaven that there is peace when there is no peace." For many months the American government had preserved between right and wrong a "neutrality" that would have "excited the emulous admiration of Pontius Pilate—the arch-typical neutral of all times." Unless the country acted with "immediate decision and vigor," declared TR, "we shall have failed in the duty demanded by humanity at large, and demanded even more clearly by the self-respect of the American Republic."[30] A furious Colonel wrote to Kermit that if he "were president, this country would be at war with Germany, unless Germany had completely backed down," which he thought she probably would have done if seriously challenged over the *Lusitania*.[31]

While the diplomatic dance with Germany over the *Lusitania* continued, on May 23 Italy finally renounced at least one of her former Triple Alliance partners by declaring war on Austria-Hungary and joining the Allies, who had secretly promised more satisfactory territorial gains in return.[32] The same day Roosevelt was thrown from a too-spirited horse at Oyster Bay and suffered broken ribs, which were very painful for several weeks. The simple fact was, he confessed to Arthur Lee, that he "tried to ride a horse that was too good for me." TR had to admit to himself that he was old and stiff. He could still sit a horse fairly well, but he could not "mount him if he misbehaves." This animal had thrown him before he got his right foot into the stirrup, and he "struck the ground a good deal as if I had been a walrus."[33]

The horse had been given to the Colonel as a present from Edith and Archie for his victory in the Barnes libel case the day before his accident. He had feared a hung jury, but in six days of cross examination by William Ivins, Roosevelt won over the fascinated jury with a masterful public performance, though it took forty ballots to find him innocent. As Elihu Root had warned William Barnes's lawyer, it was *his* skin and that of his client that in the end were "nailed to the fence." In his usual dramatic fashion, a euphoric TR proclaimed that the verdict marked the "death knell of bossism," and the influence of Barnes, who had hoped a victory would catapult him into the US Senate, fell into serious decline.[34] At the same time, Roosevelt was judged to have bounced back from his party's electoral defeat of only six months before.[35] There was also continued talk that the Colonel was ready to return to the Republican fold. To William Howard Taft it was evident too that Roosevelt was "taking a running jump back into the party."[36] A deluge of congratulatory letters on the court room victory flooded into Oyster Bay. The noted literary critic and essayist Hamilton Mabie wrote from his desk at the *Outlook* that he had "no doubt Mr. Barnes will at once buy the horse that threw you. Perhaps it would be a good idea to sell him for use in Albany."[37] Leonard Wood was "delighted with the outcome," as, he said, were "most decent people."[38]

With the Barnes trial over and Edith recovered from her operation, Roosevelt could again concentrate on preparedness, to which he returned with a renewed energy. Wood informed him that he had raised sufficient money to go forward with student training camps in California and the Plattsburg Barracks in upstate New York.[39] Roosevelt also met with Stuart Blackton, whose Vitagraph studios had prepared a "working scenario" for the preparedness film to be called *The Battle Cry of Peace*.[40] However, the continuing public antipathy to preparedness and sympathy for peace was symbolized by a popular song of the day, "I Did Not Raise My Boy to Be a Soldier," about which the Colonel commented there should be a companion song, "I Did Not Raise My Girl to Be a Mother." Henry Cabot Lodge commiserated with TR that it was "melancholy to think" that people applauded the pacifist song, because it manifested "the spirit which has been provided by the Carnegie propaganda."[41] A few months later a more patriotic songwriter sent a request that he be allowed to dedicate his own "I Am Proud to Be the Mother of a Soldier Boy" to Edith. If this was agreeable, he asked for a photo and a few lines from her.[42] Edith's retort for the whole musical flap was, "I didn't raise my boy to be the *only* soldier."[43]

On June 5, TR departed for a Southern trip. At Pass Christian, Mississippi, he was again the guest of the New Orleans cotton broker and Progressive politician John M. Parker. The Colonel took the opportunity to tour several bird refuges at the mouth of the Mississippi with Parker and his two sons, accompanied by officials of the Louisiana State Conservation Commission and the Audubon Society. Their guide was Captain William Sprinkle, whom TR while president had appointed game warden to protect the refuges.[44] In his account of the outing, the naturalist Roosevelt painted a striking picture of the varied wild fowl and other fauna, including the huge rays that sprang out of the waters, while their even larger cousins, called devil fish, swam slowly near the surface with "their mouths wide open as they follow their prey." TR also noted that the two Parker boys did credit to their father and the country. The oldest, John Jr., had run the Parker stock farm since he had been 16, while his brother Tom had just received an appointment to Annapolis. Roosevelt could not help but comment how refreshing it was to see two such "fine healthy, manly young fellows" at a time when "so large a section of our people, including those who claim in a special sense to be the guardians of cultivation, philanthropy, and religion," deliberately made a "cult of pacifism, poltroonery, sentimentality and neurotic emotionalism." Parker's sons were "emphatically neither 'too proud to fight' nor too proud to work, and . . . hard work and gentle regard for the rights of others and the joy of life all went hand in hand."[45]

While Roosevelt was on this trip, Wilson sent Germany a second, somewhat stiffer, note, which challenged the claims that the *Lusitania* had been armed and carried troops and contraband that contributed to the rapid sinking. If the Germans had evidence to the contrary, the note stated, they should produce it, but regardless, they were not justified in the sinking. Wilson concluded with a request that Germany respect the rights of Americans "bound on lawful errands" to travel on belligerent merchant vessels and asserted that the lives of noncombatants "cannot lawfully or rightfully be put in jeopardy by the capture or destruction of an unresisting merchantman."[46] Bryan, who feared war would result, and felt he had lost his usefulness to an administration that did not heed his repeated warnings, resigned. After a last cabinet meeting, he told his colleagues that he believed he could "do more on the outside to prevent war than I can on the inside."[47] The Hearst press, which agreed that the sinking was not a casus belli, veered from years of criticism to newfound praise of the former secretary of state.[48] Bryan was replaced by Robert Lansing, but the real direction of foreign policy as before would remain in Wilson's hands, and the diplomatic notes composed on the keys of his White House typewriter.

When the news of Bryan's resignation reached the Colonel in Louisiana, he hoped it meant strong action at last and dictated to reporters on hand a rare statement of praise for Wilson. But then no action came. For a moment,

THE CASTAWAYS.

Figure 4. "The Castaways," *New York World*, June 15, 1915
Theodore Roosevelt Collection, Harvard College Library

Roosevelt confided to Arthur Lee, he thought the split between Wilson and Bryan meant that the president at last had "waked up to the national needs, national duty." But when the second note was published, TR was "unable to see that he had changed in the least." Wilson and Bryan apparently agreed "with cordiality that our policy should be one of milk and water," disagreeing only as to the "precise quantity of dilution in the mixture," and this did not seem important enough to Roosevelt to "warrant a quarrel." TR told Lee that he tried not to denounce Wilson, but that it was "extremely hard effectively to attack crime without attacking the criminal." In his opinion the country as a whole had also behaved badly by not turning against Wilson, and it was a "very difficult thing to arouse our people to a knowledge of how badly they have done except by pointing out the shortcomings" of those responsible.[49]

The Colonel's old Harvard classmate and friend, the historian Albert Bushnell Hart, defended Wilson, asserting that the president was "ably and courageously standing by the interests and the lives of his fellow countrymen." This, Roosevelt retorted, was "just exactly" what Wilson was not doing. In his opinion, if Wilson had acted in the "*Gulflight* matter the thousand lives lost on the Lusitania would have been saved." His policy was "words merely," which he tried to make strong enough to satisfy the people that something was being done and at the same time "enable him to dodge out of doing anything to Germany." It was entirely possible, TR told Hart, that Wilson might "drift us into war" just as Jefferson and Madison had done a century before. He had always regarded Jefferson, "in spite of his having rendered great services to the people, as also having been one of the most mischievous enemies of democracy" and one of the weakest presidents. Jefferson was politically very successful, as Wilson might very well be also, but this would not alter Roosevelt's "opinion in one case any more than it has altered it in the other." Wilson even more than Jefferson had been "the apologist for and has given impetus to our very worst tendencies."[50]

For TR, these tendencies came to be embodied in a new organization, the League to Enforce Peace, a product after many years' gestation of the efforts of the New York Peace Society.[51] The league leadership included many notables, such as Harvard President A. Lawrence Lowell and Alton Parker, whom Roosevelt had defeated for the presidency in 1904, as well as some friends, including Hamilton Holt, editor of the *Independent*. After Roosevelt's 1910 Christiana Nobel Peace Prize address, the *Independent* had praised his call for a world league as nothing less than the "Federation of the World" and said that not since the "Great Design" of France's Henry IV in the seventeenth century had anyone comparable to Roosevelt proposed such a comprehensive plan for world peace. The paper also thought TR the ideal man to lead the movement needed for its fruition.[52]

But following his return to America, the Colonel had cooled to the league idea as unrealistic and unworkable in the present international climate, and leadership passed to his presidential successor Taft, who allied himself with Andrew Carnegie's peace initiatives.[53] The Taft administration had negotiated a series of all-inclusive arbitration treaties not unlike Bryan's, which had been similarly ridiculed by TR and blocked by the Senate. Soon after came the 1912 political row that ended their friendship. This wound had not yet healed when TR and Taft saw each other for the first time in years on April 13, 1915, at the New Haven funeral of a mutual friend, the Yale Chaucer scholar Professor Thomas Lounsbury. To make matters even worse from the Colonel's point of view, Taft supported Wilson's course in the *Lusitania* crisis, calling his first note "admirable in tone" and "dignified in the level the writer takes with respect to international obligations."[54]

At its June 17, 1915, organizational convention of an elite three hundred at Independence Hall in Philadelphia, the League to Enforce Peace (LEP) installed Taft as its president. The fundamental idea of the league was declared to be that "no war can take place between its members until they have resorted to the machinery that the League proposes to furnish to settle the controversy likely to lead to war."[55] The league covenant required regular conferences to formulate and codify a legal code and an international court. It also called for compulsory settlement of disputes that member states could not resolve by negotiation, including matters of "vital interest" and "honor" that the league court declared justiciable. Nonjusticiable disputes would come before a council of conciliation, following an idea put forward by Lord Bryce. What distinguished the LEP from other peace societies was enforcement. Any member that went to war without first submitting the dispute to the court or council would be subject to automatic economic and military sanctions.

A month later the league secretary, William Short, sent TR a packet of literature stating its principles and plans and an invitation to the initial meeting—which entitled him to charter membership if he so desired.[56] He did not. The combination of Taft and the New York Peace Society was anathema to him. But beyond the personal, there were also substantial differences with the more cautious league model Roosevelt had earlier endorsed. He did not believe nations would bow to any court when it came to their vital interests and honor, and he agreed with Elihu Root that the court itself might constitute a dangerous "suprasovereignty." TR's league would act against defiance of a ruling, but the automatic sanctions proposed by the LEP might punish the wrong party. "Your proposal," the Colonel wrote to Lowell, was that "in the future if Germany sank another Lusitania, and the United States proceeded to instant hostilities, the League should make war on the United States in the interest of Germany!"[57]

The day the Philadelphia convention met, Roosevelt commented to Arthur Lee that the "antics of the peace people here pass belief." Taft, Andrew Carnegie, "and the rest of the crowd" were at the moment holding a "grand Peace Conference to insist that everything should be arbitrated everywhere." Californians particularly applauded the movement with enthusiasm and said how splendid it was. Then when they paused for a moment, they insulted the Japanese and invited future war. Though "sick at heart over affairs in the world at large," and particularly over the course of his own government and people, TR tried to be philosophical and to remember that there came "long periods when you agree with the bulk of your fellow countrymen and long periods when you don't." At times the world seemed to go "very wrong and at times very right," and "one's duty" was to "struggle for the right and not get cast down."

The most "sad and irritating thing," Roosevelt told Lee, was that so much of the current malaise was a matter of leadership. When he had greeted the return of the Great White Fleet just before leaving office in 1909, the American navy was second only to England in fighting efficiency. US diplomacy was "courteous, respectful to others, self-respecting and absolutely firm." The nation's word carried great weight, and the United States was "working cordially with England for the common good of the British Empire and the United States"—and, he thought he could say "without cant," for the "common good of humanity as a whole." He had brought both Japan and Germany to "sharp account" and made them both "instantly back water when we came into conflict on points where I thought they were wrong." But, TR went on, he supposed that "even then the flabby peace propaganda was gaining weight." He admitted that he had not himself been at all "awake to the need that America should have universal military service." No one had been awake to it at the time, and "hardly any of our people" were "awake to it now." Nevertheless, if he had been president in 1914, he would have from the beginning taken a stand "which would have made the Germans either absolutely alter all their conduct or else put them into war with us." If the country had done what it should have after the *Lusitania*, Roosevelt and his four sons would have been in the army getting ready to serve in Flanders or against Constantinople.[58]

Two days after the League to Enforce Peace was organized in Philadelphia, Bryan put forward in a Carnegie Hall speech his now private doctrine of idealistic isolationism. In the ex-secretary of state's view, Taft's organization was not the peace group it appeared to be but one whose "intent and effect" were to "aid rather than obstruct the Roosevelt propaganda" for large-scale preparedness and conflict. Its program was a "policy of fighting the devil with fire" by using an international police force to "COMPEL peace and COMPEL IT BY THE USE OF FORCE." This would fly in the face of both Washington's warning against alliances and the Monroe Doctrine for the sake of making the United States "partners with other nations in the waging of war." Bryan afterwards continued his denunciations of the League to Enforce Peace in his newspaper, the *Commoner*.[59]

At the same time, but on completely different grounds, Roosevelt used a *Metropolitan* article to attack the "infinite folly, the discreditable folly" of the LEP, because it sought world peace before America had acquired a "military force sufficient to entitle us to speak with the voice of authority in international matters." He went on, "Let us not live in the realm of childish make-believe. Let us not make new and large promises in a spirit of grandiloquent and elocutionary disregard of facts unless and until we are willing by deeds to make good on the promises we have already made."[60] Taft commented drily to a league ally that when Roosevelt and Bryan were "both opposed to us," it was a "fairly good indication that we are nearly right."[61]

On July 11, TR departed with Edith for the West Coast on a week-long train trip that included a leg through the scenic Canadian Rockies. On the platform at New York, the Colonel was asked to comment about the latest German note on the *Lusitania*, which had repeated the argument that Britain was to blame and offered a ludicrous safe conduct scheme to American ships painted like red, white, and blue barber poles, which the press immediately ridiculed as "barber ships." He referred the reporters to his remarks of a month before, stating that the action he demanded then was still required and "in the end the United States will have to recognize the fact." TR—who, according to the press, "never looked better" and was "bubbling over with vitality"—refused to discuss politics and indicated that he did not plan to hold "a single formal conference" with any Progressive leaders. It was widely known, however, that he would hold informal chats with "various politicians" on the train along the way.[62] Roosevelt arrived on July 19 at Portland, Oregon, where he promptly told reporters that if the Republicans nominated Charles Evans Hughes for president, it would be proper for Progressives to support him: "Our progressive idea could be embraced in such a candidate."[63] It was a statement he would come to regret.

At San Francisco, TR was greeted with a twenty-one-gun presidential salute from warships in the harbor. He spent July 21 at "Theodore Roosevelt Day" at the Panama-Pacific International Exposition, a ten-years-in-the-making celebration of American technological prowess embodied by the Panama Canal, dubbed "Hercules's thirteenth labor" and the "colossal achievement of mankind" in the exposition's literature. The fair had also become a rallying point for rebuilding the city after the devastating 1906 earthquake and fire.[64] The Colonel toured the grounds, which included a three-acre recreation of the canal zone; witnessed a flying exhibition by the famed aviator Art Smith; and saw exhibits from industry, the states (complete with the actual Liberty Bell at Pennsylvania's pavilion), and nations around the world from Japan to Argentina. France's offering was housed in a recreation of the *Palais de la Légion d'honneur* in Paris, complete with Rodin's original *The Thinker* stationed at the entrance. The displays inside included the sword carried by Lafayette in the American Revolution.

Roosevelt capped his visit with an address to a crowd of sixty thousand at the Universal Court. He was introduced by Hiram Johnson, California's governor and his 1912 vice-presidential running mate. TR declared that he took a "peculiar pride" in the Panama-Pacific Exposition because if he had not acted as he had in 1903, "with absolute justice to all other nations, to benefit all other nations," no canal would have been built for fifty more years and there would have been no exposition to celebrate. The building of the canal, he went on, had nearly doubled the "potential efficiency" of the United States Navy, as long as it was "fortified and in our hands," but if left unfortified the canal would at once become a "menace to us."

What was true for the canal, in Roosevelt's view, was "no less true as regards our proper attitude concerning the interests of the United States taken as a whole." The canal was a "great agency for peace . . . exactly in proportion as it increased our potential efficiency in war." It was the "highest duty" of the United States to prepare itself against war so that it might "safely trust its honor and interest to its own strength"—to do as a nation regarding its general interests "what we have already done in Panama." If 12 years before, TR went on, the country had "confined ourselves to debates in congress and diplomatic notes"—in other words "treated elocution as a substitute for action"—it would have done nobody any good and "earned the hearty derision of all other nations." Unfortunately, outside Panama, in recent years the United States had "failed in our duty of national preparedness," and he feared that there was in the world just such a consensus of derisory opinion "primarily due" to America's unpreparedness. He was not for war and wanted peace, but he didn't want "peace for Uncle Sam because outsiders don't think him worth kicking."

William Jennings Bryan had preached peace to a huge July 4 crowd at the exposition, and TR struck back by attacking the "professional Pacifists, the peace-at-any-price, non-resistance, universal arbitration people" who were "seeking to Chinafy this country." The Colonel concluded with a favorite verse from Ezekiel: "But if the watchman see the sword come, and blow not the trumpet, and the people be not warned; if the sword come, and take any person from among them, he is taken away in his iniquity." This elicited a wild ovation from the multitude that continued until Roosevelt's car had driven out the gates of the Exposition.[65] That same day, July 21, Wilson sent Germany a third *Lusitania* note, which declared that any further sinkings would be considered by the United States to be "deliberately unfriendly" acts.

At San Diego three days later, Roosevelt spoke at the Panama-California Exposition, a more limited affair than San Francisco's, which concentrated on exhibits from the American Southwest and Latin America.[66] He again denounced the betrayal of America by pacifists and politicians. First and foremost, TR argued, the country must seriously prepare for war and show itself able to maintain its rights and make its weight felt in the world again. Next it must abandon both the "policy of poltroonery" practiced in regard to the *Lusitania* and Mexico and the policy of "recklessly making promises which neither can be or ought to be kept," such as the "unspeakably silly and wicked thirty all-inclusive arbitration-commission treaties" negotiated by the present administration.[67] The Colonel also conferred with California Progressives. Leaving one of these meetings at the Grant Hotel, he was invited to speak at the Advertising Club, which he was told Bryan had also addressed. In that case, TR quipped to the assembled newspapermen, "they most certainly can't have me. Let them get a two-headed calf now."[68] He reported to Arthur Lee that the San Diego and San Francisco speeches were not met with "wild enthusiasm," but it was true to say that the audiences listened "with utmost attention and with substantial assent" for two

Figure 5. TR "damning the mollycoddles" at the San Diego Panama-California Exposition, July 27, 1915
Theodore Roosevelt Collection, Harvard College Library

hours. And he had never before received a comparable response in cards and letters. This was "important enough to make it necessary for Wilson and those like him to consider just how far it was safe for them, from the standpoint of their own future, to go in refusing to prepare to defend our-selves and in truckling to Germany."[69]

Before he left San Diego, Roosevelt heard the news of the sinking of the *Leelanaw*, an unarmed American merchant ship. This, he told reporters, was a "deliberate insult" and a "damnable outrage, but one that was to have been expected." He wondered "what our pacifist friends will say to this? Wait for a whole year to discuss it, I suppose?" In his view this was the condi-tion to which "our peace-at-any-price policy has brought us." When asked whether he would be candidate for the presidency, TR replied that he did not know and it did not make any difference what anyone said at this time. He was touring the country to "preach national defense" and "instill and arouse in the American people" a spirit that would make them "ready should the occasion arise." Any talk to the contrary was "all rot and tomfoolery."[70] Roosevelt's preaching was making at least some Progressives uncomfortable. Soon after he left the state, California Representative William Kent confided to Gifford Pinchot that the Colonel was "talking too much like a war lord to suit my taste."[71]

Back at Oyster Bay from California on August 2, the Colonel found a letter from J. Stuart Blackton announcing that he had arrived home at "just the psychological moment" when his nine-reel preparedness film, *The Battle Cry of Peace*, was "about ready for its initial showing." Blackton invited TR to the first press screening that week in New York, which propreparedness Mayor John Purroy Mitchel had promised to attend.[72] The next step was to take the film out to the country's big cities for exhibition to government officials, army and navy groups, and finally the public at large.[73] The movie was in five parts. The first, "The Warning," had the author Hudson Maxim, and many other celebrities, in the role of prophets of doom. Next, "The Invasion" depicted an unnamed foe in suspiciously Germanic uniforms and helmets landing at New York harbor. "In the Hands of the Enemy" recre-ated the bombardment and capture of greater New York, followed by "The Price," an allegory in which "Columbia, crushed and bleeding, captive of the God of War," finally throws off the "yoke by Virtue of the spirit of America revivified." The film concluded with "The Remedy"—properly preparing the nation. Blackton had tried to get TR to appear in the film, but he had declined, saying, "When you have the Army, the Navy, Church, and State, you don't want anything else."[74]

Popular reaction to the film, which exhibited a militancy and antipacifism not seen before on the screen, was predictably split between the preparedness and antipreparedness camps. There was also some comment on the "racial animosity" that might be generated by the on-screen atrocities perpetrated on New York by the spike-helmeted invaders, who, one critic remarked, were "certainly not Portuguese." Hudson Maxim's connections to the munitions industry led to charges by antipreparedness leaders such as Henry Ford that the film was simply mercenary industry propaganda. After the master auto-maker took out a full page ad to this effect titled "Humanity and Sanity" in 250 newspapers nationwide, Blackton responded by calling Ford "spineless" and proclaiming that *Battle Cry* had been produced solely to "further the interests of practical preparedness." All this publicity simply added to the box office returns. Roosevelt joined the fray, declaring that the men who opposed the film were "thoroughly bad Americans" and engaged in "an action hostile to the vital interests of the United States." Every good American, TR went on, should be grateful to Blackton for having produced *Battle Cry*, and every "uninformed but well-meaning American should attend the exhibition and profit by it."[75] The film was "the most educational drama" the Colonel had "ever witnessed" and represented the "primary, the public school, and the college of preparedness."[76]

The preparedness agitation, reinforced by the sinking of the *Lusitania*, led Wilson on July 21 to request that the navy and war secretaries investigate and submit recommendations for programs adequate to the needs of the nation. The president, Lodge informed TR, had evidently come to the conclusion that there was "a rising popular feeling for preparedness and, seeing votes in it, is prepared to take it up." Last winter, Lodge recalled, Wilson had done everything he could to stop improvement in the army and navy, dismissing Augustus P. Gardner's calls for preparedness, depicting him as "as merely trying to make political capital because he was urging then, as he is now, the necessity of doing something, backed by an array of facts which have never been successfully impugned at any point." Now, after more than two years in office, it was being "announced with great pomp" that Wilson had sent for reports on the state of the army and navy from the respective departments. It seemed to Lodge, "an old fashioned person," that the president, as commander-in-chief of the armed forces of the United States, really "ought to learn about the Army and Navy as soon as he enters office."[77] Roosevelt agreed with Lodge's analysis of Wilson's motivation for taking up preparedness. Whether the president could make people believe he was right depended, he told Lodge, "precisely and exactly upon how widespread our national folly is."[78]

That month three of the Colonel's sons attended the United States Military Instruction Camp at the Plattsburg Barracks in upstate New York. Leonard Wood had been organizing similar camps for college students throughout the country for two years before the *Lusitania* crisis led a group of professional men, mainly in their twenties and thirties and including TR's eldest son Ted, a partner at a Philadelphia investment bank, to propose the addition of a businessmen's training camp scheme.[79] This was first implemented at Plattsburg, where training began with a student camp attended by TR's youngest sons Quentin and Archie. Afterwards, the elder Archie stayed another two weeks for the businessman's cohort that followed and was also attended by Ted. Soon after the training began, Wood confirmed a visit by the Colonel who was to be provided quarters like the men "with camp cot and camp fare."[80]

Wood had also sent Woodrow Wilson an invitation, which was declined. In his demurral the president noted that he had nevertheless followed the camp movement with "the greatest interest" and sent his congratulations to all concerned "upon the success of the experiment."[81] At the same time Wilson told his future second wife, Edith Bolling Galt, that he would have an "interesting tale" to tell her about the Plattsburg camp, which he described as "a Wood-Roosevelt affair in which we spiked their guns." He explained that he "ought not to go" because a speech on preparedness would be expected of him that "Wood and his like would try to use to show that (in another sense) they had 'taken me into their camp.'" His preparedness speech, Wilson went on, "ought to be made to congress—and will be."[82] One way in which the Republican guns were "spiked" was by having prominent propreparedness Democrats on hand. These included Dudley Field Malone, the collector of the Port of New York. Malone informed the president that he thought that if "men like myself, closely identified with you and your administration," should go to the camp, it would be "one of many steps to kill any idea that the opposition party, and its returning prodigal Mr. Roosevelt, alone are vitally interested in this great problem."[83]

The prodigal meanwhile reported to his other son Kermit, still working in South America, that at the Plattsburg student camp Archie and Quentin were under a regular officer and being trained in real army work "without the slightest touch of the tin-soldier business about it," and it would do them both an immense amount of good. Ted and Ethel's husband Dick Derby were also going to Plattsburg the next month for the businessman's camp. TR was himself not doing much of anything in the way of politics "excepting to carry on ferocious war with the pacifists and to preach preparedness against war."[84] A euphoric Dick Derby wrote to his wife from Plattsburg a month later that he and Ted were having a "most wonderful time." Everything was interesting and so very different from what they had been doing. It was, he told his wife, "a wonderful feeling to be marching in a company of 125 men, with a gun on your shoulder." He felt himself to be nothing, "merely a cog in a powerful machine that is marching irresistibly on."[85]

Before Roosevelt traveled to Plattsburg on August 19, fifty miles off the coast of Ireland the German U-24 sank without warning the British White Star liner *Arabic*, bound for New York and carrying no contraband, with the loss of 54 lives, including 2 Americans. Once again many believed US entry into the world war was imminent based on Wilson's last *Lusitania* note. The Colonel issued a press release in which he declared that "what has just occurred" was a "fresh and lamentable proof of the unwisdom of our people in not having insisted upon the beginning of an active military preparedness thirteen months ago." He had seen newspaper suggestions that the sinking of the *Arabic* would be "adequately met" by dismissing Ambassador von Bernstorff and severing diplomatic relations. Roosevelt earnestly hoped the administration would not take this view, for to do so would be a "fresh sacrifice of American honor and interest." In TR's opinion, the time for words had long passed, and it was "inconceivable" to American citizens, who claimed to be the inheritors of the traditions of Washington and Lincoln, that "our governmental representatives" should not see that the "time

Figure 6. TR and Leonard Wood at Plattsburg training camp, August 26, 1915
Theodore Roosevelt Collection, Harvard College Library

for deeds has come."[86] The administration made no answer to Roosevelt, but Bryan responded, "If we use deeds we must declare war."[87]

Though House and Lansing were ready to go beyond words, any action was forestalled by Ambassador von Bernstorff's pledge a week later that in the future no more passenger liners would be sunk without making provision for the safety of noncombatants.[88] Taft, who since the sinking of the *Lusitania* had publicly supported the president against Roosevelt's criticisms, commented to a friend that TR was "deeply grieved over the fact that Wilson seems to have won a substantial victory in his stand with Germany."[89] Whatever promises the Germans made, Roosevelt did not believe for a minute that they would abandon the submarine weapon they would need to defeat England. And when Americans again were murdered on the high seas it would be Wilson, because of his failure to prepare, who would be more responsible than the Kaiser. "But for our purposes," he wrote his naturalist friend John Burroughs, "we will give Willy equal billing with Woodrow."[90]

While this crisis was still developing, the Colonel spent August 25 at Plattsburg. Arriving early, he witnessed drill and mock battle exercises, including a bayonet charge, before eating "camp chow" for lunch. In the afternoon TR led the applause as the eight companies marched by the Plattsburg Barracks for the first time as a regiment prior to the following day's hike that would end the training. After enjoying an "old-time army supper," Roosevelt, wearing a tan riding suit, military leggings, and a cream fedora hat, delivered an evening speech to a crowd of five thousand. He first congratulated the participants in the camp, and other similar ones, "upon the opportunity they have had to minister to their own self-respect by fitting themselves to serve the country if the need should arise." They had the right to hold their heads high because they were "fulfilling the prime duty of free men" and in doing so had "added to their value as citizens."

Camps like this were in Roosevelt's view "schools of civic virtue, as well as of military efficiency." They should be "universal and obligatory for all our young men," and "every man worth his salt" would wish to come to them. The government, TR noted, had "not paid a dollar for camp," which had been financed by private donation and by the men themselves, who bought their own uniforms. But for every one who could afford this there were a "hundred equally good American citizens" who would like to come but were unable to. This was "undemocratic" and would not be remedied until the nation did as Switzerland and gave the same opportunity to all by instituting universal military service. Camps like Plattsburg were also the "best possible antidote" to hyphenated Americanism. The "worst thing that could befall this country" would be to become a "tangle of jangling nationalities." If divided in such a fashion, said Roosevelt, "we shall most certainly fall." America could stand as a nation only if "genuinely united."

Turning to the world war, Roosevelt commented that for the past 13 months America had played an "ignoble part among the nations." The country had "tamely submitted to seeing the weak, to whom we had covenanted to protect, wronged." The country had seen its own men, women, and children murdered on the high seas "without action on our part," and its leaders had treated "elocution as a substitute for action." To make matters worse, during this time the government had not taken the "smallest step in the way of preparedness, to defend our own rights." It was "lamentable fact" that force was "more dominant now in the affairs of the world than ever before"—that the most powerful of modern military nations was "utterly brutal and ruthless in its disregard of international morality." In the face of this new reality, righteousness divorced from force was "utterly futile."[91] Near the end of the speech, a wire-haired terrier puppy belonging to one of the officers, bewildered by the crowd, ran frantically into Roosevelt's leg and then rolled on its back at his feet, its legs in the air. "That's a very nice dog," he quipped, "His present attitude is strictly one of neutrality."[92]

At the rail station afterwards, the Colonel spoke to the press and went further in criticizing Wilson than he had in his prepared remarks. TR told the journalists that he wanted to respond to the often-made statement that "we must stand by the president." He heartily subscribed to this but only on the condition that it was followed by the statement, "so long as the President stands by the country." It was defensible to state that "we stand by the country right or wrong," but it was "not defensible for any free man in a free republic" to state that he would "stand by any official right or wrong, or by any ex-official." The Colonel believed that once a war was on, everyone should "stand by the land," but in a crisis short of war the "prime duty of a citizen" was, by criticism and advice, to "insist that the nation take the right course of action." The right of any president was only to demand support "because he does well; because he serves the public well, and not merely because he is President." The man who believed in "peace at any price or in substituting all inclusive arbitration treaties for an army and navy," said TR, "should instantly move to China." If he stayed here, then "more manly people" would have to defend him, and he was "not worth defending." Let him get out of the country as quickly as possible. To treat "elocution as a substitute for action, to rely on high sounding words unbacked by deeds," was proof of a mind that dwelled "only in the realm of shadow and of sham."[93]

These anti-Wilson barbs drew criticism; however, the *New York Times* commented that in its main points Roosevelt's "vigorous speech" at Plattsburg represented "what most of his fellow citizens are thinking." Many of them would think his language "too emphatic" and wished he would use "more moderation in his expression but he spoke what was in their minds." The paper agreed that the "glib and senseless patter about pacifism" has had a "deteriorating and decaying effect upon the national character, though its evil effect has not gone so far as the Colonel imagines." However, after "making the necessary deductions for the excessive strength of his language," Roosevelt had stated "many features of the case with a pith and strength that makes his speech a service to the country, and himself, in this at least, the spokesman of most of his countrymen."[94]

Allowing TR's "political speech" at Plattsburg led Secretary of War Lindley Garrison to wire a reprimand to Wood, which was released to the press. Garrison told Wood that it was "difficult to conceive of anything which would have a more detrimental effect upon the real value" of the camp experiment "than such an incident." No opportunity, he went on, "should have been furnished to anyone to present to the men any matter excepting that which was essential to the necessary training they were there to receive." This was the second dressing-down aimed at Wood in six months to be linked with Roosevelt (the first being both men's association with the American Legion), and it led to serious doubts that Wood would be given field command "in a hostile emergency."[95]

After reading a morning newspaper account of that "villain" Roosevelt's speech, Edith Galt wrote to Wilson that she was "so boiling made" she could "hardly eat my breakfast" and asked if he had "stooped to read it." She wished she were a man for a few minutes, continuing, "I would go out and make him eat his words or [knock] his disgusting teeth out." Or perhaps both, for "someone ought to thrash him for the honor of *men* in America." But she supposed he would tell her again she was an "incendiary if I don't hush."[96] Wilson replied, "Bless your dear heart, how I love you for getting so furious with TR for his assault on me!" He could "almost warm his hands at those flaming hot sentences." About the Colonel they were "entirely and enthusiastically in accord!" But, he went on, what was the use of "wasting good serviceable indignation on him?" Roosevelt was "too common a nuisance to bother our minds about," and the best way to "vanquish him" was to take "no notice of him whatsoever." And, "as richly as Wood deserved the rebuke" Garrison gave him, Wilson wished that the secretary of war had followed that course as well.[97]

The public reprimand by Garrison, and Wood's public silence, led Roosevelt to issue a statement that he was "entirely responsible" for the speech. In his view, the three week's warning the War Department had of his Plattsburg visit disqualified them from criticizing Wood for not submitting the speech to the administration beforehand. If the administration had displayed "one-tenth of the spirit and energy" in holding Germany and Mexico to account for the murder of American men, women, and children that it was "now displaying in the endeavor to prevent our people from being taught the need of preparation to prevent repetition of such murders in the future, it would be rendering a service to the people of this country."[98]

The day after giving the Plattsburg address, Roosevelt granted an interview to Julian Street, which the magazine writer published later that year alongside other biographic notes as *The Most Interesting American*. This comprehensive defense of TR, in his own and Street's words, amounted to the first piece of campaign literature for the next year's presidential election. When asked about Woodrow Wilson, Street recorded that TR exclaimed, "Oh, how I'd have liked to praise" him if the president had given him the chance. "I'm not for Roosevelt; I'm not for any man; I'm for the United States." He believed every president had the right to time to formulate his policies, and through the early part of Wilson's term he had "waited and hoped," in spite of a belief he had "long held that the pedagogic mind is generally too theoretical and abstract for politics."

Even now, the Colonel went on, if the president were a business man and "had not familiarized himself with history," he might be forgiven. But in Wilson's own *History of the American People*, Roosevelt pointed out, Wilson had criticized Jefferson and Madison "for some of the very same errors of which he himself" was guilty: "Bryan! Mexico! No fleet maneuvers for the first two years! 'Too Proud to Fight!' And all these letters to Germany!" It had led TR of late to come "almost to the point of *loathing* a bee-you-ti-ful, *pol*-ished *dic*-tion." In response to Street's query about precedents for the ex-president's criticism of Wilson, Roosevelt noted that John Quincy Adams had attacked the Mexican and slavery polices of Tyler and Polk. But, TR went on, the "most striking" example of this character he knew of was made by a president on an ex-president: the "offer of twenty-five millions to Colombia by Mr. Wilson because of what I did, as President, about the Panama Canal."

Turning to the European war, the Colonel told Street that he felt "very strongly" that Wilson should have "taken action concerning Belgium" in the last days of July 1914 but had "held my tongue." Even though it was clearly "our duty to protest," he had waited and said nothing, "thinking that perhaps the President wanted to assemble a long list of atrocities so that the people would be behind him in protesting." Instead the country was instructed to be "'neutral even in thought' toward those who had broken faith with us and with civilization." Further, if the United States had "acted with strength in Mexico," Roosevelt was convinced that "the poor souls who went down on the *Lusitania* would still be alive." But we had shown Europe "by our Mexican performance what to expect of us." The recently invaded Haiti, he added grimly, was "apparently the kind of country we can handle now. Our conduct of foreign affairs so far as that vast and powerful nation is concerned, seems to have been admirable."

To those who called him an opportunist for taking up preparedness, and in particular the Swiss system of universal service when he did not champion it as president, TR responded that he had been "shouting preparedness at the top of my lungs for thirty five years." He had in fact looked into the Swiss system years before, but the "need of universal service, and likewise the folly of such treaties as the Hague Convention," did not come out clearly until the start of the present European war. No one should blame Wilson for not being for preparedness when he took office, "but certainly he ought to be for it now." Turning to the navy, TR pointed to his own record of getting through Congress a program to build two battleships a year. Not the four he desired, but the most public opinion and congress would support. He also got a general staff for and built up "our little army" and made it as efficient as he could, but he chose to concentrate on the navy as the nation's first line of defense. When he had left office, the United States Navy had been second only to Britain's; now it was fourth or fifth.[99]

Back on the war fronts, the failure of the Royal Navy to take Constantinople had led to an Allied army, mainly composed of "Anzac" troops from Australia and New Zealand under British command, being tied down for several months in the bloody Dardanelles campaign that followed. TR sent the British overall commander, General Sir Ian Hamilton, a handwritten note of encouragement from Oyster Bay. Hamilton responded that the scenic name recalled "peace and plenty and safety." Roosevelt's note had reached the commander "at the end of four days and four nights continuous bloody fighting." He said, "at the end," but of course admitted that "if man appoints, God and the enemy sometimes disappoint." Enver Pasha, the Turkish secretary of war, was personally "on the Peninsula urging them to drive us back into the sea, and we may have another big attack at any given moment."

The old tactics, Hamilton went on, had "clean vanished." Whether your entrenched were on the top of a hill or on the bottom of a valley mattered "precious little." A trench was a trench in any case, and airplanes could spot for guns in a hollow just as well as they could for guns up on a height. The only thing to do was "by skill, or great expenditure of life," to win such a position that the enemy was "bound, for military or political reasons, to attack." Then you could "begin to kill them pretty freely; so freely indeed that if the process goes on long enough you bleed the fellow to death." Hamilton bid TR, "Goodbye for the present," telling him, "I wish very much you were here. I would then let you take back Jerusalem for you to give to Congress to run."[100]

Despite Hamilton's bravado, that August the failed Suvla Bay landing brought the campaign to a crisis. To further complicate matters, revelations concerning the Dardanelles operation were brought before the British cabinet in a damning report by the Australian journalist Keith Murdoch. TR's correspondent Hamilton had allowed Murdoch to visit the Anzac zone on an inspection of postal arrangements for the Australian government.[101] The journalist had been shocked by the squalor, sickness, and depression he saw during a brief visit to the Australian beachhead. His dire report, addressed to Andrew Fisher, the Australian prime minister, pointed out the extremely tenuous position of his countrymen and indicted Hamilton and the British for ignorance and incapacity in their treatment of the Anzac forces.[102] This was before the British government's Dardanelles Committee, when the decision was made to send Kitchener for a direct inspection of the situation.

On the western front, things were hardly better, and the Battle of Loos in September and October proved to be the final failure for Sir John French, who was replaced as commander of the British forces by Sir Douglas Haig. When Kitchener returned from the Dardanelles the government decided on evacuation. This was carried out at the year's end with an almost miraculous lack of casualties. Lord Northcliffe's London *Daily Mail* characterized the withdrawal as the government's admission that the operation had been a "stupendous blunder," declaring that "too late" was "written in letters of fire upon the record of the Asquith's administration. We were 'too late' in aiding Belgium, we have been 'too late' to save Serbia, and we sent our expeditionary force to the Dardanelles 'too late.'"[103] Meanwhile, in the United States, TR continued to direct similar dramatic salvos at his own government.

CHAPTER 5

FIRST AMERICAN CITIZEN

SEPTEMBER 1915 TO MARCH 1916

> There is only one way to meet calculated terrorism and that is by making
> evident a spirit which will not brook it. This is the duty of neutrals just
> as much as belligerents . . . Nothing is sillier than the pacifist talk of the
> effect of "the opinion of civilized mankind" upon an erring nation. In
> the first place the erring nation usually does not know that there is such
> an opinion; and in the next place if the nation wins it is certain to find
> innumerable apologists among the very creatures who have previously
> shrieked loudest that force is unnecessary because civilized opinion will
> serve as a substitute.
>
> —TR to F. S. Oliver, July 22, 1915

While the war raged on in Europe, Roosevelt spent much of the month
of September on holiday in Quebec, as a guest of his old hunting friend
and physician Alexander Lambert, at the doctor's camp in the wilderness
preserves of the Tourilli Club. This refuge for animals from beaver to moose
was a joint venture of a group of American and Canadian sportsmen who
had leased 250 square miles of wilderness northwest of Quebec City from
the Canadian government. Tramping the ground with his party, helping to
portage the canoes between the local tributaries of the Saint Anne River, and
feasting on freshly taken game and fish had a rejuvenating effect on the Colonel. While in the wilderness he witnessed for the first time a moose diving to
the bottom of a lake to feed on the bottom grass, and from his canoe he shot
another large bull moose standing on the bank.[1]

In Canada, Roosevelt found the time to make half a dozen brief speeches
in which, while he avoided commenting directly on politics, he expressed
his admiration for the way the country had stood by the British Empire and
urged her men to continue volunteering. After reading a report of one of
these addresses, an American serving in the British army felt compelled to

"drop him a line" and tell him "how magnificent it was and how it echoed the hearts of us few Americans who are over here fighting for the Big Ideal." Holbrook Bonney, a second lieutenant in the royal field artillery, confided to the Colonel that most Englishmen considered TR "the representative American" and respected his aims and opinions. He knew what TR had to "contend against" at home and only hoped his country would "see its path of duty before it is too late." He asked himself again and again, "Is this my U.S.A.? Where are all her ideals of justice and liberty?" Bonney continued that it was "sickening to all full blooded Americans to see our country shirk its responsibilities to Humanity." He hoped to be "in at the finish, and to feel that I have done my bit and to uphold what I consider to be my country's honor."[2]

Henry Cabot Lodge echoed this sentiment, writing TR that the "melancholy thing" was the apparently general satisfaction with Woodrow Wilson, "so long as he keeps us out of war, without any reference to the methods by which he does it, and the same indifference on the part of the people to the humiliation of the long and pointless diplomatic discussion about the *Lusitania* and the *Arabic*, on which nothing has been accomplished." The senator also complimented TR's latest *Metropolitan* article, which defended the right of America to sell munitions to the Allies despite German protests of the policy's unneutrality. In seeking to prevent these shipments, Roosevelt had written, the "professional pacifists, hyphenated Americans, and beef and cotton Americans; in short, all the representatives of American mollycoddleism, American greed, and downright treachery to America," were "playing the game of a brutal militarism against Belgium and against their own country." The United States, from the standpoint of international law, had an "absolute right to make such shipments," and every president since Washington had refused to let "this right be questioned." Further, TR pointed out, up to the beginning of the present war, this was a right insisted on by Germany "more strongly than any other nation."[3] This argument, Lodge told the Colonel, was received with "utmost approval" everywhere he spoke.[4]

The Colonel was back at Oyster Bay on October 1 and on Columbus Day traveled to New York to give a speech to the Knights of Columbus at Carnegie Hall. The thousands of Italian casualties in the war had solemnized the holiday celebration and as a result, for the first time in 18 years, there was no great street parade to mark the day. Catholic Vicar General Joseph F. Mooney introduced Roosevelt, to loud applause and cheering, as the "first American citizen." In every act of his life, said Mooney, TR had "exhibited every quality of true American manhood." The long address that followed returned to the Colonel's favorite themes: the twin dangers of unpreparedness and hyphenated Americanism. There was no place, he declared, for the hyphenated American, and the sooner he returned "to the country of his allegiance the better." For an American citizen to vote as a German American, an Irish American, or an English American was to "be a traitor to American institutions; and those hyphenated Americans who terrorized American politicians by threats of the foreign vote" were "engaged in treason to the American republic." Even worse than hyphenated Americans, in his estimation, were the rich men who kept the wages of immigrants so low that they could not "enjoy life and fostered discontent which tended to prevent true allegiance to the United States."

Turning to preparedness, the Colonel repeated his clarion call for the country to take up the Swiss system of universal service. His dream was to have "the son of the multi-millionaire and the son of the immigrant who came over in the steerage, sleep under the same dog-tent and eat the same grub." This, he went on, "would help mightily to a mutual comprehension of life." He pointed out to the individuals who sang about the mother who didn't bring up her son to be a soldier the fact that "if the song had been popular from 1776 to 1781 there wouldn't be anyone to sing it today." TR also attacked Germany and Austria for trying to stir up troubles in the munitions plants of America, while he equally condemned non-foreign-inspired labor troubles. This must cease, he said, "if we were to have the true American spirit."[5]

Roosevelt reported to Kermit that he had chosen "Americanism" as his title and gave "straight doctrine" to the audience, which must have been 95 percent of foreign birth or parentage but "went right with me." The Colonel went on that Wilson, with his usual "shifty astuteness and entire lack of sincere conviction," had concluded that "as regards preparedness and hyphenated Americanism he must follow me, and is doing so." But the president would do as little as he thought safe and strictly with the aim of getting votes. Consequently, Wilson would "refrain from playing any honorable part in the world war or in Mexico." The president had made up his mind that the bulk of the people cared for "nothing but money-getting, and motors, and the movies," and dreaded nothing so much as "risk to their soft bodies, or interference with their easy lives." And the dreadful thing was that he was right and that the people were behind him. To Roosevelt, things were just as they were a century before when Jefferson, "another shifty phrase maker who was 'too proud to fight,' was president." He also dragged the country's honor in the dust and was responsible for the "ignoble conduct of the war that followed; but he pandered to the worst side of the people, and they supported him with enthusiasm."[6]

That month Germany presented the Allies with another propaganda coup when, despite diplomatic protests from the United States and many other neutral countries, on October 12 the German army executed Edith Cavell, a British nurse working in occupied Belgium. The firing squad protocol included the usual pistol coup de grâce to the head, and Cavell thus became the latest martyr to German barbarism. The nurse had been convicted on charges of treason, which she did not deny, for helping several hundred British soldiers escape the country. In a subsequent *Metropolitan* piece, Roosevelt listed Cavell's death as only one of the "dreadful deeds" that had been carried out while the United States "sat tamely by." Cavell, he pointed out, had been executed for deeds that thousands of women on both sides had committed in the American Civil War. But if either Lincoln or Jefferson Davis "had ever dreamed of putting any of the women to death, a deafening howl of execration would have gone up from both sides." The unrepentant Germans, however, showed no hesitation and no remorse in killing the British nurse, and once more "there was no disapprobation expressed by our administration."[7]

Soon after this, TR was able to compare the "black horror" of Germany's action in the Cavell case to Britain's more merciful treatment of an unbalanced young American, Kenneth Triest, who had joined the British navy and then been arrested in England for espionage after a botched attempt to betray wireless secrets to the enemy—potentially a hanging offence. Answering a plea from the young man's parents, the Colonel asked for him to be returned to the United States on account of his unstable mental health. Foreign Secretary Sir Edward Grey and First Lord of the Admiralty Arthur Balfour were skeptical of this defense, but they relented and informed the Colonel that Triest would be sent home. When the young man was returned, he visited Sagamore Hill, where Roosevelt administered a stern lecture.[8]

A week after Nurse Cavell's execution, on October 19, 1915, the United States gave de facto recognition to the Carranza government in Mexico—a step, Roosevelt pointed out in the *Metropolitan*, that Wilson had insisted he would never take, after having refused with "far less justification" to recognize Victoriano Huerta. While the followers of Huerta had committed "foul wrongs" on Americans, the followers of Venustiano Carranza had done worse. Carranza himself "derided and insulted" Wilson, and his adherents had committed "every species of outrage" on American citizens and, according to several reports, literally on the American flag. But the Wilson administration sheltered itself behind the Latin American states it had "unwisely invited to do the duty which the administration itself feared to undertake." It then "bowed with abject submission" to the man who had defied it, and with "servile eagerness" served Carranza against his rivals. The Colonel deliberately chose the word "infamy" as the only one that could describe with "scientific accuracy the policy of poltroonery that the representatives of this government had now for five years into effect as regards Mexico, and, above all, the policy that has obtained for nearly three years."[9]

Many Progressives, however, were attracted to Wilson's calm and deliberate Mexican policy. The *New Republic* disagreed with Roosevelt on the issue, and Walter Lippmann commented that his latest *Metropolitan* "performance" showed that "T.R. will not do." The editor wrote to a sympathetic Liberal British journalist, C. P. Scott, that Wilson's attitude toward Mexico was "proof of his radical benevolence towards the weak and his hatred of conquest and aggression." And in Lippmann's view, when the Wilson administration had refused to protect Americans in Mexico, "it struck a great blow against nationalism." Another writer and Wilson supporter, Ray Stannard Baker, believed that in no way did the president show his "fundamental progressiveness and democracy" more than in his "attitude towards Mexico," while in contrast Roosevelt urged the country "with might and main to think only of ourselves; of our honor, our commerce, our integrity."[10] To Baker, TR's foreign policy reflected "the morals of 1825, with the gentlemanly code of the duello!" And it was this same code, "on its way to eternal damnation," that had caused the war in Europe.[11]

Two days after recognizing Carranza, the Wilson administration dispatched a lengthy note to Great Britain protesting the Royal Navy's continued interference with American trade. This called the British blockade "ineffective, illegal, and indefensible" and insisted that Anglo-American relations be determined by international law. It did not appear in the newspapers until November 7 on account of the tardiness of Ambassador Walter Hines Page in presenting the note, which he considered an "uncourteous monster" that would hurt relations. The British press agreed, while American papers were more favorable. The *New York World* commented that the British blockade had not killed Americans, but it had killed American rights. The difference between the policies of Britain and Germany, said several editors, was the difference between "robbery" and "murder."[12]

Meanwhile in Paris, Edith Wharton was finishing off the details of *The Book of the Homeless*, a charity project for which Roosevelt wrote an introduction. Wharton insisted on this despite the fears of the publisher, Charles Scribner, that TR's unpopular criticisms of the Wilson administration might hurt sales. Wharton had gathered contributions for this mélange of prose, poetry, art, and musical composition from her many famous friends, including Sarah Bernhardt, Joseph Conrad, Thomas Hardy, Igor Stravinsky, W. B. Yeats, Paul Cezanne, Claude Monet, and John Singer Sargent, to name but a few. The net sales proceeds went to support her refuge and other charities. To raise even more money, several of the original works submitted were auctioned off for a total of $15,000. The auction items included a handwritten manuscript of the Colonel's introduction, which, she wrote him, might be sold to the "Tru-fool who wants your handwriting; we even hope to find two or three & pit them against each other." Wharton was disappointed that she could not persuade him to come to France and see the front, as she believed his description of the scene would shake America out of its neutrality. She agreed with TR that the Wilson apologists were largely "responsible for our shame." It was, she thought, the "saddest moment of my life when I realized that my country wanted him to be what he is; & shook in its shoes for fear he wouldn't understand how thoroughly they were 'behind' him & meant to stay there."[13]

Roosevelt continued his attacks in the November 1915 *Metropolitan*, focusing attention on the "professional German-Americans" and their newspapers that, with "President Wilson's ardent supporters in New York, with the connivance of the Administration, and by the direct instigation of the German Government," had "deliberately campaigned against the United States," had "exulted in German atrocities," and had "openly stated that the support of the German-American vote was conditioned on the Administration's attitude towards Germany." Further, they asserted that Germany would let Wilson play a part in the peace negotiations "only if he actively or passively helped Germany in the war."

The article also again attacked the Wilson administration for allowing the navy to deteriorate "with frightful rapidity" in the previous two years This was partly because of the "way it was handled in connection with our absurd and humiliating little make-believe war with Mexico" but also because there had been no maneuvers or training in fleet or squadron gunnery. This in TR's view "should be accepted as an impeachable offense." At any rate, the fleet was "not fit at this moment to defend us from serious attack." The navy and the army, he declared, should both be maneuvered "every year in mass." On land, the nation needed a mobile army of 100,000, kept ready to meet any challenge. And unless some form of universal service was instituted, the regular army needed to be increased to a total of 500,000 men, if the country's needs were "adequately to be served." The "much-praised 'volunteer' system" meant nothing but "encouraging brave men to do double duty and incur risk" so that "cowards and shirks and mere money-getters" might sit at home in a "safety bought by the lives of better men."[14]

Roosevelt mailed a copy of the *Metropolitan* piece to his friend John St. Loe Strachey, the editor of the London *Spectator*, who in reply to the Colonel's pessimistic appraisal of US politics asserted that he believed there would be a reaction in TR's favor and that he would return to "public life, in spite of American traditions and other idiotic lumber." Roosevelt had also sent Strachey a letter for Rudyard Kipling, whose son John had been listed missing in action. The editor reported that the young man had now been confirmed killed and that he had sent on TR's message. Kipling, he reported, had "behaved as he was sure to do, very well indeed," and he had written Strachey "quite a splendid letter the other day in answer to one from me." Strachey also recounted the "baptism of fire" in combat of his son-in-law, who, though "not particularly keen on soldiering," was "full of pluck and determination" and had a good heart. He certainly had, in TR's words, "seen the vision and been true to it."[15]

In late October, in answer to the criticism of Roosevelt and the preparedness movement, the Wilson administration offered its own proposals. Secretary of the Navy Josephus Daniels unveiled a five-year, $500 million naval construction program including ten battle ships and six battle cruisers. This plan, Roosevelt believed, was inadequate to bring the navy up to his standard: second place in the world behind only Britain. Secretary of War Lindley Garrison put forward a scheme to increase the regular army to 230,000 with a reserve under federal control, dubbed the Continental Army, to bring the force strength up to 500,000, with the National Guard left as a third reservoir of men. In a *Chicago Daily News* interview, TR called the proposed Continental Army "utterly undemocratic" because it denied "to the patriotic man of small means" the chance to train that it gave to the "well-to-do brother." Employers, if they were to "compete with their rivals in business," could not afford to give the men the proposed two months leave. It was a "simple imitation" of prewar England's Territorial Army, which had "proved a flat failure as soon as the crisis came." What was needed was universal service, which meant every young man should be trained.[16]

Hoping to unite all shades of opinion under a nonpartisan banner, the president introduced his administration's preparedness program in a speech to the Manhattan Club on November 4, 1915. "We have it in mind," said Wilson, "to be prepared, not for war, but only for defense; and with the thought constantly in our minds that the principles we hold most dear can be achieved by the slow process of history only in the kindly and wholesome atmosphere of peace, and not by the use of hostile force."[17] Although the plans fell well short of what TR and his allies were demanding, they were sufficient to shock and antagonize pacifists and other opponents of militarism, as well as anti-preparedness Democrats such as William Jennings Bryan, Speaker of the House Champ Clark of Missouri, and Congressman Claude Kitchin of North Carolina. Kitchin, the new House majority leader and spokesman for several dozen progressive Democrats, told Wilson four days after the Manhattan Club speech that he could not support the War Department program. At the same time, outside of Congress, the radical Emma Goldman also condemned the president's "betrayal" and concluded that there was no longer any difference between Roosevelt, "the born bully who uses a club," and Wilson, the "history professor who uses the smooth polished university mask."[18]

The Colonel blasted Wilson's preparedness plan as a "shadow program," a policy of "adroit delay and make-believe action" put forward for political purposes. He called instead for "immediate action" to make the United States Navy second only to Britain's. Wilson's plan, TR pointed out, would be followed mainly by the next administration and, if lived up to, would in five years perhaps put the fleet where it was three years before. It was in reality "merely an adroit method of avoiding substantial action in the present." Not only were the naval proposals a sham, but the projected increase in size of the regular army was "utterly inadequate to serve any real purpose." It was "one of those half-measures which are of service, if at all, only from the political standpoint." The Colonel therefore earnestly hoped that, since their official leaders refused to lead them, the citizens of the country would "themselves wake to their own needs and lead the should-be leaders" to take action "this year and not the year after next."[19]

Wilson, Roosevelt reported to Kermit, "astute, cold-blooded, absolutely a time server—has made up his mind that the country wishes preparedness, at least as regards the navy; and with entire calm and shamelessness he has eaten his words of a year ago." TR went on that his own speeches and articles had a "rather curious effect" on the people. They violently objected to him, but "after a time they come round to my doctrines, proclaiming that this shows what I have preached is useless, because they would be for it anyhow!" So he was inclined to think that in an "indirect fashion I accomplish a certain amount of good."[20] The Colonel commented similarly to Baltimore District Judge John Carter Rose that Wilson was now "following afar off in the paths of preparedness and of Americanization" that TR had "blazed for him more than a year before." And to TR's "immense amusement," Wilson had even used the same verses from Ezekiel that TR had proclaimed at San Francisco and then again "commended to his prayerful consideration" in the August *Metropolitan*.[21]

The *New York Times* also noticed that both men had used the same verses and quoted two: "If the people be not warned and the sword come and take any person from among them his blood will I require from the watchman's hand" and "Whosoever heareth the sound of the trumpet and taketh not warning his blood shall be upon his own hand." The paper pondered whether Wilson's "gracious amenability" would "fail to melt the Colonel's heart, dissolve the green-eyed suspicion and uncharitableness which have possessed him." Both men were "on the patriotic side, the common sense side," and *Ezekiel* had established "between them the tie that binds."[22]

William Jennings Bryan, meanwhile, took issue with the interpretations both men put on the verses to justify their brands of preparedness. It was not surprising to the former secretary of state that Roosevelt quoted from the "Old Testament rather than the New, because he would class Christ with the mollycoddles." But why should the president, who was a Presbyterian Elder, "pass over the new Gospel in which love is the chief cornerstone" and build his defense on a passage "written at a time when the children of Israel were surrounded by enemies?" But even if the passage came from the New Testament, it would not support the president's plan, because the words quoted by him had "reference to an actual attack." At present the sword had not come upon the land and no enemy was in sight, as Wilson himself had said at New York. It was "all right for Mr. Roosevelt to sound the trumpet," because all colors looked red to him, and he saw "armies marching against us from every direction." But the president was a man of peace and was in a position to know that no one was threatening attack. What the world needed, in Bryan's opinion, was "a Pentecost, not an Armageddon."[23]

One defender of Wilson's preparedness program, particularly as it concerned the navy, was Senator "Pitchfork Ben" Tillman of South Carolina, the chairman of the Committee on Naval Affairs. Tillman assailed both Bryan and TR and blamed the problems faced by Navy Secretary Daniels on the previous Republican administrations. Bryan, the senator noted, was the "evangel of peace at any price" and "bitterly opposed to any and all increase either in the army or the navy." He had been Bryan's friend for many years, but the "Great Commoner" seemed to be "simply obsessed on this subject" and had "lost his usual poise." Roosevelt, on the other hand, who "snorts and roars like a veritable Bull of Bashan, poses as the god of war and clamors for a very large standing army and great reserves." He reminded Tillman of the giant in Mother Goose:

> Fe, fi, fo, fum.
>> I smell the blood of a German man.
> Be he live or be he dead.
>> I'll grind his bones to make my bread.[24]

The white-supremacist Tillman had led those who loudly condemned Roosevelt 14 years before when he had dared to dine with Booker T. Washington at the White House, and on the day of Tillman's latest attack, TR learned of the black leader's death. A month later he eulogized him at Washington's beloved Tuskegee Institute in Alabama, of which Roosevelt was a longtime Trustee and beneficiary of its political clout among African American voters.[25] When he was president, said the Colonel, "Dr. Washington" was one of the few men to whom he turned to for advice, because Roosevelt knew "he would not give me one word based on a selfish motive" and would "state what in his best judgment was for the best interests of the people of the entire country." Booker T. Washington, he went on, "did justice, loved mercy, and walked humbly." He taught "honesty, cleanliness and efficiency." His "every step helped others," and his "monument lies in the minds and memories of those whom he has served and uplifted."[26]

Back on the preparedness front, Robert Shaw Oliver, who had briefly been acting secretary of war under William Howard Taft, sent Roosevelt a copy, for his "careful consideration," of a "Brief on the Organization of Our Land Forces," by Captain George V. H. Moseley of the General Staff Corps. Oliver considered Moseley "one of the cleverest of a very able group of young officers on the General Staff & now at the War College." Like TR, Oliver was an opponent of the "Continental" plan to build up the army presently before Congress. He told Roosevelt that "long experience with 'civilian soldiers'" had convinced him that the scheme based on voluntary service was "eventually doomed to failure."[27] Roosevelt wrote directly to Moseley to express his overall support for his alternative plan, which included a scheme of compulsory national service. He "emphatically" agreed with Moseley not to use the word "conscription," which gave the wrong idea. *Universal training* was the "right term." However, he did not think the American people would accept Moseley's idea for two types of such training: one for the college educated and one for the rest. TR believed "every man in this country should serve with the colors."[28] Roosevelt repeated many of these points in a *Chicago Daily News* interview in which he declared that advocates of "half-preparedness," such as Wilson and Taft, were "more dangerous to the body politic" than the "pitiable spectacle" produced by peace-at-any-price men like Bryan and Henry Ford, rendered less threatening by their "very absurdity" and "unspeakable silliness."[29]

Whatever Roosevelt might think of him, by November 1915 Henry Ford had emerged as perhaps the most prominent and popular opponent of preparedness and militarism. That month the automobile maker extraordinaire decided to back a peace expedition to Europe to get the boys "out of the trenches by Christmas, never to return."[30] To carry out this quixotic project, the Detroit industrialist booked passages for himself and his assorted confreres on the Danish ship *Oscar II*, set to depart from Hoboken on December 4.[31] At the same time TR, along with other preparedness leaders, was attacked by Oswald Garrison Villard, another leading pacifist and owner of the *New York Evening Post*, as a tool of the munitions makers that Ford had decried, along with money lenders, as the cause of all wars. The Colonel commented about Ford and Villard that it was "sometimes necessary to skin skunks," but it was also "necessary to choose the skunk!" He might have to attack Ford, but he did not think Villard ought to be so honored: "To change the metaphor," he was the "kind of crawling thing we step on, provided the resulting crunch won't leave too large a stain on the floor. But we ought not to fight it."[32]

On the eve of the Peace Ship's departure, Roosevelt remarked that Ford's mission to Europe would "not be mischievous" only because it was "so ridiculous," but it was nevertheless "a most discreditable thing to the country."[33] Many newspapers agreed with at least part of TR's assessment, dubbing the mission "Ford's Folly" and "much adieu about nothing." The departure turned into an embarrassing bit of comic opera as one intoxicated acolyte fell overboard to the accompaniment of a brass band blaring "I Didn't Raise My Boy to Be a Soldier."[34] Bryan was present to bid the travelers bon voyage, but Ford was the only real notable who in the end sailed. And very soon after arriving in Europe the tycoon lost the true faith and abandoned ship at Christiana, Norway, on Christmas Eve. Before long a comedic film, *Perkin's Peace Party*, satirized the whole affair with a tale of an absent-minded professor and his bungling companions who failed to stop the European war.[35] Despite this embarrassing episode, Ford's commitment to peace remained strong and his personal popularity high.

Four days after the *Oscar II* sailed, Wilson, in his message to Congress, stole much of Roosevelt's preparedness and antihyphenate thunder. First, the president laid out his administration's plan to increase the standing army to 140,000, with a force of 400,000 in reserve—Garrison's Continental Army. Then Wilson denounced those "born under other flags but welcomed under our generous naturalization laws" who had "poured the poison of disloyalty into the very arteries of our national life." They had "plotted to destroy our industries, conspired against our neutrality," and "pried into the confidential affairs of the Government with intent to betray its secrets." He called on Congress to pass laws to "crush out" this grave "threat to our national safety." Wilson did not mention TR by name, but went on, "Some men among us have so far forgotten themselves and their honor as citizens as to put their passionate sympathy with one or the other side in the great European conflict above their regard for the peace and dignity of the United States." By doing so, according to Wilson, they too preached and practiced disloyalty.[36]

As might have been expected, Roosevelt assailed Wilson for simply extending his absurd "milk and water" policies in defense and foreign policy, and for omitting any mention of sorely needed aid to industry. There would have been no need, said TR, for Wilson's "wail" to congress that he was unable to control anarchy without their passing laws "the nature of which he does not indicate," if ten months before when he had written his "strict accountability" note to Germany he had "meant what he said and had made it evident he meant what he said." Such action would not provoke war; it would "prevent the cumulative outrages which lay the foundation for war."[37] In this criticism of the presidential message, Secretary of the Interior Franklin K. Lane confided to a close friend that TR "did certainly write himself down as one large and glorious ass," particularly in his attack on what Lane considered the "bully" section of the speech on the "hyphenated gentlemen." He wished he did not have to say this about the Colonel, because he was extremely fond of him, but a "poorer interview on the message could not have been written." Lane, a progressive Democrat whom a decade before Roosevelt had appointed to the Interstate Commerce Commission, was convinced that TR hated Wilson so much that "he has just lost his mind."[38]

On the political front, Roosevelt had by this time reconsidered his July declaration that Progressives could support Charles Evans Hughes for the presidency, writing to Lodge that he had discovered a "considerable feeling" that it was "not wise to establish a very bad precedent and take a candidate from the Supreme Court." Further, TR was unsure whether Hughes was "all right about preparedness and defense and foreign policy generally." He also complained that Hughes "got me in the fight against Barnes; and then his memory proved conveniently short on the subject when the libel suit came up." Consequently, TR proclaimed, "I thoroughly dislike him." Roosevelt's former secretary of state, Elihu Root, was even worse. To the Colonel and other Progressives Root's central role as chairman of the 1912 Republican convention that steamrolled Taft to the nomination was "morally exactly as bad" as the actions for which many Tammany and small Republican politicians who had committed election offences were now serving or had served "terms at Sing Sing." Consequently, only a "national cataclysm" could get Progressives to support him.[39]

The Progressive National Executive Committee had also decided not to place Roosevelt's name in the Republican primaries, reversing the course of 1912 in which TR (before he became the Progressive candidate) had won 11 of the 13 held, including Taft's home state of Ohio. The Colonel thought it would be "useless to precipitate an open fight again" and did not want to give the "entirely erroneous impression" that he was receptive to being a candidate. However, he had told the Chicago Progressive leader Raymond Robins that he would be gratified if it could be made known that there was a "growth of sentiment in favor of my ideas and of what I stand for." But he refused to make an open declaration, having had enough of announcing "unalterable decisions in public."[40] The Colonel was likely also swayed by his friend Lodge, who wrote him that the only thing that could save Wilson would be "your running as the Progressive candidate for President." It seemed to Lodge that "feeling as you and I do our first duty to the country is to remove this administration from power."[41]

On December 18, 1915, 16 months after the death of his first wife, Ellen, Woodrow Wilson married Edith Bolling Galt, and the two departed for an extended honeymoon. The love-struck Wilson had only met the Virginia-born widow that March and proposed two months later. During his first marriage, whispers of dalliances with various women had circulated widely, but Roosevelt had refused to countenance their use against Wilson in 1912,

Figure 7. *Metropolitan* Cover, January 1916
Theodore Roosevelt Collection, Harvard College Library

telling his political managers that such tactics would not work, and besides, "You can't cast a man as Romeo who looks and acts so much like the apothecary's clerk."[42] The 1915 presidential wedding caused many eyebrows to be raised in proper society. Lodge called it "a vulgar marriage," but TR again made no public comment.[43] Privately, however, he remarked to a fellow Rough Rider, Charlie Bull, the assistant chief ranger at Yosemite National

Park, that in marital affairs, "the worthy gentleman's motto" seemed to be "My wife is dead! Long live my wife!"[44]

In print Roosevelt held his fire concerning Wilson's private affairs, but a week later in the *Metropolitan* revealed the public "sins of the Wilson Administration" in "America First—A Phrase or a Fact." This latest jeremiad began with the by-now-standard vitriolic attack on Wilson's wicked neutrality and Mexican policies, but it also did not spare the feelings of Taft. The present administration, declared TR, with its conviction that phrase making was "an efficient substitute for action," had "plumed itself" on the campaign slogan "Safety First" when in practice it had acted on the theory of "America last" both at home and abroad, in Mexico and on the high seas. "Safety First," the Colonel went on, certainly expressed "their attitude in putting honor and duty in the second place, or, rather, in no place at all." This was the motto on which in a shipwreck the men "crowd into the life boats ahead of the women and children—although they do not afterwards devise a button to commemorate this feat." In his estimation, there could be "no more ignoble motto for a high-spirited and duty-loving nation."

Lest his words be dismissed as a mere partisan attack, Roosevelt acknowledged that the present state of affairs had begun in the previous administration, when Taft "surrendered to the peace-at-any-price people, and started the negotiation of its foolish and wicked all-inclusive arbitration treaties." In Mexico for the last three years, Wilson had "merely followed in the footsteps" of the previous administration's policy. Further, concerning the European war, Taft had gone out of his way "heartily to commend" the present administration for the "outrages and humiliations" America had suffered thanks to its actions. Taft had accepted the presidency of the League to Enforce Peace, while he must know that in a crisis like the present war, "unless the United States had an army of two or three million men, it could do nothing at all towards enforcing peace." And yet, according to the press, Taft had stated that even a standing army of a tenth that size meant "militarism" and "aggression" and must be opposed. Lumping Taft in with Bryan and Ford, Roosevelt went on that America would never be able to "find its own soul or to play a part of high nobility in the world" until it realized the full extent of the "damage done to it, materially and morally, by the ignoble peace propaganda" for which these men, and others like them, were responsible.[45]

As if to underline Roosevelt's words, on January 11, 1916, Pancho Villa raided a train at Santa Isabel, Chihuahua, killing 16 of the 17 Americans on board. Despite this, and in the face of heated congressional demands for action, Wilson remained opposed to armed intervention and left it to the Carranza government to punish the bandits responsible for the massacre. The president pointed out in the administration's defense that the slain Watson party had been warned by the State Department not to enter that part of Mexico. This latest "dreadful outrage," Roosevelt told reporters, was "merely an inevitable outcome" of the policies that had been followed in Mexico for the previous five years, and particularly the past three. Wilson's policies of "watchful waiting," of not interfering with "blood spilling," of asking the

Central and South American republics to "take from us the responsibility that we were too timid to take," had all "borne its legitimate fruit." And in the past the Carranzistas, whose leader Wilson had recognized as forming the government of Mexico the previous October, had done exactly the same thing as the Villistas.

It was only a year, TR went on, since Wilson had sent the army chief of staff down to Mexico to make a treaty with Villa, who had by then already committed "outrages of this kind and outrages not only against men but against women." Wilson had permitted these "different bandits" to get from us, or with our permission, the arms with which they had killed American private citizens, soldiers and the "husbands and fathers of women whom they have outraged." In Roosevelt's opinion, there was a "hundred times" the justification for interfering in Mexico that there had been for interfering in Cuba. The regular army, not volunteers, should be sent into Mexico, and led by General Leonard Wood, who "did the job in such fine shape in Cuba."[46] This was a course the administration was already unlikely to follow, and even less so after Wood testified a few days later before a Senate committee that compulsory service was the only way to build an army adequate for protection in the present war-torn world—words not designed to curry favor with his commander-in-chief. Meanwhile in London, Ambassador Page was also weary of Wilson's timid diplomacy and had taken, like TR, to comparing him to Jefferson, doing so to a shocked Colonel Edward M. House, who had returned to continue his peace endeavors. A frustrated Page recorded in his diary that there was "a feeling here (no doubt premature, at least) that as Roosevelt by his Bull Moose defection elected Wilson, Wilson by his war-timidity may now elect Roosevelt."[47]

That month the Colonel spoke at a meeting of the Advisory Board and the Trustees of the American Defense Society (ADS), a self-declared "patriotic society for the systematic distribution to the American people of our program: military efficiency for the United States." This was in essence a Republican branch of the National Security League, from which it had split the previous August.[48] TR served on the advisory board and endorsed the program of the ADS, which demanded that the United States "have a strong navy, fully manned, of 48 Dreadnoughts and battle Cruisers in proportion" and the additional necessary number of support vessels, submarines, and other ships, with construction to begin immediately. In addition, the nation "must have a standing army of 200,000 men and 45,000 officers," backed by a national force of fully equipped citizens, numbering no less than 2,000,000, "trained in arms under a universal and obligatory system." This, declared the ADS program statement, "shall be America's insurance against war, against invasion, against a foreign flag over Washington—a force of defense which makes the Monroe Doctrine a living fact. And this shall be the true meaning of preparedness. Half measures are useless and a waste of money."[49]

Another group, the National Americanization Committee (NAC), cooperated with Roosevelt in coordinating an Americanization push with the activities of the preparedness societies he supported. The NAC had begun an

"America First" campaign three months before aimed at "internal preparedness" and called for the exclusive use of English in schools and required lessons on patriotism in naturalization classes.[50] In a January 20, 1916, speech
at the Philadelphia Opera House sponsored by the NAC, TR appealed to
America to fulfill her promises of liberty and equal opportunity to people
who came from foreign lands, which he declared to be the "first essential in
transforming them into desirable citizens."

The "larger Americanism," said Roosevelt, demanded that "we insist that
every immigrant who comes here shall become an American citizen and
nothing else." If the immigrant then showed that he still remained "at heart
more loyal to another land, let him be promptly returned to that land." If
on the other hand, the immigrant showed that he was "in good faith and
whole-heartedly an American, let him be treated as on a full equality with the
native-born." TR compared the man who loved another country as much as
his own with the man who loved other women as much as he did his own
wife. Further, the professors of every form of hyphenated Americanism were
"thoroughly the foes of this country as if they dwelled without its borders
and made active war against it." Lincoln had said truly at the time of the Civil
War that the United States could not survive half slave and half free. Today it
was "true that it cannot endure half American and half foreign." The hyphen
was "incompatible with patriotism."[51]

On February 3, Roosevelt had lunch at Oyster Bay with Rear Admiral
Bradley Fiske, one of the fathers of naval aviation, and the US navy's Leonard
Wood. Since August 1914, Fiske had worked ceaselessly inside the administration for increased naval preparedness and had published recent articles
on the subject in the *North America Review*, which TR praised.[52] In the
end, Fiske's unvarnished testimony before Congress would lead to his forced
retirement that June. Meanwhile, in St. Louis, Wilson upped the preparedness stakes when he called for "incomparably the greatest navy in the world."
Was it possible, asked the *New York Tribune*, that the president who retained
Josephus Daniels, whom the paper derided as the "court fool" of the administration, as secretary of the navy was "actually and sincerely a convert to
policy of naval expansion which makes a 'little navy' man out of Theodore
Roosevelt?"[53] Whether Wilson was sincere or not, TR's rejoinder was that it
would "be asking too much of this people to get them to try to rival Great
Britain and her Navy, just as it would be too much of them to try and get
them to rival Germany and her Army." The navy was as vital to Britain as the
army was to Germany, and "neither could afford to let another power rival
it." But if the US navy was second to Britain, as it had been briefly while he
was president, it would be able to hold its own against any other nation.[54]

That month a German note announced that, after February 29, its U-boat
commanders had orders to sink armed merchant ships. Consequently, several members of Congress in both houses, most notably representative Jeff
McLemore of Texas, introduced resolutions to warn Americans not to travel
on armed merchantmen and to place an embargo on arms and ammunition
sales. In the end, after a bitter political battle, Wilson saw to it that all these

were tabled in the House with the aid of 93 Republican votes. This was seen by the *Evening Post* as a victory over "pro-German agitation conducted for the purpose of embarrassing the President and besmirching the nation."[55] The bulletin from Berlin that submarine warfare was to recommence against armed vessels, Sir Cecil Spring Rice reported to Sir Edward Grey, was "hailed by the press here as a further proof that a good understanding prevailed between the United States and Germany." The ambassador went on that Wilson had recently made a speech at St. Louis, the "headquarters of the German population here," announcing that the German submarine campaign had in the main been carried out "in accordance with accepted law" and his adherence to the principle that Americans "had an indefeasible right to trade in innocent goods with the civil population of Europe." Concerning American politics, Spring Rice also reported that Roosevelt was considered Wilson's "most dangerous antagonist."[56] By this time, Wilson rarely received Spring Rice, whom he dismissed to Colonel House as a "highly excitable invalid."[57]

Wilson's envoy House had returned to the European capitals with a renewed peace initiative but was having his own difficulties. Aristide Briand, who had replaced René Viviani as French prime minister four months before, dismissed House, who did not speak French, as "*M. Nul.*" The British premier, Herbert Henry Asquith, considered House to be the impresario of Wilson's reelection and an unimpressive figure, dubbed "sheep-face" in the cutting drawing room repartee of the day.[58] Nevertheless, as the president's personal ambassador, he could not be ignored, and that month Foreign Secretary Grey initialed a draft of what would be called the House-Grey Memorandum.[59] This outlined a scheme to call a peace conference to end the war, and if Germany refused to attend, the United States would "probably" enter the war on the side of the Allies. Wilson added the "probably" to the language, and though House tried to downplay its importance, Grey believed it completely changed the proposal's meaning.[60] Though this initiative came to nothing in the end, Wilson's diplomacy yielded a success in Germany's final *Lusitania* note, dated February 16, 1916, which expressed "profound regret" for the American dead, assumed liability, and offered to pay "a suitable indemnity."[61]

This apparent victory dampened a blow the administration had suffered a week earlier when Secretary of War Garrison had resigned after Wilson surrendered to those in Congress who loudly objected to reducing the role of the National Guard and deserted his army reorganization plan for a rival proposal. This more politically popular measure, sponsored by Congressman James Hay of Virginia, the chairman of the House Committee on Military Affairs, dropped Garrison's Continental Army idea and instead simply enlarged the National Guard.[62] To replace Garrison, Wilson chose a like-minded antimilitarist, Newton D. Baker, who openly stated his anti-army prejudice and was a member of several peace organizations, including Oswald Garrison Villard's League to Limit Armaments. The diminutive former mayor of Cleveland even rejected an honorary post as leader of Ohio's Boy Scouts because he thought the organization too militaristic.[63] To TR and his allies, a more ridiculous choice could hardly have been made to lead the War Department. And tragically for the country and its war effort, it would be two years before Baker would take any serious measures to clean up his department and change the army's antiquated bureau system organization in Washington.[64]

By this time, however, Theodore and Edith were on their way to the Caribbean. They had departed on February 11 for a five-week cruise to the Lesser Antilles and Demerara, British Guiana, and planned to be gone through March 16. Roosevelt had reported to his sister Anna that the trip would do Edith's health good, and it would save him "much pointless fussing and resultless worry," as he was "totally out of sympathy with the currents of public opinion." The Republicans were "very little better than the Democrats," and Wilson was "infinitely more astute" than Root, Lodge, and the other party leaders. TR did not see that their convictions were much deeper. They were letting the fight, in the popular mind, be between Wilson and Bryan. Neither on defense nor on foreign affairs did they venture to take "any stand for decency" that would "sharply differentiate" them from Wilson. They were all of them, Republicans and Democrats, "timid, absorbed in their own selfish hopes, shortsighted or indifferent about the country's honor and future welfare, cowed by the German Government and afraid of the German vote."[65]

Before departing, TR had been introduced to Marjorie Sterrett, a Brooklyn girl who had become a national symbol for the preparedness cause after the February 4, 1916, *New York Tribune* published her letter to the editor with which she had enclosed her weekly "errand money," one dime, to "help build a battleship for Uncle Sam." The 13-year-old schoolgirl told the editor that she had read a lot about preparedness in the paper and believed "a lot of other kids" would give their money too if the paper would start a fund. A postscript added, "I am a true blue American and I want to see Uncle Sam prepared to lick all creation like John Paul Jones did." The Colonel wrote Marjorie a letter with which he enclosed a dollar, representing four dimes for his four grandchildren and six more as a reserve for the future. He told Marjorie she was doing "great work" and to remember that "battleships and grandchildren go together."[66] Within a year 200,000 dimes would be collected, but Josephus Daniels rejected the money, citing legal restrictions. However, a law was eventually enacted in 1918 allowing the contribution.

In an interview aboard his ship, the *Guiana*, reporters asked the Colonel to comment on War Secretary Garrison's resignation. He referred them to his new collection of articles, *Fear God and Take Your Own Part*, which had published just the day before. In its pages, said TR, they would find his views on preparedness and answers to "every question raised by Mr. Garrison's resignation or by our entire foreign policy."[67] Roosevelt told Kermit that the book was an effort to get the nation to "take a heroic attitude; and this nation is not in a heroic mood—few peaceful, industrial nations are, when danger on a giant scale does not so immediately impend that even the most short-sighted must see it."[68]

That month Houghton Mifflin published another book of interest, *Theodore Roosevelt: The Logic of His Career*, in effect a campaign biography by the Colonel's friend and supporter Charles Washburn. Declaring that "ROOSEVELT IS LOOMING LARGE IN OUR POLITICAL WORLD," the publicity sheet claimed the book was written "with a zest that recalls the style of the ex-president himself," while the "new light" Washburn shone on Roosevelt's career would be a "revelation to even his closest followers."[69] It might have added that TR gave Washburn his complete cooperation in the laudatory project, which recorded his life and career through the 1912 campaign.

The *Guiana* arrived on February 17 at St. Thomas in the Dutch West Indies, where the Colonel inspected the recently completed harbor works and took an automobile tour of the town, which became a standard practice everywhere he and Edith landed. He refused to talk politics with reporters, telling them he had come for a rest. The annual Carnival Ball was postponed two days so that Theodore and Edith could attend. At a dinner before the ball they received a cable from Buenos Aires that a son had been born to Kermit and his wife. After brief stops at St. Croix, St. Kitts and Antigua, and Guadeloupe, the *Guiana* arrived at Roseau, Dominica, in the British West Indies on February 20. Thousands of people lined the shore to greet the "King of America." In a brief speech, Roosevelt recounted the history of the island and praised its loyalty and contribution of volunteers to the British Empire's war effort.[70]

On February 24 the travelers arrived at Barbados, from which they sailed to British Guiana to visit the tropical laboratory that had been set up in the Demerara district by Roosevelt's friend and fellow naturalist William Beebe.[71] Beebe, who greeted Theodore and Edith when they landed at the Georgetown dock, had been trained as an ornithologist at Columbia University and the American Museum of Natural History by TR's old friend Henry Fairfield Osborn. However, at the Demerara station Beebe had broadened his research horizons from birds to the whole tropical ecosystem. Before they went upriver to Beebe's station, they visited the botanical gardens so that TR could, if lucky, see a manatee. The two men stood on a curved Japanese foot bridge for ten minutes, Beebe recalled, without a ripple in the water below. When he wondered aloud if fortune would smile on them, Roosevelt remarked that he would "willingly stand for two days to glimpse a wild manatee." Then, wrote Beebe, "St Francis heard, and, one after another, four great backs slowly heaved up; then an ill-formed head and an impossible mouth with the unbelievable hare-lip, and before our eyes the sea-cows snorted and gamboled."[72] TR reported to Kermit that he and Edith were devoted to Beebe and they had had a visit to remember. Especially interesting was their stay at the home of a local rubber planter, "a true tropical house," where they had "about as much privacy as a gold fish," but both thoroughly enjoyed the experience.[73]

The travelers spent the first week of March in Trinidad, where they had sailed in a very comfortable British ship that, Edith noted, wore gray war paint and had veiled lights on account of the submarine menace.[74] They were once again greeted enthusiastically everywhere they traveled on the island. At a dinner at the Union Club, TR spoke on conservation and the Panama Canal. International progress, he declared, depended "just as much on the refusal to submit to wrongdoing as it did on refraining from committing a wrong." He added that if a nation was "powerless either to hold its own or to secure respect for the rights of others, or to do right within its own borders," if it fell into a "condition of misrule and anarchy," then it had "no right to be treated as a self-respecting and independent power." In world affairs, Roosevelt concluded, "we shall have to take steps with regard to disorderly nations that do not behave themselves, and are festering sores in the international body politic."[75] On March 17 the Colonel and Edith boarded the steamer *Maura* bound for New York, where they arrived a week later. The voyage home was plagued by seas so stormy that one night a pajama-clad Roosevelt was forced at two in the morning to bail water out of his stateroom with a bucket.

During his Caribbean tour the Colonel gained at least one political convert: Mrs. Henry Stoddard, who had traveled to Trinidad with her husband, the editor of the New York *Evening Mail*. The editor, who had come at Roosevelt's invitation, confided to him that he surely had broken "up a once happy home!" Before his wife went to Trinidad she took "mighty little interest in politics"; now she was a "real politician, and, of course, a prophet" who insisted that TR was to be, "MUST BE, our next President." Instead of reading one morning newspaper, she now read them all and ignored all but political news. She also demanded front row seats at both the Republican and Progressive conventions in Chicago planned for the same week that June, "to make sure her views are carried out by both!"[76] Roosevelt could only hope that others would be as enthusiastic in his cause over the following months before the two nominating conventions met at Chicago.

CHAPTER 6

NOT IN HEROIC MOOD

MARCH TO JUNE 1916

> I most earnestly hope the Republicans will not nominate me; for my belief is that the country is not in heroic mood; and unless it is in heroic mood and willing to put honor and duty ahead of safety, I will be beaten if nominated. Wilson is a very adroit . . . hypocrite; and the Republican leaders have neither courage nor convictions and therefore can do little against him.
> —TR to Anna Roosevelt Cowles, February 3, 1916

While he was in the Caribbean, Roosevelt used the good offices of his newspaper ally Henry Stoddard to release what came to be called the "Trinidad Statement."[1] This political manifesto was in part meant to head off supporters in Massachusetts and elsewhere who wanted to enter his name in the Republican presidential primaries. The Colonel declared that he was not a candidate, nor was he "in the least interested in the political fortunes of himself or any other man." What he was interested in was "awakening my fellow countrymen of facing unpleasant facts." He was interested in the "triumph of the great principles for which" with all his heart and soul he had "striven and shall continue to strive." However, at the same time he left an opening for his supporters by declaring that it would be a mistake to nominate him *unless* the country had "in its mood something of the heroic—unless it feels not only devotion to ideals but the purpose measurably to realize those ideals in action."

In the Colonel's view, "nothing was to be hoped for from the present administration," and the struggles between Woodrow Wilson and his party leaders in Congress were merely struggles as to whether the nation would see its government "adopt an attitude of a little more or a little less hypocrisy" and follow a policy of "slightly greater or slightly less baseness." All they offered was a choice between "degrees of hypocrisy and degrees of infamy."

In a "crisis so grave," Roosevelt believed that it was impossible "too greatly to magnify the needs of the country or too strongly to dwell on the necessity of minimizing and subordinating the desires of individuals." The next administration could do "an incalculable amount to make or mar our country's future," and the delegates to the Republican and Progressive conventions set to meet in Chicago that June would "have it in their power to determine the character of the administration" that was to "do or leave undone the mighty tasks of the next four years." Therefore the men chosen to decide such a question should be the "very best men that can be found in our country, whose one great mission should be to declare in unequivocal terms" a program of "clean-cut, straight-out, national Americanism, in deeds not less than in words."[2]

Of course no one of consequence took seriously this act of political humility and theater. All and sundry believed that TR sought both the Progressive and Republican nominations so that there would be no repetition of the divisions of 1912 that had delivered the White House to the reviled Wilson. Roosevelt the politician believed his popularity was on the rebound, but he was unwilling to test this in divisive primary battles in states he might well lose. Better to appear above the fray and to be seen as a statesman ready for the Republican and Progressive conventions to turn to when no other candidate appeared strong enough to defeat Wilson. The weakness of this course was that it relied on a calculation that no Republican savior would emerge.

At TR's request there was no public greeting at New York when the *Maura* arrived from the Caribbean. He and Edith were met only by his secretary, John McGrath. Reporters, however, came out to the ship in quarantine and the Colonel agreed to speak briefly with them. Roosevelt told the journalists that he had greatly enjoyed the trip and was more impressed than ever with the islands and Demerara as tourist resorts and future sites of industry. He was also struck by the loyalty with which the British and French islands had come forward to support their homelands, by contributing between 20,000 and 30,000 men to the war effort. He at first refused to talk politics or international affairs for the record, again referring them to his recently published book for enlightenment. His only reference to the Trinidad statement was that he "had meant every word he said."

But TR did state, concerning Mexico, that his prophesies had come true, in particular what he had written about "furnishing arms and munitions to one set of bandits in order to help them against another set of bandits instead of helping Uncle Sam against all of them." This referred to the March 9 attack by Mexican irregulars under Pancho Villa on Columbus, New Mexico, where 19 Americans were killed. Six days later, without the permission of the Carranza government, a 7,000-man punitive expedition, led by General John J. Pershing—not Leonard Wood, as TR had recommended—crossed the border in pursuit. Though Roosevelt was mum on politics, the *New York Times* commented that he "looked in every way fit" for the strenuous campaign the political leaders believed was ahead of him.[3]

Back at Sagamore Hill, at least somewhat refreshed by his Caribbean holiday, TR's Massachusetts Progressive supporters Charles S. Bird and Augustus P. Gardner called to apologize because the primary laws of their state did not allow his name to be withdrawn as he wished. After the Oyster Bay visit, Gardner told the press that the Colonel was "neither an active nor a receptive candidate for President" and was doing nothing to win delegates. Gardner added that TR was not the man of four years before: his "blood did not appear to run so warm," and he was not thinking of his personal ambition to be president so much as he was the "election of a Republican President who fitted into the present situation in the United States." The Colonel had told Gardner that he "stood for men who stood for American ideals" and mentioned the names of several other possible candidates, including Charles Evans Hughes.[4]

A "boom" had begun for the heavily bearded Supreme Court Justice and former governor of New York, who, like the Colonel, had stated in a public letter that he was not a candidate and, further, would not disclose his positions on preparedness or foreign policy. The idea of running a "mare with no record"—someone who, unlike Roosevelt, had taken no stand on the vital questions of the day—appealed to many Republicans, including Henry Cabot Lodge, who had come to believe his friend Theodore could not win. Lodge told a mutual acquaintance that he would rather have Roosevelt in the White House than anyone else, but there was one thing that weighed more, and that was the defeat of Wilson.[5]

On March 31 Roosevelt attended a preparedness luncheon in New York at the Park Avenue home of his friend Robert Bacon, briefly secretary of state at the end of his administration. Bacon also had in mind reconciliation between the Colonel and Elihu Root, who met on this occasion for the first time since Root had abetted William Howard Taft's "naked theft" of the nomination at the 1912 Republican convention. For his part, Root professed to be ready to forgive and forget and claimed not to hold any bad feelings for all the "hard things" Roosevelt had said about him. Lodge and Wood were also on hand, and the general recorded in his diary, "All passed off well." The Colonel "cussed out Wilson as did Root and Lodge" and blamed the president for the country being in such low standing internationally. There was also "much talk about Mexico" and "what they would have done had they been in power." Roosevelt reported to Hiram Johnson about the meeting that he wanted the Progressives to understand what he was doing and that the men had "talked only of preparedness and of the necessity from the public standpoint of doing something that would enable us to get rid of Wilson."[6]

It is unclear whether Bacon was attempting to gain TR's support for Root as president or vice versa, but in the aftermath political confusion reigned. Many Republicans speculated that the meeting meant Roosevelt would support Root, while Progressives were sure that Root would support the Colonel.[7] This previously unthinkable reunion between TR and Root stunned the press and politicians equally and was called "the most significant happening of the political campaign," which "paled into insignificance" the dinner earlier in the year at the home of the steel magnate E. H. Gary at which Roosevelt had broken bread with a score of financiers. Consequently, the Colonel's chances of picking up the Republican nomination were estimated to have "jumped 100 per cent."[8] The impression of former President Taft, still bitter himself over 1912, was that the lunch would be a "nine day's wonder" and that it would so alarm the regular Republicans that it would only make the "trend to Hughes more certain." A week after the lunch the boom for Root was officially started in a statement signed by 74 New York notables, including Joseph Choate, who had been at the Bacon lunch. Roosevelt, however, felt the Republicans would never unite around Root and a month later told the former governor of New Jersey that the move to nominate Root was a "movement to cut the throat of the Republicans from ear to ear."[9]

At Sagamore Hill on April 5, Roosevelt met with several delegates to the Republican National Convention. Afterwards, one of them told the reporters on hand that he had confessed to TR that he might have to put his name forward in nomination. The Colonel advised the men that if they had "any doubt on the subject do not nominate me." If they did so, "it mustn't be because it is in my interest, but because you think it is your interest and the interest of the Republican party, and because you think it is in the interest of the United States to do so." Further, the men should not do it if they expected Roosevelt to "pussy foot on any single issue" he had raised. They must be prepared to say, as did TR, that "every citizen of the country has got to be pro-United States first, last, and all the time, and not pro-anything else at all," and "whatever his birthplace or creed, and wherever he now lives . . . we demand that he be an American and nothing else, with no hyphen about him."[10]

The *New York Times* sarcastically noted the Colonel's use of campaign rhetoric on this private occasion, and the verbatim accounts that appeared in all the papers, that it was "as spontaneous as a performance of 'Hamlet' after a run of a hundred nights." The paper then recounted the reforms TR had put forward in 1912 guaranteed to cost him the support of the wealthy men at the recent Gary dinner. "The soft feline footfall" of Roosevelt "backing away from these," said the *Times*, would "not be detected by the sharpest ear." The Colonel's call for America First, the editorial also noted, read "like an endorsement of the Wilson administration." Last December in his annual address Wilson had said all this "and much more—some will think the President said it better." If Roosevelt had had time for more thought, perhaps he would have put forth "some issues as to which he could claim prior discovery and use." But that was only "one count in the arraignment of the Republican visitor at Sagamore Hill who abused his host's hospitality by a base betrayal."[11]

Among the many political callers at TR's *Metropolitan* office in New York was James Garfield, Roosevelt's secretary of the interior, who had just returned from a trip to the West Coast. After their meeting, Garfield told the press that he had been amazed to find the sentiment for Roosevelt as strong as in 1912. He did not doubt that the Republican convention "would have to answer the call of the people and put Roosevelt in the field as the opponent of Wilson." A visitor even more familiar with California, Colonel D. C. Collier, commissioner general of the San Diego Exposition, declared that TR was as good as nominated and that he had told him this two months before and "now all hell can't stop it." In his opinion the support for Hughes was "all manufactured," as no one knew where he stood on any of the issues.[12]

While the political maneuvering continued, TR also kept a close eye on the critical situation in Mexico, where in his quest to capture or kill Pancho Villa, Pershing had led his troops 500 miles south of the border. But instead of finding Villa, they had skirmished several times with the forces of Carranza, most recently on April 12 at Parral. Though he had recommended Wood for the command, Roosevelt was not unhappy with the choice of "Black Jack" Pershing, who had acquired that nickname as a captain with the Tenth Cavalry, known as the Buffalo Soldiers, who had fought side by side with the Rough Riders at San Juan Hill. After subsequent distinguished service in the Philippines, TR had promoted the tough and determined Captain Pershing to brigadier general over 862 more senior officers, leading to charges of favoritism, since the president had attended Pershing's 1905 wedding to the daughter of Wyoming Senator Francis Warren. In September 1915, while Pershing was serving at Fort Bliss, near El Paso on the Mexican border, his wife and all but one of their children had been killed in a fire at the Presidio in San Francisco. Pershing had taken his surviving son Warren with him back to El Paso, where the general found solace in his soldier's duty.

From Mexico, Pershing sent Roosevelt a "sidelight" on the "so-called punitive operation." The general used "so-called advisedly" because, he confided to TR, since the "treacherous" attack on his forces at Parral, the situation had been brought into the "domain of international diplomacy," and his expedition had been "practically standing fast ever since." Pershing described the hunt for Villa as "something like looking for a needle in a haystack with an armed guard around the stack forbidding you to look in the hay." In the general's opinion, the Carranza government was "but a name which other subordinate leaders cling to for present purposes." No one respected it or thought it would last. In Mexico the "ordinary restraints of civilization" had almost been obliterated, and anarchy was "in fact supreme." The only way to get the cooperation of the people and have the natural leaders come forward to help restore order, Pershing believed, would be for the United States to announce and carry out a military occupation of the country. It was not wise, Pershing knew, to underestimate an opponent, but it was the "truth to say that the soldiery of Mexico today, when measured by any modern military standard, may be regarded as well-nigh negligible." His force, he told TR, had done some hard work and had "accomplished much despite its handicap." The supply departments had learned some new lessons with a line of communications five-hundred miles long. The cavalry especially had made a "splendid record for dash and endurance." Pershing's command was, he declared, "ready for anything."[13]

Roosevelt replied that he was "prepared to find the situation as bad as you describe it," but Pershing etched in his knowledge and gave "effect to the facts." What he said of the Carranzistas in general was about what the Colonel had supposed, and he was relieved to hear of the "worthlessness of Mexican soldiery of today." If Roosevelt had been president, he told Pershing, he would have handled the Mexican situation along the lines the general recommended, which were substantially what had been done in Cuba. He went on that it had not been easy "for an American to be proud of much during the past two years," but that he was "proud and pleased" with Pershing's "brilliant handling of the situation."[14] The Wilson administration would also be pleased with Pershing's performance, and after a warning by Army Chief of Staff Hugh Scott the general ceased his epistolary grousing about not being allowed to march on to Mexico City. This cleared the way for much bigger things in the not-so-distant future.

Back in the political arena, after the Republican *New York Tribune* pledged its support, TR declared that he deeply appreciated what the paper said of him but appreciated "infinitely more what it says in advocacy of things" for which he stood. The last sentence of the *Tribune* editorial—"We are choosing which way the country shall go in the era that is now opening, just as our fathers chose the nation's path in the days of 1860"—the Colonel said, should "be in the mind of every man who at Chicago next June takes part in formulating the platform and naming the candidate." The men at Chicago should "act in the spirit of the men who stood behind Abraham Lincoln." TR disagreed with those who said the presidential election would be fought mainly on the tariff issue. Such an appeal, he said, would be an "appeal to the belly and not to the soul of the American nation." He believed in a protective tariff and that if the United States did not return to such a policy before the end of the world war, "we shall face widespread economic disaster." But this was not the "great issue" on which the fight should be made "if the highest service is to be rendered the American people." National honor was a "spiritual thing" that could not be "haggled over in terms of dollars"; America "must find its own soul."[15] George Perkins had Progressive headquarters distribute 15 thousand copies of the *Tribune* statement.

The old adage that politics makes strange bedfellows proved particularly true that April, when William Randolph Hearst, Roosevelt's sworn press and personal enemy since the days of the 1898 race for governor of New York, invited him to lunch. The press magnate's hatred for Wilson was so intense that he was willing to at least consider throwing his newspapers behind the Colonel, who had ten years before described Hearst as "the most potent single influence for evil" in American life.[16] Though Hearst vehemently disagreed with Roosevelt about supporting the Allies in the European war, he shared his fervor for action in Mexico and for preparedness—though only for home defense, and not for use abroad. The Colonel was unable to lunch but, swallowing his own distaste for an old enemy, invited Hearst to meet him at the Langdon Hotel. With his reply TR enclosed a copy of *Fear God and Take Your Own Part* with a friendly note that this violated the "principle laid down" by his uncle Robert B. Roosevelt "many years ago when he said he had done a good many mean things in his life, but he had never asked anyone to read one of his books."[17] Hearst replied with equally forced cordiality that he looked forward to their meeting and that TR did not have to ask him to read his books, as he did so without invitation. After their talk Hearst went so far as to ask TR to write for his papers or to choose any of his correspondents to "report your acts and utterances fully faithfully and sympathetically." Hearst consequently assigned himself to cover the Republican convention with the idea that he might be able to "engineer a Roosevelt nomination."[18]

Meanwhile, the latest crisis with Germany over submarine warfare led Wilson to call a joint session of Congress to meet April 19. This had been brewing since March 24—the day Roosevelt arrived back at New York from the Caribbean—when a German U-boat torpedoed without warning the French liner *Sussex* in the English Channel. The vessel was not sunk and no Americans were killed, but eyewitness testimony made it absolutely clear that, despite German denials, it was a submarine attack. An irate Wilson dispatched the ninth, and by far the stiffest, American note yet on U-boats to Germany warning that the use of the vessels "for the destruction of an enemy's commerce" was "utterly incompatible with the principles of humanity," the rights of neutrals, and the "sacred immunities of non-combatants." Unless the German government "should now immediately declare and effect an abandonment of its present methods of warfare," the American government would have "no choice but to sever diplomatic relations."[19]

Consulting Congress, in Roosevelt's opinion, was a mistake. It was the duty of the president to lead. A successful foreign policy could not be carried out by "town meeting." It was Wilson's responsibility and he should not try to pass it on to any individual or group. The president was also "wholly responsible" for the fact that the country was in a state of "utter unpreparedness" for such a critical situation. Further, Wilson's speeches and "diluted mush and milk" foreign policy had left the people in a "dazed state of mind" and unable to "grasp the real extent of the indignities which have been heaped upon the citizens of this country by some other nations." It was impossible to tell if Wilson was "retreating or adventuring, threatening or preparing for further concessions," which did not fit well with the "upholding of the honor of the country among the nations of the world."[20]

After Wilson spoke to Congress, TR's verdict was that the address, and the man, were both "wanting." If Wilson had stood by the "strict accountability" note of 14 months before, the present crisis would never have happened, and it was "unpardonable" in the meantime not to have instituted the strong measures of preparedness needed to "back up the brave words of the *Sussex* note." If the Germans yielded now, it would prove that lives could have been saved by a sterner policy, and if Germany rejected the demands, Wilson was responsible for the fact that the country was "unready" to respond with military force.[21] As it fell out, Germany chose not to hazard the possibility that the United States might enter the war and on May 4 issued the "*Sussex* Pledge," which agreed to restrict submarine attacks—but on the condition that the United States insist Britain also follow the rules of international law. When asked to comment on the apparent success of Wilson's *Sussex* note, the Colonel declared that he had no "interest in ultimatums that fail to ultimate" and that the latest note was up to Wilson's "usual standard," whether applied to Villa, Carranza, or the German Empire.[22]

On April 28, at the *Metropolitan* office in New York, Roosevelt told a delegation from the Congressional Union for Woman Suffrage that he favored a constitutional amendment permitting women to vote. One of the delegates, Alice Carpenter, was also president of the Women's Roosevelt League, which supported both his candidacy and preparedness.[23] The Colonel declared the league could "do a tremendous lot to aid in the campaign for preparedness" and that the time had come for a "greater and truer nationalism" concerning other issues that affected both men and women.[24] He then departed for Chicago on the Twentieth Century Limited, arriving there the next day.

An enthusiastic crowd greeted Roosevelt's train at the La Salle Street Station with cries of "We Want Teddy," recreating the scene at the 1912 Republican Convention. That evening, he gave the keynote address at the annual meeting of the Illinois Bar Association. This speech, on "National Duty and International Ideals," was interpreted by the thousand or so lawyers and reporters present as a "straight declaration of the issues"—military and industrial preparedness and Americanism—on which the Roosevelt campaign would be based. TR first reviewed the Wilson administration's failure to prepare, declaring that he believed that a great majority of Americans, when they took the time to think on the problem at all, would refuse to consent in the "Chinafication of this country." They would refuse to follow those who make "right helpless before might, who would put a pigtail on Uncle Sam and turn the Goddess of Liberty into a pacifist female huckster, clutching a bag of dollars, which she has not the courage to guard against aggression."[25]

By this time in England the German submarine attacks and the needs of the war had combined to make many items scarce, including food.[26] For years Britain had imported much of her supply and now relied on the Royal Navy to get staples through.[27] That year's poor harvest made necessary the adoption of severe measures. Food queues were common and a source of alarm to many. There was also a reawakening of the Irish problem, which had been overshadowed by the war. The executions carried out by the British in the aftermath of the bloody April "Easter Rising" centered in Dublin only created martyrs and radicalized Irish opinion in favor of Sinn Fein, which had not been involved in the insurgency. The rash British action also brought cries of indignation from the American government and public and further complicated British relations with the most powerful neutral nation. David Lloyd George had been enlisted to tackle this latest Irish crisis. The

London *Daily Mail* loudly applauded the choice, calling the Welshman the "handyman of the Coalition."[28]

A few months earlier, Roosevelt had asked Arthur Lee to convey to Lloyd George his "heartiest regards" and his admiration for the character he was "now showing in this great crisis." TR had always agreed with his radical social program, but he wished it had been complemented with Lord Roberts's "external" preparedness program. It was often, he went on, that the "only way to render great services" was by "willingness on the part of a statesman to lose his future" or at any rate his present position in politics, "just as the soldier may have to pay with his physical life in order to render service in battle." The Colonel felt that "in a very small and unimportant way" he had done this himself over the last 18 months, paying no heed to the effect on his own fortunes in what he had said. What he was trying to do was "to make the country go right," and he did not "give a damn as to what my countrymen think of me in the present and in the future," provided only he could "make them wake up to the sense of their duty."[29]

After the Easter rebellion and the executions, Roosevelt confided to Lee, for Lloyd George's information as well, that he wished "your people had not shot the leaders of the Irish rebels after they surrendered." It was a "prime necessity" that the rebellion be "stamped out at once, and the men should be ruthlessly dealt with while the fighting went on," but TR thought it would have been "the better part of wisdom not to exact the death penalty," since before the war Sir Edward Carson, the Ulster leader, had been "uncomfortably near doing the same thing" in Northern Ireland, and he and his followers had been "unconditionally pardoned."[30] However, not even the "Welsh Wizard" could calm Ireland in 1916, and Lee reported to Roosevelt two months later that he was sorry about the aborted Irish settlement on which Lloyd George had been working. He called the failure "one of the greatest political tragedies of my time" and complained of his chief's treatment by his colleagues over the issue.[31]

Back on the American political front, Colonel George Harvey, the influential editor of the *North American Review*, castigated Roosevelt while making a case for the nomination of Hughes. The Trinidad Statement and the repeated and theatrical protestations recorded in the newspapers that TR had no desire for the presidency led Harvey to quip, "Whoever says Our Colonel is a candidate is a liar." He was no "hill climber"; he was "Mohamet. If the mountain sees fit to come to him, it may bask in the glories of Heaven; if not it can go to Hell." The article also chronicled Roosevelt's drift back toward the Republican Party, while he declared himself still a Progressive. Surely, said Harvey, history did not record a "political act so fully laden with audacity and presumption as that of a statesman, however heroic, who in one breath defiantly heralds his allegiance to a party which has become a remnant, and in the next arrogantly defines the terms on which he will accept the nomination from the party which he assassinated." If TR had read his bible more closely, he might have "profited from the knowledge that it was not the Prodigal Son who possessed the fatted calf." In March, Harvey went on, the

Republican party might have accepted "Anything To Beat Wilson," including Roosevelt as president and Root as secretary of state, but that possibility had in the editor's estimation been changed by the emergence of Hughes, the man "nobody wants."[32]

At the same time, Wilson gave a rare glimpse of his opinion of Roosevelt in a wide-ranging talk with the muckraking journalist Ray Stannard Baker. In answer to whether the president would rather face the Colonel or Hughes in the election, Wilson told Baker that it mattered very little. "We have definite constructive things to do & we shall go ahead and do them." The Colonel, he went on, dealt in "personalities & not arguments upon facts & conditions," so one did not need to "meet him at all." But Hughes was of a different type. If he was nominated, he would "have to be met." After their meeting, Baker, a Wilson partisan, commented that their talk was not an interview but a "conversation the purpose of which was to enable me to found soundly & truly whatever I may write about him & his policies." To Baker a thoughtful and great leader like Wilson needed interpretation. TR, on the other hand, "interprets himself."[33]

On May 13, Edith Roosevelt marched in a massive New York City preparedness parade, the first and largest of its kind, which the *New York Times* described as the "greatest civilian marching demonstration in the history of the world."[34] General Wood stood on the reviewing stand next to Mayor John Purroy Mitchell as 200 bands and 125,683 marchers strode by. Back at Oyster Bay, Edith's husband applauded a somewhat smaller group of visiting Boy Scouts as they carried out maneuvers on the lawns of Sagamore Hill. He told the crowd on hand that his wife "felt she must go and march because we both regard it as the prime duty of the country at this moment to prepare." Unless a nation was "true to itself it will be false to everyone else." No nation could help any other if it could not protect its "own national honor and its sons and daughters wherever they are." This it could never do without preparation, and he believed that the significance of the many thousands marching with Edith was that the country was "waking up to understand that the weakling never earns anything but contempt, for contempt is all he deserves."[35]

The Colonel decided to strike a blow himself against the forces of anti-preparedness by traveling to the center of support for Henry Ford's popular brand of pacifism, Detroit, where on May 19 he made one major and two minor speeches on military, industrial, and social preparedness.[36] This was in part a response to Ford's recent victory in the Michigan Republican primary and the popularity of his antiwar sentiments with voters in Nebraska and Pennsylvania. In Washington, this pacifist trend translated into more congressional votes to defeat a proposal to increase the army to 250,000 men. Ford and the Colonel had corresponded earlier in the year but did not see each other on this visit, even though the car maker had sent Roosevelt an invitation to meet. He likely did not appreciate the blunt reply that TR wanted "to go over at length with you this pacifist business" and that it had been a "real grief" to him when Ford took the stand he did. After the great industrial and social services he had rendered the country in his automobile factories, Roosevelt hated to see Ford "fall into the trap of pacifism."[37]

In his principal Detroit address, in a packed opera house, the Colonel spoke "with courtesy but with entire frankness of what the success of Mr. Ford means" and told his audience that he chose Michigan, where the Ford movement began, to say what he had to say on the subject. As he had in his letter to Ford, TR conjured up in comparison the Northern Copperheads of the Civil War who demanded an immediate peace and that the "boys" of the Army of the Potomac be "out of the trenches" before Christmas 1864, a course that would have would have "utterly ruined this nation." It would have "purchased peace at the moment by ignoble submission to wrong, by ignoble cowardice." And this, said Roosevelt, was what the "neo-Copperheads" of the present day would do if they achieved their purpose. After the Revolutionary and Civil Wars, the Colonel considered the present situation facing America the "third great crisis" in its history and one that coincided with "a tremendous world crisis." The issue was, "are we prepared with a sane and lofty idealism to fit ourselves to render great service to mankind by rendering ourselves fit for our own service," or was the nation "content to avoid effort and labor in the present by preparing to tread the path that China has trodden?" The nation must choose one course or the other. Unfortunately, after 22 months Congress was still in the "conversational stage" in the matter of preparedness.

In Roosevelt's view, the "ultra-pacifists as represented by Mr. Ford" had made their showing only because there had been no "real and resolute opposition" to them. The Wilson administration, backed by the majority in Congress, had "taken no step for preparedness" and done "nothing efficient to sustain our national rights." As far as deeds were concerned, it had stood for "applied pacifism." But even this did not satisfy the ultrapacifists, who objected "even to make-believe preparedness" and insisted on "even more thorough-going helplessness" than that "so amply provided at Washington." The government had proved, in his estimation, "96 per cent feeble," but the ultrapacifists "demanded a clear 100 per cent." The pacifists had told the country that if it remained helpless, "we shall escape all difficulties with other nations and earn their good will."

In answer, the Colonel asked them to ponder what had happened in Mexico, where for five years the United States had followed the principles of the pacifists. After all the bloodshed, the trouble had "only begun and we are no nearer a solution than we were three and a quarter years ago." America had not "gained the good will of the Mexicans." They hated and despised the United States "infinitely more than they hated us five years ago—at which time they did not despise us at all." The practical application of pacifism in Mexico had resulted in incalculable loss of life and property and gained the United States only the "utter contempt of the people with whom we dealt; and it has brought us to the verge of war with them."

Exactly the same was true, Roosevelt went on, regarding Germany. For 16 months, the country had been "employed in sending Germany ultimatum after ultimatum in monotonous succession," while Germany sank ship after ship, "drowning our men, women, and children by the hundreds." Consequently, the United States had learned that note writing was "not an antidote to murder." The Colonel firmly believed that if "at the onset we had clearly made it evident that our words would be translated into deeds," that the "first ultimatum sixteen months before was really an ultimatum," Germany would have yielded and the *Lusitania* and other ships would not have been sunk. It was "our own attitude of culpable weakness and timidity—an attitude assumed under the pressure of the ultra-pacifists—which" was "primarily responsible for this dreadful loss of life, and of our national humiliation."

To make matters worse, America's shortcomings were not restricted to military preparedness, as the country was just as unprepared industrially. The Colonel believed in cooperation between the nation and industry, but instead of emulating Germany's "admirably successful method of dealing with her industries so as to insure their efficiency in time of war," the Wilson administration had taken "no step whatever" except the "thoroughly mischievous" one of endeavoring to "cripple a great private industry by the creation of a government armor plant." This, in his view, the country did not need and could do better by regulating and controlling the private industry in question. In his view, there must be overall organization of both capital and labor and there "must be a deliberate purpose to see that the health and well-being of the workers, their standard of wages and living and of the education of their children," were held up to the level that would "insure the greatest national efficiency."[38] A few days later, 13 Detroit industrialists representing such concerns as the Chalmers, Cadillac, Paige, and Hudson motor car companies signed a petition pledging their support to Roosevelt for the presidency.[39]

The greatest car maker of them all, Henry Ford, replied to TR's criticism that he was not disturbed by what was said about his work. In fact, he thought the attacks did his peace propaganda good, and he thanked Roosevelt for "again bringing to the attention of the public his views and thereby arraying the public against his armament crowd," who were so prominent in the "Detroit demonstration." Ford knew them and that their motivation was "not all patriotism." Ordinarily, the automaker went on, "one considers an ex-president a little different from the everyday citizen," but Ford considered Roosevelt "so antiquated that the 'ex' business" did not mean anything; he was merely "an ordinary citizen" because he did not "keep up with the times." It had been seven years since he left office, and in that time he had "entirely failed to understand the trend of events and the sentiments of the people." The people, said Ford, were what was important, and they would "attend to Roosevelt at the proper time."[40]

Back in Washington, on May 27 Wilson spoke at the Willard Hotel to a meeting of Taft's League to Enforce Peace. Colonel Edward M. House had wanted the president to use the speech to make an appeal for an immediate peace conference to settle the European war, but Wilson decided instead to make a general statement of his administration's foreign policy and idealistic hopes for the future. Though he did not call for a conference, Wilson laid out a three-point plan for peace that called for the right of self-determination for important national groups, the right of small nations to have their sovereignty respected internationally, and the right of the world to be free from disturbances of its peace. As a corollary to the last point, said Wilson, there should be some sort of association of nations that would make war impossible. He was not concerned with the "causes and objects" of the "present quarrel" and went on that the "obscure fountains from which its stupendous flood has burst forth we are not interested to search for or explore"[41]

This last sentiment was wildly applauded by Wilson's audience, but by ignoring German militarism he infuriated Allied public and press opinion. In England Ambassador Walter Hines Page, sounding very TR-like, offered the explanation that the president had been speaking "to the gallery filled with peace cranks—Bryans, Fords, Jane Addams."[42] Meanwhile, Roosevelt wrote to Arthur Lee that Wilson was "now playing the exact game" as in the American Civil War when Prussia, through its foreign minister (the father of the present German ambassador, Count Johann von Bernstorff), brought pressure to bear for peace and neutral rights on the United States. After that von Bernstorff "in the name of humanity besought Lincoln to make peace, the copperheads and pacifists of that day warmly applauded the Prussian King" and other European diplomats for their similar efforts for peace, which would have destroyed the United States.[43]

On the same day that Wilson spoke to the League to Enforce Peace, a throng of 2,500, sponsored by the Roosevelt Non-Partisan League, gathered at Sagamore Hill to voice their hearty approval of the Colonel's candidacy. Three special trains brought the bulk of the participants, who marched the three dusty miles from the Oyster Bay station, accompanied by the Seventh Regiment Band. To the tune of "Glory, Glory Hallelujah," the marchers sang,

> We'll vote for Theodore Roosevelt
> Because we know that he'll be true,
> He loves our starry banner—
> Our own red, white, and blue;
> We know that he'll defend it
> From the enemy in view, as we go marching on.

Roosevelt burst out of the house and onto the broad back porch to greet the flag-waving visitors, who chanted, "We Want Teddy!"

Speaking for the visitors, Richard Hurd, president of the Lawyers Mortgage Company, made a brief address. He told TR that the multitude had come to reaffirm "its unalterable devotion to the high principles and ideals upon which our ancestors founded this republic" and that Roosevelt personified. He repeated the Colonel's declaration that the nation could not "endure half hyphenated and half American." In the present crisis, said Hurd, the country needed a man who would "rouse the soul of the nation." It was for this purpose they called on Roosevelt. "Alone among our public men," he went on, the Colonel had "raised his voice in these troubled times for American rights and for American honor." They were confident that when the voice of the nation called the Colonel to "these heavy responsibilities," TR would "be willing to thus serve your country." Roosevelt replied that he without qualification stood by what Hurd had said and then invited the crowd to file into the house to be greeted in the North Room. The press of people momentarily threatened to collapse the porch, but order was soon restored and all those gathered got to shake hands with the Colonel.[44]

The next day, Roosevelt departed for a western speaking trip to Kansas City and St. Louis, stopping at Chicago briefly en route to confer with Progressive leaders, as well as what the *New York Times* described as "prominent men of German extraction," including Henry Olson and Otto Butz.[45] At Kansas City, 50,000 greeted the Colonel at the rail station, and as many more lined the route to his hotel. At a luncheon for 300 at the Commercial Club, Roosevelt commented to the gathering that he had been told that the West was not interested in preparedness because it would not suffer in a foreign war. This, he exclaimed, was a lie. "I'd shrink with shame, I wouldn't have the courage to bring this message to you, if I felt there was one American who was not interested in the welfare of another." TR shared his table with Kansas City Progressives and the evangelist Billy Sunday, who also supported preparedness. Sunday commented that he had been out "among the plain people," and they wanted Roosevelt. And if he were nominated at Chicago, Sunday predicted, TR would receive "the biggest vote given a candidate in the history of the country."[46]

The Colonel capped off a long Memorial Day with an address before 16,000 at Convention Hall titled "A Message to all Americans." His appeal, TR told his audience, was to the "spirit of thoroughgoing Americanism in all our people in whatever portion of the land they dwell." But he made no appeal to the "peace-at-any price men" who put "peace above duty, who put love of ease and love of money getting before devotion to country." 1916, Roosevelt declared, was "one of the great years of decision in our national history," and the way in which the country now decided would "largely determine whether we are to go forward in righteousness and power or backward in degradation and weakness."

If peace in Europe should come the next day, TR went on, it should make absolutely no difference to America's need for preparedness, since it was possible that one of the combatants, being fully armed, would see the United States as a "rich and helpless prize" for the taking. On the other hand, it was also possible there would be "temporary exhaustion among the combatants," who would claim they were peaceful and harmless. He feared the "apostles of unpreparedness" would then influence the American people once more to "shirk our duty of getting ready." To those skeptical of invasion, Roosevelt offered in evidence the Dardanelles operation of the previous year, in which hundreds of thousands of troops were transported across the world's oceans. If such a force landed near New York or San Francisco, the United States could send against it only "an army of ill-trained men—an army about one third the size of the invading army, untrained, badly armed, and without the necessary artillery." The country would be dispatching its young sons "to be butchered, to make good for the fact that we had not prepared in advance." Therefore, said Roosevelt, the prime needs that could be immediately met were to give the country, first, a navy inferior only to the British fleet and, second, a small, highly efficient regular army of 250,000 men. Such an army and navy would be "our best insurance against war and for peace."[47]

The next day the Colonel spoke three times in St. Louis, considered the center of pro-German sentiment in the United States. The greatest applause came when he denounced the German-American Alliance as an "anti-American Alliance," adding that he was happy that at its recent convention the organization had denounced him "a little more bitterly than it has denounced Mr. Wilson or Mr. Root." Referring to Wilson's Memorial Day address, TR accused the president of using "weasel words" in advocating a universal military training program that would allow those unwilling to do their part to escape service. This meant Wilson was in fact advocating "only the compulsion of the spirit of America." One prominent St. Louis Republican commented that "no one had dared to talk out like that before, and no one but Roosevelt would dare to do it." It was the "most magnificent exhibition of nerve" he had ever seen, "to talk like that in this city."[48]

The day Roosevelt spoke at St. Louis, May 31, 1916, in the North Sea off the coast of Denmark the British and German fleets fought the only major dreadnought engagement of the war at the Battle of Jutland. The dramatic action involved 150 ships on the British side and 100 on the German. When the smoke had cleared and the long-range guns ceased firing, Jutland had cost the British 14 ships including 3 battle cruisers, while Germany lost 1 battle cruiser and 11 ships total. The Royal Navy's losses in tonnage sunk and casualties were roughly twice that of the outnumbered German fleet. However, even though Jutland was not the decisive victory the British sought (and the newspapers claimed at first), afterwards the German fleet would mostly stay anchored at Kiel and never again challenge the British fleet in any force. The battle helped convince Germany that submarines offered a more promising path toward challenging British dominance on the high seas.[49]

Among the British battle cruisers that went down at Jutland was the *Invincible*, commanded by Admiral Sir Horace Hood, to whom TR had been introduced by Lord Bryce in 1914. The Colonel wrote to Bryce that he had been "greatly struck" by Hood's "evident strength and gentleness of character." His illustrious ancestor, Viscount Hood, had been a British admiral in the Revolutionary period and was one of Roosevelt's favorites from naval history, "because he was one of those men in history of whom we can say with practical certainty that it was fate and chance that prevented him leaving a name equal to the greatest." It was a "sad and terrible thing to have such a fine young fellow" as Hood die, but, TR told Bryce, "as we must die" and as it was a matter of "a very few years whether we die early or late," the vital thing was that "our deaths should be such as to help others to live." This was what Hood, and many thousands of other British sailors and soldiers, had accomplished with their deaths in the past two years.[50]

On the battlefields at midyear 1916 the British and French were hard pressed at Ypres and Verdun. The Germans, believing the Russians weakened enough that they could turn back to the west, had hoped to bleed the French out of the war at Verdun, but once again their plans failed at the cost of horrific casualties on both sides. Roosevelt's old Harvard classmate and friend Frederick Allen wrote to him from Verdun, where he was given a tour of the battlefield and "had a view that covered most of the positions where names have become famous." He shared TR's reply with the general in command, Robert Nivelle, and it pleased him greatly. Allen wished Roosevelt could witness the "calm bravery of these officers and soldiers under this tremendous ordeal." As a soldier himself, Allen believed TR "could appreciate it more than I, but really I feel like taking off my hat to every man I see."[51]

As the British prepared to launch an offensive on the Somme River to take some pressure off the French, the problem of what to do with Lord Kitchener was settled by the fortunes of war. While a fine recruiter of men, the war secretary had proved a positive hindrance to the efficient running of the overall British effort. He was sent on a mission to Russia that June to get him out of the way, and his cruiser, the *Hampshire*, struck a mine and sank with almost all hands. On hearing the news, Lord Northcliffe reportedly proclaimed, "Providence is on the side of the British Empire after all."[52] Putting aside his own personal dislike, Roosevelt issued a statement that, while it said nothing of his war work, praised Kitchener the imperialist as one of the "great figures in that work of spreading civilization which has been the greatest permanent achievement of the civilized powers of the world in recent decades." The death of a man who had been so prominent in this work illustrated "in striking fashion what a lamentable and evil thing" it was that these "great civilized nations should now be tearing out one another's lives."[53] To replace Kitchener, once again Herbert Henry Asquith turned to David Lloyd George.

Arthur Lee followed the Welshman to the War Office from the Ministry of Munitions as TR had hoped he would. The new war secretary seemed to Roosevelt "to be about the only one of the big men" who had made good. The difference between England and America in the last few years, he told Lee, had been that "you have one Lloyd George, whereas we have no one!" Asquith, TR thought, really believed that "a parliamentary victory offsets a disaster at the Dardanelles or Mesopotamia," and as such the prime minister represented a type that Roosevelt felt "more dangerous to a democracy than any other." This was fundamentally the Wilson type, and both differed from the Taft type "chiefly by being a little abler" and self-satisfied, and "therefore a little more dangerous." Roosevelt agreed with Lee that the greatest danger at present was that a premature peace would be made with the Central Powers, who after 22 months of war were "on the whole victorious." They had successfully beaten off all Allied attacks and were in possession of great stretches of French and Russian soil as well as practically all of Serbia and Belgium.

Both men feared that "weak and irresolute minds among the Allies" might be influenced by the "cold-blooded opportunism" of men like Wilson and Pope Benedict XV. The last had refused to take sides in the war and the previous month requested that the neutral powers make a direct offer to secure a negotiated peace. Roosevelt bemoaned the fact that the previous pontiff, Leo XIII, who had been about as much like Benedict as TR was like Wilson, was not alive, as the Vatican then would have been "emphatically on the side of the Allies." The Colonel attempted to buck up his overworked and anxious friend, telling Lee that it was no wonder he felt as he did. Roosevelt had to keep an "iron hand" on himself "simply to keep my soul from being fretted into a frazzle by beating against the immense mass of selfishness and cowardice, love of ease, love of luxury, love of money-getting" and above all the "spineless sentimentality" that was "merely a mask for cowardly materialism," and that when "not merely materialistic" was "equally noxious because unspeakably foolish."[54]

As the Republican and Progressive delegates gathered in Chicago in the first days of June, Roosevelt returned to Sagamore Hill after making his last preconvention speech at a Newark industrial exposition, where he called for "Americanization of our industries" to confront Europe after the war.[55] The Colonel kept in touch with developments at the conventions by a direct telephone line laid in to the room of George Perkins at the Blackstone Hotel. When asked by reporters what the Progressives intended to do, Perkins replied, "My first choice is Roosevelt; my second choice is Roosevelt, and it is in that spirit that I go to Chicago."[56] There was no doubt who the Progressives wanted to nominate; the question was whether the Republicans could accept the Colonel after his "betrayal" of the party four years before.

Unfortunately for Roosevelt's already slim chances, Colonel Harvey had been correct in his analysis of the previous month. By June, Charles Evans Hughes had emerged as a safe choice to save the Republican Party, or at least its leaders, from the specter of TR. As a Supreme Court Justice, Hughes had not taken a stand in the 1912 Republican split, nor since then on any conceivably divisive campaign issue, and in addition he had a mildly progressive record as governor of New York. Against these safe attributes, Roosevelt's revived popularity with the people counted little with the Republican convention leadership, or as TR described them, "a very sordid set of machine masters." TR summed up the boom for Hughes as a "politician's movement" made for the "very reason that no one knows where he stands," and therefore Hughes represented the "ideal, dear to the soul of the politician, of the candidate against whom no one can say anything."[57] It was a state of affairs certainly not enjoyed by the Colonel.

On June 7, the day the Republican and Progressive conventions both officially opened, Roosevelt reported to Arthur Lee that he was in the "throes of a nominating convention" and was being "called up all the time to answer every form of question from Chicago" and to give "advice on every species of

Figure 8. "How Roosevelt Writes It," *New York World*, June 9, 1916
Theodore Roosevelt Collection, Harvard College Library

crisis and problem—for the most part ridiculous but nevertheless important
for the time being." TR confided that he did not think the Republicans had
"any intention of nominating me," even though in the last six months he
had developed a considerable following. But this was still not yet sufficient
to make an impression widespread enough "to reflect itself among the politicians." At present it appeared that Hughes would be the Republican nominee.
The Colonel appraised Hughes to Lee, more kindly than he had to others
in the past, as a "man of integrity and courage, with a purely lawyers mind"
and a "natural predilection for peace projects" and no real understanding of
international or military affairs. The German Americans, TR went on, were

enthusiastically behind Hughes, "not because they know him, but because they know *me*." The prospective nominee was, in Roosevelt's eyes, a man of the "Wilson type, but a better specimen." If he came out "unequivocally and emphatically for Americanism and Preparedness," TR believed Hughes would make a much better president than Wilson. However, he very much doubted if Hughes would be "the kind of man demanded, not only by this country, but by the world at large, in this present crisis."[58] Sir Cecil Spring Rice, who came to Chicago as an observer for the British government, was struck by the conversations he shared with Republican delegates who all were "united in asseverating that they hated Teddy like hell" but at the same time felt he was the "only man who could save the country."[59]

The Colonel's press ally Julian Street, on hand to report political developments for *Collier's Weekly*, attended sessions at both the Progressive and Republican conventions. He aptly described the first as "all fire" and the second as "all ice." One convention, said Street, was "all soaring spirit; the other all machine." The Progressive delegates went mad whenever Roosevelt's name was mentioned and would have nominated him immediately by acclamation had not the chairman, Raymond Robins, done a masterful job of keeping them under control. The Colonel hoped to use the threat of his nomination (thereby effectively reelecting Wilson) as a weapon to force his acceptance by the Republican convention members involved in the ongoing two-party conference talks that Perkins reported to Sagamore Hill by phone. From the beginning the Republican conferees were adamant against Roosevelt but offered no alternative candidate.

While these interparty meetings continued, at the Coliseum, the "calm, arrogant, determined" Republican convention, chaired by Warren G. Harding, carefully excised Roosevelt's name from the official roll call of party heroes from Lincoln on, even attributing the famous demand "Perdicaris Alive or Rasuli Dead" solely to John Hay. Julian Street recorded that the only really prolonged and heartfelt demonstrations came first, when TR's name was merely mentioned in passing, and then again when it was put into nomination on June 9 by Senator Albert Fall of Arizona, leading to a 36 minute outpouring of emotion from the galleries and many of the delegates on the floor, the longest of the convention. At the same time six blocks away in the Auditorium theater, the Progressive convention was "struggling, hoping against hope, and determined, if hope failed, to batter itself to pieces against its stronger adversary, like an aeroplane flying against a Zeppelin: willing to destroy itself in order also to destroy its foe." Both conventions talked of peace, wrote Street, but while they talked peace, the leaders "trained their guns on one another." The Progressives were headstrong and positive; the Republicans bullheaded and negative. The Progressives had but one demand: that both conventions should choose the Colonel. The Republicans "likewise insisted upon but one thing: that the nominee should *not* be Roosevelt." It was a deadlock that meant war, at least to some. But there was "no Bryan with a one-year arbitration treaty to postpone the fight."[60]

William Randolph Hearst had come to Chicago in the vain hope of influencing a Republican nomination for TR, or another progressive candidate other than Hughes, who had bested him the 1906 New York governor's race with Roosevelt's help. At the hall, Hearst met Alice and urged her to have her father come in person to the convention. He also made a *New York Journal* appeal to the Colonel to travel to Chicago and use his "splendid ability and mighty influence" to establish a "permanent, patriotic, radical party." At the convention, Roosevelt could do "your real duty" and "embrace your real opportunity."[61] However, TR ignored Hearst's advice and stayed put at Sagamore Hill. The Colonel's apparent rapprochement with the Old Guard Republicans led Hearst to note sarcastically that TR was "eagerly searching for a brand new plutocratic suit of Republican clothes."[62]

On June 10, shortly before the Republican convention nominated Hughes, who had been well in the lead from the first ballot, the Progressives, disregarding the pleas of Perkins who spoke for TR, nominated the Colonel. John Parker of Louisiana was added to the ticket for vice president. However, a telegram soon arrived from Sagamore Hill, which was read to the expectant crowd. Though Roosevelt was very grateful for the honor, he notified the convention that he could not accept the nomination "at this time" as he did not know the attitude of Hughes toward the "vital questions of the day." If the convention desired an immediate decision, TR went on, he must decline. But if they preferred he suggested that his "conditional refusal" be placed in the hands of the Progressive National Committee so that if "Mr. Hughes's statements, when he makes them, shall satisfy the committee that it is for the interest of the country that he be elected, they can act accordingly and treat my refusal as definitely accepted." If they were "not so satisfied," they could so notify the party, and at the same time "confer with me and then determine on whatever action we may severally deem appropriate to meet the needs of the country."[63]

For a moment, William Allen White recalled, there was silence among the delegates. Then a "roar of rage" filled the hall. With tears in his eyes, he witnessed hundreds of brokenhearted men "tear the Roosevelt picture or the Roosevelt badge from their coats, and throw it on the floor." After Perkins managed to get a resolution passed empowering the national committee to "fill any vacancies that may occur on the ticket," the last Bull Moose Progressive national convention adjourned.[64] Those who had labored since the beginning in 1912 were particularly bitter. White later wrote that he felt as though he had had his "face blown off and that I can never turn to the world again."[65]

After Hughes pledged himself to preparedness, progressivism, and Americanism, Roosevelt endorsed the Republican candidate. In a long letter to the Progressive National Committee, TR declared that it was "impossible for us Progressives to abandon our convictions," but they were faced with the fact that as things actually were the national organization could no longer offer the "means whereby we can make these convictions effective in our national life." Under these circumstances, their duty was to "do the best we can, and not to sulk because our leadership is rejected." In his judgment, the nomination of Hughes met the conditions set out in the statements of the party and himself, and to run a third ticket would be "merely a move in the interest of the election of Mr. Wilson." His "one purpose," said Roosevelt, was to serve "our common country," and it was his deep conviction that at "this moment we can serve it only by supporting Mr. Hughes."[66]

When TR's letter was published in the newspapers the next day, the *New York Times* commented, "Tenderly but inexorably Mr. Roosevelt draws the cruel steel along the throat of the Bull Moose. He introduced it to the political fauna. Now he bids it join the dodo. The animal was his. For him it must die." If the platform of 1912 was, as the Colonel had written, "the most important public document promulgated in this country since the death of Abraham Lincoln," the paper asked, "why doesn't Mr. Roosevelt stick to it?" Where was the platform now? Thrown "into the ash heap of history," forgotten even by the Progressives at their Chicago convention. In his letter to the party the Colonel had declared it was impossible for Progressives to abandon their convictions, but he had abandoned them. Roosevelt was thoroughly tired of the Progressive party, and his letter might aptly have been titled, "I Must Get Back into the Republican party." The Colonel was "a mighty engaging character, but too worldly wise for 'the conscience of the people.'" He wanted a conscience that could "deliver more votes."[67]

After all these developments, so many telegrams flooded into Oyster Bay that three operators were needed to handle the tide. Some correspondents applauded Roosevelt for his stand against leading a third-party ticket. Others denounced his abandonment of the Bull Moose, while a third group berated the Republican Party for its failure to nominate him. One disappointed Detroit supporter, Huey Chalmers, who reflected the views of many others, wrote that he was "very much disappointed" that the Republican leaders were "so blinded by prejudices that they could not see that your nomination was the best for the party as well as for the country." However, at least some of the principles for which Roosevelt "fought so hard" and was so "self-sacrificing, have triumphed," and he knew that after all, "that is what you most desired." He hoped that these "principles of yours will be put into effect for the safe-guarding of the country's interests and their adoption by others at this time will not turn out to be merely a lip service but a genuine wholehearted service to this and future generations."[68] TR replied to another such letter that there was only one thing to do and that was to support Hughes. But he added that he wished "the bearded iceberg had acted a little differently during the last six months so as to enable us to put more heart into the campaign for him."[69]

In a letter released for publication in the newspapers, Hughes expressed to Roosevelt his appreciation for the "capital letter of endorsement you have sent the Progressive Committee." No one was "more sensible" than Hughes "of the lasting indebtedness of the nation to you for the quickening of the national spirit, for a demand for an out and out—one hundred per cent—Americanism, and for the insistence upon the immediate necessity of a thorough-going preparedness, spiritual, military and economic." Hughes knew that TR had been "guided in this emergency by the sole desire to be of the largest service to the United States" and had "sounded the trumpet that shall never call retreat." He wanted the Colonel to know that in the campaign he wished to "have all the aid you are able and willing to give," and he wanted "the most effective cooperation with all those who have been fighting by your side. Let us work together for our national security, and for the peace and righteousness and justice."[70] In a private note to TR, Hughes added the personal message that he was "anxious to see you and have a good talk with you over the whole situation." The time and place he left to Roosevelt, although he thought it would be best to have "no guests—just a good time together."[71]

At their three-hour meeting at the Hotel Astor on June 28, Roosevelt urged Hughes to fight the election campaign on the issues of preparedness, Americanism, and Wilson's Mexican and neutrality policies. He also urged Hughes to strike at Wilson immediately, but the Republican candidate, following the traditions of the time, ultimately held his fire until he officially accepted the nomination at the end of July. Hughes afterwards wrote to TR that it was "very satisfying to have such a good talk with you and I hope you will not fail to give me from time to time any suggestions you think will prove helpful." He added in ink at end of this, "Response on all sides encouraging."[72] Roosevelt reported to Lodge that he was "very much pleased with my talk with Hughes" and with his letters. He believed as did Lodge that Hughes would make a "straight-out fight for preparedness and national defense." Hughes had told him personally that he believed in universal service, "but was doubtful as to the expediency of coming out for it at this time." TR went on that he was "simply unable to understand" how the American people could tolerate "this creature" Wilson. But in retrospect he was also unable to understand how they could have tolerated Jefferson and Madison a hundred years before. Andrew Jackson also had his faults, "but at least he was a fighting man, and had some idea of the correspondence between words and deeds."[73]

From London, Arthur Lee wrote of his disappointment with the Hughes nomination and added that the candidate had made a "singularly depressing" impression when they had met in New York before the war. He told TR that it was "nothing short of an international tragedy that you should have been swindled out of the greatest opportunity that a man ever had to serve his fellow men." He almost despaired when he thought of "all that it might have meant to the settlement of this war and the cause of Peace if you could have held the position of arbitrator when the final stages of exhaustion are reached by the various combatants."[74] Roosevelt undoubtedly heartily agreed with all this, but he now went forth to campaign for Hughes and, more importantly, to remove Woodrow Wilson at all costs from the seat of power.

CHAPTER 7

A SHADOW DANCE OF WORDS

JULY TO NOVEMBER 1916

There should be shadows enough at Shadow Lawn; the shadows of men, women and children who have risen from the ooze of the ocean bottom and from graves in foreign lands; the shadows of the helpless whom Mr. Wilson did not dare to protect lest he might have to face danger; the shadows of babies gasping pitifully as they sank under the waves; the shadows of women outraged and slain by bandits; the shadows of Boyd and Adair and their troopers who lay in the Mexican desert, the black blood crusted round their mouths, and their dim eyes looking upward, because President Wilson had sent them to do a task, and had then shamefully abandoned them to the mercy of foes who knew no mercy. Those are the shadows proper for Shadow Lawn; the shadows of deeds that were never done; the shadows of lofty words that were followed by no action; the shadows of the tortured dead.

                                        —TR at Cooper Union, November 3, 1916

At the Oyster Bay Fourth of July celebration, Roosevelt broke the self-imposed silence he had maintained since the Chicago conventions with an impromptu speech. His cheering audience included a force of 116 sailors from the cruiser USS *Baltimore*, which had seen service in the Philippines during the Spanish-American War. The Colonel had agreed to come down to listen to an address on Americanism and review the sailors and a local parade, but he had not been expected to speak. However, after seeing the marching bluejackets, and the red, white, and blue decorated floats representing the 13 original colonies, he could not restrain himself. The crowd had listened to a reading of the Declaration of Independence, and TR noted that, if the men who wrote and signed that document had then "gone home and let it execute itself, we should not be here today." The Declaration was "made good by the sword of Washington" and the men who fought with him through six years of war. No nation, he went on, was "either fit to be free" or would "permanently be permitted to be free" unless it was able to "protect all its own rights with all of its own power." Therefore he believed with all his heart in universal military training in time of peace and universal service in time of war.

In his remarks, Roosevelt stayed away from politics, but he declared his intention to raise a force for service in Mexico in the event of war. He told the gathering that he would pick no one to do anything that he and his sons would not do, and he promised all the unmarried young men from Oyster Bay a chance to join. (TR would not take any married man with a family depending on him and considered it an outrage that such a system was permitted in the recent militia muster for duty on the border.) He called for a "dog-in-the-manger" policy toward Mexico after the European war was over, to keep foreign powers from intervening to protect their citizens being murdered by bandits. Unless the country did its duty now, said the Colonel, the United States would have to "fight one of them for the Monroe Doctrine."[1]

War appeared imminent between Mexico and the United States because of the June 21 skirmish at Carrizal between Carranza's troops and elements of John J. Pershing's punitive expedition. In this engagement both sides had suffered numerous casualties when the Mexican force obeyed orders to halt any movement of American troops except back toward the border. The losses included Mexican General Felix Gomez. On the other side, 23 Americans were taken prisoner and Captain Charles T. Boyd and Lieutenant Henry R. Adair killed. A month before, Carranza had sent such a bitter diplomatic note about the American incursion that Woodrow Wilson had in response called up 100,000 National Guardsman for border duty. Sending the Guard to the border had, in TR's opinion, "simply been wicked." It was an action, he told the writer Julian Street, which provided "most of the hardships of war, without the benefits of efficient war." The Guard could not be properly trained, and half the men had people depending on them and were themselves depending on jobs that could not be kept open indefinitely. Roosevelt knew of a case of a soldier whose wife and children were already suffering in the interests of a policy that was "neither Peace nor War, and which has nothing to do with humanity," but was hoped would "help Wilson win the election."[2]

Anticipating a declared war with Mexico, TR's supporters moved forward with the plans for a volunteer force—to be led, of course, by the Colonel. The deluge of letters from volunteers for the prospective Roosevelt Legion was taken in hand by the Colonel's military secretary at Oyster Bay, Walter Hayes, and his friend Regis Post, a former governor of Puerto Rico, working out of the *Metropolitan* offices in New York. The applications came from close friends and complete strangers, from nurses to newspaper correspondents. One old friend, Seth Bullock, reported that he was raising a force of men in the Dakotas but had signed up only one officer so far: Kermit Roosevelt.[3] The newspapers reported that officers had been accepted and printed the localities where they would recruit, including western Colorado, Wyoming,

Utah, and Nevada. At least one cavalry regiment, it was rumored, had been accepted to receive training at Fort Douglas, Utah, or Fort D. A. Russell, Wyoming, before joining the rest of the division at Fort Sill, Oklahoma.[4]

In early July, Roosevelt wrote to Secretary of War Newton Baker respectfully requesting permission, if war was declared, to raise and command a volunteer division.[5] A week before this, Baker had been asked by reporters about the Colonel's efforts to raise volunteers and whether he was within the age limit for appointment as a major general. It must have been a delicious moment for Baker, whom TR had for months belittled at every opportunity in his speeches. The war secretary remarked with a smile that there were "some men, like Cleopatra," who were "not withered by age and cannot have their infinite variety staled by custom."[6] Roosevelt was nevertheless hopeful and commented to his preparedness ally Julian Street that he thought it possible that he would be allowed to raise a division—since, when he was in uniform, "I must stop being a critic."[7]

As it fell out, however, the Wilson administration was saved from having to reply to Roosevelt's request when this latest crisis did not lead to wider hostilities. Carranza had the American prisoners released and announced that he would resume negotiations to restore order in Northern Mexico. This allowed Wilson once again to proclaim that he had "kept the peace." Henry Cabot Lodge confessed to TR that he was aghast that the administration celebrated a "diplomatic victory" when American dead were returned and prisoners given back. They "made a point of getting the prisoners back," he told the Colonel, "but American dead, whether civilians or soldiers, on sea or land, do not seem to interest them at all." As long as they were dead, "that apparently, in the mind of this administration, closes the incident." It seemed to Lodge, as it did to Roosevelt, that voting for Wilson constituted "moral degradation," and he looked on "with amazement at the newspapers and the people that were supporting him."[8]

Some of these Wilson supporters were Progressive Party renegades, including Matthew Hale of Massachusetts, vice president of the Progressive National Committee; Bainbridge Colby of New York; and Francis J. Heney, a San Francisco Progressive. The last in particular had been a staunch supporter of Roosevelt, and his defection to Wilson was a political coup that the Democrats were quick to exploit. In a letter to Wilson released to the newspapers, Heney praised the president's foreign and domestic policies and legislative achievements, while declaring that the Republican nomination of Charles Evans Hughes represented the "fruition of the political corruption" that had been successfully practiced at the Republican National Convention four years before. Heney would have "loyally and vigorously" supported Roosevelt if he had accepted the Progressive nomination, but he could not follow TR in backing Hughes while the Republican Party was guided by sinister Old Guard figures such as Senator Boies Penrose of Pennsylvania and Elihu Root and William Barnes of New York.[9] The Wilson campaign openly courted Progressives, and the Democratic platform of progressivism, "reasonable" preparedness, and peace (including a "feasible" association of nations for collective security after the war) attracted a number of them. By the end of June the newly elected chairman of the Democratic National Committee, Vance McCormick, announced that he had received "assurances of sufficient Progressive support to make the re-election of President Wilson certain."[10] This was only campaign rhetoric at the time, but it was prescient of the final outcome.

That summer, whatever caustic criticisms Roosevelt might have continued to make on the preparedness issue, Wilson's credentials in the matter were considerably bolstered by the passage of two major pieces of legislation. The Naval Act authorized contracts for the construction of 156 new ships over the next three years, including 10 new battleships and 50 destroyers, an undoubted victory for the "big navy" forces. The National Defense Act (which TR dubbed "flintlock legislation") enlarged the US army to 175,000 over five years and increased the first line of reserve, the National Guard, from 100,000 to 400,000. The act ignored the universal service demanded by Leonard Wood and TR for the old voluntary methods and left the country reliant on the National Guard, from which Wilson had had trouble raising 100,000 men for service on the border. Nevertheless, these measures allowed the president—justifiably, in the minds of many worried about the issue—to stake a valid claim to be the candidate of reasonable preparedness promised in the Democratic platform. Wood had correctly forecast that the Army Bill, though weak, would satisfy many people and wrote to Roosevelt it was "one of the most iniquitous bits of legislation ever placed on the statute books."[11] With the Army and Navy Acts law, the *New York Times* dubbed the Colonel's continued demands on this front "belated," as the new legislation had "drawn the teeth" of his attacks and "provided liberally for national defense."[12]

In addition, the St. Louis Democratic Convention that nominated Wilson sent him out for the fight complete with what turned out to be the winning campaign slogan: "He Kept Us Out of War." (It cleverly made no promises about the future.) Roosevelt described the event as "one of the most degrading spectacles we have ever seen" and told his sister Anna that he despised Wilson but even more "our foolish, foolish people who, partly from ignorance, and partly from sheer timidity, and partly from lack of imagination and of sensitive national feeling," supported him.[13] The attitude of the Democrats at St. Louis, he told another correspondent, "was one of greater infamy" than any political convention had taken since the Democratic conventions of 1860 and 1864 that had nominated Breckenridge, McClellan, and Seymour. Wilson was not only the worst president the country had had since Buchanan "but even a much worse President than Buchanan."[14]

While Wilson studiously refused publicly to answer Roosevelt, his running mate Thomas Marshall eagerly commented on the duplicity of the Colonel in abandoning the Progressives he had promised in 1912 to "lead at Armageddon" but had, "alas! deserted at Bull Moose Run." In his acceptance speech, Marshall admitted that the Progressive upheaval had led to Wilson presiding over the last three years of "most fateful history in the annals of mankind." TR, the former leader of the crusade, had "turned his back on the Holy land." He now cried that the "great mission" of the Progressive Party had been accomplished and it was time to turn the country over to the "very men he condemned." If the Progressive mission had been accomplished, said Marshall, then it was the Democrats that had done it. The average American wanted to know who was in the partnership with candidate Hughes in "firm Americanism." Did the firm consist of "Hughes and Roosevelt, of Hughes and Hohenzollern, or of Hughes, surviving partner of the firm of Hughes and Huerta?"[15]

Meanwhile, on the European war front, British troops went "over the top" yet again on July 1 to open the Battle of the Somme, a new offensive meant to relieve the German pressure on the French army at Verdun. Tragically for the soldiers involved and the Allied cause, the preceding unprecedented artillery barrage failed to clear away the German defenses, and the British army suffered more than 50,000 casualties on the first day—with only meager gains to show for their sacrifice. As the toll mounted over the following weeks, the commander, Sir Douglas Haig, stubbornly continued the bloody frontal assaults, despite the dreadful human wastage. Lord Kitchener's successor as secretary of state for war, David Lloyd George, viewed the Somme as a larger repetition of the previous Neuve Chappelle and Loos failures. The Welshman aimed to reduce the carnage in France and Flanders—if necessary by diverting troops elsewhere or holding them in Britain.[16]

Arthur Lee had followed his chief Lloyd George from the Ministry of Munitions to the War Office and was rewarded for his work with a KCB (Knight Commander of the Bath). Lee wrote to TR that he knew that "despite your austere republicanism you will be pleased." To take advantage of Sir Arthur's good relations with the soldiers, his superiors shifted him from parliamentary to military secretary, and he confided to Roosevelt that he hoped to help bring about "harmonious and whole-hearted cooperation" between his chief and the army leadership. Recent developments at home and on the battlefield, Lee reported, had helped to make things "considerably more cheerful here about the military situation." There was "no doubt whatever" that things were "brighter for the Allies," because they were pulling together more effectively "than at any time since the beginning of the war."[17]

A much less cheery appraisal of events came from Sir Cecil Spring Rice, whose fifty-year-old brother Gerald was among the dead on the Somme. Gerald, who had immigrated to Canada some years before, had pulled strings to enlist and had been serving as a lieutenant in the transport service when he was killed by a shell. Downcast over the fate of his brother, and also by what he saw as a lack of Allied and American resolve and war effort, Cecil wrote to his friend Theodore, "I must have a talk with you or bust!" He supposed they shouldn't talk politics, but he confessed that Roosevelt's July 4 Oyster Bay speech "did one good to read."[18]

Roosevelt consoled his friend with the thought of how "finely and gallantly" Gerald had acted. "Your pride," he went on, "must outweigh your sorrow. I would like to finish in such manner." England, he told Spring Rice, was "passing through the flame and will come out cleansed and refined to lofty nobleness." He agreed with his friend that America, on the other hand, was "passing through the thick-yellow mud streak of 'safety first,'" and its high places were "held—and not only in one party—by the men of little soul who desire only sordid ease." Perhaps, he went on, "we will have to be shot over, and eat the bitter bread of shame, before we find again the spirit of high desire."[19]

On a more pleasant note, Sir Henry Rider Haggard, who was on a tour of the Dominions looking into possibilities for postwar immigration of soldiers, came down from Canada that very hot July to see Roosevelt at Sagamore Hill. "Heaven, how we talked!" Haggard recalled. "Of all sorts of things; of the world and its affairs, of religion, of heaven and hell, of the fundamental truths, and the spirit of man; for when Roosevelt and myself meet—men who are in deep and almost mysterious sympathy with one another, there are many vital matters on which we need to know each other's mind." As a keep-sake TR gave his friend a photo of himself jumping a horse over a fence and sent him a copy of *Fear God and Take Your Own Part*. This he inscribed, "To Sir Rider Haggard, who has both preached and practiced fealty to the things of the soul. With the regards of his friend, Theodore Roosevelt." Haggard recorded in his diary that the inscription was "perhaps the greatest compliment that was ever paid to me." In return, six months later Haggard dedicated his next Alan Quartermain adventure, *Finished*, to TR, "in memory of certain hours wherein both of us found true refreshment and companionship amidst the terrible anxieties of the World's journey along that bloodstained road by which alone, so it is decreed, the pure Peak of Freedom must be scaled." The Colonel responded that he was "very proud" of the dedication and that he would never forget Haggard's visit, which was one of the "most enjoyable afternoons I have ever spent with any friend." Roosevelt added that he wished he could see Haggard again. This was not to be.[20]

As the official opening of the campaign season drew near in late July, the Colonel confided to former New Hampshire Governor Robert Bass that he thought Hughes would be a good president, but no one could tell whether he would "rise level to the great international needs of the moment" or if he possessed the "knowledge and power to undo the frightful wrongs committed on this nation by Wilson." TR went on that a "more sordid set of creatures" than the Republicans who nominated Hughes could not be imagined. They had no thought whatever for the welfare of the country, had no appreciation of the international dangers or proper international relations, and did not know their candidate's views on the most vital questions and "hoped to escape talking about them at all." Of course, he went on, it was "very galling" to have to take any action that helped such scoundrels.[21]

Nevertheless, Wilson had to be defeated, and Roosevelt dutifully attended the July 31 Carnegie Hall event at which Hughes formally responded to his notification of the Republican nomination. From a lower tier box shared with Theodore Jr. and Robert Bacon, the Colonel watched Hughes give a ninety-minute speech, "America First and America Efficient," which attacked the Wilson administration's foreign policy and preparedness record. With a glance at Roosevelt, Hughes noted that Wilson had changed course on preparedness "under the pressure of other leadership." This led to an outbreak of cheering directed at the Colonel that lasted several minutes. Hughes also declared that he would protect domestic American interests from sabotage such as the previous day's "Black Tom" explosion on the New Jersey waterfront, which had caused massive destruction when two million pounds of munitions awaiting shipment to the Allies blew up.[22]

The acceptance speech attracted less attention than did TR's presence at his first official Republican function since 1912. Afterwards, he praised Hughes's address as "admirable" and called particular attention to several points. First, the Colonel was pleased at Hughes's "exposure" of Wilson's Mexican policy and the way it had brought "humiliation to the United States and disaster to Mexico itself." He also congratulated Hughes for his "straightforward" declaration concerning outrages against munitions plants, whether by "citizens of foreign nations or nominal citizens of our own," declaring that the Republican candidate would punish offenders with the "fearlessness and thoroughness that he showed in dealing with the powers of evil at Albany" when he was New York's governor. The next day TR joined Hughes at the Hotel Astor for tea with the Women's Roosevelt League, which soon after joined the Hughes Alliance and officially threw its support behind the Republican nominee while at the same time calling for the Colonel to be made secretary of state in the prospective Hughes administration.[23] This looming possibility would be used in the campaign by the Democrats in their appeals to German American voters.[24]

The Hughes camp feared that Roosevelt's attacks on hyphenates would cost the party votes. During the Republican convention the German-American Alliance had pressured the party to nominate "anyone but Roosevelt," ultimately supporting Hughes as "the Bismarck of America" and the "new Lincoln."[25] In a telephone conversation the candidate shared as tactfully as possible his fears that the Colonel's attacks were being "misunderstood." TR responded that he would "profit by your suggestion as to my use of the hyphen" and thought it "admirable." The trouble was, as Hughes had said, that "many good people of foreign birth or parentage" were "entirely unable to differentiate" and thought that he attacked "all of the naturalized voters, or the sons of the foreign-born," when, in fact, he only attacked those who endeavored to "remain foreigners as well as German-Americans." Roosevelt admitted that in a political campaign, "with all of its turmoil and misrepresentation," his method of stating the case seemed to "have lent itself to misunderstanding," so he would do as Hughes suggested and avoid using the phrase while continuing to "set forth my principles just as unequivocally." Hughes agreed with this strategy.[26]

The Colonel's campaign for Hughes opened on August 31 at the packed City Hall Auditorium at Lewiston, Maine, with a speech that had been read and approved by William Willcox, Hughes's campaign manager.[27] TR told the audience he had come to advocate to "all good Americans" the election of Hughes and a congress to support him. Though as promised he did not use "hyphen," he lost little time in condemning the "professional German-Americans" and any divided loyalty between "this country and the country from which any of our citizens, or the ancestors of any of our citizens, have come." Americanism, he told the crowd, was a "matter of the spirit, of the soul, of the mind; not of birthplace or creed." Roosevelt not surprisingly laid the present divisions at the feet of Wilson, who lacked the courage and vision to lead the country "in the path of high duty." Further, the president's failure to provide "affirmative leadership" had "loosened the moral fibre of our people" and weakened the national spirit. To the Colonel, Americanism was "inseparably connected" with preparedness, where Wilson again had failed the country as he had in Mexico when he halted "between feeble peace and feeble war."

Turning to the Democratic cry that Wilson had "kept us out of war," Roosevelt declared this a claim that could be "seriously made" only by individuals who endorsed the president's belief that "deeds are nothing, and words everything." For evidence, he chronicled in detail the many American interventions in Mexico made after Wilson had said repeatedly that the country would not do so. In this "peace" more Americans had been killed by Mexicans than by the Spanish in the Spanish-American War. While "waging peace" the United States took Vera Cruz with the loss of 75 Americans killed and wounded, more than it took to capture Manila in 1898. Wilson then "became frightened" and abandoned Vera Cruz, whereas President McKinley did not abandon Manila. One was war as much as the other; the difference was that Wilson was beaten in his war, a war "entered into pointlessly and abandoned ignobly." It was a war that not only failed but also "did damage both to the Mexicans and ourselves, and which in its outcome reflected infinite dishonor upon our nation." Then, last March, Pancho Villa, whose "career of successful infamy had been greatly aided by Mr. Wilson's favor and backing," attacked Columbus, New Mexico. The president had announced the next day that adequate force would be sent into Mexico after Villa "with the single object of capturing him" and claimed that they would stay until he was taken "dead or alive." These were fine words, only they meant nothing. Villa was not dead nor had he been captured. And on May 12 the formal pursuit of Villa was abandoned.

In conclusion, Roosevelt asked his audience if, between Hughes and Wilson, there was any doubt which was the man who would "with austere courage stand for the national duty." Wilson's words had contradicted one another, "and all his words had been contradicted by his acts." Against the president's combination of "grace in elocution with futility in action; against his record of words unbacked by deeds or betrayed by deeds," the supporters of Hughes set his "rugged and uncompromising straightforwardness of character and action" in every office he had held.[28]

After weeks of "milk and water," the *New York Times* commented that Republicans and converted Progressives had been "yearning for pepperpot," which Roosevelt had delivered at Lewiston in a speech that "amusingly, and no doubt sincerely," the Colonel described as "no merely partisan appeal." And after Hughes's "silence and egg-shell walking his advocate's hearty bewhacking of the hyphen" was good to read. So far, Roosevelt did Americanism, while Hughes proclaimed "we are a united people." Concerning TR's attack on Wilson as the font of all recent evils, the paper remarked wryly that it was now clear that there would have been no war if the Republicans had been in power. A "single demand" would have prevented the invasion of Belgium and "all the diversions of the Germans and Turks." The Colonel's notion seemed to be that the United States, like the Knights of the Round Table, "should ride abroad redressing human wrongs." The paper pointed out that there had been Armenian outrages in 1908 about which President Roosevelt had taken no action; nor had he condemned the Austrian annexation of Bosnia that year, which had made the Treaty of Berlin a "scrap of paper." It appeared TR, like Wilson, was "blind to his duty." But the editorial writer found it a waste of time to argue against a foreign policy "so quixotic, perilous and impossible as Mr. Roosevelt proposes."[29] Nevertheless, half a million copies of the Lewiston speech were printed by the Republican National Committee for use in the campaign. Hughes, campaigning in Kansas City, sent Roosevelt his hearty congratulations on the speech and his warm appreciation for his "effective support."[30]

All the attention paid to Roosevelt's entry into the campaign, including posing for motion pictures with Hughes supporters, drew the fire of the Democratic leadership. Vance McCormick, the dour chairman of the Democratic National Committee, announced that President Wilson was not at all worried that the Colonel had been called in to invigorate the Republican campaign. "Why should the President," asked McCormick, "feel nervous over what the Colonel is going to do?" In his view it was just another example of "proxy campaigning" and a repetition of the "Henry L. Stimson affair" in which TR "dictated the nomination, ran the campaign, and the result was history." Roosevelt, said McCormick, could "not be injected into the campaign too much to suit us."[31] Wilson continued his policy of publicly ignoring the Colonel's attacks, commenting that it was a good rule not to murder a man who was committing suicide.[32]

Hughes's failure to repudiate the support of "professional" German Americans and Irish Americans gave Wilson an opening. In September he underlined "Americanism" as one of his own campaign issues when a New York lawyer and Sinn Feiner, Jeremiah O'Leary, sent Wilson a telegram denouncing the administration for "truckling to the British Empire." O'Leary was the president of the virulently anti-British American Truth Society, which in their monthly publication, *Bull*, loudly condemned both the unneutral actions of the administration and the pro-British bias of most newspapers. "Anglomaniacs and British interests may control newspapers," Leary warned the president, "but they don't control votes." Voters, he went on, did not approve of Wilson's "dictatorship of Congress," his foreign policies, his "failure to secure compliance with all American rights," his "leniency with the British Empire," nor his "approval of war loans" and the "ammunition traffic."

These nonneutral actions, O'Leary said, made it impossible for him or other Irish Americans to vote for the president.[33] Replying in an open telegram, Wilson declared, "I would feel deeply mortified to have you or anybody like you vote for me," and since O'Leary had "access to so many disloyal Americans and I have not," the president asked him to "convey this message to them."[34]

At the same time, the United States continued to offer mediation to Europe through Wilson's personal envoy, Colonel Edward M. House, who hoped Romania's entry into the war on the side of the Allies at the end of August might tip the balance and offer an opportunity.[35] However, Lloyd George instead gave a statement to Roy Howard of the American United Press, who had stopped in London on his way to Germany. Their conversation, published internationally on September 29, 1916, became famous as the "Knock-Out Blow" interview. In this the Welshman declared that any peace move by a neutral, whether the Vatican or the United States, would be regarded as pro-German. Lloyd George told Howard that Wilson "must understand that there can be no outside interference at this time" and that the "fight must be to a finish—to a knockout!"[36] Lord Northcliffe's *Daily Mail* printed the interview and congratulated the war secretary for his "straight from the shoulder language that Americans appreciate." This bold and unauthorized statement by Lloyd George bolstered domestic and Allied morale and sent a clear signal to Germany and the United States, where it was less-than-enthusiastically received by the Wilson administration.[37]

After the Lewiston success, speaking requests for TR poured into Republican National Campaign Headquarters, and the Colonel agreed to make several more major addresses at important cities in a tour on the way to the Pacific coast. His next appearance was scheduled for September 30 at Battle Creek, Michigan, one of the states he had won in 1912. This was billed in advance as "skin-em-alive" speech that would savage both the president and the Adamson eight-hour railroad bill.[38] For a change, Wilson responded to a press query about Roosevelt's declaration that at Battle Creek he planned to "tear the shirt off" the president as he had done in his Grand Rapids speech in the 1912 campaign, commenting that the "funny thing about this campaign" was that it "doesn't make any difference." The Republicans, said Wilson, were "the happiest family, considering its differences of opinion," that he had ever seen.[39]

The Colonel gave his Battle Creek address from the top of a table on the speaker's platform in a huge circus tent, which underlined the revivalist nature of the event. He began the speech, as he would many others that followed, by addressing those who protested any criticism of Wilson, noting that the newspapers and individuals who took this position were the same ones who, when he was president, "spread every species of calumny and slander about me." In office, TR had taken the view that no one should speak untruthfully about the president, or anyone else, but that "even less than anyone else ought the President to escape from truthful criticism." He had never complained of any attack on him unless it was false, and if the man making it was important enough, he "clearly showed its falsity." Now he only applied to others the standard by which he had asked to be treated. Roosevelt had not "uttered one word of criticism" of Wilson for a year and a half after he was elected president, and in fact he had actively tried to support him. But at last, when Wilson's policy of "tame submission" to insult and injury from all whom he feared had invited the murders of Americans by Mexican bandits and German submarines, TR could keep silent no longer.

Nearly a year and a half had passed since the sinking of the *Lusitania*, after which Wilson had made his famous "Too Proud the Fight" declaration. "In all our history," said TR, there had never been another president who had used a phrase that had "done such widespread damage to the good name of America." It was one of those "dreadful phrases which, as by a lightning flash, illumines the soul of the man using it and remains forever fixed in the minds of mankind in connection with that man." And when that man was president of the Unites States, it was a "sad and dreadful thing" that the shame was "necessarily shared by the nation itself" and would be "completely assumed by the nation if it fails to repudiate the man who uttered the phrase." If the Colonel had been president when the *Lusitania* was torpedoed, he would "instantly have taken possession of every German ship interned in this country." Then he would have said, "Now we will discuss, not what we will give, but what we will give back." This statement drew wild applause.

Turning to domestic affairs, and in particular the recent eight-hour-day legislation for the railroad brotherhood found in the Adamson Act, the Colonel declared that in his years of public service he had on every important issue supported the unions. But it was the duty of every good American to judge questions that arose between capital and labor on their merits, and in TR's opinion, there had been few things more "discreditable to our representatives" and more "ominous for the future of the nation" than the "spectacle" of the president and Congress being required to "pass a certain bill before a certain hour at the dictation of certain men who sat in the gallery with their watches in their hands threatening ruin and disaster to the nation if there was the smallest failure to satisfy their demands." Wilson had been "cowed by the big labor leaders exactly as he had already been cowed by Germany and by Mexico." Once more, in "our internal affairs, as in our external affairs, he had stood for peace at any price."

In conclusion, Roosevelt appealed to his audience to elect Hughes and "repudiate Mr. Wilson," because only by doing so could they "save America from that taint of selfishness and cowardice which we owe to Mr. Wilson's substitution of adroit elocution for straightforward action." The permanent interests of the American people did not lie in "ease and comfort for the moment no matter how obtained, as Mr. Wilson would teach us," but in "resolute championship of the ideals of national and international democratic duty, and in preparedness to make this championship effective." President Wilson embodied "that most dangerous doctrine" that taught that "when fronted with really formidable responsibilities we can shirk trouble and labor and risk and avoid duty by the simple process of drugging our souls with the narcotic of meaningless phrasemongering." Hughes, to the contrary, embodied the ideal of "service rendered through conscientious effort in the face of danger and difficulty."[40]

Wilson ignored this latest attack, but Vance McCormick responded for the Democrats, in particular to the Colonel's comments about seizing the interned German ships and his opposition to the eight-hour-day legislation. The chairman of the Democratic National Committee challenged Hughes to endorse TR's stand on the German ships, declaring that, according to this admission, "the United States would have been at war with Germany today" had Roosevelt been president. McCormick went on that he hoped in his next speech TR would tell the people whether, if he were president, he would repeal the eight-hour law or would insist on its repeal if Hughes (who had come out for the eight-hour day in principle) should be elected. McCormick concluded by asserting that all Americans who wanted continued peace and prosperity would vote to reelect Wilson, while those who wished war should vote for Hughes. There could be no mistaking the issue. There was only one alternative to peace and that was war.[41]

On October 1 Roosevelt was back at Oyster Bay and two days later attended a reception for Hughes at the Union League Club, a New York Republican stronghold since its founding in the cauldron of the Civil War.[42] This event was hosted by the club's president Elihu Root, and the main point of interest soon became a potential political reunion of TR and William Howard Taft. When their joint appearance was announced, the *New York Times* commented that a funeral had been the last occasion at which the two men were "visible in the same place," and now they were to "commemorate the funeral of the Progressive Party by being present at a love-feast at the Union League Club." Turning to Root, the editorial went on that Roosevelt had once declared that he would walk on his hands and knees down Pennsylvania Avenue to make him president of the United States, but for the last four years, the Bacon lunch "being but a show," the Colonel had labeled Root the boss "burglar, porch-climber and crook." And, the paper continued, the old friendship of Will and Theodore was equally "past renewal," and TR's opinion of the "malefactors" of 1912 unchanged. It was because Roosevelt hated Wilson more, not because he hated Root or Taft less, that he had consented to this "tableau of handshaking."[43]

This was an apt description of the reception, as, behind closed doors and out of the sight of the newspapermen on hand, a smiling TR and Taft did shake hands and share a formal greeting, but only as part of a long reception line that included many other of the Colonel's Republican political enemies, such as Senator Boies Penrose of Pennsylvania, with whom Roosevelt, it was noted, proved more jovial in his greeting. The reporters were told that the two ex-presidents had addressed each other with the "greatest cordiality," but Taft's version (given through a friend) was that the two men simply "shook hands as any gentlemen might and not a word was spoken."[44] However brief it was, the joint appearance nevertheless delighted Hughes and his supporters. Diehards on both sides, however, were disgusted by even this small gesture of unity between the old foes of 1912.

A few days later, in a speech to 3,500 prominent professionals and businessmen at his New Jersey home, Shadow Lawn, Woodrow Wilson for the first time, still without mentioning his name, made a public reference to Roosevelt to underline the key theme of the campaign's final month: Peace or War. Speaking of the divisions within the Republican Party, Wilson referred to the "only articulate voice, a very articulate voice," who professed "opinions and purposes at which the rest in private shiver and demur." Noting the Colonel's support of Robert Bacon in the New York Senate primary, the president declared that "one collateral branch backed a man whose position in respect of international affairs was unneutral" and whose intention was to "promote the interests of one side in the present war in Europe." Therefore, if the Republican Party should succeed in the coming election, it would mean that "one very large branch of it" would insist on a complete reversal of policy that could only be "a reversal from peace to war."[45] When asked by reporters, Roosevelt uncharacteristically made no comment on Wilson's speech.[46]

TR's next address was scheduled for Wilkes-Barre in Pennsylvania, another state he had carried in 1912. This was to be followed in short order by a western tour through Kentucky, Arizona, New Mexico, Colorado, and Illinois. Before the Colonel departed, however, a raid on neutral shipping just off the East Coast by the German submarine U-53, which had first popped up in Newport Harbor with a message for Ambassador Count Johann von Bernstorff, moved TR to unleash another broadside at Wilson. The president had claimed leadership of the neutral powers in the most recent note sent to England protesting her blockade. Now by not acting similarly against Germany after the U-53 sinkings, Wilson had "betrayed" this proclaimed leadership. Once again the Colonel chronicled the many failures of the administration since the outbreak of war and declared that the "Pontius Pilate-like construction which Wilson put on neutrality" was responsible for "the complete breakdown of the code of international rights." In the election season the president's "ignoble shirking of responsibility" had been "misclothed in an utterly misleading phrase, 'He kept us out of war.'" In actuality, war had been "creeping nearer and nearer until it stares at us from just beyond our three mile limit," and the country faced it "without policy, plan, purpose or preparation." The time for Wilson's "head-in-a-hole" policy was past. America could not afford to continue playing that part among nations, least of all could she afford to be "an elocutionary ostrich."[47]

Wilkes-Barre was the headquarters of the coal-mining industry in which Roosevelt had won union support with his militant stand against the intransigent mine owners in the 1904 anthracite strike. His address at the Armory was meant as a bid for labor votes lost to Wilson and the Democrats for passing the Adamson eight-hour bill. While union picketers outside marched with signs reading, "We Love You, Teddy, but Wilson is a friend of labor," TR spoke to 5,000 mainly nonunion listeners.[48] The Colonel contrasted his handling of the coal strike with what Wilson had done "in connection with the law for the increases in wages on railroads"—for this, he again asserted, was the question at issue, not the eight-hour day. Roosevelt went on that he believed in the eight-hour day as the "ideal toward which we should tend," but there must be "common sense as well as common honesty in achieving the ideal." The president had "laid down the principle" that there was something sacred about the eight-hour day that made it "improper even to discuss it." If this was so, TR thought it proper for Wilson to apply it in his own household for the butlers and maids at the White House. If there was only principle involved, he further asked, why not bring under the Adamson Bill standard the railway postal clerks over which he had full power? The only possible explanation for his inaction was that only 400 men were affected where the government had full control of hours, whereas 400,000 men were "supposed to be affected by the Adamson bill."

Roosevelt was proud to be an honorary member of a labor union, but he was first of all a member "in the Union to which we all belong, the union of the people of the United States." In the coal strike, he had followed the proper course by seeking arbitration and investigation to come up with a fair settlement, which remained, with small adjustments, in place. Wilson, on the other hand, had yielded to the threats of labor and afterwards admitted this pattern should not be followed again. TR championed Hughes against Wilson, because in every crisis, international and domestic, the president had shown by his public acts that he "will yield to fear, that he will not yield to justice," whereas the public acts of Hughes had "proved him to be incapable of yielding in such a crisis to any threat, whether made by politicians, corporations or labor leaders."[49]

On the way to speak at Phoenix, in 100 degree heat, Roosevelt gave a rear platform speech at Gallup, New Mexico, which set off what he described as a "rare diversity of entertainment." As soon as TR showed himself, an ex–Rough Rider, Joseph Richie, "shedding tears of joy," leaped onto the platform and wrapped his old Colonel in a bear hug. After disentangling himself, Roosevelt declared to those gathered how much New Mexico had helped his career by providing more than half of the First Volunteer Regiment, without which "I never would have been President." A few minutes later a railroad brakeman yelled from the crowd about the Mexican situation, "If you were in Wilson's place what would you do?" TR quieted the assembly and responded, "I would have protected men, women and children." The brakemen continued, "Yes, but what would you do for a working man in a crisis?" "Exactly what I did do," Roosevelt shouted in response, "I would do justice to both sides and I would not stand for any bullying from either." The crowd liked this response, but the unimpressed brakeman asked, "Did we ever have eight hours before?" "You have not got it now," the Colonel replied, "It's a sham."

"How do you like Wilson, Teddy?" shouted another man. "I'll bet you like him in the bottom of your heart." To this TR answered, "Then I have skillfully concealed it even from myself." When the Colonel spoke of Wilson being "too proud to fight," the same brakeman bellowed, "Aw, we ain't fighting here—we're working" and added "we was not working in 1907 and 1908 when you were in." "Friend," countered Roosevelt, his face dripping with sweat, "I never in my life ask for you to vote for me on the ground that I would keep your belly full. I have no claim on the man who puts his belly before his soul. It is true that the country was prosperous in my administration, but my appeal is to patriots, not such men as you." As TR began to read his speech proper, there were no more interruptions except cheers and applause.[50]

At Denver, Roosevelt rode in three parades and spoke as many times. In his main address, to the Hughes Women's Campaign, TR returned to the familiar ground of preparedness. At this moment, he declared, the country was not "ready in any way, physically or spiritually, to face a serious foe." This "lamentable fact" was due to many causes, but especially to the "evil leadership given our people in high places." Wilson had been not only too proud to fight but also too proud to prepare. The administration was not really interested in preparedness or the defense of the country. They thought only of their own "political fortunes in the immediate future." They refused to provide "expert military legislation," instead giving the country "political military legislation" designed to secure votes next November "at the cost of the lives of the gallant officers and men of the regular army; at the cost of the lives of civilians, men, women and children on the border, and in Mexico; and at the cost of the well-being" of thousands of the families of the national guardsmen sent to the border "not to make war for the country, but to help Mr. Wilson wobble between feeble peace and feeble war until after the election."[51]

Before the campaign train reached Chicago, where he was scheduled to give two addresses, TR rejected out of hand the request of several Illinois Republican leaders that he tread softly on the hyphenates. His response was that he would "not speak at all if my silence would benefit Mr. Hughes," but that if he did speak he must say what he thought "the vital needs of this country at this time demand."[52] This would include putting the "hyphen" back into his addresses, beginning with an extemporaneous speech from the back platform of the train at Cedar Rapids, Iowa. Both Chicago speeches that followed continued in this vein, which led his former supporter George Sylvester Viereck to declare in his pro-German periodical *The Fatherland*, "If Mr. Hughes is defeated, he owes his defeat to the Colonel."[53]

In Chicago, Roosevelt focused on Wilson's scandalous handling of the navy. The Colonel reminded his audience that when he left office, after the Atlantic fleet's triumphant circumnavigation of the globe, there was "no other navy in the world at such a high point of efficiency and enthusiasm." In the final year of his presidency he had supported the plan of the navy's General Board to construct four super-dreadnought battleships each year, and if his recommendation had been followed there would now be no fear of attack by any Great Power. But as it fell out, only the last spring, "after three years of halting and folly," had Wilson "turned a characteristic somersault" under public pressure and declared himself for what TR had supported nine years before. The difference was that Wilson was "wise after the event and I before the event." Nine-tenths of wisdom was "being wise in time!"

Consequently, Roosevelt declared, on the president's shoulders rested "the entire responsibility for our lamentable failure" to prepare the navy—one of the "gravest offenses against the nation" committed by Wilson and the Democrats in control of Congress for the last six years. And during the last three years more harm had been done to the navy by the politicians in power than in the preceding thirty. Wilson and Navy Secretary Josephus Daniels now assumed the credit for passing the recent Naval Bills, but they never took "the slightest action upon them until forced to do so by the people." The "activity and energy" of the Navy Department under Wilson had been "primarily concentrated on schemes aimed at vote-getting or advertising," and the present administration took "no action whatever until, with the opening of the present political campaign, it became politically unsafe longer to delay."[54]

In the opinion of one of the newspapermen covering the campaign trip, Ned Lewis, who spoke frankly with the Colonel every day of the journey, TR realized full well that while the crowds were for him personally, and cheered whenever he showed his face, they were not in accord with the doctrine he preached. The Republicans in general were up against a hopeless situation. Roosevelt's plan for compulsory service and preparedness were not practical because they did not have widespread support. The crowds came to hear TR, but they were "too busy making money and planning how to make that money make some more" to receive the "deep-rooted appeal of Theodore Roosevelt to their Americanism."[55]

And TR could only do so much. The candidate he supported, Hughes, played it safe in his "lackadaisical and legalistic" addresses. Six years on the Supreme Court had tamed the platform ardor that had led to his being described as an "animated feather duster" in the 1908 New York governor's race. Crucially, when campaigning in California, Hughes managed to offend Progressive supporters of Governor Hiram Johnson, praising a political rival as "California's favorite son" and neglecting to meet with Johnson when the two were at the same hotel during his tour. This proved politically fatal.[56]

Seeing the light at the end of the campaign tunnel, an upbeat Roosevelt celebrated his fifty-eighth birthday on October 27 while passing through Indiana, where he made several more speeches. At South Bend, the Colonel told his audience that he was "flying back to New York" to "take off my coat" and make the closing speeches of the campaign. He vowed to go into the fight with "every ounce of strength I have to secure the election of Governor Hughes," even though it entailed "a tremendous sacrifice on my part and will be an actual menace to my health."[57] To a heckler who called out "Three cheers for Woodrow Wilson," Roosevelt reportedly replied, "Yes, cheer for him! Cheer for the murdered babies on the Lusitania!"[58] He arrived back at Oyster Bay on the October 29 for a few days of rest.

Roosevelt was back in New York on November 3 for his final major address before Election Day, which he described as "a new speech with kick in it," at Cooper Union.[59] He told his audience in the Great Hall that there could be "no greater misfortune for a free nation" than to find itself under "incapable leadership when confronted by a great crisis." This was "peculiarly the case" when the crisis was "not merely one in its own history" but was due to "some terrible world cataclysm" such as that which had at this moment "overwhelmed civilization." The times needed a Washington or a Lincoln, but unfortunately the country had been "granted only another Buchanan." Wilson's supporters argued that the nation should not change horses when crossing a stream, but Roosevelt reminded his audience that the United States had just entered the greatest crisis in its history "when we 'swapped horses' by exchanging Buchanan for Lincoln," and if the country had not made the exchange, "we would never have crossed the stream at all." The failure now, Roosevelt went on, to exchange "Mr. Wilson for Mr. Hughes would be almost as damaging."

Wilson, said the Colonel, had "adroitly and cleverly and with sinister ability" appealed to all that was "weakest and most unworthy in the American character." And many men and women who were "neither weak nor unworthy" had been misled by Wilson's "shadow dance of words" issued from the White House and his New Jersey home, Shadow Lawn. Near the end of the speech, TR made his most vivid campaign condemnation of Wilson:

> There should be shadows enough at Shadow Lawn; the shadows of men, women and children who have risen from the ooze of the ocean bottom and from graves in foreign lands; the shadows of the helpless whom Mr. Wilson did not dare to protect lest he might have to face danger; the shadows of babies gasping pitifully as they sank under the waves; the shadows of women outraged and slain by bandits; the shadows of Boyd and Adair and their troopers who lay in the Mexican desert, the black blood crusted round their mouths, and their dim eyes looking upward, because President Wilson had sent them to do a task, and had then shamefully abandoned them to the mercy of foes who knew no mercy. Those are the shadows proper for Shadow Lawn; the shadows of deeds that were never done; the shadows of lofty words that were followed by no action; the shadows of the tortured dead.

Roosevelt concluded with a warning that if the country elected Wilson, it would be "serving notice on the world that the traditions, the high moral standards, the courageous purposes of Washington and Lincoln have been obscured," and that in their stead, "we have deliberately elected to show ourselves for the time being a sordid, soft and spineless nation; content to accept any and every insult; content to pay no heed to the most flagrant wrongs done to the strong and weak; allowing our men, women and children to be murdered and outraged; anxious only to gather every dollar that we can; to spend it in luxury, and to replace it by any form of moneymaking we can follow with safety to our own bodies."

"We cannot for our own sakes," TR exhorted his audience, "we cannot for the sake of the world at large, afford to take such a position." In place of the man in the White House who had "brought such shame on our people, let us put in the Presidential chair, the clean and upright Justice of the Supreme Court, the fearless Governor of New York," whose whole public record had been that of a man "straightforward in his thought and courageous in his actions, who cannot be controlled to do what is wrong, and who will do what is right no matter what influences may be brought against him."[60]

The passage about Shadow Lawn in his last speech, Lodge wrote to TR, showed "eloquence in a very high degree" and was "imaginative and moving." He hoped the speech would "pass into the school books and be used for declamation in the days we shall not see." In fact he found all Roosevelt's speeches as reported in the newspapers "wonderfully strong and effective" and told his friend that they made "a record which the future historian will have to reckon with when it comes to Wilson."[61]

In the final days of the campaign, on November 3 and 4, several New York papers carried the following Democratic advertisement:

> You Are Working—*Not Fighting!*
> Alive and Happy;—*Not Cannon Fodder!*
> Wilson and Peace with Honor?
> or
> Hughes with Roosevelt and War?

> Roosevelt says we should hang our heads in shame because we are not at *war* with Germany in behalf of Belgium! Roosevelt says that following the sinking of the Lusitania he would have foregone diplomacy and seized every ship in our ports flying the German Flag. That would have meant *war!*
> Hughes says he and Roosevelt are in Complete Accord!
>
> . . .
>
> The Lesson is Plain;
> If You Want War, vote for Hughes!
> If You Want Peace with Honor
> Vote For Wilson![62]

In the initial tallying of the ballots after the November 7 election, for several days it appeared Hughes would triumph and the outcome would be a stunning defeat for Wilson, who seemed destined to join Grover Cleveland as the second Democratic president to win a popular majority but lose in the electoral college. After the *New York Times* and *New York World* declared victory for Hughes, Roosevelt joined the chorus, issuing a statement that he was "thankful as an American for the election of Mr. Hughes," which was a "vindication of our national honor." He added in answer to "some charges that had been made" that he would "not, under any circumstances," make any recommendations to Hughes about appointments or legislative policy.[63]

Wilson, realizing full well that Germany was poised to unleash its submarines at any time, hatched a plan to be implemented if he lost. Rather than have the president-elect wait the four months until his inauguration in March, he would appoint Hughes secretary of state, so that after Wilson and the vice president resigned, Hughes would become president immediately. But in the end the close electoral count turned on Ohio and then California, where Democratic newspaper revelations tying Hughes to the Old Guard Republican disdain of Hiram Johnson likely lost the few thousand votes that threw the state, and with it the presidency, to Wilson.[64] O. K. Davis commented that Roosevelt "fought as valiantly for Hughes as he could." Wilson alone he might have beaten, but it was "impossible to defeat the combination of Wilson and Hughes."[65]

In reality, and infuriatingly to TR, a more important factor was probably the antiwar feeling in the country, so well-captured by the Democratic slogan: "He Kept Us Out of War." The feeling about Wilson that "he kept us out of war," the Colonel told William Allen White, had not the "slightest particle of foundation in morality." The men or women who voted for him for that reason "did not in the least object" to going to war with Santo Domingo or Haiti and the killing or wounding of some "badly armed black men." They did not care that "some gallant fellows of our own were killed." All such people meant when they said Wilson "kept us out of war" was that he kept "their own worthless hides safe." This "plain, sheer and undiluted yellow fear of danger, and delight in the gross materialism of prosperity," along with "hatred of the Republican machine," had cost the Republicans the election.[66] Roosevelt's belligerent speeches also cancelled out at least some of his personal popularity and by association cost Hughes votes, particularly in the Midwest and West, much of which went for Wilson.[67]

A Democratic victory rally at Oyster Bay on the night of November 10 was transformed by the many "T. R. Democrats" in the crowd into a bipartisan affair. The five hundred participants marched by torchlight around Oyster Bay with a "Teddy Yes; Hughes No" banner and chanted "Teddy and Nineteen Twenty." The celebrants did not make the two-mile tramp out to Sagamore Hill, but Roosevelt could hear them in his library. When asked by the reporters on hand about the "Nineteen Twenty" sentiment, the Colonel only threw up his hands and would make no statement for publication. He also refused further comment on the election.[68]

This TR saved for a *Metropolitan* article in which he declared his keen disappointment that the nation had responded to the Democratic appeal to vote for Wilson in essence "because he had kept us out of war and we were prosperous." He went on that it would have been "highly creditable to the average man if he had possessed the vision and disinterestedness to disregard such an appeal." And the fact that "he did not disregard it" merely meant that the Republicans "were not able to make the issue clear to his eyes." It did not mean that "he would remain morally obtuse if he could be shown in convincing fashion that where his duty lay." Roosevelt concluded his article with a declaration that "we who supported Mr. Hughes will always be glad that we supported him. We believe that his triumph and the national welfare were closely interwoven. We now, for the sake of the nation, earnestly hope Mr. Wilson will meet with every success in the task that lies ahead of him."[69]

In private Roosevelt was less magnanimous. He wrote to his son Quentin that victory would have been a "certainty if Hughes had had it in him to make a straight-from-the-shoulder fighting campaign—which would have shown courage, disinterestedness, vision and intensity of conviction."[70] A letter to Benjamin Wheeler, one of his advisors in California, revealed TR's "utter disbelief in permanent good" coming from a victorious Democratic Party that had selected "an adroit, insincere hypocrite as its leader" and "disregards cowardice in that leader and in the nation, and applauds his breaches of faith and his mendacity as proofs of intellectual acumen."[71] He had supported Hughes, Roosevelt confessed to William Allen White, only because he felt that Wilson's reelection would damage the "moral fibre of the American people." He had grimly accepted, "at great personal cost, a man whose election would have been hailed as a great personal triumph over me by the standpatters." Hughes and the Republicans "tried to beat skimmed milk with cambric tea; they earned their defeat." The Colonel added that the other day five newspapermen had lunched at Sagamore Hill. Three had been on the Hughes train and all voted for Wilson. Two had been at Shadow Lawn with Wilson and voted for Hughes.[72]

Down the ballot, Roosevelt's efforts had not been completely in vain. In Maine a TR stalwart, Colonel Frederick Hale, took the Senate seat held by Charles F. Johnson, a strong Wilson supporter. From Montana another winner, Jeannette Rankin, the first woman ever elected to Congress, sent thanks for Roosevelt's endorsement. She felt sure that his "kind message had much to do with my election," and she felt "deeply grateful" for what he did.[73] Had he known that five months later Rankin would be one of the 57 members of Congress to vote against the war resolution, TR would certainly have not given her his blessing. And in 1918 she consequently would have to run for reelection as an independent.

Charles Gray Shaw, Professor of Philosophy at New York University, had predicted Hughes would lose because the Republican candidate used "poor psychology" in his campaign. The victor Wilson, on the other hand, represented the "new will" recently discovered by psychology. This was a will that turned "inward upon the brain instead of passing out through hand or tongue." To Roosevelt, Wilson seemed "weak and vacillating," but that was because he knew nothing of the new will. The Colonel had a "primitive mind, but one of the most advanced type." In the "T.R. brain," *will* meant "set teeth, clenched fist, hunting and rough riding." Shaw gave Roosevelt credit "for having raised the old will to the nth power" by means of the old Hindu philosophy of Hatha Yoga, of which, presumably, he was "ignorant." The Colonel was a good man of the old school who meant well and "paved the road to Oyster Bay with good intentions." Wilson, in Shaw's view, might be regarded as "either creating the new volition or as having discovered it." And it was significant to observe that the Germans, who were psychologists, recognized the "fact that a new and important function of the mind" had been focused on them. The Germans feared and respected the "Wilson will of note writing more than they would have dreaded the T. R. will with its teeth and fists."[74] If so, in the following months Germany did not reflect this fear in its actions toward the newly reelected president and his country.

CHAPTER 8

THE CURSE OF MEROZ

DECEMBER 1916 TO APRIL 1917

> When fear of the German submarines next moved Mr. Wilson to declare for "peace without victory" between the tortured Belgians and their cruel oppressors and taskmasters; when such fear next moved him to utter the shameful untruth that each side is fighting for the same things, and to declare for neutrality between wrong and right, let him think of the prophetess Deborah, who, when Sisera mightily oppressed the people of Israel with his chariots of iron, and when the people of Meroz stood neutral between the oppressed and the oppressors sang of them: "Curse ye Meroz, said the angel of the Lord, curse ye bitterly the inhabitants thereof; because they came not to the help of the Lord, to the help of the Lord against the mighty."
> —TR speech at Chicago, January 28, 1917

After six months spent in northern Mexico, John J. Pershing and the American forces under his command still had not caught Pancho Villa and had long since given up serious efforts to do so. On December 9, 1916, Villa issued a defiant proclamation condemning both the Venustiano Carranza government and Pershing. From El Paso, one of TR's journalist friends covering the crisis, W. R. Rucker, sent a letter about the situation. He assumed that Roosevelt had seen Villa's manifesto, which "we patriots sent out to the country last night." In it Villa followed the Colonel's lead, grouping the "barbarians of the north with the Chinese" and calling on "all good Mexicans and true to drive out Carranza and Pershing." It looked very much like a declaration of war; the "only trouble was" that Villa at the moment had "not the numbers nor equipment to carry out his declarations." Moving from Mexico to the recent election, Rucker jokingly asked TR to permit him "a Missouri subtlety—to congratulate you on the outcome of what happened around 7th November. Eh what? You know me. I'm a Tee-Arr-Ista from who laid the chunk." He only hoped the country remained "in one piece till four years hence."[1]

There had also been political developments in London, where a new government led by David Lloyd George was formed a month after the American election. This came in part as a consequence of the Battle of the Somme, which by its end in November 1916 had cost 400,000 British casualties with precious little to show in exchange. In the new regime, a five-man War Cabinet was instituted to run the effort in a more efficient manner. In a United Press article, "Fashioning the New England," Lord Northcliffe reviewed the progress of the war and roundly praised Lloyd George for his courage. On this occasion, the press lord broke his own rule about newspaper prophecy. To those who asserted that the new government and Lloyd George would not last, he declared, "I believe that he will be at the head of the Government that wins the war: that brings a settlement of the Irish question and maintains that essential factor goodwill between the people of the English speaking nations of the British Empire and the people of the United States."[2]

Whatever hopes of goodwill Northcliffe might have had for relations with America, the newly reelected Wilson administration watched the political upheaval in Britain with dismay. Democratic sentiment in Washington lay with the Liberalism of Herbert Henry Asquith and Sir Edward Grey, not Lloyd George, who after the "Knock-Out Blow" interview was dismissed as a reactionary.[3] The president's advisor Colonel Edward M. House had warned the president that if the Lloyd-George faction succeeded "in overthrowing the Government and getting control," England then would be under "a military dictatorship" and there would be "no chance for peace until they run their course."[4] Despite these words, he suggested to Woodrow Wilson that the House-Grey memorandum might now be revived, even though his friend Grey had been replaced as foreign secretary by Arthur Balfour. But Wilson, well aware of the pressure on the German government to unleash its upgraded and enlarged U-boat fleet, had other plans. With Anglo-American cooperation now more problematic, and bolstered by his election victory on the issue, Wilson meant to stand for peace, alone and independent of others. He told House that if the Germans responded favorably, he would work with them. And if the Allies resisted, he would attempt to force them.[5]

The Allies, confident of their prospects, rejected a disingenuous December 12 proposal from Germany to discuss a peace conference. Wilson responded by having Secretary of State Robert Lansing send identical notes to Britain and Germany asking them to state their war aims. This was intended to call attention to the fact that the "objects which the statesmen of the belligerents on both sides have in mind in this war" were "virtually the same as stated in general terms to their own people and to the world." Each side desired to "make the rights and privileges of weak people and small States as secure against aggression" as those of the "great and powerful states now at war."[6] Henry Cabot Lodge commented to TR that he had "no doubt" that it was by "prearrangement to help Germany" that Wilson jumped "out this morning with a torrent of fine words and empty phrases" at the "precise time when she holds allied territory & is growing weak internally." And the "worst of it was the American people—a majority of them like it & believe in him."[7]

Feeling was different across the Atlantic. From London, Ambassador Walter Hines Page warned Lansing that the British felt the struggle was "a holy and defensive war which must be fought to a decisive conclusion to save free government in the world," and that they were angry because the American note seemed to place the Allies and the Central Powers "on the same moral level." He went on that Northcliffe had assured him that his papers would continue to say "as little as possible," but that "the people are mad as hell."[8] This was illustrated in the music halls, where references to an unexploded shell as a "Wilson" drew big laughs.[9] In the House of Commons on December 19, in his first speech as prime minister, Lloyd George continued in knockout vein, announcing that his country was determined to "continue the war till we have made it certain that the Allies in common have achieved the success which must, and ought to be theirs."[10]

The Allied ambassadors in Washington were also incensed. Cal O'Laughlin reported to TR their indignation, not only at Wilson's "intervention, but at his assertion in the note he transmitted that their countries did not know what they were fighting for and that the object of both sides was identical." Jean Jules Jusserand exploded that it was "not for a stranger to say when a nation shall stop dying" and declared that France would "never forgive the United States and that the ground had been laid for an everlasting misunderstanding." Sir Cecil Spring Rice, O'Laughlin added, was "in practically the same frame of mind." He was also concerned about Spring Rice's position in Washington, as the ambassador had "a number of enemies in this country who have been urging his removal." Spring Rice's well-known friendship with TR and Lodge, his occasionally short temper, and his sharp tongue all had been problems for years. Like TR, O'Laughlin believed Spring Rice had done splendidly for both his country and the United States and realized that the "single spirit which should guide international relations" was that of "mutual accommodation." He asked Roosevelt to write to Foreign Secretary Balfour in support of the ambassador and hesitated to think what might happen if Spring Rice was replaced by "another man who might want to do the Bernstorff trick" and interfere in American domestic affairs.[11]

Newspaper accusations that the war aims note made the United States the de facto "agents and purveyors of a German peace" led Robert Lansing to call the press to the State Department, where he issued a denial of any collusion with Germany. The secretary of state, however, went on to muddy the waters by speaking of the "critical" nature of America's international position, by which he said he meant that "we are drawing nearer to the verge of war ourselves, and therefore we are entitled to know exactly what each belligerent seeks in order that we may regulate our conduct in future."[12] This confusing "clarification" only led to rumors that the country was on the brink of war and that the president wanted the war aims to decide which alliance to join. A furious Wilson ordered Lansing to issue an immediate explanation that he had been "radically misinterpreted" and that it was "not at all in your mind to intimate any change in the policy of neutrality" that the country had "so far so consistently pursued" in the face of "accumulating difficulties."[13] Lansing promptly did so while at the same time apologizing for the confusion and disavowing any looming crisis.

O'Laughlin confided to TR that, as far as he could learn in Washington, Wilson had "acted because of the knowledge conveyed to him that a huge new fleet of submarines would begin operations against commerce in the spring." He expected they would conduct a "ruthless warfare and that this will lead to war with Germany." Lansing had told the exact truth in his first statement the day before "but was forced to apologize for making it because the President was concerned about the effect on the stock market and abroad."[14] In the Senate, Republicans blocked a resolution of blanket support for Wilson's note, while in the House a similar resolution brought an "explosion in the Republican ranks" when Minority Leader James R. Mann defended Wilson's peace efforts and urged bipartisan support. Mann, who represented a largely German American Illinois district, was denounced as a "tool of the Kaiser" but survived as minority leader.[15]

In the end, Germany declined to state her war aims while suggesting that a conference of belligerents was the best way to end the war and that, afterwards, the imperial government would be pleased to cooperate with Wilson in preventing the outbreak of future wars. The Allies on the other hand formally replied with a list of aims, which included the restoration of Belgium, Serbia, and Montenegro; the evacuation of invaded territory in France, Russia, and Rumania; reparations for war damage; the reorganization of Europe in accordance with the rights of the nationalities in question; and the expulsion of Turkey from Europe. While he withheld public comment at first, Roosevelt wrote to his friend John St. Loe Strachey in London that he greatly admired the Allied reply to Wilson's "poisoned chalice" peace note. The president had been "playing an evil part by his action" and in TR's view was "trying now to bring about a peace as wicked as the peace which Prussia, France and a minority of English leaders tried to force on Lincoln." The Colonel believed that Germany was in the position of the Confederacy in the summer of 1863 and that if the Allies stood firm they would win.[16]

While this diplomatic drama played itself out, TR resumed an old Oyster Bay Christmas tradition by playing Santa Claus at the local Cove School. Roosevelt told the students to remember that "you are all of you little Americans, first, last and all the time, and nothing else." He went on to say, "I haven't got a bit of use for a bully, but on the other hand, I haven't got the least use for a 'softy.'" He told the children of his Christmas in Africa, where he dined on elephant he had bagged himself. Then he distributed gifts, including a flashlight (such as he had used in Africa to ensure there were no snakes in his tent), hatchets, knives, and garden utensils—"not a mollycoddle present among them."[17] Roosevelt saw in the New Year 1917 with Edith quietly at Sagamore Hill.

Several correspondents, American and British, urged Roosevelt to visit the war front in Europe. He told Arthur Lee, who early that year was assigned the essential but thankless task of overhauling British food production, that he would like to "visit the Front at the head of an American division of 12 regiments like my Rough Riders—but not otherwise."[18] John Wheeler of Wheeler Newspaper Features offered TR $2,500 a week plus expenses to go to Europe for the syndicate exclusively any time until the end of peace negotiations. "Outside the remuneration," claimed Wheeler, he was "very anxious to accomplish this" because he realized that "at this critical time in the world's history you would contribute something to contemporaneous history that no other living American can," and Wheeler would "like to have my humble share in helping to accomplish this." He went on that many writers had found dealing with a syndicate "far more satisfactory" than single newspapers and renewed a standing offer, if TR did not go to Europe when his present contract expired, of $25,000 a year for 26 articles.[19] At the same time others were attempting as well to capitalize on TR's name and image. Since Roosevelt had lodged previous complaints about a doll and "a wretched portrait" in 1900, the US Patent Office warned the Colonel of an application to patent a nutcracker with the likeness of his jaw, and asked if he objected.[20]

On January 3, 1917, Roosevelt broke his public silence on Wilson's war-aims note and Lansing's contradictory explanations of it. Since the note had been issued, the Colonel told a reporter for the *New York Times*, he had been "revolving in his mind the wisdom of another attack on the administration." But Wilson's note, in TR's view, took "positions so profoundly immoral and misleading that high-minded and right-thinking American citizens," whose country it placed in a "thoroughly false light," were "in honor bound to protest." It was "palpably" and "wickedly false" to say that "thus far both sides seem to be fighting for the same thing," and it brought into question Wilson's "judgment, his wisdom, and his courage." To say that the Germans, who had "trampled Belgium under heel" and were at the moment transporting 100,000 Belgians to serve as "state slaves in Germany," were fighting for the same things as their "hunted victims" was not only a "falsehood, but a callous and a most immoral falsehood, a thing shocking to every high-minded man who loves the peace of righteousness." Wilson further said that "at some unknown date in the hereafter" the American people intended to safeguard the rights of small nationalities against "big and ruthless nations." Unless this was "sheer hypocrisy," the Colonel called on the president to "begin now" and "promptly withdraw" this note, which had given "comfort and aid only to the oppressors of Belgium" and in which he had "not dared to say one word in behalf of the rights of Belgium."

The defenders of the administration, TR declared, were "still actively discussing whether the President's recent manifesto was a peace note or a war note," since the secretary of state had interpreted it "in two precisely opposing directions within six hours." To be sure, he went on, this represented "a rather longer interval than usual between the changes of mind of the administration," but in the present instance, there seemed to have been "more design than usual in the change of mind." And while "neither the

dream nor the two interpretations thereof" had the slightest effect in securing peace in Europe, they had an "extraordinary effect on the stock market
in New York." To judge from what Roosevelt had read, the "net effect, and
the only net effect of this supposed action for peace was to ruin an immense
number of small investors who were not forewarned for the benefit of a very
few persons, who, if they did not know of these events prior to their publication for the information of the public, then certainly showed that on this
occasion they were inspired by prophetic insight concerning the handling
of our foreign affairs." The allegations made since then had prompted him
to demand a thorough investigation of the charge that Wall Street profited
through a previous "leak" of Wilson and Lansing's statements. In this he
planned to back to the fullest demands for an investigation by congressmen
W. R. Wood of Indiana, Augustus P. Gardner of Massachusetts, and other
Republicans. He also planned to support Senator Lodge's fight in the Senate
against an endorsement of the peace note and the League for the Enforcement of Peace.[21]

The Colonel assailed the league in a *Metropolitan* article as the unwitting
agent of Germany, a country eager to end the war "so long as it can be ended
to her advantage." And to this end it seemed likely she would "encourage
and praise her dupes on this side of the water in the movement for a league
to enforce peace." The leaders of the league, still presided over by William
Howard Taft, were "following in the footsteps of (and in many cases were
identical with) various pacifist agitators" who, in the last quarter of a century,
had "so deeply discredited the whole peace movement." TR admitted there
were "honorable and upright" men who had taken part in the league movement, but they had been misled and because of a "failure to know the facts"
seemed to regard the league as "promising something of worth." These men,
he believed, "should have the facts put before them."

Roosevelt opposed the proposals of the league because under existing
conditions, "and in view of the past performance of most of the leaders
of the movement, and especially in view of the action of our Government
and people during the last two and half years, the agitation or adoption of
the proposals would be either futile or mischievous." In view of "our utter
national unpreparedness, and of our utter recklessness in making promises
which cannot be, or ought not to be kept, and our utter failure to keep
promises we have made which ought to be kept, the movement can do no
possible good" and might, "if adopted by our Government, do very serious
harm."[22] Agitation for such a league was in the Colonel's opinion "infamous
and immoral in general" and on the part of Wilson constituted a "mean and
odious hypocrisy."[23]

The League to Enforce Peace responded with a statement issued from
its New York Fifth Avenue headquarters, which asserted that it was a "militant and not a pacifist organization." Further, since TR's secretary of war,
Taft, was president of the league and the present secretary of war, Newton
Baker, was also a member, it did not seem "instantly apparent" that league
was made up of "apostles of feeble folly with piping voices" as the Colonel

claimed in his article. The league believed, with President Wilson, that there would be no neutrals in the next war and that it was up to the people of the country to decide "right now" whether they were to "prepare for national self-preservation in the future, not merely by increased armament and military training, but also by such diplomatic arrangements as may be feasible."[24]

That January, a week apart, TR learned of the deaths of his friends Sir Frederick Selous and "Buffalo Bill" Cody: the first in combat, the second of kidney disease. Roosevelt accepted an invitation to become vice president of the Colonel William F. Cody Memorial Association, which proposed to erect a monument near Denver. In accepting, TR described Cody as "the most renowned of those men, steel-thewed and iron nerved, whose daring opened the West to civilization."[25] Selous, meanwhile, had been the greatest of the all the African Big Game hunters and had closely advised the Colonel on his 1909 safari and accompanied him on its first leg.[26] He had enlisted in 1914 at age 63 and been killed in East Africa fighting with the British Legion of Frontiersman against the sole diehard detachment of Germany's imperial forces still in the field, and so he had gained a heroic death envied by the old Rough Rider. According to the brief press accounts, he had been mortally wounded but continued to urge his men forward until he was shot a second time and killed.[27]

In the obituary he wrote for the *Outlook*, TR noted that the British War Office had at first refused to use Selous though he was "hardy as an old wolf" and "much stronger and more enduring than the average man half his age." Finally, displaying the "wooden dullness" that reminded Roosevelt only too well of the bureaucracy in Washington, the British had sent him out with the transport service. However, Selous "speedily pushed his way into the fighting line" and accounted himself so well that the home authorities "grudgingly accepted the accomplished fact" and made him a lieutenant. By the time Selous was killed, he had gained a captaincy and the Distinguished Service Order. In TR's opinion, his friend had "closed his life exactly as such a life ought to be closed, by dying in battle for his country while rendering her valiant and effective service." Who could wish a "better life or a better death, or desire to leave a more honorable heritage to his family and his nation?"[28]

Dying a glorious death in battle was a world away, literally and figuratively, from the contrary vision put forward by Woodrow Wilson on January 22, 1917, when he delivered to the Senate his famous "Peace Without Victory" address, borrowing a phrase coined in the *New Republic* a month before.[29] This appeal to the peoples of the world over the heads of their governments called for a negotiated end to the war in Europe, freedom of the seas as the "*sine qua non* of peace equality and cooperation," limitations of armies and arms, and the creation of a postwar league for peace. A secure settlement, said Wilson, must be one without victory—a peace between equals. Victory would mean a "peace forced upon a loser, a victor's terms imposed upon the vanquished." It would be "accepted in humiliation under duress" and such terms of peace would rest "only as on quicksand."[30]

Roosevelt's response was pointed and immediate. As for Wilson's statement that there could be "no real peace with victory," he told reporters at Oyster Bay that, so far as Belgium was concerned, it stood "on a par with a similar statement, had there been such, after Bunker Hill and Lexington, that there could be no real peace if victory came to the forces of General Washington." If the men of Bunker Hill were right, then the Belgians had been "right, and to say that the victory of the oppressed people struggling for freedom" was incompatible with peace deserved "no more consideration in one case than in the other." Regarding freedom of the seas, the Colonel declared that the most important element in it was "freedom from murder," and until the Wilson administration had taken an effective stand to prevent the "murder of its citizens on the high seas," it made itself "an object of derision for the freedom of the seas." Interfering with life was worse than interfering with property.

Before the United States asked for the limitation of armies, TR went on, the country would "do well to remember" that so long as "we keep ourselves nearly on a level of military strength with China, our words will not carry much weight." And further, the country would not command respect as long as its government sought to "conceal the pitiful ignominy and the pitiful shirking of duty toward itself and toward others, so evident in its conduct in recent years by making grandiloquent promises" that there was "nothing in its past record to indicate that it would seriously attempt to keep." As far as Wilson's nonspecific call for an international league, Roosevelt referred the reporters to his 1910 Nobel Prize speech at Christiana and to his book *America and the War* published two years before.[31]

On January 28, TR renewed his attack on Wilson, telling the press at Oyster Bay that by calling for "peace without victory," the president was asking the "world to accept a Copperhead peace of dishonor, a peace without victory for the right, a peace designed to let wrong triumph, a peace championed in neutral countries by the apostles of timidity and greed." When fear of the German submarines next moved "Mr. Wilson to declare for 'peace without victory' between the tortured Belgians and their cruel oppressors and taskmasters," when such fear next moved him to "utter the shameful untruth that each side is fighting for the same things, and to declare for neutrality between wrong and right," Roosevelt went on, "let him think of the prophetess Deborah, who, when Sisera mightily oppressed the people of Israel with his chariots of iron, and when the people of Meroz stood neutral between the oppressed and the oppressors sang of them: 'Curse ye Meroz, said the angel of the Lord, curse ye bitterly the inhabitants thereof; because they came not to the help of the Lord, to the help of the Lord against the mighty.'" Wilson had brought the biblical "Curse of Meroz" on America because he had not "dared to stand on the side of the Lord against the wrongdoings of the mighty."[32]

At least one of TR's political allies and friends cautioned him about going too far in his rhetoric and worried about the quality of his advisors. Congressman Medill McCormick wrote that he believed the Republicans would need all his "wisdom and reserve strength" to defeat Wilson. This was the time for "argument and not for adjectives," and Roosevelt's "utterances should not be prompted only by chivalric or quixotic emotion." He should "not be guided by generous or unselfish indignation, but by your considered judgment." McCormick thought that TR saw too many men "whose candor and patriotism exceed their discretion and not enough politicians in the best sense of the word." This opinion reflected that of many of their other mutual friends. McCormick added in pen at the end of this letter, "If the suggestions I offer seem to be impudent—I would have you remember the obligation of friendship and affection which I have so many reasons to bear—no less than the long years I have followed your leadership—& so excuse me."[33]

As it fell out, however, Roosevelt's utterances were made to seem less extreme by the German note handed to the stunned administration by Ambassador Count Johann von Bernstorff on January 31, 1917, which declared that from the next day an unrestricted submarine war zone around Britain would be in effect. The *New York Evening Post* commented that a "Malay pirate could not have made the announcement more brutally."[34] America's full-fledged entrance into the war now seemed certain, but Germany calculated that the already weakened British and French could be brought to their knees by the U-boat assault before the unprepared United States could make a significant impact. In fact, had the Germans not made this fatal blunder, the Wilson administration would have unleashed a weapon of its own against the Allies, using the Federal Reserve Board to restrict their credit, which might well have forced Britain and France, near the end of their financial tether by this time, to the negotiating table. But miraculously for them, the precipitant German action forestalled this. One British treasury official, fully cognizant of the situation, commented that the German government had "as usual been more stupid than ourselves in our dealings with the United States."[35]

Roosevelt had planned a trip with Edith to Jamaica, but he wrote again to Newton Baker on February 2 that, given the new situation, he did not want to leave the country if there would be a call for volunteers. Once again the Colonel put his prospective division at the service of the country and asked Baker to notify him if the war secretary believed there would be a need. Baker replied the next day, "No situation has arisen which would justify my suggesting a postponement of the trip you propose," and he said he would put his letter on file for further "consideration should occasion arise."[36] That day, February 3, Wilson again went before Congress, this time to announce that the United States had broken diplomatic relations with Germany, but— incredibly, given their record in the war—the president still could not believe the Germans intended to carry out their threat. Only "overt acts on their part," he declared, could "make me believe it even now."[37] Roosevelt, on the other hand, had no doubt about Germany's intentions and cancelled his trip. That day, in his view with war now imminent, he pledged "hearty support" to the president, offering his own life and the life of his sons to the effort "in case hostilities could not be averted." The plans under way since the sinking of the *Lusitania* for a volunteer division commanded by the Colonel now "jumped to the fore."[38]

On February 7, Roosevelt again wrote Baker, this time asking for the War Department's permission to go forward in raising his force. The papers also revealed that TR had had a long conference with Henry Stimson concerning the prospective division, for which the former war secretary would be commissary general. Baker replied to the Colonel's "patriotic suggestion that in due time you be authorized to raise a division of troops for service abroad," though Congressional approval would be needed before he took any concrete action. Should the "contingency" that TR had in mind take place, it was expected that Congress would complete its legislation and provide, "under its own conditions, for the appointment of officers for the higher commands."[39]

A frustrated Roosevelt confided to Lodge that he did not believe Wilson would go to war unless Germany "literally kicks him into it." He could not criticize the government until the issue was decided, for if Wilson gave him a division and sent him to war he had vowed to "serve him with single-minded loyalty."[40] In the same vein, TR wrote to William Allen White that "with the dreadful creatures we have at Washington" he would have his "hands full getting to the front." He did not intend to die, "if it could be legitimately avoided," but he believed at this point the most good he could do the country would be by "dying in a reasonably honorable fashion, at the head of my division in the European War."[41]

Foiled by the Wilson administration in his attempt to get into the fight, Roosevelt turned to his friends Spring Rice and Jusserand, offering his services and a volunteer division of 20,000 men to fight with the British or French forces if the United States entered the war but did not send an expeditionary force or did not allow him to join it. TR confided to the French ambassador that if the United States entered the war he would be "profoundly unhappy unless I got into the fighting line." He believed that in six months he could get a division ready to for the trenches. He did not want to be a nuisance, but he thought it would be "worth their while" for the British or French "to have an ex-President with his division in the trenches." He vowed not to be "a political general" and that he would "expect no favors of any kind, except the great favor of being sent to the front." He asked Jusserand, as he did Spring Rice, to "inquire confidentially of your Government" whether they would care to call on him and whether he should raise his troops in Canada and take them over for final training in France, or whether it would be better that he should be under an English or French general.[42]

At least one of TR's preparedness allies had the courage to challenge the wisdom of his burning desire to fight and die overseas. The agrarian activist Henry Wise Wood was "greatly disturbed" by the announcement that the Colonel might go. In Wood's opinion there was "only one man, yourself, in whose hands this country will be safe in the event of a serious war." By leaving at "such an hour, with its fortunes in the hands of so weak a government," TR would, he believed, "be giving a wholly wrong expression to your patriotism." What was needed at home was a "great, strong, statesman," about whom all the opposition forces could gather, in order that they might be effective in "imposing on the government a vigorous, a masculine prosecution of the war." Roosevelt alone, in Wood's estimation, could "perform this indispensable service." If TR departed, the country would be "left wholly in the hands of a pacifistic government, afraid lest its blows be too hard to assure an early peace." He suggested that instead the Colonel "organize at once a Committee of National Safety, to be made up of the strongest men to be found who are opposed to the administration." Wood had sent such a plan to Roosevelt the previous December. The United States government, he went on, was "at sea about many important matters" and required the "help of just such a body" as TR could "create to bring all of our industries and people efficiently behind it."[43]

On February 17, Roosevelt, accompanied by Edith, observed army exercises at Governor's Island with General Leonard Wood. TR told the reporters on hand that he had seen outmoded airplanes and "rookies drill with broomsticks." He admired their "wonderful patriotism, but was filled with wonder and shame that such a great people like ours should be in such a state of unpreparedness." His final remark was that he wished "Congressman Mann would come here and see these men drill. He might get a few ideas on elementary patriotism."[44] During this visit Wood complained to the Colonel that there had not been "one particle of effective preparation" in the two weeks since relations had been broken with Germany.

"Heaven only knows," TR wrote to Hiram Johnson, whether the country would go to war, and "certainly Mr. Wilson doesn't." The Colonel did not believe Wilson "capable of understanding the emotion of patriotism, or the emotion of real pride in one's country." He had no shame, and "if anyone kicks him, he brushes his clothes and utters some lofty sentence." By his "side-stepping trickery, timidity and shuffling," the president had created the pacifist party and furnished it ready-made to men like progressive Wisconsin Senator Robert La Follette and Representative Claude Kitchin, who opposed any war measures. Wilson, "having himself called it into being, whines for sympathy and support because it is in being" and offers it as an excuse for "his not taking fearless and honorable action in international matters." Meanwhile, Taft, Charles Evans Hughes, Elihu Root, and the rest had joined the howl that everyone must "stand by the President, thus signing blank checks for him," instead of doing what they ought, which was to say that they would stand by him "to the limit" as long as he stood for the "honor and the vital interests of the United States." Roosevelt told Johnson that if Wilson "would give me a free hand and send me to the front," he would "support him as loyally as any man possibly could." This would follow the examples of the Civil War commanders David Farragut and George Thomas, who were "not in sympathy with the party in power."[45]

On February 26 Wilson asked Congress to authorize the arming of merchant vessels, a measure seen by the antiwar party as a point of no return and fought tooth and nail by a group of 11 senators including a filibustering

Robert La Follette of Wisconsin. Wilson famously described them as a "little group of willful men, representing no opinion but their own," who had "rendered the great government of the United States helpless and contemptible."[46] Even though Roosevelt considered the Armed Ships Bill in question almost worthless and representing "nothing but timid war," he nevertheless declared the senators opposed to it guilty of treason. But, he told Cal O'Laughlin, Wilson was "a thousand times more to blame, than all the senators combined." They did badly, but it was only because of all the shameful things Wilson had "done, and the good things he has shamefully left undone, during the past four years." The 11 had reached a lower depth than the president, but only by a little, because he was so far down there wasn't "much room to get lower."[47]

The battle in Congress was overshadowed at the end of February when Wilson released to the press the Zimmermann telegram. In this shocking document, German Foreign Secretary Arthur Zimmerman offered Mexico an alliance against the United States if America came into the war on the side of the Allies and suggested Japan also be asked to join. In return Mexico was promised the territory along the border lost in the previous century, from Texas to California. After the British turned the decoded cable over to the administration, Wilson's response when Lansing read it to him was, "Good Lord! Good Lord! Good Lord!" This added revelation of German perfidy electrified large parts of the country that had heretofore seen the war as a distant thing and set off a national firestorm of anti-German protest. Even the *New York World* now declared that Germany had been "making war upon the United States for more than two years." It had not been an "open and honorable war but a sneaking and despicable war." Some, including William Randolph Hearst, at first dismissed the telegram as a forgery, but incredibly, when asked, Zimmermann freely admitted sending the message.[48] Roosevelt wrote to Kermit, who returned to New York as the war clouds gathered, that now "even the lily-livered skunk in the White House *may* not be able to prevent Germany from kicking us into war."[49]

Both the shadow of war and terrible weather put dampers on Wilson's subdued public inauguration. That day, March 5, 1917, Myron Herrick wrote from Cleveland to TR that "many, many thousands of Americans will be thinking of you when they have read what they can read of the president's address." In the opinion of the former ambassador to France, it was "the poorest inaugural address ever delivered," especially to have it come "at this supreme moment, when all ears were attuned to hear the first words of patriotism and inspiration." Four years was a long time to wait. Everyone was ready to "stand by the president" if they could only find "where he was standing." Herrick now feared the next four years would be "disintegrating ones." The American people were all right, but, asked Herrick, "where do they turn for their leadership?" This was a moment when America needed "inspiring words from a leader such as you have never failed to be."[50]

The *Baltimore Sun* agreed with Herrick to a degree about the inaugural speech, commenting that there were "few occasions when the Roosevelt style is preferable to the Wilson style," but this was one of them. "An anonymous female admirer of Roosevelt" took issue with this in a letter to the editor, declaring that there were no occasions when Wilson's style was preferable, "unless perhaps a funeral." The president's style was "admirably adapted to the funeral oration"; she only hoped that "he will not be called on over the dead body of our national honor." In the writer's opinion, courage was "the greatest virtue in a man." And this "Mr. Roosevelt had in fullest measure." He was not afraid of "lions, Kaisers or newspapers," he spoke his mind freely, and he was "always willing to stand by the results of his words." If he had said "strict accountability," he would have meant it.[51]

Despite the imminent threat of war, Wilson allowed the session of Congress to expire, an action that infuriated Roosevelt. He wrote Lodge that he was not "overpleased" with Congress, but to leave Wilson alone in the face of a foreign crisis was "like leaving Pierce or Buchanan or Tyler alone in the presence of secession." If the session continued at least there would be "some brave and honorable men to point out the nation's duty." The "chatter" about "standing behind the President" when Wilson was "nervously backing away from his duty," TR found "sickening." He could say nothing publicly because of his continued hopes for a fighting division, but he hoped Root would speak up. Wilson's blaming Congress for the present situation was "idiotic." The president alone was culpable. In Roosevelt's view, Wilson was "so purely a demagogue" that if the people were "really aroused and resolute—as they were in '98—he would give them leadership in the direction they demanded," even though to do so "stirred with fear his cold and timid heart." But Wilson's "extreme adroitness" in appealing to all that was "basest in the hearts of our people" had made him able for the time being "to drug the soul of the nation into a coma." Wilson was responsible for Germany's "brutal wrong doing to us" and for the existence of the "very peace party" that he brought forward "as an excuse when told he ought to act boldly."[52]

Outside of Congress, William Jennings Bryan and his allies continued to fight for peace. At an emergency peace meeting in Washington, Bryan called for "prompt and concerted action" by the American people in a "peace at any price movement" to prevent war with Germany. The "Great Commoner" also demanded a national referendum on the decision for war and urged the convening of an official conference of neutrals.[53] Roosevelt turned down another challenge to debate Bryan and released a letter to the press in which he commented that he regarded it as a "waste of time to debate nondebateable subjects." To debate with the former secretary of state "his views against national preparedness would," in the Colonel's judgment, "be precisely on par with debating the undesirability of monogamous marriage, or the morality of abolishing patriotism, or the advantage of the re-introduction of slavery, or the right of judges to accept bribes from suitors"—or lastly, "the propriety of actions such as that of Benedict Arnold."[54]

The *New York Times* commented that TR's letter abounded in the "humor, the marrowy vigor, sound sense, the Americanism" that made "even those who have to quarrel with occasional errors or excesses of that diversified and compound genius admire him more than ever." Bryan, the editorial continued, "fled from Washington the other day, bowing before the storm, conscious that his doctrinarism was not welcome among men facing pitiless facts." His part, however well intentioned, in the disgrace of the Senate and the dishonor of the nation, the paper left to history. But it did not doubt that Bryan's own "sleek conscience would acquit him." Since he had preached peace so long on the Chautauqua circuit, "much of whatever of deafness to national need and supine reliance upon improvised national defense" had "crept into the Middle West" was due "in large measure to him." It was therefore just for Roosevelt to remind Bryan that professional pacifism was not a high ideal but "profoundly immoral." Judged by its fruit, in America it had been "the timid apologist and potent ally of the ruthless brutality of German militarism."[55]

On March 11, Roosevelt attended a New York dinner given by the Republican financier Cornelius N. Bliss Jr., which included prominent men from New York, New Jersey, and Connecticut such as J. P. Morgan Jr., Elihu Root, Mayor John Purroy Mitchel, General Wood, and Franklin D. Roosevelt. At this affair the men discussed preparedness and area defense in case war broke out, including such topics as safeguarding the Port of New York and the eastern seacoast. TR released a statement that the dinner had "absolutely no political significance" and the concern of all those present was to do anything they could to stand by the administration, provided it would "fearlessly and without equivocation stand by the honor of the American flag and safeguard the life of every American citizen on land or sea."[56] Nevertheless, he reported to Lodge that when Root took up the "stand by the President" call, the senator would have enjoyed watching him "stand Root on his head"—so much so that Root "promptly reversed himself."[57] Lodge was in the middle of the Senate fight over the Armed Ship Bill and passed along the inside story.[58] In Roosevelt's opinion, Wilson was more to blame than the "wilful [sic]" senators. He told Lodge that he was "as yet holding in," but if Wilson did not go to war with Germany, TR vowed to "skin him alive."[59] On March 12, Wilson ordered the arming of US merchantmen using a century-old antipiracy statute.

Meanwhile, in Russia Nicholas II abdicated and a provisional government was established, removing the objection some in the United States had offered to fighting alongside the autocratic Czarist regime. Roosevelt declared in the *Metropolitan*, "Now, at last, we can say that this war is everywhere a war not only for right against wrong, for civilization against military barbarism, but for democracy against absolutism."[60] Some optimists hoped this first, liberal Russian revolution of 1917 might bring a new efficiency, as had happened in 1790s France, but such dreams of an improved war effort were soon dashed by the reality that military and industrial conditions grew worse, not better. The amounts of munitions and other supplies sent to the eastern front never satisfied Russian demands, and the eastern ally refused to coordinate major military support for a proposed grand offensive in the west planned for 1917 under the leadership of the French army's commander Robert Nivelle, a hero of Verdun who promised the war-weary politicians that he had "the formula for victory."[61]

On the morning of March 19, TR received the news that German submarines had served up three "overt acts" in the previous days by sinking American merchantmen with loss of lives. He again, temporarily at least, postponed his departure for Florida. The news, he declared in a statement from Oyster Bay, made it "imperative that every self-respecting American should speak out and demand that we hit hard and effectively in return." Words were wasted on Germany. What was needed was "effective and thorough-going action." Seven weeks had passed, said Roosevelt, since Germany had notified the United States of her intention to renew "her never wholly abandoned submarine war against neutrals and noncombatants." This notification was in itself a declaration of war and should have been treated as such. And since then Germany had waged a "war of murder upon us; she has killed American women and children as well as American men," sunk American ships, blockaded American ports, and "asked Mexico and Japan to join with her in dismembering this country." If these were not overt acts of war, then Lexington and Bunker Hill were not overt acts of war. Under such conditions, any American citizen who was now a pro-German was a "traitor to this country; as much a traitor as any Tory who upheld the British cause against Washington." And as for the pacifists, they were "on a level with the copperheads who in 1864 denounced and assailed Lincoln."[62]

The same day, in view of the fact that Germany was now at war with the United States, Roosevelt sent yet another telegram to Newton Baker asking for permission to raise a division to be sent to France for intensive training after six weeks preliminary drill in America. He asked no favor of any kind "except that the division be put in the fighting line at the earliest possible moment." He also asked for the department to allow the division to assemble at Fort Sill, Oklahoma. And if the government would furnish arms and supplies, as it did for the Plattsburg camps, he would raise the money to prepare the division until Congress could act, thereby giving a month's head start in making ready. He asked that Captain George Moseley be detailed to him as chief of staff and for Lieutenant Colonel Henry Allen, Major Robert Howze, and Major James Harbord as brigade commanders.[63] Baker again replied that no additional armies could be raised without the "specific authority of Congress," which by the Act of February 27, 1906, had also "prohibited any Executive Department" to involve the government "in any contract or other obligation for the future payment of moneys in excess of appropriations" unless authorized by law. He went on that a plan for a "very much larger army than the force suggested in your telegram" had been prepared "for the action of Congress whenever required." Militia officers of high rank would "naturally be incorporated with their commands," but the "general officers for all volunteer forces" were to be drawn from the regular army.[64]

Roosevelt in turn told Baker that he understood that a "far larger force than a division" would be called out. He merely "wished to be permitted to get ready a division for immediate use in the first expeditionary force sent over." In reference to Baker's final comment about officers, TR respect-fully pointed out that, besides his field experience in Cuba, he was a retired commander-in-chief of the United States Army and therefore eligible for any position in command of American troops to which he might be appointed. For his fitness to command troops, he referred Baker to his three immediate superiors in the field, Lieutenant General S. B. M. Young, Major General Samuel Sumner, and Major General Leonard Wood.[65] The "patriotic spirit" of Roosevelt's suggestion, Baker responded, was "cordially appreciated" and the "military record to which you call my attention" was, of course, part of the permanent records of the department and "available in detail for consid-eration."[66] The war secretary also passed along TR's letter to Wilson, who responded that it was "one of the most extraordinary documents" he had ever read and thanked Baker for "letting me undergo the discipline of temper involved in reading it in silence!"[67]

An increasingly frustrated Roosevelt sent his correspondence with Baker to Lodge, asking him to bring up the matter with his friends in the Senate and, when legislation was passed, if they could "try to have it made proper to employ an ex-President—a retired Commander in Chief—in such fashion?" In case this did not work, he told Lodge that he had renewed his offer to Jusserand to fight under the American flag with the French and also held in reserve the possibility of raising an American division similarly to fight with the Canadians, as he understood they needed men. Since he had done all the preliminary work he could on the division, and there was nothing he could do further until Congress gathered, TR told his friend he was going for a ten-day trip to Florida (rather than the month originally planned) for devil fish and would be back when Congress was set to meet.[68] Before he left for the fishing grounds, Roosevelt attended one last war meeting at the Union League Club in New York, which included Root, Hughes, and the Repub-lican lawyer and preparedness activist Joseph Choate. Afterwards, a group gathered in the grill room and the Colonel held forth about his proposed division, appealing to all for help obtaining Wilson's permission to go to Europe. He declared dramatically that if he went he did not expect to return but hoped he would be buried in the soil of France. With mock solemnity, Root asked TR to repeat that statement, which he did with even greater vehemence. "Theodore," Root then replied, "if you can convince Wilson of that I am sure he will give you a commission."[69]

The same day Woodrow Wilson's cabinet urged him to declare war, March 24, Roosevelt arrived at Jacksonville, Florida. Before going on to the fish-ing grounds at Fort Myer, and to the strains of a band playing "Dixie," TR announced that "he would like to hear that tune against von Hindenburg's line in France." He also told the crowd he could have a division of American soldiers in the trenches in France within four or five months, that the United States should carry the war to Germany, and he again pleaded for universal service.[70] Meanwhile, at a New York mass meeting celebrating the Russian Revolution, the chairman expressed the regret of all present that TR was not there. He wished the Colonel had stayed, for there were "plenty of devil fish for him to harpoon in New York City in German spies, Austrian plotters, and mad pacifists without number." Though he was absent, Roosevelt sent a message to the gathering that declared, "I rejoice from my soul that Russia, the hereditary friend of this country, has ranged herself on the side of orderly liberty, of enlightened freedom, and for the full performance of duty by free nations throughout the world."[71]

From a thirty-foot launch in the waters off of Punta Gorda, Florida, Roosevelt took two devil fish, the larger of which was 16 feet long. His host, Russell Coles, told reporters that he and TR had come upon the largest school of the manta rays that Coles had ever seen. After the Colonel harpooned the largest of the group, the fish put up a 26-minute fight, towing the boat two miles. At the end, the giant ray threw itself against the vessel with enough force to lift both out of the water. Roosevelt then finished it with a spade lance.[72] Before leaving Florida, a tanned TR gave brief speeches on April 1 to one thousand at Punta Gorda and to three thousand at Lakeland. At the first, he told the crowd at the train station that there were "only two classes in this country now": Americans and anti-Americans. He did not care "what a man's religion or politics" was if he knew he was a "red-blooded American." The fact that the Germans had "proposed to dismember us" and made war on defenseless men and women made it "a more despicable war, and one to which we must rise the more quickly." The country had to handle this situation now and to do it right had to send an army to France. TR's final comment, that if the government accepted his offer of a division he wanted some "Florida crackers in it" like those he had been associating with for the past week, drew wild cheering from the crowd. When his train stopped at Lakeland, the Colonel told those gathered that he had formulated no plan as to his line of action when he reached the capitol, but he went on, "You know my position and I'll be governed by circumstances in what I do on behalf of what I believe is necessary for this country."[73]

In Washington, with war clearly now on the horizon, the question of what to do about Roosevelt's volunteer division continued to trouble the president and his advisors. House confided to Wilson that a "leading republican" told him that TR had 54,000 men pledged. He doubted this number but believed a great many were willing to go with him. The same man had suggested the United States send three regiments of regulars to France as soon as war was declared, "thus taking the wind out of Roosevelt's sails." House doubted that TR would go with a "second contingent after the first had received all the notoriety and enthusiastic reception from the French." He had also been told that the French would rather have the three regiments at once rather than a division with Roosevelt later and in fact did not desire "any considerable force at this time."[74]

By this time, the Council of National Defense, an advisory body created the year before, had recommended to the cabinet the enactment of selective service, which meant that volunteerism, and—most significantly in the opinion of some—Roosevelt's services, could be avoided.[75] Two days after he had sent TR's last letter to Wilson, Baker informed the president that the army would be "raised and maintained exclusively by selective draft."[76] This was in line with both the realities of modern warfare and the desires of the professional soldiers not to have amateurs and politics intrude into their sphere. Further, had the Colonel been allowed to raise his force, it would have stripped the regular army of many of its best officers and men, who were sorely needed as the core of the new mass army planned at first to be one million strong.

The previous year's National Defense Act and Naval Construction Acts had been merely long-range authorizations yet to be realized. The army remained by European standards pitifully undermanned and underequipped, with no tanks or gas masks, less than 2,000 mostly obsolete machine guns, not even a thousand pieces of artillery, and no air arm at all by the latest standards. The navy was in somewhat better shape but had no practical experience in the antisubmarine warfare that would be its first and most important task. In February, German submarines sank 536,000 tons of Allied shipping and in March 603,000 tons more. This two-to-one ratio of sinkings to launchings decreased dramatically the shipping available to send over American aid, and troops, when she joined the fight.

On April 3, en route to Oyster Bay from Florida, the Colonel stopped at Washington to offer his congratulations to Woodrow Wilson, who had the day before asked Congress for a declaration of war against Germany.[77] When the president, meeting with the cabinet, was unable to see him, TR left a card. Wilson's war message proclaimed the purity of American motives and most famously that "the world must be made safe for democracy." The president was careful to designate the country as an "Associated power," not an Ally, of Britain, France, Italy, and Russia. Though Roosevelt disagreed on these matters, there was much in the president's speech behind which he could rally, such as Wilson's declarations that "the right is more precious than the peace" and the warning that, though most German Americans were "true and loyal Americans," disloyalty would be dealt with "with a firm hand of stern repression."[78] Edward Grey, who had accepted a peerage and taken a seat in the House of Lords as Viscount Grey of Fallodon, cabled Roosevelt, "President's noble message has swept all clouds from our sky causing us to rejoice forever hereafter that all English Speaking people walk hand in hand as joint protectors rights of mankind we are all grateful to you for your part in bringing this all about."[79]

Three days later the United States officially entered the conflict against Germany. TR wrote to Arthur Lee that he feared it was "too late for us to do very efficient work, but thank God we are in and able to look men in the eyes without flinching."[80] For public consumption, Roosevelt released a statement at Washington that Wilson's war message was a "great State paper which will rank in history among the great State papers of which Americans in future years will be proud." It now rested with the people of America to see that "we put in practice the policy" the president had outlined, and that "we strike as hard, as soon, and as effectively as possible in aggressive war against the Government of Germany." To this end, America must send troops to the firing line as rapidly as possible. He hoped to be allowed to raise a division for immediate service and guaranteed that "no finer body of fighting men could be gathered together than there would be in that division." It would be one composed of "men who mean business."

When asked as he left Washington what his plans were on reaching New York, Roosevelt replied they would "depend altogether on the 'course of events.'"[81] TR had got his wish and the United States was at war, but this did not mean he would be permitted to lead troops to France as he had to Cuba. The world had changed, but the Colonel of the Rough Riders had not. It would be a hard lesson.

CHAPTER 9

A SLACKER IN SPITE OF HIMSELF

APRIL TO JULY 1917

> I doubt whether the President lets me go: and surely he will try his best
> to cause me to fail if he does let me go. We all have our troubles! Quentin
> has grave difficulty with his back; the other three boys, at Plattsburg,
> have no idea what they will be sent to do. It is exactly as if we were
> fighting the Civil War under Buchanan.
> —TR to Anna Roosevelt Cowles, May 17, 1917

Three days after the United States joined the war, the delayed Anglo-French assault devised by French Army Commander Robert Nivelle began, despite the criticisms of British Commander Sir Douglas Haig and Philippe Pétain, another French hero of Verdun, and the fact that the Germans had withdrawn to a more defensible line. The April 11 *Daily Mail* editorial, "The Battle of Arras, Haig's Great Results," poured praise on the field marshal for his "consummate generalship" in the new Allied offensive. However, Nivelle's accompanying attack, which cost 100,000 casualties with no appreciable gain, was soon countered and the push collapsed along with the fragile morale of the French army.[1] By the end of the month there were widespread mutinies among the French troops, which, luckily for the Allied cause, the Germans did not discover until they had been put down.

Meanwhile, on April 10 Roosevelt traveled to Washington again to press his case for leading a division overseas, first with Woodrow Wilson in the Red Room of the White House where he offered in return his aid combatting congressional opposition to the administration's draft measure. The bill, which followed the General Staff's recommendation to build a million-man conscript army, set off a hysterical revolt among some congressional Democrats. Senator James A. Reed predicted the streets of America would run red with blood as in the Civil War draft riots in New York, while in the

House Claude Kitchin denounced the measure as a tyrannical invasion of civil rights.[2] TR assured the president he would support the conscription bill, but he argued that it needed a provision for volunteers outside the age limits to supplement the draft army, which would take a year or more to gather and train. The Colonel told Wilson that he could in a few months prepare such a division of men, which might then be sent to France for final training. He and the division would be under the command of the regular army general in charge of the American army sent overseas. TR argued that it would be "criminal" not to supplement the draft by providing "at once for the hundreds of thousands of volunteers which it would not touch, and who could be used for the first expeditionary force."

He subsequently wrote to Cal O'Laughlin that Wilson seemed pleased that Roosevelt was going to support his bill and "ask for action supplementary to it, and not contradictory to it." The president also told TR that he had felt for some time what he had said in his war message, but that the American people had before this not been "awake to the need, and that he had to bide his time." Many people, though not Roosevelt, Wilson went on, had misunderstood him. The Colonel then assured the president that what he and others had said and thought in the past was "all dust in a windy street if now we can make your message good." If it could be translated "into fact," the war address would rank as a "great state paper" standing with those of Washington and Lincoln. What Roosevelt asked was that he be allowed to do all that was in him "to make good this speech of yours."[3]

In their 45 minute interview, Wilson refused to commit himself to using Roosevelt or volunteers, telling him that the days of "The Charge of the Light Brigade" were over, but TR's boyish enthusiasm thawed the initial coldness, and by the end the president was laughing and "talking back." And when the Colonel left, accompanied by Wilson's secretary Joseph Tumulty, the usual rule against newsmen and cameras on the White House portico was relaxed, and he was "filmed and interviewed to his heart's content."[4] Edward M. House wrote Wilson that he was glad he saw Roosevelt (and hoped he would see Henry Cabot Lodge as well), as the president would need Republican support to pass his war measures.[5]

Later that day at the Longworth house, where TR stayed during this two-day visit, he repeated his arguments with Secretary of War Newton Baker. He also met with Oregon Senator George Chamberlain and Alabama Congressman Stanley Dent, the heads of their respective military affairs committees, to push the draft legislation while also arguing that in order to plant the American flag on the firing line "at the earliest possible moment" there should be a provision added for volunteers to be used in connection with a portion of the regular army.[6] That evening he conferred with Jean Jules Jusserand and Sir Cecil Spring Rice about their governments' views of his request to serve. Jusserand openly lobbied the Wilson administration to send a division led by Roosevelt to France as soon as possible, while Spring Rice felt he had to be more circumspect. He told Roosevelt, however, that he always said there were two things, after ships, which the British most desired: "(1) the

American flag over a detachment however small; (2) men, to any extent." Of course, he went on, "your presence would be immensely popular," but he had to avoid making any suggestion "as to any particular force or any particular man." The British ambassador was given to understand that the administration "didn't ask for suggestions" and felt that any requests he made would hurt more than help his friend's cause.[7]

After considering their conversation in Washington for two days, Baker wrote to Roosevelt that, though he did not doubt his patriotic intentions, he could not approve the sort of unit TR proposed. No final decision had yet been made about the disposition of an expeditionary force, but in the war secretary's judgment any Americans sent to Europe to "expose their lives in the bloodiest war yet fought in the world" should be led by the ablest and most professional and experienced officers available, "men of the Army who had devoted their lives exclusively to the study and pursuit of military matters." He also could not consent to send troops until they had been "seasoned by most thorough training for the hardships they will have to endure." This, Baker assured Roosevelt, was a "purely a military policy" that followed the recommendations of the War College Division of the General Staff and did not attempt to "estimate what, if any, sentimental value would attach" to a representation in France by a former president, but in his estimation there were "doubtless other ways in which that value could be contributed apart from a military expedition."[8]

Before Baker's letter arrived, TR had departed for Boston to join the family gathered for Archie's marriage to his fiancée Grace Lockwood at Emmanuel Episcopal Church. Quentin served as best man. The nuptials, like many across the country, were hurried by the prospect of the groom going overseas to fight, and perhaps die. And Archie soon after joined his already married brothers Ted and Kermit at the Plattsburg officer training camp. All of them, like their father, wanted to see action as soon as possible. Ted and Archie had spent the previous summers at Plattsburg in supplemental drill, while Kermit was starting fresh, which would delay his being commissioned and sent to Europe. The swiftest path for Quentin to fulfill his long-held passion to be a flyer at first appeared to lie in Canada with the Royal Air Corps. But as it fell out, Quentin, who left Harvard after two years of study, instead joined the American forces. He reported "Wild Excitement" to his fiancée Flora Whitney when his Signal Corps aviation section was assigned for training at the Hazelhurst Field at Mineola, Long Island, close enough to buzz Sagamore Hill when he began solo training flights at the end of the next month.[9] Sharing the poor eyesight of his father, Quentin had to memorize the eye chart to pass the test. He also suffered chronic back pain resulting from an accident on a mountain trail during an Arizona hunting trip three years before when a pack horse rolled on him.[10] It was not a list of physical attributes ideal for surviving the rigors of combat flying.

After his youngest son joined the American forces, Roosevelt asked Spring Rice to thank the Canadian authorities for their trouble. He also told his friend that Baker did "not intend to send troops speedily to the front, nor to employ me." The Colonel had not yet given up in his quest, however, and went on that he was going to send the war secretary a long letter (that he copied to Spring Rice and Jusserand) suggesting that Baker ask the British and French governments if they would like to have such a division with him in command, or if not in overall command then as a brigade commander. TR understood that their governments did not want to do anything counter to the wishes of the American administration, but if asked he hoped they would respond, as they had to him, "that they believed to have such a division sent over at the earliest moment would be a very good thing."[11]

In the Senate debate on the issue, the newly elected Hiram Johnson rallied the defense of Roosevelt and his volunteer division against the criticism led by Missouri's Senator William Stone, who had voted against the declaration of war but now had taken up the same cries of preparedness and Americanism that TR had been repeating for two and half years. Johnson urged Wilson to let the Colonel take a division to France, declaring that

> Roosevelt's was the clarion voice that first demanded preparedness in this land. We listened with little attention at first, and then . . . embraced his doctrine. Roosevelt's tongue was the first to demand Americanism undiluted . . . At first little did we heed him, but finally all of us adopted all that he said. Roosevelt typifies to-day Americanism and American citizenship in its highest type.
>
> We are now asking simply that in these late years of this great patriot's life he be permitted to give that life, if need be, to the country that he loves and to the country that he has served. Was there ever a time in any nation's history when a man knocked at the door of the council chamber of that nation and begged merely that he might lay down his life for his county, that he was denied by that nation that he served?
>
> And so we ask you . . . send this man of dynamic force, of ability, of virility, and of red-blooded courage, typifying the American Nation, over to France, there to bear aloft the American flag for world democracy.[12]

After the Colonel read a copy of Johnson's speech, he wrote him, "I am deeply touched and pleased . . . I should be well content to have it as my epitaph."[13]

In the end Senator Warren G. Harding of Ohio, who as chair of the 1916 Republican Convention had helped deny Roosevelt the nomination, offered an amendment to the Army Bill that did not mention Roosevelt but provided for four divisions of volunteers.[14] While Congress debated, on the oceans an armed American steamer, the *Mongolia*, sank a German submarine. "Thank heaven," the Colonel told reporters at Oyster Bay, "some Americans have at last begun to hit." The country, he went on, had been "altogether too long purely on the receiving end of this war Germany has waged on us." He "beamed with pleasure" when told the gun crew had named their weapon "Theodore Roosevelt."[15]

The Colonel was in Chicago exhorting a luncheon gathering to "Farm and Arm" when the news reached him of the Harding amendment's passage in the senate. A smiling TR read the dispatch aloud to the cheers of the audience and declared, "Bully! Bully!" The amendment, he told the gathering, had been "carefully drawn not to interfere in the slightest degree with the President's plan for obligatory service." He wanted to put himself in a position "not to say 'Go to the front,' but 'Come to the front.'"[16] In reply to those inside and out of Congress who criticized his efforts to serve abroad, he told the same audience that to regard his attitude as unpatriotic because of a "fancied interference" with the president's recommendations was "mere hysteria."[17]

Harding responded to Roosevelt's telegram of thanks and congratulations that he did not see how the other house could reject the amendment.[18] Lodge, however, wrote TR about the deliberations of the conference committee that he thought Wilson would make a "bitter personal fight" against the amendment and might "turn the Democrats." But if the president did nothing, said Lodge, "we shall win."[19] The next day Hiram Johnson reported that the conferees had made some headway and if there were "not such a despotism here we would surely succeed," but Wilson having transmuted democracy in Washington into "autocracy," he did not feel "over confident."[20] No matter what Congress did, Roosevelt's daughter Alice was correctly convinced that the present administration hadn't the "remotest intention" of letting him raise a division. She also reported to her father that she had seen their cousin Franklin, who was "profoundly downcast" at the way everything was going.[21]

Unlike TR, who in 1898 resigned as assistant secretary of the navy to "join the fun" in the Spanish-American War, Franklin stayed at his post, a course that became a subject of some bitterness between his wife Eleanor and "Uncle Ted," who urged her husband on several occasions to get into the fight more directly. Until this point FDR had purposefully followed TR's career path, but in the end he was not the Colonel, and World War I was not the Spanish-American War. Franklin did not have Theodore's restless need to be at the center of the action, and besides, there was no volunteer cavalry to join and no French San Juan Hill for him to ride up to glory had he joined it. Franklin was aware that the Colonel's war record had been instrumental in his rise to the presidency but became convinced that he could make a much more important contribution by staying in Washington to keep the US naval effort on track. Many influential friends in and out of the administration let him know in no uncertain terms that he would be "crazy or derelict" to enlist. Among these was Leonard Wood, who told a mutual friend for Franklin's benefit that it would be a "public calamity to have him leave at the present time."[22] And so he stayed.

While the congressional fight over the draft bill and a volunteer provision for it continued, the Colonel attended a New York Harvard Club farewell dinner for Wood, whose Eastern Department had been divided in three. Rather than allow himself to be shifted out of the way to "more important" posts at Manila or Hawaii put on offer by the administration, Wood accepted command of the new Southeast Department with headquarters at Charleston, South Carolina, but he also applied to go over to Europe with the first American contingent.[23] Wood wrote TR from Charleston that he did not know how his request would be acted on, but in the meantime he would "try to do my level best here."[24] Roosevelt thought the transfer of Wood to a noncombat command "ominous of grave failure to do what ought to be done in this great crisis."[25] Still, he held out hopes to command a division in an army corps under Wood. Neither man would get his wish. Nor did Baker, who may well have hoped Wood would resign when he did not get the over-all command in Europe a few weeks later.

On May 5, an exasperated Baker replied to another long TR letter arguing his case. All the questions raised in it, wrote the war secretary, when stripped of personal considerations, became simple. The war in Europe was "stern, steady and relentless," a contest between the "morale of two great contending forces." Any force sent to this contest by America should be chosen to depress the morale of the enemy, to stimulate the morale of our associates, to be as efficient as possible from a military point of view, and, finally, to be organized and led to minimize its losses and sacrifices. And all these four objectives would be better served by a professional army rather than a "hastily summoned and unprofessional force."[26] In private, Baker was more frank about the personal factor, telling an associate that as war secretary he was obligated to see that the American forces were as well equipped and led as possible. "We could not risk a repetition of the San Juan Hill affair, with the commander rushing his men into a situation from which only luck extricated them."[27] Further correspondence from Roosevelt had no more effect than the previous letters.

Newspaper editorials, however, continued to urge the government to "Let Roosevelt Go," and the surge of wartime patriotism led to a raft of songs dedicated to the Colonel. These included such rousing titles as "Oh! Teddy, Take Our Boys to France"; "If We Only Had a Million Like Teddy (The War Would Be Over Today)"; "I Tried to Raise My Boy to Be a Hero"; and "I Didn't Raise My Boy to Be a Slacker."[28] Roosevelt uniformly refused to allow his photo to be used on the sheet music covers, but his image continued to be popular in movie productions. One example was the Vitagraph film *Womanhood: The Glory of the Nation*, which was, according to its advertising, a "big startling patriotic spectacle." In addition to airship raids, naval battles, and "terrible submarine warfare," its final enticement was that "Col. Theodore Roosevelt, America's foremost citizen, personally appears in the production."[29] The film was endorsed by the National Security League, the American Defense Society, and other patriotic organizations, while the army set up recruiting booths at the theaters where it was being shown.[30]

When the United States joined the war, France, Britain, Russia, Belgium, Italy, and Japan all dispatched war missions to Washington, and by early May they had arrived to "state their needs and to discuss the best means of cooperation."[31] The Wilson administration announced that its first priority was to meet the Allied need for food and supplies and that troops would be sent later when vessels were available.[32] On May 9, TR attended a dinner at the home of the industrialist Henry Clay Frick for the French delegation, led by former French Premier René Viviani and Field Marshal Joseph Jacques Césaire Joffre, the former Commander in Chief of the French Amy and hero of the Battle of the Marne. Alice was also on hand and described Joffre, though a warrior, as having the "engaging quality of a huge pink and white, blue-eyed Mellen's food baby." Everyone liked the war hero, who had the nickname "Papa Joffre." Viviani on the other hand was to the "American eye rather a comic-supplement type of Frenchman," who employed the services of a *coiffeur* every morning and was in a bad temper all day if the man arrived late. He was jealous of Joffre, who was frank about the desperate conditions in France, which Viviani wanted to conceal.[33] Roosevelt heartily concurred with Joffre's public call for the United States to send at least a token force to France immediately, and the Frenchman told the Colonel that if he was allowed to come to Paris and march down the Champs-Élysées "if only with a fife and drum corps," the effect on French morale would be "electric."[34] As it fell out, TR's son Ted would play this role.

In meetings with Newton Baker and Army Chief of Staff Major General Hugh Scott, Joffre urged the administration to adopt a national plan for compulsory service. He was also sympathetic to American wishes to form an independent army and did not support his own government's proposal to amalgamate US troops with the French. He later wrote that "no great nation, having a proper consciousness of its own dignity—and America perhaps less than any other—would allow its citizens to be incorporated like poor relations in the ranks of some other army and fight under a foreign flag." Joffre's successful strategy was to have US forces fight beside the French (rather than the British), and he offered his country's aid to train and supply the American troops. This would be accepted, and approximately 80 percent of the American Expeditionary Force was trained by the French and used their artillery, machine guns, and airplanes. While most of its troops were brought over in British ships, a majority of American units fought in conjunction with the French army.[35]

Roosevelt saw Joffre again at a dinner two nights later at the Waldorf Astoria, later telling his sister Anna that he enjoyed his conversations with the Frenchman and at neither dinner was there "another soul who could speak French to him."[36] At this affair the French were joined by representatives of the British War Mission, led by Arthur Balfour, the foreign secretary and one of the few world political figures who shared TR's intellectual bent. In their duel for American aid with the French, the British were handicapped by a public opinion that viewed the French more favorably, a tradition stretching from Lafayette and George III to the more recent wartime blockade and economic blacklist policies. German propaganda broadcast with some success the notion that the French had done most of the fighting in the trenches, while the British held men back. On May 13, after lunching with Colonel House in New York, Balfour had dinner with TR at Oyster Bay. Quentin came over from Mineola to join them.

While Roosevelt's volunteer division was still being debated in Washington, New York Governor Charles S. Whitman offered a generalship in the state militia. However, TR was not interested in home-guard duty any more than the men who wanted to follow him to Europe, and he politely turned this down. On May 15 the congressional conferees agreed on the Harding amendment, which authorized, but did not direct, the president to accept the enlistment of four volunteer divisions. The newspapers revealed that "sentiment in army circles" was against sending Roosevelt to France, which would have "no beneficial effect from a military standpoint and would tend to disrupt military organization and authority." If Wilson heeded his advisors, the Colonel would not go. The papers also noted that the administration had given the French mission a "virtual promise" that American troops would be sent to the fighting as soon as transport could be arranged.[37]

More than a few people laid the blame for the holdup in enacting the draft legislation at the feet of Roosevelt. At the raising ceremony of a twenty-by-thirty-foot American flag at the New York Customs House, Collector Dudley Field Malone told reporters that the delay over the previous weeks had come "by the ambitions of one man." He was willing to let the Colonel go when it was "decided to have him do so." The country should not discourage volunteers above draft age, but "we should remember that we have a Commander in Chief upon whose shoulders responsibility for the successful prosecution of the war rests." Men in this room, he went on, "may yet be lying dead in French trenches." It was "no time for illusion."[38]

On May 18, the War Department announced that John J. Pershing, the only senior officer since the Spanish-American War with experience leading a large force in the field, was to command the American Expeditionary Force (AEF).[39] He and his punitive expedition had been recalled from Mexico that January without capturing Villa, but the public had not blamed the general and the newspaper coverage of his exploits in Mexico made him a popular figure. Though known to have ties to Roosevelt and the Republicans, Pershing, unlike Wood, was canny enough to keep both his politics and his criticisms private. He replied to TR's message of congratulations that he could only repeat what he had said 11 years before when Roosevelt had promoted him from captain to brigadier general: "I shall do my best to make good." He went on that he feared "our people have not yet begun to realize the seriousness of this war nor the enormity of the loss in blood and treasure that we must pay." The Colonel's own patriotic attitude had, in Pershing's opinion, "done much," but there remained "much to be done." In reply to TR's request that Ted and Archie be allowed to join him, the general told Roosevelt that he would be glad to have them and he would request them as officers once he arrived in Europe and was able to expand his organization.[40] The Colonel had added a postscript to his letter of congratulations to Pershing that if he were "physically fit, instead of old and heavy and stiff, I should myself ask to go under you in any capacity down to and including a sergeant." But at his age and condition he supposed he could "not do work you would consider worthwhile in the fighting line (my only line) in a lower grade than brigade commander."[41]

The same day Pershing's appointment was announced, Woodrow Wilson signed into law the Selective Service Act, which, after weeks of acrimonious congressional back and forth, allowed for four volunteer divisions but left calling them up to the president's discretion.[42] This gave Roosevelt an opening to send a final plea for permission to raise two divisions "for immediate service at the front." Wilson replied to TR's telegram, "I very much regret I cannot comply with the request . . . The reasons I have stated in a public statement made this morning and I need not assure you that my conclusions were based entirely upon imperative considerations of public policy and not upon personal or private choice."[43] The statement announced that the president had decided "at the present stage of the war" not to make use of the volunteer divisions provided for by Congress. TR's force, Wilson went on, would have taken "some of the most effective officers of the regular army," men who could not "possibly be spared from the too small force of officers at our command for the much more pressing and necessary duty of training regular troops." It would be "very agreeable" to him to "pay Mr. Roosevelt this compliment and the Allies the compliment of sending to their aid one of our most distinguished public men." Politically, too, it would "no doubt have a very fine effect," but the compliments could not be paid. The business now in hand, said Wilson, was "undramatic, practical, and of scientific definiteness and precision." Other means were required, which the president had heard of "from the mouths of men who have seen war as it is now conducted, who have no illusions, and to whom the whole grim matter is a matter of business."[44]

The administration, Cal O'Laughlin wrote to TR, did just what he expected about the volunteer division. Failing to beat the legislation, as Roosevelt said, "under the table," Wilson was "forced to make the statement he did last night." Of course, he had no intention of sending him, but the "suggestion" that he may do so was found in the clause "at any rate not at the present stage of the war." This was obviously put in to stem criticism. Wilson realized that the draft army would be "called to the Colors in September," and then he would say "there is no need for your division." O'Laughlin hoped the Colonel would make a statement; he was sure that it would appeal to the country. Only one thing would change Wilson's mind, and that was the "persistent pressure of public opinion."[45]

Roosevelt, however, realized that the die had been cast, and after consultation with many of the leaders involved, he prepared a message to be sent to the men in the various states who had volunteered to raise and command troops freeing them from their commitment to his force. This published statement, dated May 20, 1917, declared that in light of the president's announcement that he would not allow the divisions to be organized or allow the Colonel to lead them, the only course open was "forthwith to disband and to abandon all further effort in connection with the divisions, thereby leaving each man free to get into the military service in some other way." "Our sole aim," TR went on, was to "help in every way with the prosecution of the war and we most heartily feel that no individual's personal interest should for one moment be considered save as it serves the general public interest."

Further, the men rejoiced at the news that a division of regular soldiers "under so gallant and efficient a leader" as Pershing was to be sent abroad, and they had a right to a "certain satisfaction in connection therewith." As evidence of this Roosevelt quoted the previous day's *Brooklyn Eagle*, which had "stated authoritatively" that the "sending of this expedition was a compromise between the original plans of the General Staff, which favored no early expedition, and the request of Col. Roosevelt for authority for an immediate expedition." This "agitation," backed by the expressed desire of such leaders as Joffre and Pétain, "unquestionably had its effect in bringing about the Pershing expedition." The compromise was that France got American soldiers, but Roosevelt would not "lead or accompany them." The paper went on that it was believed in Washington that any criticism for turning down TR would be "fully answered by the fact that American soldiers were going over." If this newspaper article, the Colonel went on, gave "the explanation of the matter," he could "gladly say that we are all unselfishly pleased to have served this use, although naturally we regret not to have been allowed ourselves to render active service."

As good American citizens, Roosevelt and the men would of course "loyally obey the decision of the Commander in Chief," but he felt it necessary to "respectfully" point out "certain errors" in Wilson's announcement. First, the Colonel took issue with the contention that he sought an "independent" command in Europe, since TR had several times stated he wanted only brigade command under a general such as Pershing, Wood, Barry, or Kuhn. Roosevelt also denied that any "political consideration whatever or any desire for personal gratification or advantage" entered into the matter. "Our undivided purpose was to contribute effectively to the success of the war." TR also took on Wilson's implication that "our offer would have been mischievous from the military standpoint" by draining "effective" regular officers from the army needed for training purposes. Roosevelt pointed out that his first division contained only about fifty regular officers, one-tenth of the number going with Pershing's division. Therefore the "present plan will take ten times as many men from the 'most pressing and necessary duty'" than would have his proposal.

The president objected to the volunteers on the ground that "undramatic" action was needed that was "practical and of scientific definiteness and precision." In Roosevelt's view there was nothing "dramatic" in their proposal "save as all proposals indicating eagerness or willingness to sacrifice life for an ideal are dramatic." It was true that the division would have contained the sons and grandsons of numerous Civil War heroes of both sides, including Phil Sheridan, Stonewall Jackson, James A. Garfield, and Nathan Bedford Forrest. But all these men would have "served like the rest of us; and all alike would have been judged solely by the efficiency—including the 'scientific definiteness'—with which they did their work and served the flag of their loyal devotion."[46]

With his last hopes of taking a force to France dashed, Roosevelt wrote to Kermit at Plattsburg, more bravely than he must have felt, that he had "hoped that we might round out Africa and South America by a 'greater adventure' together," but as it was he was "not to serve at all . . . Well, we have to abide by the fall of the dice!"[47]

The Colonel wrote much more bitterly to William Allen White that the administration would rather "make this a paper war if possible, but if not that then they want to make it a Democratic war." They were "much more anxious to spite Leonard Wood and myself than to uphold the honor of the nation or beat Germany."[48] White in reply consoled TR that he should not be "very discouraged." This was going to be a long war, and the time was going to come when the administration "will know that they need you as badly as we know they need you now." The editor of the *Emporia Gazette* would "hang onto the willows and sing low." He added a postscript meant to be humorous (which it must be doubted Roosevelt found so): "There is this to say of the President: He at least kept *you* out of war!"[49]

On June 5, after an intensive publicity campaign, almost ten million men, ages 21 to 30 inclusive, presented themselves at their polling places to register for the draft from which would be built the National Army, the largest arm of a three-branch, mutually supportive land force that also included the Regular Army and the National Guard. This first of three wartime registration days was a resounding success. By the end of the war there were more than 500,000 regulars, almost 400,000 National Guardsman, and more than 3,000,000 men in the National Army, out of which 2,000,000 would reach France. The draft machinery was put in the hands of Judge Advocate General Enoch Crowder, whom TR considered one of the few capable appointments made by the administration.

A week before the first registration, Pershing and the rest of his staff, all dressed in civilian clothes, had departed for Europe in secret on the SS *Baltic*. A force of 12 thousand men soon followed them: an advance guard to reassure the French while decisions were made about future American troop numbers. Pershing's chief of staff, Colonel James G. Harbord, one of the officers who had been slated for duty in Roosevelt's division, wrote to the Colonel that he was "very much disappointed at the action in regard to your division" but there seemed to be no appeal possible. Consequently, the war from the American side would "wholly lack the element which only a division led by yourself could have supplied." It would have "aroused the American people" as he felt nothing now could do "except some great loss." Concerning TR's request that his sons join Pershing, he advised him that this was impossible at present. They should stay at Plattsburg where they were training and not enlist. He repeated that once they got to Europe, Pershing would be able to request them.[50]

In Paris, the newspaper editor and politician Georges Clemenceau, who before the end of the year would be premier, published an open letter to Wilson in his paper, *L'Homme Enchaîné*, which called for the Colonel to be dispatched to France. In all candor, said Clemenceau, at the present moment there was in his country "one name which sums up the beauty of American intervention" and that was Roosevelt, who was "imbued with simple vital idealism," which explained his "influence on the crowd, his prestige" with the soldiers and people of France. He asked Wilson, therefore, to give them "before the supreme decision the promise of reward, believe me—send them Roosevelt."[51] The Colonel expressed his private thanks to Clemenceau for the editorial and his bitter regret that Wilson had refused his offer to raise troops and give France immediate help before the draft army could be shipped over. His only comfort was that his four sons were in the army, and he hoped they would all "get to the other side." The fundamental trouble with Wilson, TR confided, was that he was "merely a rhetorician, vindictive yet not physically brave." The president could not face facts nor help believing that since "sonorous platitudes in certain crises win votes they can in other cases win battles."[52]

To win battles, the Army War College recommended that shipments of troops to Europe should begin on August 1 and continue at the rate of 120,000 men a month until June 1918, when more than a million would be in place. The mission of the American army in Europe should be to "enforce peace upon the enemy at the earliest possible moment," and training would be carried out in the United States and France, which, since America had only declared war on Germany to this point, would be the theater of operations. This was similar to a plan devised by Pershing, who wanted to build a separate and independent United States Army, while the French and British pressed for the new troops to be dispersed among their forces.[53] Pershing realized that his men needed training in trench warfare, but he did not want them to be trapped in a defensive position as the Allies were. His plan was to forge an American army to be used as an offensive weapon to win the war, while Wilson also wanted a separate American army as an instrument to enforce his will on the peace settlement.[54]

At the same time, to allow Wilson to wield the "hand of stern repression" against disloyalty that he had demanded in his war message, the administration began to put into place mechanisms for the purpose by Executive Order, passing laws, and forming committees. The first of these, the Committee on Public Information (CPI), was created on April 14 using Wilson's emergency powers and put under the leadership of George Creel, a minor muckraker, sycophantic supporter of Wilson, and caustic critic of TR. Consequently, it was not long before Roosevelt and the Republicans saw the committee as more or less a propaganda arm of the Democratic Party. The CPI (which was funded out of a special $100 million war-powers allotment unaccountable to Congress) was tasked with controlling war news through voluntary censorship methods and persuading the mass of the American public, which had supported neutrality, to a view of the war consonant with Wilson's new moral vision of a crusade to "Make the World Safe for Democracy."[55] Using speakers, pamphlets, press releases, films, and other novel methods, Creel and his organization did their job all too well, helping to incite a wave of patriotic anti-German hysteria while at the same time also carrying out political propaganda and damage control for the president and the administration.[56]

The government's power to suppress opposition was also bolstered in the clauses of the Espionage Bill, an amalgamation of 17 proposals much broader in scope than the antispying focus the title implied. Once passed it would become the basis for extending federal jurisdiction over speech, the press, and general dissent in the war.[57] The spying and antisubversive clauses of the measure drew little congressional criticism, and TR and the Republicans were at first perfectly happy at the prospect of the government moving against aliens, socialists, hyphenates, and others. But a censorship provision against disloyal expression soon ran into trouble when the political opposition and the press realized it could be used as a weapon against them. In the Senate, Lodge condemned the censorship clause as a "gross infringement on the right of every newspaper to print what it wanted about the war." The *New York Times* led the press criticism, calling the act a "tyrannous measure" that would undermine democracy.[58]

Wilson defended the measure in a direct appeal to Congress, arguing that the "authority to exercise censorship over the press" was "absolutely necessary to the public safety."[59] Nevertheless, after nine weeks of political wrangling, the censorship provision was excised from the Espionage Act signed by the president. But two of its remaining provisions concerning interference with the armed services or the war effort could and would be used by federal officials to punish "individual casual or impulsive disloyal utterance." Under these began wartime prosecutions of more than two thousand violations with over a thousand convictions, the most celebrated being the case of the socialist leader Eugene V. Debs, who received the maximum penalty of twenty years in prison.

The Espionage Act also gave Postmaster General Albert S. Burleson discretionary power to ban from the mails any published matter "advocating or urging treason, insurrection, or forcible resistance to any law of the United States." Another provision empowered the postmaster general to use his own judgment whether mailing certain kinds of matter constituted "willful obstruction to the progress of the war." If so this matter could be excluded from the mails without court order, and the burden of proof in any legal action would fall on the person who mailed the allegedly subversive matter. While Wilson announced that such powers would not be used to suppress civil liberties, Burleson gave directions to his local postmasters to do just that and to stay alert even for matter that might simply embarrass the administration's conduct of the war.

Burleson, a narrow-minded Bryanite whom Wilson dubbed "the Cardinal," was the scion of an old Texas political family and became the self-appointed guardian of the nation and administration in actions mainly against the "subsidiary press," particularly socialist and foreign language newspapers and magazines, 15 of which were excluded from the mails within a month.[60] Despite much criticism, Wilson refused to rein in Burleson, and before long the post office also began to interfere with more mainstream publications, and this would run Burleson afoul of Roosevelt. Despite these new powers, administration officials continued to demand even more explicit legislation to act against "dangerous utterances."[61]

Roosevelt was already in the habit of leaving his return address off messages he did not want opened by the American postal authorities, and Sir Henry Rider Haggard wrote him that his recent letter had been opened by the British censors, he believed, for exactly that reason. The writer and his friends were all rejoicing over the entry of the United States into the war, for which he had "ceased to hope," and he told TR that he had attended a mass of thanksgiving at St. Paul's and a Pilgrim's dinner celebration. America's entry, Haggard believed, was "full of hope for the future and destined, possibly, to bring about that drawing together of the two great divisions of the English-Speaking peoples" that he and TR had discussed when he visited Sagamore Hill. Haggard's greatest hope was that the American navy could help to defeat the German submarine campaign that threatened Britain with starvation, something he reminded the Colonel that he had warned of for years.[62]

Navy and administration figures were stunned when the British revealed that the U-boats had sunk nearly a million tons of merchant shipping in April, and helping the Allies to conquer the submarine menace would be the first tangible military contribution of the United States. The leader of this effort was one of the Colonel's naval protégés, William Sims, who had been promoted to vice admiral and given command of the American Naval Forces Operating in European Waters. The tall and handsome Sims, who sported a white Vandyke beard appropriate for a naval officer of the period, reached London four days after the declaration of war and was instrumental in pressing the British and American naval commands into a convoy system that would eventually end the shipping crisis.[63] Still it was a very near thing—at one point that summer Britain had only a six weeks supply of food on hand. In the end, of 5,090 vessels convoyed in 1917, only 63 were lost.[64] "Nothing could have gratified me more," Sims wrote TR, than TR's letter of congratulations. It was perfectly apparent to him that if Roosevelt when president had not supported his "campaign for the improvement of gunnery and for the improvement of the design of our vessels," he would have been "turned down and my naval career ended." The Colonel could imagine, therefore, how grateful Sims was to him. And the admiral felt, as some of the papers stated, that he was one of the "Roosevelt men."[65]

Before Ted and Archie departed June 20 on the USS *Chicago* for Europe to join Pershing's division as promised, the family gathered for a farewell party at Sagamore Hill. Ted's wife Eleanor was less than happy when TR loudly declared that he expected at least one of his sons would be wounded and possibly killed in France.[66] Two days after the boys sailed, Ambassador Jusserand wrote his friend Theodore that he had seen the news in the papers and taken note that Roosevelt was "not idle. You will never be; anything that happens; and the results of your efforts are already apparent." In his opinion, "the going of General Pershing" and the others was "certainly one of those results."[67] Similarly, Arthur Lee wrote the Colonel, "You are more responsible than the rest of all your countrymen put together for bringing America into the war," and he continued that TR had "rescued her honor and perhaps averted a great disaster." He had also "forced the immediate intercession of troops in Europe" and thereby had done to France a service that was "incalculable."

Lee was angry at TR's treatment by Baker and sorry his friend was kept from the battle, but he could not "help feeling glad for Mrs. Roosevelt's sake that all her pet lambs have not frisked off together and that you can help her through the anxious days ahead." Lee went on that the war fronts were not everything; the world struggle had a "back" as well, and he was not sure that the home front wasn't equally important. And there Roosevelt had a lot to do. Lee had enjoyed his own time at the front but had done more to "beat the Boche" since he took off his uniform and "speeded up the shells and the food." The last he had now been at for six months, and he found it the most strenuous task he had ever undertaken. He hoped to get two million more acres under the plow by the 1918 harvest.[68]

Not long afterwards, Rudyard Kipling wrote that, for once in his life, he was "thoroughly in accord with Wilson's attitude." The "present game of war" was "no show for a middle-aged man." It meant collapse at the end of a few days. He knew that if Roosevelt went out, "you would go out— with no corresponding advantage to your country." But as long as Roosevelt remained in America, there was "always the element of strength . . . *and* drive for the world to rely upon in the days when (as surely will happen) your paci-fists, doubters and general slimers begin to bleat." Then TR's "prestige and power" could "steady and rally and keep your faint hearts up to the mark." This would be a service "inestimably beyond any other" that the Colonel could "render to mankind." So he applauded the "great and good Wilson— though I don't know what was in his mind."[69]

Roosevelt's main concern now became ensuring that Kermit, whose pre-war work in South America had kept him from officer training with his broth-ers, should get a commission and join the fighting as swiftly as possible, if not with the American forces then with the British, who he knew to be in need of junior officers. TR had warned Kermit that he did not know if he could ensure this, as the Allies might be "afraid to offend the malignant coward in the White House."[70] Nevertheless, he dispatched letters to Arthur Lee, David Lloyd George, Sir Edward Grey, and Sir Henry Lowther, a member of the British General Staff, requesting that Kermit be given a lieutenant's commis-sion in the British army and posted to Mesopotamia for the fighting in the open there to which he thought his son best suited. Otherwise, he feared Kermit might be kept at home for a year or more in training. The Colonel knew this was asking an extraordinary favor, but the favor was "that the boy shall have a chance to serve and if necessary, be killed in the fighting." He had asked the same from the American military authorities for his other sons and his son-in-law, Ethel's husband Richard Derby, all of whom were going to the front. Roosevelt was trying to give Kermit the same chance. Whether their mother and wives and TR would ever see them again or not, no one could tell, but he was "very genuinely proud that they are all eager to prove their truth by the endeavor."[71]

The Colonel also put Kermit's dilemma before Lord Northcliffe when, newly arrived as successor to Balfour as head of the British War Mission, he visited Sagamore Hill to speak of the war and Anglo-American cooperation.[72] The press lord's informal dress (usually a blue serge suit, soft white collar, red checked tie, and gray soft hat) and equally informal manner aided his general popularity and the ease with which he could work with Americans, particularly the business leaders. His style was in marked contrast to Arthur Balfour's starched-linen, frock-coated formality, which had led the foreign secretary to be described in the American press during his visit as "an interesting survival."[73] Though the choice was widely criticized at the time, in England and America, Northcliffe had the expertise needed to organize both the business and the publicity sides of the mission. Lloyd George was well aware of Northcliffe's many trips to the United States, his reputation there, and his belief in its absolute importance. A final, and perhaps decisive, factor was that the press lord's loose-cannon activities had been a constant irritation to the prime minister, and the mission would remove him for an extended period.[74] Wilson might have been wise to do the same thing with Roosevelt.

During his visit to Sagamore Hill, Alice recalled, Northcliffe "said oracularly that the war would go on for years," though they felt that this was "perhaps not quite his real opinion, and intended largely to impress upon us the necessity of giving everything the Allies wanted." The British were competing in particular with the French for money and supplies, and the press lord commented about their Gallic recital of woes, "What actors they are!"[75]

Not without dramatic skills himself, Northcliffe added his considerable weight to the entreaties on Kermit's behalf, and whether or not this was crucial, as TR believed, permission to join the British forces in Mesopotamia was soon forthcoming from War Secretary Lord Derby. Roosevelt immediately sent the news to his son that he was "not to be behind!" He reminded Kermit that he had a "heavy weight of responsibility on your shoulders" in an obligation to "England, to America, to yourself and to me." He must not only "*do* what is right, but also *seem* to do what is right." There could be no looking back or "acting so as to cause even a suggestion that you are expecting any favor or behaving save as any subaltern, eager to get to the front, would behave."[76]

On the Home Front, Leonard Wood had assumed his duties as commander of the Southeast District at Charleston, and after he praised Confederate bravery in the Civil War in an early speech, he made a tour of Southern states to select army training camp sites, which became "one continuous triumphal progress" of cheering crowds. Roosevelt wrote him that he could not "help grinning over the way in which the attempt to exile you" had turned out. He also shared his amusement when the senior military member of the British War Mission, General Tom Bridges, who had lost an arm in combat, told him that Wilson claimed he had sent Wood south "because of the great work he knew you would be doing down there!" TR asked Bridges if that was the reason the president had first tried to get Wood to go to the Hawaiian Islands. Bridges also made the Colonel smile when he voiced his doubt whether his volunteers would have done well, giving as justification the fact that he did not think the Canadian and Australian volunteers were as "good as the British tommies and expressed disapproval of their discipline." Roosevelt appraised Bridges as a good fellow but of the "somewhat thick-headed British type."

Unfortunately, in TR's estimation, woodenheaded behavior also prevailed in Washington and made the situation, in his estimation, "fraught with ugly possibilities of delay and disaster." If Wood had been given a "free hand, not merely in the South but in the country at large," Roosevelt was sure that he could have had 500,000 men ready for training in Europe by November, rather than the 100,000 forecast. He agreed with Wood's contention that never had there been "such an effort as now to keep concentration and control in Washington." With Wood, TR was trying to "do the best that can be done." He had not publicly criticized the president since April 2, but neither did he "lie about him!" The Colonel went on that he fully intended to "tell the truth, and point out the criminal folly of our having failed to prepare, and to speak plainly of the dangers ahead."[77]

On June 28, two days after the first American troops landed in France, Balfour cabled House that the British were "on the verge of a financial disaster which would be worse than defeat in the field. If we cannot keep up exchange neither we nor our allies can pay our dollar debts. We should be driven off the gold basis and purchases for the U. S. A. would immediately cease and Allies' credit would be shattered."[78] Northcliffe was sent a similar message and, because Spring Rice was out of Washington, was instructed to take matters in hand and call on the president if necessary.[79] Wilson directed him to the secretary of the treasury, his son-in-law William Gibbs McAdoo, who imagined himself the president's heir apparent.[80] Northcliffe called his visit to the treasury (and his overall job) "an urgent begging mission of colossal scale."[81] Wilson certainly saw the potential, and he seemed to have no qualms about using America's financial domination to force the Allies to accept his preferences for a peace settlement, about which he had been quiet since the United States joined the war. He told House that when the war was over, "we can force them to our way of thinking because by that time they will, among other things, be financially in our hands: but we cannot force them now, and any attempt to speak for them or to our common mind would bring on disagreements which would inevitably come to surface in public and rob the whole thing of its effect."[82]

While these fateful financial arrangements were being brokered in Washington, on July 3 Archie and Ted arrived at Pershing's headquarters in Paris. Colonel Frank McCoy, another officer who would have been on TR's staff if his division had been authorized, reported to him that his sons had that day "turned up in fittest and fightenest [sic] mood." Pershing and Harbord had "fixed them up at once for duty, and Archie went off bang to join his regiment, the Sixteenth Infantry." Ted, however, would still be in Paris for the next day's Fourth of July parade arranged by the French, who had declared a national holiday. So, McCoy told TR, "a Roosevelt would march through

Figure 9. "The Roosevelts in the War," *Leslie's Illustrated Magazine*, July 5, 1917
Theodore Roosevelt Collection, Harvard College Library

Paris tomorrow and on to the training camp in the zone of the armies the day after."[83]

On July 4, while Roosevelt gave a patriotic speech in Forest Hills, New York, denouncing "conscientious objectors" and "fifty-fifty allegiance," American troops, along with their French comrades, marched in Paris from the Hôtel des Invalides, the shrine of the French army where Napoleon was buried, five miles through an exultant multitude to the Picpus Cemetery and the grave of Marquis de Lafayette.[84] There, Pershing's aide Colonel Charles Stanton famously announced, "*Lafayette, nous voici!*" So many garlands were thrown at the marching troops that Pershing commented that the parade "looked like a moving flower garden."[85] Along the way the whole city turned out to cheer the Americans, and the newspapers reported that the calls of "Sammies" (after "Uncle Sam" but a name the all-white soldiers did not like because of its racial overtones) were replaced by cries of "Teddy!" and "Long live the Teddies!" as word spread that Roosevelt's son was in the parade.[86]

The same day, Conklin Mann, the managing editor of *Leslie's Illustrated Magazine*, sent TR a copy of the July 5, 1917, issue with a note referring him to page six for "a smile."[87] It depicted, in a full page of photographs, "The Roosevelts in the War." Surrounding TR's grinning portrait in the center were uniformed shots of Ted, Kermit, Archie, Quentin, and cousins Nicholas, J. A., and Franklin Roosevelt.[88] The magazine soon could have added a female Roosevelt auxiliary, as Ted's wife Eleanor refused to stay at home and offered her services to the YMCA in recreational work for the AEF. In one of the few direct orders she could remember him giving, the Colonel, perhaps recalling the strain Ethel had suffered in 1914, had "declared emphatically" that no women in the family were to follow their husbands to Europe. But he finally relented in her case and offered any help he could render. Eleanor's service soon after gave Roosevelt a golden opportunity, when he was told by newspapermen that Wilson's son-in-law was going to France with the YMCA, to comment, "How very nice. We are sending our *daughter-in-law* to France in the Y.M.C.A.!"[89]

The YMCA had forbidden wives to be stationed near their husbands, but before too long Eleanor was in Paris performing a variety of duties, running a canteen in the Avenue Montaigne during the day while giving elementary French lessons to American soldiers in the evenings. The Colonel sent Ted a note, through Eleanor, wishing him "every luck." Like the Civil War–era humorist Artemus Ward, TR went on, he had been "straining every nerve to get all my wife's relations to the front! (My sons are my wife's relations ar'nt they?)." Quentin had finished his basic training and, he reported, would sail in ten days. Kermit, thanks to Northcliffe, had been offered a staff position with the British in Mesopotamia and was to sail immediately. The Colonel signed the letter, "Your Loving Father The Slacker Malgré Lui"—the slacker in spite of himself.[90]

Later that month, Major Theodore Roosevelt Jr. was given command of the First Battalion of the Twenty-Sixth Infantry Regiment in the AEF's First Division. Lieutenant Archibald soon after joined the Twenty-Sixth as well. Though he did not at first approve of one brother being under the command of another, TR was "delighted" when Ted reported that he had got a fighting command, a rarity for a reserve officer. He wrote his son that he knew of his desire to be in the line but had "no idea you could make a regular regiment in a line position." He went on, "You have the fighting tradition! It is a great thing you have done. I am very pleased." Ted's hard work and ability, his toughness and fairness, before long won over most of those American officers and enlisted men in France who believed he had been given preference on account of his father. He would later turn down promotion to brigade adjutant to stay with the troops he forged into one of the most efficient units in the AEF.[91] The Colonel reported to Archie that Kermit would soon sail for Mesopotamia (via England) and that Quentin was to go over with the first ten American flyers to the French aviation school. Consequently, "Everybody works but father," and this, he told his son, would become "my motto hereafter." All he could do was to "wade into the pacifists, pro-Germans and rioters here," which was a "pretty poor substitute for work at the front."[92]

The first leg of Kermit's journey to Mesopotamia, on the SS *Carpathia*, ended in England, where he received his orders and was outfitted for battle in London. At lunch with Lord Derby, the war secretary offered a staff position and the rank of major, but Kermit chose instead to take a captaincy with the promise of field action. Arthur Lee reported to TR from Chequers on July 25 that Kermit had "come on" tremendously since he last saw him three years before. Lee went on that he was trying to get Kermit to give up the idea of Mesopotamia and to "go crusading" in Palestine, where Lee thought there were greater opportunities for significant fighting. "Kermit Captures Jerusalem," he wrote, would make a much better headline than "Swatting Flies on the Tigris." So far as he could make out, Kermit's main objective in life at present was to "kill Turks, associate with Arabs and other unclean tribes, and to live under conditions of heat, sand & flies which would be quite unendurable to me." Whatever he decided to do, Lee would help all he could.

Lee also confided that Lloyd George was growing impatient with what TR called the "stern foremost" method of United States aid. It was more "important than anything else in the world" that America speed up bringing over manpower to assist France. Three years of effort had "badly frayed the nerves of all involved," and Lee was convinced that "the secret of final victory" lay quite as much in "keeping our heads as in conducting successful offensives." There was across Europe a state of "unstable equilibrium," which gave America a chance to tip the balance. If "she shoved now and shoved hard," the Central Powers might "topple at any moment."[93] A few weeks later Ruth Lee wrote to Edith that she was happy to see her son and his wife, Belle, who was going to Spain with their boy Kim to stay with her parents while Kermit went to war. She also proudly reported that the day before the Stars and Stripes had flown from the Victoria Tower at Westminster. All London had lined the streets to see a parade of American troops go by, and they had made a "splendid impression." The men were so "tall and slender, lean and wiry looking with such intelligent faces—but all so young poor dears!"[94]

Nineteen-year-old Quentin was the last of TR's sons to sail for Europe—on July 23 with the Ninety-Fifth Aero Squadron, a tiny advance guard of what was dreamily envisioned by Newton Baker to be "the greatest air fleet ever devised" and "perhaps America's most speedy and effective contribution to the Allied cause from a military point of view."[95] The reality would be tragically different. Theodore and Edith saw their son off at the Hudson River pier. Quentin's fiancée Flora Whitney, heiress of one of the largest fortunes in the country, was also on hand, and his parents left early so that the two young lovers could say their good-byes in private. Neither set of parents had much regard for the other. The Whitneys deplored TR's radical politics, while he had an even lower opinion of "the dull purblind folly of the very rich."[96] However, Theodore and Edith would both become very fond of Flora, who while Quentin was in France came to prefer the simplicity of Sagamore Hill over her family's opulent but empty life at Newport and on Fifth Avenue. Quentin reported to her from his ship, the SS *Olympia*, that as the youngest of the squadron he had been labeled "Babe" or "The Kid," and he was to "have my baptismal party when we get to Paris!!!"[97] After Quentin departed, Jusserand wrote to his old friend Theodore, "So they are all gone! May they return safe and victorious, having taken part in the grand defilé under the arc de triomphe de l'etoile." He also told TR that he had notified his government of the sailing so that Quentin "may not find that he lands in a country where he is unknown."[98] It was very hard for Edith to see the last and youngest of her boys go, but she commented to a friend, "You can't bring up boys to be hawks and expect them to turn out sparrows."[99]

An old preparedness ally, the writer Julian Street, reported to TR that he had spent an evening with Charles Hanson Towne of *McClures's*, and both men were "deeply impressed" with the restraint Roosevelt had shown in "refraining from attacks on the administration" when, as they knew, many things had occurred that "must be sickening to you." They felt he should continue this course until the "psychological moment" for change arrived. Street was sure that TR was fully aware of the "undercurrent of discontent" building all over the country. This was "bound to grow," and as grave mistakes were made "and come home to the people" an outcry would inevitably arise for Roosevelt. Even if the "storm was slow in breaking," Street and Towne would rather "see it originate with the mass of the people than with you." They believed this would happen "in due course" and were against TR "letting them have it" in the near future, though the temptation would be great as "new reports of slyness and incompetence reveal themselves."[100] However, with his sons now safely in the bosom of the military and his own chances of field service defunct, patience was not a virtue Roosevelt would or could cherish. As in 1914, when he had waited three months to see Wilson's course before unleashing his guns, TR now again prepared to fire.

CHAPTER 10

CHILDREN OF THE CRUCIBLE

AUGUST TO DECEMBER 1917

It was the most colossal misfortune of the century that in this great
crisis . . . our President should be an absolutely selfish, cold-blooded
and unpatriotic rhetorician. Wilson has a great deal of ability of the most
sinister type . . . above all in appealing to whatever is evil or foolish in
the average man, who . . . also has very noble qualities to which the right
appeal could be made. The average man has in him both the Mr. Hyde
and Dr. Jekyl [sic]. Lincoln could successfully appeal to one side of him;
Wilson does successfully appeal to the other.
                                    —TR to Arthur Lee, August 17, 1917

Roosevelt opened fire on the Wilson administration in the *Metropolitan*,
where he published his complete correspondence with Baker on the matter of
the volunteer division. This action, he explained, was taken to set the record
straight in response to scurrilous rumors that he had demanded command
of all the volunteers, and that adding the volunteer provision purely in his
selfish interest had needlessly delayed both the passage of the draft bill and
the dispatch of troops to France. First, TR declared, the correspondence
clearly showed that he had never suggested that he be given command of an
expeditionary force, only to serve under a regular army general like John J.
Pershing. Second, if the volunteer force he had offered in February had been
accepted immediately it would have been ready to sail with Pershing's Regular Army Division. Finally, the Colonel asserted, it was only the agitation led
by himself and "strongly endorsed by Gen. Joffre" that obliged the Wilson
administration to reverse its decision not to send troops immediately. Consequently, the country was "saved the humiliation of taking no military part in
the war through 1917 and part of 1918."[1]

"Every trouble we have at this moment in this country," TR wrote to
Arthur Lee, was "primarily due to Wilson." All those who were opposing

the war, or attacking England, or praising Germany were "merely quoting what Wilson said as late as December or January last." The great danger now was the present "Peace Without Victory" agitation led by the Hearst press, the German papers, and all the pro-Germans and pacifists.[2] William Randolph Hearst supported conscription and the Liberty loans to arm the nation for self-defense, but he crusaded against transporting a large army overseas, much of which, he feared, would be drowned in the Atlantic crossing by marauding submarines. The Anglophobe press magnate continued to rail against the British, writing in the *New York American* that the "painful truth" was that the United States was being used as a "mere reinforcement of England's warfare and of England's future aggrandizement."[3]

In response, Roosevelt laid out his own 11-part plan in the *Metropolitan* for a "Peace of Victory," which included redrawing the map of the postwar world. This scheme began with the restoration and indemnification of Belgium. In addition TR proposed that Luxembourg be joined to either Belgium or France and that the last should get back Alsace and Lorraine. Further, the Danes of North Schleswig should be able to vote whether they wanted to be part of Denmark. To the south, Italy should receive *Italia irredenta* ("unredeemed Italy"; the 800,000 or so Italian speakers under Austrian rule in the Trentino and around Trieste) with the proviso that Austria be allowed "commercial access to the Mediterranean." Elsewhere in Austria-Hungary, the "Czechs and their close kinsman outside Bohemia" should be given a new commonwealth, the Southern Slavs joined in a Greater Serbia, and an effort made to keep the Magyars and Roumans together as independent nations. To the east, in TR's view a democratic Russia "should be entitled to and would not abuse the possession of Constantinople." And such a Russia could also be safely trusted to "stand as the sponsor" of autonomous states in Finland, Poland, and Armenia, while Lithuania should also have its claims to statehood considered. In a last European point, Roosevelt argued that "surely the time has come" to give Ireland Home Rule within the British Empire "on a basis of resolute justice," while beyond Europe, Britain and Japan "must keep the colonies they have conquered."[4]

But before any maps could be redrawn the war still had to be won, which seemed a doubtful prospect for the hard-pressed Allies. When word reached Washington on August 21 from Russia that Riga had fallen, leaving the capital Petrograd (as St. Petersburg had been renamed) vulnerable to attack, Roosevelt's cousin Franklin commented to his chief Josephus Daniels that if they had "sent TR over to Russia with 100,000 men" this would "not have happened." Captain Josiah McKean, one of the Naval Operations Officers present, later told Daniels, "It was strange how many folks TR had fooled."[5] What Russia would do, Roosevelt wrote some weeks later to Archie about the deteriorating situation, "neither I nor any other human being can possibly foretell." He hoped the nation would "continue to make war, no matter how inefficiently," but it was impossible to prophesy about "such seething chaos."[6] Taking advantage of the chaotic situation, the Bolshevik party led by Lenin took control that September of the Petrograd Soviet, positioning themselves to overthrow the provisional government that had ruled following the revolution.[7]

Back on the American political front, on September 8, Roosevelt opened the New York women's suffrage campaign with a speech, "Suffrage and the War," at Oyster Bay. The war, he declared, had brought the day "nearer in every country" when women should be given the same political rights as the men, because in each warring nation the "woman force has had to be put squarely behind the man force to carry on the struggle." People had said to him that women should not be given the vote because they would be pacifists. To this he replied that the Lord knew he despised pacifists, but TR had "failed to notice that among them the shrieking sisterhood" outnumbered the "bleating brotherhood." He had absolutely no doubt that suffrage must come "as a matter of right, if we are to continue our Democratic experiment of Government—it must come."[8]

The "woman force" in France still included Ted's wife Eleanor, who while continuing with her YMCA duties had set up a Paris refuge for the Roosevelt men when they got leave in a spacious house with a lovely garden on the rue de Villejuste (now rue Paul Valéry) owned by her aunt. She wrote to Ted's sister Ethel on September 1 that it was not possible to be nearer her husband and she had only seen him once since she arrived. They had to be "very careful about appearing to have pull," but Eleanor was nevertheless glad she came, as she was also able to acquire needed supplies and provisions for the brothers and their men.[9] The same day, the Colonel wrote to "Dearest Ted," whose present command as a Major in France was larger than that TR had as a Colonel in Cuba. "You have had grueling work," he told his son, "but, Lord, it has been worthwhile." He passed on with pride that he had received a letter from a French Colonel who had been involved with their training that complimented Ted and Archie's "fine energy and soldierly eagerness." Because it all seemed so trivial in comparison to the real work at the front, it was difficult for TR to write of anything at home, but General Leonard Wood, he confided, had been given the new Eighty-Ninth Division of the draft army to train, at Camp Funston in Kansas, and "naturally he feels very bitter" at being kept out of the fighting. Roosevelt himself remained "so emphatically out of kilter with the Administration" that he could do little except "war on the Hun within our Gates" and try to spur the people on to "constantly speedier and more effective action."

Along these lines TR was about to publish another collection of his articles, for which, he revealed to Ted, Edith had supplied the title—*The Foes of Our Own Household*. He also reported that starting October 1 he would be writing for the *Kansas City Star*, at a salary of $25,000, while he would continue to write a monthly *Metropolitan* editorial for $5,000. This, he told his son, would allow him to earn enough money to give Archie and Quentin a start after the war. But his and their mother's "real task," the "raising of you four boys, in such shape that we lift our heads in pride whenever we think of you, or whenever anyone asks of you," was done.[10] Besides the generous remuneration, TR's new connection with the daily *Star* offered an immediate and powerful voice for his pronouncements, which could be broadcast nationally by syndication within 24 hours.

Roosevelt reported to Archie that the National Guard regiments were just going into their camps and the draft army contingents were slowly beginning to assemble as well. He feared their officers would have their work cut out for them and was glad that Kermit was "not in it." TR went on that General Franklin Bell, who had succeeded Leonard Wood as commander at Governor's Island, had told him that if the government refused to send him abroad he intended to retire and "cross the seas as a volunteer" and that Bell hoped TR and Wood would "go with him—as the Three Elderly Musketeers," Roosevelt supposed. He feared they would not be "very welcome auxiliaries."[11] By this time it had become customary for the parents of soldiers at the front to display flags with a star for each son who had gone over, and TR proudly told Archie that such a banner with four stars now flew at Sagamore Hill.[12]

At the same time the Colonel wrote to Quentin in France that he supposed he was "hard at work learning the new type of air-game" and that he was immensely proud of all four boys. He went on that he felt that "*mother*, and all of *you* children have by your deeds justified my *words*!!" For his own part, TR reported that he gave a few speeches, which he loathed doing because he always feared to "back up the administration too strongly lest it turn another somersault." At the moment, he went on, New York City, "having seen the National Guard, fresh from gathering at the Armories, parade, believes that Germany is already conquered!"[13] That month Roosevelt visited one of the National Guard regiments, the New York Sixty-Ninth at Mineola on Long Island, commanded by Colonel Charles Hine, who had been at Santiago with TR. This occasion also afforded him the opportunity to go aloft, outfitted in goggles and helmet, for half an hour in an airplane equipped with the new Liberty engine in which the administration put high hopes. The flight, which ascended to 5,000 feet at a speed of 100 miles an hour, he told reporters, was "remarkable" and a "great pleasure."[14] TR wrote to Ted that he wished "mother could have gone; she would have enjoyed it, for we go fast and yet it is entirely safe."[15] The new Liberty engine, he reported to Quentin, was not yet perfected, but it was a "big improvement on what we have had," though he did not know if it was "anywhere near equality with the models now in use on the war front."[16]

On September 9 the newspapers printed Roosevelt's "Children of the Crucible" appeal to "crush sedition in the United States." According to the appeal, the American crucible "must melt all who are in it" and turn them out in the "one American mold . . . shaped 140 years ago by men who under Washington founded this as a free nation separate from others." The "true test of loyal Americanism to-day" was "effective service against Germany." Further, it would be an "act of baseness and infamy, an act of unworthy cowardice and a betrayal of this country and mankind to accept any peace except the peace of overwhelming victory, a peace based on the complete overthrow of the Prussianized Germany of the Hohenzollerns."[17] The papers also announced that TR had formed a related antitreason "Vigilantes" organization. Vigilance, he declared, was the best method of fighting the evil of pro-Germanism, and the original task of the group was to monitor and report on the seditious speeches of "soap-box" pacifists and pro-Germans.[18]

However, the Vigilantes soon grew beyond this original mandate into a self-described "patriotic, anti-pacifist, non-partisan organization of Authors, Artists and others," with offices at 505 Fifth Avenue. Its logo was the silhouette of a suspiciously Rough Riderly Paul Revere on horseback, lantern in hand with the Old North Church in the distance. The stated purposes of the society were to "arouse the country to a realization of the importance of the problems facing the country"; to "awaken and cultivate in the youth of the country a sense of public service and an intelligent interest in citizenship and national problems"; to "work vigorously for preparedness; mental, moral and physical"; and finally to "work with especial vigor for Universal Military Training and Service under exclusive Federal control, as a basic principle of American democracy."[19]

As Roosevelt and his allies moved to rouse the country, the Wilson administration ramped up its own relentless propaganda effort under the auspices of the Committee on Public Information. Besides printed appeals along the lines of the Vigilantes, the CPI also dispatched across the nation thousands of "Four Minute Men" giving ultrapatriotic speeches as extreme as or more than those TR had been criticized for over the previous years. Taking advantage of the motion picture boom, these addresses were often delivered in theaters while reels were being exchanged for sensational commercial films and serials such as *The Kaiser, the Beast of Berlin* and *Wolves of Kultur*. One such speech, "What Our Enemy Really Is," proclaimed that the "first step" toward learning this must be to "wake up and realize that an enemy exists and then urge such awakening on our neighbors." The people must remember that if the "Sword of the Kaiser should ever hang over America," it would be a sword not for the service of humanity but a "sword of cruelty, oppression and slavery." To protect "our civilization" from such disasters and tragedies as those that had befallen Belgium and elsewhere was the reason "our khaki-clad 'Soldier-Boys'" were "today in service in France" and others were training to follow in their footsteps. "KAISERISM" was an "International Cancer with the words of truth and promise on the lip, but with the spirit of the devil and falsehood in the heart."[20]

While this publicity blitz was carried out at home, Roosevelt sent Kermit birthday greetings, telling his son, "What a full twenty-eight years you have had!" He knew "no other man of your age who has had such an experience; adventure and wandering in many lovely lands, the life of courts and cities, love and war—you have had them all." And when his son came back again to Sagamore Hill, how much there would be to tell as they sat "before the great fireplace in the North Room." General Wood, TR went on, had written "with greatest bitterness" about his division of drafted men training near Ft. Riley, Kansas, and had only one hundred rifles for twenty thousand men. The troops were drilling with sticks and had been outfitted by Wood in blue overalls because they had no uniforms. It was "cruel to think," wrote the Colonel, "how well we would have done if this wretched creature in the White House had not been such a white rabbit." Luckily, Kermit was where he was and not "paying in person for all the blunders and crimes of the administration."[21]

On September 20, Roosevelt departed for a trip west to Illinois, Missouri, and Kansas. Along the way he visited several military camps and gave speeches for the National Security League at several cities. Before he left, TR told the press at Oyster Bay that the keynote in his addresses would be "Americanism and the War."[22] The Colonel arrived at Kansas City at the beginning of "Old Glory Week" and was welcomed at the station by a crowd of 10,000 with the United States Navy Band, led by Lieutenant Commander John Philip Sousa, playing the "Star Spangled Banner." This tour also allowed him to inspect the offices of the *Kansas City Star*, which he joined as a contributing editor. When he was introduced to the rest of the staff at the newspaper office, TR joked that he had joined them as the newest "cub" reporter. He told Archie, who had refused promotion to a staff position to stay in the line, that he "was able to size up fairly just what it was they wanted from me."[23]

In his speech at Kansas City on September 24, Roosevelt declared, "If we take heed of any peace utterance Germany prepares we will show that we are not yet prepared to go out into the world without a guardian." America, he added, must make good the words of President Woodrow Wilson to make the world safe for democracy, and for this reason the country should declare war against Austria and Turkey. TR also proclaimed that if he was a member of the Senate, he would be "ashamed to sit in that body until I found out some method of depriving Senator La Follette of his seat in that chamber which he now disgraces by his presence."[24] La Follette had incurred TR's particular wrath by introducing a senate resolution calling for a restatement of US war aims conducive to a negotiated peace. This led to his being branded a traitor by other members of the body who refused to consider the measure. Then in an inflammatory September 19 speech before the agrarian Nonpartisan League convention at St. Paul, Minnesota, the senator claimed, not for the first time, that the *Lusitania* had been carrying munitions and that the "technical right" of American citizens to ride on such foreign vessels, this "comparatively small privilege," was "too small to involve this government in the loss of millions and millions of lives!"[25]

At St. Paul nine days after La Follette's speech, on the same platform where the senator had made his remarks, TR classified him among the "Huns within our gates" whom he would like to send, with all the other "Shadow Huns," as a "free gift to the Kaiser." La Follette's assertion that the *Lusitania* carried munitions was a "falsehood," and the senator knew it. And any man who excused and condoned such "infamy" did not represent the American people. Roosevelt abhorred Germany and the "Hun without our gates," but he abhorred more the "Shadow Huns" within. He repeated his charges in a Minneapolis speech the next day.[26] Though he loathed doing it when action was needed, TR wrote to Kermit, speaking was all he could contribute these days. And "as La Follette had become a real menace" and other public men feared to "attack him boldly and to assail the German newspapers and Alliance in concrete form," he thought it worthwhile to do so in the senator's "home neighborhood." Roosevelt believed he did a certain amount of good, for "my attack undoubtedly inspired the senate to take notice of what he was doing."[27]

While on his Midwest tour, Roosevelt visited Camp Grant, near Chicago at Rockford, Illinois, and gave another speech under the auspices of the National Security League. The army, said TR, had not even begun to prepare and could not at the moment "fight 60,000 German soldiers."[28] General Barry's "big drafted men's camp," Roosevelt reported to Archie, had uniforms for the men but only 5,000 old Spanish War Krag rifles for 20,000 draftees. Since there was no artillery, they had made wooden guns with which to drill. Roosevelt laid part of the blame at the feet of the "very inefficient" Major General William Crozier, the Chief of Ordnance, but the real fault in his view lay "at the head" with Baker and Wilson. The next day, TR spoke at Fort Sheridan, Illinois, and the nearby Great Lakes Naval Training Station. At the first he addressed 4,000 officer candidates, whom he described as an "admirable body of men." At the naval station 14,000 sailors were being trained under Captain Moffatt, who Roosevelt gleefully confided to Archie had gone ahead despite a lack of orders from Washington. The men applied to Moffatt "a modification of Farragut's order—'Damn the Department; Go Ahead.'"[29]

Roosevelt's public criticism was answered by Crozier, who announced that there were sufficient weapons in the camps for drills, that a six-month delay in supplying rifles was "perfectly endurable," and that by the time any soldier was ready to go to Europe there would be a rifle for him. Having trained raw recruits himself, TR considered Crozier's response "utterly unworthy" and the general's statement about the "perfectly endurable delay" in supplying weapons "entirely wrong." After a week's basic training the best officers, the Colonel wrote the publisher Frank Munsey, always wanted to get rifles into the hands of recruits and then wanted to train the men afterwards with their rifles and on how to take care of them. Two generals in charge of training cantonments had complained privately to Roosevelt that they were "gravely handicapped" by the shortage of rifles and by the "complete absence" of guns for the artillery units. Crozier, he went on, was at one time "a very good bureau man for bureau work," but for the last few years his work "had not been done in a way that should make him the head of his bureau at this time."[30] TR repeated these points in a scathing October 14 *Kansas City Star* editorial, "Broomstick Apologists."

The delay in supplying rifles came in part because Crozier had promoted a plan, objected to by Leonard Wood and TR, to change the caliber of the British Lee-Enfield rifle being mass produced for the army to match ammunition already on hand for the old Springfield Model 1902. Therefore, in Roosevelt's view, Crozier was "directly responsible for our not having many hundreds of thousands of the new rifles now." He also took exception to the declaration in Frank Munsey's New York *Sun* that "naturally, we have no million new rifles stored in arsenals." There was nothing "natural" about this, TR reproached Munsey, and it was the "gross fault" of Wilson and his War Department officers including Crozier. The *Sun* placed the "real responsibility" on Congress when in the Colonel's estimation it lay with Wilson, who remained deaf to the cries for preparedness and "misled Congress and the people by his attitude." For a year and a half the president did everything in his power to "prevent all preparedness." And then for another year and half "went every which way, speaking for preparedness sometimes, sometimes speaking, and *always* acting, against it." And after War Secretary Lindley Garrison was "turned out" for standing even for an "insufficient measure," it was "utterly impossible to expect that Congress would act favorably."[31]

One of TR's first editorials for the *Kansas City Star* lampooned the administration war effort so far by portraying Uncle Sam as still taking off his coat and boasting in "grandiloquent pronunciamentos" what he was about to do, eight months after "Germany went to war with us, and we severed relations with Germany as the first move in our sixty days' stern foremost drift into, not going to war." Roosevelt went on more seriously that in those eight months the country had "paid the penalty for our criminally complete failure to prepare during the previous three years" by not having "yet to our credit one single piece of completed achievement." One day, he went on, it was announced that the country had an "infallible remedy against submarine attack," and the next day it was announced that the submarine toll was "heavier than any previous month." At the same time it was proclaimed that America was going to have "an immense army of aircraft—some time next spring." Meanwhile America's allies were actually accomplishing things.[32]

Roosevelt's editorial was carried in hundreds of newspapers. One of these, the *Fort Worth Star Telegram*, received an outraged letter to the editor from the mayor of Abilene, Texas, which called the article "nothing short of the expression of the thoughts of a seditious conspirator who should be shot dead." Further, the editor who was responsible for printing it should be tarred and feathered and the paper excluded from the mails of the United States. The *Star Telegram* published this side by side with a response that invited the mayor to bring his tar and feather party to Fort Worth, where he would "find no difficulty in locating the said Editor-in-Chief," and assured him that his reception "would not be lacking in hospitality or warmth."[33] Roosevelt responded that, although "differing in method of expression," the "slightly homicidal bleat of the gentle-souled" mayor was "exactly similar in thought to the utterances of all these sheep-like creatures who raise quavering or incoherent protests against every honest and patriotic man who points out the damage done by our failure to prepare." Yet none of these people could deny "one fact" that he had stated in detailing shortages from guns to uniforms. Covering up the truth by "bluster and brag and downright falsehoods," said TR, might deceive "ourselves, but will deceive no one else, whether friend or foe." Let the country, he concluded, "learn from our past folly, future wisdom."[34]

"Teddy's Ravings" against the administration's handling of the war in the *Kansas City Star* and on the stump drew the attention of the cabinet. William Gibbs McAdoo denounced the Colonel's "utter hypocrisy and lack of patriotism in trying to make the rest of the world believe" that America was as "feeble and as weak as he represents her."[35] Josephus Daniels noted in his October 5 diary that "T.R. at large, writing and speaking in disparagement of America's preparation for war" was "helping Germany more than the little fellows" who were being arrested for giving seditious "aid and comfort" to the enemy. He wondered if the Kansas City paper that printed TR's "allusions to soldiers training with broomsticks" could be excluded from the mails (as authorized by the Espionage Act) along with the other papers that spread what was "construed as seditious." Postmaster General Albert S. Burleson told him that the *Star* was being watched and he would "not hesitate to act."[36] In fact a postal inspector did visit the newspaper office in Kansas City, but no further action was taken.[37]

Meanwhile in France, the first American casualty of the war was announced: Dr. William T. Fitzsimmons, killed in a German air raid on a military hospital. This prompted Roosevelt to comment that the death should "cause us more pride than sorrow," for in striking fashion it illustrated the "two lessons this war should especially teach us—German brutality and American unpreparedness." The country should feel "stern indignation" at the attack on the hospital, which was "merely one among innumerable instances" of Germany's "calculated brutality." But the country should feel "even sterner indignation towards—and fathomless contempt for—the base or unfeeling folly of those who aid and abet the authors of such foul wickedness." And these included all men and women who in any way apologized for or upheld Germany, who assailed any allies, who opposed "our taking active part in the war," or who desired an "inconclusive peace." Because of America's unpreparedness, the country had not in France a "single man on the fighting line" eight months after Germany "went to war against us" and was still "only on the receiving end of the game." The military work now being done was the work of preparation that should have been done three years before. Nine-tenths of wisdom was "being wise in time."[38]

By this time Roosevelt had regained all the weight, and more, lost in the South American ordeal, and the rigors of the war years had left him, in the estimation of both his doctor and his wife, sorely in need of rehabilitation. Their mutual friend Henry Adams commented to Sir Cecil Spring Rice that TR's "egotism has grown on him" and "so has his fat."[39] Consequently, at Edith's gentle prodding, he spent ten days in mid-October 1917 at Jack Cooper's training camp at Stamford, Connecticut. The Colonel explained to Ted's wife Eleanor that he had come to the camp to "lose a little weight and gain a little wind." Cooper, he went on, was an "old-time skin-glove fighter who had made training almost into a fine art." The men in camp with him ranged from "professional athletes, touching the underworld, on one side, and gilded youth and frayed gilded age on the other," and everyone accepting it all "as simply as so many June bugs."[40]

After a physical exam showed TR's heart and lungs were sound, Cooper set up a daily regimen for the Colonel that included a three-mile hike before breakfast, a massage, and then several hours of exercises under the tutelage of the camp instructors. Though the people at the camp amused him, Roosevelt soon complained to Kermit that he hated to be doing "foolery things now" when the need was for action, but "Darling Mother" thought it would "rest" him, which it would not, as he was "bored to extinction."[41] Cooper estimated that the Colonel needed to lose 35 pounds—by modern standards, probably closer to 50. Unfortunately, Roosevelt was unwilling to curb his huge appetite, which Cooper said a "dragoon would envy," and the camp made little dent in his weight, although he did lose a few inches from his waist. In an admission he would soon regret, the day he departed the camp, while bantering about boxing with reporters, he revealed that he had been blind in his left eye since a White House sparring match with a young artillery officer. This had not been known of before outside family and close friends, and it only made the press more curious about what other infirmities he might have kept secret.[42] When he returned, Edith thought her husband looked tired and feared the camp "was too much of a strain on his nerves."[43]

On November 2, the United States suffered its first combat deaths of the war after the same AEF battalion that had marched through Paris on July 4 moved into a front line trench, in a "quiet" sector of the French line. That night the newcomers were welcomed by a well-executed German raid in which three Americans were killed and 11 captured. Two days later the French, with much ceremony, buried the three Americans.[44] To the north in the British sector yet another great battle, Third Ypres, entered its final phase at Passchendaele, slogging toward its end, mired in nightmarish mud created by a combination of rain and shelling. Sir Douglas Haig, still the British commander-in-chief, nevertheless pressed his generals to keep up the attacks, while being less than honest about casualties and results. Based on army information, the newspapers printed stories of success, but once again after three months little progress had been made while the British army suffered grievous casualties.

Things appeared even worse in Italy when at Caporetto a combined German and Austrian attack routed the Italian army, which fled back to the Piave River with the loss of 300,000 men taken prisoner and probably an equal number of desertions. The front was only saved from complete collapse when British and French reinforcements were rushed into place in the first days of November. This led to the replacement of the Italian commander, General Luigi Cadorna. The disaster in Italy, declared Roosevelt, should make "every American worth calling such awake to the real needs of the hour" and "arouse in him the inflexible purpose to see this war is fought through to a victorious conclusion, no matter how long it takes, no matter what the expense and loss may be."[45] In a letter to TR, Rudyard Kipling put down Germany's "desperate whack at Italy—and all the propaganda that made the break in the Italian army" to a Hunnish "Holy dread of the U.S.—not only on military but on economic grounds." He admitted that it was a "long,

long, and peculiarly bloody business that we are in for," but he nevertheless maintained that the "Hun's temperament" would in the end "impose his own destruction upon him."[46]

Several correspondents suggested that TR raise an Italian American division to go to Italy's rescue, and Joseph Dixon, the former chairman of the Progressive Party, wrote that the "biggest wisdom the President could display would be to send you to Italy to become the Garibaldi of the nation, and save the cause of the Allies, and thus the cause of Liberty."[47] This was a course the Wilson administration was no more likely to follow than it was to send Roosevelt to France, but any military action in support of Italy was further complicated by the fact the United States was not at war with Austria-Hungary or Turkey, a situation TR longed to remedy and spoke of in the *Kansas City Star*. "A limited liability war in which we fight Germany ourselves and pay money to Italy and Russia to enable them to fight Austria and Turkey, with whom we are at peace," savored to the Colonel of "sharp practice and not of statesmanship." In his view it was a "good rule either to stay out of war or go into it, but not to try to do both things at once."

American war policy, TR went on, also tested "our sincerity when we announced that we went to war to make the world safe for democracy." This phrase was obviously "used in a somewhat oratorical fashion," as the United States had in the last years made the world "entirely unsafe for democracy in the two small and weak republics Haiti and the San Domingo." Therefore the phrase must have meant that "we intended to make the world safe for well-behaved nations great or small, to enjoy their liberty and govern themselves as they wished." If it did not mean this then the phrase was "much worse than an empty flourish, for it was deliberately deceitful." But if it did mean this then "we are recreant to our promise unless we go at once to war with Austria and Turkey," both of which were "racial conglomerates" in which one or two nationalities "tyrannize over subject nationalities." The world would not be safe for democracy, argued Roosevelt, until the Armenians, the Syrian Christians, and the Arabs were "freed from Turkish tyranny" and until the Poles, Bohemians, and Southern Slavs "now under the Austrian yoke" were made into separate independent nations and until the Italians of southwest Austria were restored to Italy and the Romanians of eastern Hungary to Romania. Unless America proposed in good faith to carry out this program, "we have been guilty of rhetorical sham when we pledged ourselves to make the world safe for democracy."[48]

The Allied setbacks on the battlefield made it possible for the European leaders, and particularly David Lloyd George, to enjoy a victory over their generals, who fought hard against any political interference.[49] At Rapallo in Italy on November 7, the Allied leaders agreed to set up a Supreme War Council at Versailles to superintend the overall conduct of the war and coordinate Allied and US military efforts.[50] At the same time, in a second 1917 Russian revolution, the Bolsheviks under Lenin moved to seize power at Petrograd under the slogan "Peace, Land, Bread." And true to at least part of their words, the Bolsheviks soon after opened peace negotiations with

Germany at Brest-Litovsk. On November 9, Roosevelt wrote to Kermit that the Russian "break-up, and the Italian disaster" were very grave. But they only emphasized the "criminal folly of Wilson in having failed to prepare before we went into the war, and in having acted with such indecision, procrastination and feebleness since."[51] On that same date TR sent Quentin a letter of congratulations for his twentieth birthday, telling his son, "I am very proud of you, old boy; I hold my head higher when I think of you."[52]

The situations on the Eastern Front, TR confided to Lord Bryce, left him "pretty despondent." However, he still hoped, and was inclined to believe, that the Russians could not make a "really separate peace" and therefore the Germans would not get any food from them. He confessed he was also "pretty melancholy" about Italy and "puzzled and perplexed" about the

BALANCING THE BOOKS.

Figure 10. "Balancing the Books," *New York World*, November 17, 1917
Theodore Roosevelt Collection, Harvard College Library

political crisis in France, where Georges Clemenceau emerged as premier with the self-imposed mandate of keeping his country in the fight until decisive American force could be brought to bear. As for the Germans, TR told Bryce he did not know whether "most to admire their efficiency or to abhor their hideous moral degeneracy."[53]

In the meantime, Lord Northcliffe had returned to England, where he dodged Lloyd George's attempt to muzzle him by bringing him into the cabinet as head of a new air ministry. The press lord turned this offer down via a letter published in the *Times* of London that also praised American virility and effort, which, he warned, must not be squandered. This bald exhibition of bad form drew much criticism in England, but American opinion in the main was positive.[54] Northcliffe reported to Roosevelt that he had accepted the leadership of the London end of the British War Mission, where he hoped to be "of use to our two countries and to the Earl of Reading," the new head of the British Mission in Washington. Reading, whom Northcliffe considered "very able," was particularly experienced in matters of finance, which had been the press lord's admitted weakness. "My present position," Northcliffe told TR, "leaves me ungagged & able to work for efficiency."[55]

The similarities of their respective positions did not go unnoticed. The *New York World* printed a cartoon titled "Balancing the Books," which showed Roosevelt and Northcliffe writing on both sides of an open ledger, the one inscribing "The U.S. government does everything wrong," the other "The British government does everything wrong."[56] The paper dubbed both men "War Naggers" and claimed that the American effort had been "magnificent" aside from a few minor blunders, understandable in light of the vast scale of the affair.[57] The day Northcliffe's letter was published in the *Times*, Edward M. House and Lloyd George had lunch with the royal family and joked about the prime minister's predicament. When House asked if Northcliffe was to return to the United States, Lloyd George replied, "I hope you will ask for him because I would like to send him. I would even be willing to take Roosevelt for a while in exchange, although," the Welshman added, "not permanently."[58]

From Oyster Bay, TR and Edith motored over to visit Camp Upton at Yaphank, Long Island, where they lunched with their old friend Henry Stimson, now a lieutenant colonel in the field artillery despite being almost fifty and blind in one eye himself. Unwilling to serve in an administrative post, he had used his and Roosevelt's connections to gain an appointment at Camp Upton.[59] At the giant camp in two great meetings (one for white soldiers and one for black soldiers), TR praised the National Army and preached military sermons to the choirs on preparedness, antipacifism, universal service, and a "square deal" for black troops.[60] He was greatly impressed with the officers and men he saw, who were eager to serve and hoped to be sent abroad soon. But, he wrote to Kermit, they only had one-fourth of the rifles and one-tenth of the cannon they needed for proper training. Even worse, they had no ammunition, and after almost three months had still "not fired a shot" in target practice of any kind. This he again put down to Wilson's failure to prepare.[61]

On Thanksgiving at Oyster Bay, Alice tried to persuade her father that he was needed in Washington, since "he alone could steer and eventually lead the Republicans."[62] TR reported to Quentin that he and Alice "saw some Republican senators and congressmen who came out to see me and talk over what action was necessary in order efficiently to speed up the war."[63] Senator Reed Smoot of Utah and Representative Martin Madden of Illinois were among those who lunched at Sagamore Hill. But when it was announced that the Colonel would visit Washington and stay with his daughter, Smoot was quick to deny any political significance, telling reporters that while the Colonel was hugely interested in war affairs and there was "no doubt he would talk to some leaders in the war program," he felt safe in saying there was "no 1920 boom about it; nothing of that nature."[64]

Two days after Thanksgiving, TR departed for Canada, where he gave several speeches at the invitation of Conservative Canadian Prime Minister Sir Robert Borden. Edith, Ethel, and Quentin's fiancée Flora Whitney all came along. The Roosevelt party had a private railway car and stayed at Government House at Toronto. In his address there, the Colonel supported Canada's Victory Loan program and conscription, the central issue in the approaching election in which Borden and the Conservatives would triumph over Sir Wilfrid Laurier and the Liberals. TR declared that he spoke the "literal truth when I say that what has been accomplished by you Canadians," and by their brethren across the British Empire, was "without parallel in history." He thanked heaven that "you men and women of the North" had "spurned the councils of a mean and blind timidity" to play their part in such fashion that their "children's children" would hold their heads high and could "look all the world in the face without flinching." Roosevelt told his audience that he had refrained from speaking formally in Canada until his own country had joined the war and gave him the right to "come there with pride speaking as an equal to equals."[65] Flora was very excited by the crowds and speeches, but she wrote to Quentin from Toronto that she hoped he would not to go into politics, as she had been "severely terrified all the time" and feared she would never make a "good diplomat's wife." When people asked her questions, she told him, "my tongue becomes paralyzed & my brain gets 'paresis' or something," and she was "incapable of articulating."[66]

TR reported to Ted that in Canada he was greeted with "frantic enthusiasm." He also told his son that he had a letter of praise from Pershing for Ted having his men at a "razor's edge" of efficiency and that there was a "curiously marked agreement of everybody as to how well you are doing—and Archie's belief and devotion to you are quite touching." The proud father also passed along to Ted that he had had a letter sent from Baghdad by Kermit, who had been made a captain of sappers and sent to the front where there was heavy fighting reported.[67] Kermit had written to his sister Ethel that he was trying to get into the LAMB (light armored motor battery) services, a unit that scouted, reconnoitered, and harassed the enemy in machine-gun-armed Rolls Royces. It was an interesting country, he went on, and a "good part of the war to be in," for it looked as if they were going to push on and perhaps "make up a little for the Italian disaster."[68] The Colonel told Kermit that he was "more proud of you, and pleased with you," than he could say, and he was glad he got there in time to be sent to the front to take part in the "successful fighting that seems to have occurred during the last two months." Of all the boys, he went on, Kermit had been the first to see active service, although Ted and Archie had now returned from two weeks in the trenches, in a quiet sector.[69]

After some preliminaries, on December 1 Inter-Allied Conference meetings at Versailles began between Lloyd George, the new French premier Clemenceau, the Italian premier Orlando, and Colonel House. Both the British and French, fearful of the German troops now shifting to France following the developments in Russia, pressed House to allow amalgamation of American forces with their armies. But House stood firm on the principle that the United States must have an independent force.[70] Wilson's envoy was also frustrated with the little headway made in ascertaining the war aims of the Allies and became convinced that Wilson must take the lead in a public formulation of terms.[71] Overall, the Texan was disappointed in the results of the Paris talks. He returned to the United States disheartened by the "utter lack of virile unity of purpose and control" he found in Europe.[72]

While the Paris conference had still been in session, Lord Lansdowne, a well-respected Conservative elder statesman and former foreign secretary, had a letter published in the November 29 London *Daily Telegraph* that called for negotiations with Germany for a reasonable and honorable compromise peace, including the creation of a league of nations, in order to save what remained of civilization.[73] To stop any sympathetic growth of pacifism in Britain, Andrew Bonar Law responded for the War Cabinet, declaring that the letter was "a national misfortune" and that a "peace made on this basis would be nothing less than defeat."[74] Lansdowne's proposal, which called for no postwar retaliation or reparations to be aimed at Germany, was not unlike the one Woodrow Wilson had House unsuccessfully put before the Inter-Allied Conference as a first step toward forcing a general peace conference. In fact, Roosevelt, Wood, and Henry Cabot Lodge all put Lansdowne's action down to House's "malign influence."[75]

TR labeled Lansdowne's proposal, which would leave oppressed peoples "under the yoke" of Austria, Turkey, and Bulgaria, a "peace of defeat for the Allies and of victory for Germany." In his opinion it made such a peace "worse to try and hide the shame of defeat behind the empty pretense of forging a league of nations, including Germany, to secure future peace." It would mean that Germany's "unspeakable brutality and treachery" would be "crowned by essential triumph" and would "put a premium upon her repeating the brutality and treachery at the earliest convenient moment." The only safe course to follow was to fight the war through to victory no matter the cost. After the final victory, TR concluded, the United States should join in any arrangement made to "increase the likelihood of international peace" but should treat this as an "addition to, and never as a substitute for, the preparedness which is the only sure guarantee against either war or measureless disaster." To this end, the country should immediately implement "as our permanent national policy" a system of "universal obligatory military training of all our young men."[76] When Newton Baker came out publicly against permanent universal military training, the Colonel responded that the war secretary was taking in effect the "position of Mr. Bryan, which was picturesquely phrased as being that a million men can at need spring to arms overnight." The administration's attitude was expressed "less picturesquely" but was "precisely as futile and as unspeakably mischievous from a standpoint of permanent national interest."[77]

Meanwhile, developments on the Western Front, after appearing bright for the Allies, had foundered. In the first few days following the November 20 push at Cambrai, the British army had made impressive gains using 476 tanks in an attack on a quiet sector. Two days later the *Daily Mail* hailed the assault as a "Splendid Success," and a full-page headline proclaimed, "HAIG THROUGH THE HINDENBURG LINE." Unfortunately, the momentum of the British spearhead was soon reversed when reserves were not brought up fast enough either to exploit the breakthrough or to halt the German counterattack. A national celebration of ringing church bells prompted by overenthusiastic reports of victory soon turned into anger and disillusionment at the suppression of news about the subsequent reversals. The British government, which already felt it was being misled by the generals, would not support any further costly attacks and turned as had the French already toward a defensive policy in wait of the gathering American army.

In his December 4 annual message to Congress, Wilson reaffirmed his faith in the sanctity of the cause for which the nation fought and his confidence, despite all the carping criticism being aimed at the administration, in the adequacy of the war measures being undertaken. These, he assured his audience, would lead inevitably to the defeat of the enemy, whatever their recent battlefield successes. He dismissed Roosevelt and the other "noisily thoughtless and troublesome" voices that spread doubts among the people as of no consequence and drowned out by the "voices of humanity," which demanded a "just and righteous accounting from the enemy who in the end would be compelled to yield."[78] Wilson denounced the military masters of Germany for plunging the world into war in a grab for power, but he stated that the United States had no desire to interfere with the internal affairs of Austria-Hungary. However, the address called for a declaration of war on the Dual Monarchy, as TR had demanded, and this was carried out three days later.

This rare congruence of opinion led Roosevelt to praise Wilson in a *Kansas City Star* editorial for admirably setting forth the "firm resolve of the American people that the war shall be fought to the end" until it was "crowned by the peace of complete victory." At the same time he did not fail to point out that his own calls for a declaration of war against Austria-Hungary over the last months had been mercilessly attacked by the same newspapers that now supported the administration. Nevertheless, he joined those Americans to whom the honor and welfare and high ideals of the country were dear to say "amen to the President's expressed purpose to wage this war through to the end with all our strength and to accept no peace save that of complete victory."[79]

The declaration of war on Austria-Hungary did not sooth Roosevelt for long, and he returned to the attack in the *Kansas City Star*, pointing out that in his address to Congress Wilson had mentioned the "very embarrassing obstacle" that stood in America's way to bringing the war to a "righteous conclusion": the fact that the country was not at war with Germany's allies. However, the president had only recommended declaring war against Austria and not Bulgaria and Turkey as well. In TR's view, there had been no justification whatever for not declaring war on Austria at the same time as Germany, and there was now no justification for not declaring war on Germany's two other allies. There was "no use in making four bites of a cherry" and no use in "going to war a little, but not much." Wilson had sent a pledge of support to Romania, but it was "worse than an empty form" to send such a message unless America declared war on Bulgaria. The president had set a Sunday aside for a "special expression of sympathy" with Armenia, but this was "utterly meaningless" unless America declared war on Turkey. The Austro-Hungarian and Turkish empires had to be broken up as TR had previously outlined, "if we intend to make the world even moderately safe for democracy." Only in this way "can we remove the menace of German aggression" that had become "a haunting nightmare for all civilizations, especially in the case of small, well-behaved, liberty-loving peoples."[80]

Roosevelt listed the continued wartime failures of the Wilson administration in a letter of indictment to Kermit dated December 10. The new head of the General Staff, Tasker Bliss, was "particularly no improvement" over his predecessor Hugh Scott, since both men's expertise lay in the nineteenth-century Indian Wars. And Bliss's chief Baker, said TR, continued to be a "well-meaning little humanitarian, ridiculous as the head of a great military department." But at least Kermit's theater of war had seen the capture of Jerusalem, the "one bright spot in the newspaper for the last fortnight." Elsewhere, Russia seemed "in the anarchy which brings dissolution," Italy was "on the verge of ruin," and the French were "unquestionably very much disheartened." Worst of all, after ten months, "we are still onlookers; America does not yet count." Fortunately, Kermit was having a "most interesting experience; Baghdad, the Indian troops, the ruins of cities which flourished in the immemorial past," and now "doing your part in the great hero-epic of the present."[81] TR wrote Kermit's wife Belle, in Spain with her parents, that her husband was "more fortunate than the other three boys in being with a well-organized army." The others were among the "many thousands of gallant young fellows" who were paying with their bodies for the "folly of our people, and the sharp, conscienceless political maneuvering of our should-be leaders," which were responsible for "our hideous delays and blunders."[82]

While the Hearst press and others continued to portray Roosevelt running amuck as a critic of the Wilson administration, some thought TR had not been forthright enough. Ralph Stout, the editor of the *Kansas City Star*, wrote him that he had "never worn gum shoes" and never would, but to be frank he thought the Colonel had been "speaking rather softly of late." The *Star* wanted Roosevelt to write what he thought, and the paper would print it.[83] The Colonel needed little urging, and a week before Christmas Roosevelt took off his gloves in Stout's paper, using General Crozier's admission of deficiencies in testimony before the Senate Military Affairs Committee, which laid the blame on funding, labor, and contract problems. Because the administration continued to persevere in its old policies of unpreparedness, wrote TR, it therefore assumed "complete responsibility for every blunder and delay, and for all the misconduct," while at the same time complacently announcing that all these errors had "taught us nothing, and that we are to amble onward until . . . brayed in the mortar of terrible calamity."

Eleven months since Germany "went to war with us," Roosevelt declared, the United States still had not built an airplane "fit to match the speedy battle planes of our foes." The country had not built a heavy field gun and had to rely on French artillery while the artillery regiments in the national training camps still had about ten wooden guns for every old field piece and none of the modern guns they would use in the field. There were rifles only for every third or fourth man, wooden machine guns, and improvised trench mortars. Until the previous month the troops had even lacked warm clothing. At the moment, not one-tenth of the American forces were fit to go into battle. All this was due, the Colonel went on, "solely and entirely" to the policy of unpreparedness to which the administration adhered for two-and-a-half years "when even the blind ought to have read the lesson of the Great War." It would be "criminal folly" for the American people to follow an administration that now announced that "we are not to alter this policy and that we are to continue the do-nothing policy of refusing to help."[84]

Hearst's editor-in-chief, Arthur Brisbane, complained to Woodrow Wilson that Roosevelt should not be permitted "in all the newspapers of the United States to say unrebuked that which would put in jail some Little socialist editor, and cause his newspaper to be suppressed." He believed it would be extremely popular if the president, or one of his departments, would "remind Mr. Roosevelt" that the "United States at war" was not a "playground for ex-presidents to display their foolish egotism." Brisbane also pointed out that TR's attacks were printed abroad and belittled the United States in the eyes of the European nations, particularly England, where they would be passed "BY THE CENSOR THERE AND PRINTED EVERYWHERE."

The editor further complained that Hearst's reply, which argued that the Republicans had little room to criticize the administration after their own mishandling of the Spanish-American War, was not allowed by the British to be sent abroad via the cables they controlled, because Hearst's newspapers "had not been edited to suit England." Brisbane hoped the time would come when "this government will tell England that the United States Censor" was the censor for the American press and that England "should be contented with censoring her own press." And if England was justified in forbidding Hearst the use of the mails and cables because he was "alleged to have said some things not flattering to England," would not the United States be justified in similarly "refusing Roosevelt permission to send to England by mail or by cable his statements that are intended to bring the United States government into contempt and inspire the Allies with disgust and dislike of the Americans and those that direct American affairs?"[85]

Wilson replied, through his secretary Joseph Tumulty, that though he appreciated Brisbane's letter, he really thought that the best way to treat "Mr. Roosevelt" was to "take no notice of him. That breaks his heart and is the best punishment that can be delivered." And while what TR said was "outrageous in every particular," he did, Wilson was afraid, "keep within the limits of the law." He was "as careful" as he was "unscrupulous."[86] Though he took no action against Roosevelt, Wilson's administration did see to it that England dropped its prohibitions against the Hearst publications—a victory of sorts for Brisbane and his chief.

Well aware of the demands made of the administration to muzzle him, TR reported to Archie that he could not tell him the whole truth of the situation because of the censor. Hearst, he went on, was now "hand in glove with the administration" and had been "yelling that I ought to be imprisoned," and the authorities were "merely debating about what action about me they will take." How he wished they "*would* try to act against me." He was not in government employ, and there was nothing that he would "more eagerly welcome" than any action that would make his voice carry further as he demanded the speeding up of the war and pointed out "our delays, inefficiencies and shortcomings."[87]

The 1917 Christmas season was the first at which none of the four boys were at the family gathering at Oyster Bay, but Theodore and Edith soldiered on, with Alice and her husband Nick and Ethel and her two children. Roosevelt continued the tradition of playing Santa Claus at the local Cove School, which his sons had all attended, giving out gifts to the sixty boys and girls who that year marched up to him for his season's greetings.[88] On Christmas Eve, a "hardened and wary old father" remonstrated with Quentin about his long failure to write, both to his "adamantine" mother, who had stopped herself as a consequence, and to his fiancée. Whether or not he wrote to the family, TR went on, would make no permanent difference, but Flora, who had told Ethel of the matter, was another thing. Her friends were receiving three or four letters a week from their loved ones in France, and unless Quentin wanted to lose Flora, Roosevelt exhorted his son to "write all the time!" and to send her "letters—interesting letters, and love letters—at least three times a week"—no matter how tired he was, no matter how inconvenient it was, even if he was "smashed up in a hospital" or "doing your most dangerous stunts" or when "your work is most irksome and disheartening."[89]

The Colonel's aviator son was not "smashed up," but he was in hospital with pneumonia and spent several weeks in Paris recuperating under the watchful eye of Ted's wife, Eleanor, still busily engaged in war relief work for the YMCA while looking out for the Roosevelt contingent.[90] Many soldiers in the overcrowded training camps in the United States were also suffering from pneumonia and other diseases including typhoid, cholera, and measles. In the southern tent camps the unusually cold winter found men without blankets, and in some places the disease outbreaks reached epidemic proportions, a harbinger of the more deadly influenza pandemic that would soon strike the army and the world.[91] All this only added to the criticism of the Wilson administration and elicited myriad letters of complaint to Roosevelt, while the CPI continued to issue statements defending the government.

Quentin revealed his illness in a December 16 letter, in which he also complained that his brothers had been chiding him as a shirker for his billet at Issoudun one hundred miles south of the trenches, which allowed him to enjoy the comforts of Paris. Roosevelt replied that he was "amused and indignant" that Ted and Archie had let him think they regarded him as "embusquée," and he did not for one minute believe that they really thought so. In his opinion, as a pilot Quentin had been of all of them "the one in most real danger" and the first to suffer the pneumonia. (All this was truer than his father knew, for by this time Quentin had survived two training crashes and a serious motorcycle accident while he had been out scouting the countryside for supplies for his unit.) On the home front, TR reported that he was "busy doing nothing." He spoke now and then, but it was a "mighty poor substitute for action." Seemingly, he was the only man who cared to try to "wake our officials out of their stupor of fatuous complacency" and point out a "few of our more vital shortcomings and endeavor to get them remedied." He thought of nothing but the war and its attendant industrial problems.[92] And this he would continue to do in 1918.

CHAPTER 11

THE PEOPLE'S WAR

JANUARY TO MARCH 1918

> It is a very unjust world in which my sons and their wives and their
> mother and I have to pay for the slothful and utterly selfish ambitions of a
> cold-blooded and unprincipled demagogue. History *may* never discover
> it; but when this war is over I shall write a full and truthful record of why
> we went in late and so unprepared and of the incredible baseness which
> lay behind.
>
> —TR to Archibald Roosevelt, February 8, 1918

Despite receiving numerous greetings and good wishes, including many
from those who had been critics, Roosevelt wrote to Sir Cecil Spring Rice
from Sagamore Hill on January 2, 1918, that it had been "indeed far from a
happy New Year." In large part this was because the Colonel's old friend had
been recalled to England, officially on account of his health, which had never
been good. But in truth the change was the culmination of years of criticism
concerning his suitability for the position. The handwriting had been on the
wall for Spring Rice since his champion Sir Edward Grey was replaced by
Arthur Balfour at the Foreign Office a year before, and the dismissal was carried out by cable with no previous notice and without the usual honors given
in reward for years of service in an important post. Theodore commiserated
with Cecil that his sorrow at being ignobly removed from Washington could
be balanced with national pride; whereas TR could take pride in his sons
"but certainly not yet [in] what the nation has done. Yet—who would have
thought of little Kermit, twenty-five years ago, being where he is now?" To
TR, the maddening thing was that "our people know so little, understand so
little" of what was going on.[1]

On his way home Spring Rice stopped at Ottawa to stay with the governor-
general, the Duke of Devonshire, a kinsman of his wife, Florence. The ambassador's departure from Washington that January, Alice noted at the time, had

"a Socrates death-scene feeling about it," and a little more than a month later he died while still in Canada.[2] Some claimed this came from a broken heart over the manner of his removal.[3] "We dearly loved Cecil," the Colonel wrote to Lady Spring Rice, "he was our close friend for over thirty years." Her husband had "lived a fine, gallant life of disinterested usefulness, and he died as finely and gallantly." On the whole, he thought that "no English Ambassador for a century had as difficult and important task to perform as Cecil during the last five years." It was a task of "wearing anxiety; and called for the most devoted patriotism, for infinite patience, watchfulness and keenness of vision, and for complete self-abnegation." Every one of these qualities he showed "in extraordinary degree." He and Edith had looked forward "eagerly to the time when you and he could leave care behind—when the world had passed through its present awful travail—and could come here to stay with us and to talk on the innumerable matters about which we wished to question you or which we wished to discuss with you."[4]

That month Roosevelt agreed to become the honorary president of the American Defense Society and was their guest of honor at a January 16 luncheon at the Union League Club in New York. In his remarks, TR declared that he believed it was his "prime duty to tell the truth when it was in the interest of the nation that the truth be told," just as he had done after the Spanish-American War when he called for cutting through the red tape in Washington that had hampered the conflict. To those who told him not to tell America's foes about our faults, Roosevelt responded, "Do you think that von Hindenburg and von Tirpitz don't know about them?" They had their spies in America by the thousands and knew "everything about them." There was only "one set" of people that did not know, and that was "the American people."[5]

The Colonel's name and efforts were also used by many relief drives in aid of France. For example, he was on the advisory board with Robert Bacon of the New York Committee of the "Fatherless Children of France," the secretary of which was TR's sister Corinne. His name in an appeal for the "French Heroes Fund" drew a letter and a check for $500 for the cause from Ion Perdicaris, whom TR famously had helped liberate from captivity in Morocco years before. Writing from his home in Kent, Perdicaris told the Colonel that he had already taken in Belgian soldiers and given generously to other war charities but could not refuse a subscription "to which *you* have appended your esteemed signature."[6] Countless others undoubtedly felt the same, and Roosevelt's direct and indirect fund-raising activities buoyed a multitude of appeals in the war years.

These included several for Russia, where a civil war raged on in which the Bolsheviks fought for control with several contending forces. While Woodrow Wilson tried to follow a policy of nonintervention, the United States and the Allies all struggled to establish informal relations in the forlorn hope that some eastern pressure could be maintained on the enemy. The previous December the Bolsheviks had begun publishing the secret treaties concluded with Nicholas II in which the Allies variously agreed to carve up the Middle

East, cede Austrian territory to Italy, and give over the Rhineland to French domination.[7] On December 22, a week after concluding an armistice, representatives of the Central Powers sat down at Brest-Litovsk with the Bolsheviks, who demanded that the meeting be turned into a general peace conference on liberal terms including national self-determination and invited the United States and Allies to send representatives.[8] The British and French had no intention of doing so, but Wilson, who thought peace might be at hand, decided to answer by laying out his terms.

Consequently, before a joint session of Congress on January 8, 1918, Wilson offered "the only possible programme" for world peace, his famous Fourteen Points, including open diplomacy, freedom of the seas, and a league of nations. He also made clear for the first time his views on territorial questions, supporting France's claim to Alsace-Lorraine and the creation of an independent Poland, while rejecting the claims of Italy revealed in the secret treaties. His plan, Wilson declared, was a response both to the "voice of the Russian people" reflected in the Bolshevik demand for a general liberal settlement and to the fact that the Central Powers had made it clear that they aimed at the conquest and dismemberment of Russia. The now mostly forgotten Point Six called for the evacuation of all Russian territory and the "independent determination of her own political development and national policy." Further, Wilson called on the other nations of the world to give Russia any assistance "she may need or desire" and "assure her of a sincere welcome into the society of free nations under institutions of her own choosing." The treatment of Russia would be the "acid test" of the goodwill of nations. Point Fourteen, in the end the dearest to Wilson's heart, was a call for a "general association of nations" including Germany to be formed for the "purpose of affording mutual guarantees of political independence and territorial integrity to great and small nations alike."[9]

Roosevelt dismissed the Fourteen Points, crowned with a "league of peace," as "fourteen scraps of paper" aimed not at the unconditional surrender of Germany but a "peace without victory" of conditional surrender of the sovereignty of America to an international league.[10] Wilson, TR wrote to Rudyard Kipling in a letter circulated to the British War Cabinet, did not mean to do "anything effective against the Mittel-Europe world menace," just as at present he was "underhandedly endeavoring" to urge peace terms that, "under the guise of high-sounding phrases," would leave Germany "substantially victorious." He was "entirely willing to pose as the great peacemaker" if this seemed "more personally profitable." But Wilson would leave the war the moment he could profitably do so, eating "all his past declarations without even looking uncomfortable." Since the country had entered the war, Wilson had been holding out the "furtive flag of truce to the pacifists and pro-German elements here at home," instead of prosecuting the war with "energy and singleness of purpose." And, Roosevelt prophesied, "three of my sons will probably pay in life or limb for his callous self-seeking." One member of the War Cabinet, Lord Milner, commented that, though the letter was "rather one-sided and exaggerated," there was "no doubt something in" TR's indictment.[11]

While Wilson spoke of world peace, that January widespread shortages forced the government to extreme measures, including the rationing of coal by Fuel Administrator Harry Garfield. Roosevelt decried the resulting "industrial paralysis." America had not "as yet inflicted any injury on Germany, but our unpreparedness has caused us to suffer from economic disturbances within our own borders."[12] The Colonel reported to Kermit that the administration had "closed all the factories, theaters and the like" to save fuel for the trains. The remedy he thought "was rather worse than the disease" and had aggravated the suffering among the workers. He went on that at the War Department, where "elderly mutton-heads had been put in the highest places," the delays and blunders were "heartbreaking." The administration had done nothing compared to what ought to have been done regarding the needed ships, cannon, and auto-rifles, not to mention shoes and overcoats. He feared it would be a year before the AEF was large enough to effect the result. Meanwhile, "the little army we have now in France may be sacrificed."[13] Roosevelt knew of the shoe and other shortages directly from his sons in France. That month he sent Archie, who had been promoted to Captain, one hundred pairs he had requested for his men, and TR reported to his son that the drafted men in training now mostly had rifles but still only wooden cannon and machine guns.[14]

In New York on January 19, Roosevelt attended a huge National Security League luncheon for 1,700 people at the Hotel Astor in honor of George Chamberlain, the Democratic chairman of the Senate Military Affairs Committee, and Julius Kahn, a Republican congressman from California who had come to the United States from Germany with his parents as a small boy. Though a Democrat, Chamberlain had presented a bill to provide universal military service and was a critic of the administration's war effort, and in particular of Newton Baker. In his remarks, Chamberlain charged "as an American citizen" that the military establishment of America had "fallen down." There was no use to be "optimistic about a thing that does not exist." It had "almost stopped functioning" because of the "inefficiency in every bureau and in every department of the Government of the United States." He urged the passage of a bill to create, as had the British, a Ministry of Munitions and a War Cabinet of "three distinguished citizens of demonstrated . . . ability" to direct the war.[15] Roosevelt led the applause, while Congressman Kahn added that "a few prompt trials and a few quick hangings" were what was needed.[16]

No war council would be established, a furious Wilson informed the cabinet, "until he was dead." He accused the Republicans of "conspiring to make political capital by attacks on the conduct of the war." They wanted, he went on, a cabinet that represented privilege and did not "think as we do because they wish to act for a class." Nevertheless, a shaken Newton Baker, who looked five year older to Josephus Daniels, declared that he was willing to resign. But the navy secretary advised him that Wilson would never allow it and that the opposition would not be satisfied with anyone except TR, Elihu

Root, or Leonard Wood, to which the president would also never agree.[17] Wilson defended Baker in a press release that labeled Chamberlain's accusation an "astonishing and absolutely unjustifiable distortion of the truth." His claim that there was inefficiency in every bureau and department, said Wilson, showed "such ignorance of actual conditions as to make it impossible to attach any importance to his statement." And further, the legislative proposals that Wilson had heard of would only lead to "long additional delays and turn our experience into mere lost motion."[18] The president immediately began drafting an alternative proposal that became the Overman Bill, in which ultimate power to reorganize the government agencies and departments as needed in the emergency rested with Wilson instead of some extraordinary body.

In the Senate on January 21, TR's old enemy William Stone of Missouri carried out his most virulent attack so far, and after quoting extensively from his articles he labeled Roosevelt the "most seditious man of consequence in America." The Republican leaders, Stone charged, had instigated most of the investigations under way simply to make political capital. It was a "shrewd movement," he went on, "to plant the mine and get some simple-hearted—I will not say simple-minded Democrat to fire it off." Referring plainly to the Colonel, the senator continued that "rising out of this cloud" was the "abhorrent figure of the political hag, stirring the cauldron of domestic partisanship to disturb even in this hour of national peril the sympathetic unity of the American people." Roosevelt's heart was "aflame with ambition and he runs amuck." Since the country's entrance, TR had been a "menace and obstruction to the successful prosecution of the war." His "chief thought had been of Roosevelt," as almost every day he spoke in "bitter and contemptuous disparagement of the President and of the Majority members of this Congress." He was publishing under contract "for money—think of it for money—villainous screeds in the Kansas City *Star*." This outburst set off an uproar in the chamber and was answered in more measured words by Henry Cabot Lodge and Boies Penrose.[19]

As all this played out, Roosevelt arrived at Washington to take the fight directly to Wilson, discuss party matters with congressional Republicans, and give any aid he could to Chamberlain's proposals. In a brief statement, TR declared that he was in Washington "to help every man who sincerely desires to speed up and make effective our preparations in this war." He would stand "by the efficient and against the inefficient man," as would anyone who was "really and intelligently loyal to this country." When the newsmen asked for comment on Stone's attack, the Colonel replied that he found it amusing to be accused of aiding the Kaiser by a man who had in his opinion "done everything to help Germany before the United States entered the war and since then had done everything that would help America to be inefficient in the war."[20] He also told reporters, "If they wish to arrest me, I am here."[21]

In Washington TR stayed with Alice at the Longworth house, which was kept under siege for four days by myriad callers. The residence became a rallying point for Republicans of all stripes, and some Democrats, unhappy with Wilson's prosecution of the war. Many members of Congress were further inspired in their criticisms by the death of Major Augustus P. Gardner from pneumonia, at Camp Wheeler a week before. The former Massachusetts representative, Wilson critic, and preparedness ally of TR had been the first member to resign and join the armed forces. One representative told his colleagues in the House, "If we have boys in the encampments who are being sacrificed, they ought to be sacrificed for the country and not by the country."[22] As might be expected, Roosevelt and Lodge, Gardner's father-in-law, particularly held Wilson and Baker accountable for the death.

As always, the Colonel attracted a horde of reporters. At one point Alice recalled looking over her bannister and counting "thirty-three newspaper correspondents, fairly stacked in the small hall." A representative front-page headline generated for the *Cleveland Plain Dealer* blared, "WILSON READY TO BATTLE ROOSEVELT, PRESIDENT IN HOT FIGHT FOR WAR CONTROL." The first night, Nick Longworth hosted a men's dinner at which the Colonel discussed party plans with a score of Republican political figures, Old Guard and Progressive. One of them told Alice (who had dined out with Edith) that the evening was a "great success" and that "many backbones were stiffened." And for the next three days, from breakfasts through dinners, TR held forth and rallied his forces.[23]

The pro-Wilson editor of the *Washington Times*, Arthur Brisbane, editorialized that the "spectacle of a former President coming to the capital to organize war against the Government" when the nation was at war with Germany was "something new" and the "most original of Theodore Roosevelt's many original ideas." The Colonel came to Washington, Brisbane went on, "as the spokesman of high finance" and acted as the "agent of the very rich, organizing a political fight to give the corporations control of the United States Government at the next Congressional election." Further, Roosevelt's attacks on the president had "encouraged Germany and prolonged German resistance."[24] This editorial, Wilson wrote Brisbane, was "a corker," and TR certainly was not "setting forward those purposes of harmony and cooperation which are absolutely essential just now in the counsels and in the action of the country."[25]

Roosevelt's only public appearance in Washington came before the National Press Club, where he had been the first president to speak nine years before. TR attacked the administration for "shielding incompetence," called for a speeding up of the American war effort, and supported Chamberlain's cry for a ministry of munitions and a war cabinet. He also defended himself against Stone's "partisan and mendacious speech," attacking in return the senator's own patriotism and vote against the declaration of war, which Stone had called "the greatest national blunder in history." It was the duty of all good Americans regardless of party, TR went on, to provide constructive criticism. The only mention Roosevelt made of Wilson was to quote a passage from his *Congressional Government* that called for Congress to "scrutinize" and "sift" the "acts and the disposition" of the "administrative agents of the government," otherwise the country "must remain in embarrassing, crippling ignorance" of the very affairs that it was "most important that it should understand and direct."[26]

The Colonel reported to William Allen White that he had seen a great many senators and congressmen. Three of the former group, he told White, struck him as "hopelessly reactionary, as hopelessly blind to the conditions ahead." But the great majority of the men in the lower house, and many in the senate, appeared to be "sincerely desirous of accepting the fact that we are about to face a changed world and that mere negation and obstruction and attempts to revive the dead past spell ruin." All he spoke to were anxious for him to take "some position of leadership" while equally anxious that he should not think this committed them to supporting him or to making him the candidate in 1920. In response Roosevelt told the legislators that he was "not in the least concerned about your supporting me either now or at any future time." All he was concerned with was that "you should so act that I can support you."[27]

Whatever he told White, out of all these confabulations Roosevelt emerged as the de facto leader of the Republican Party and to a growing number of people the presumed candidate in the next election. The dapper and diminutive Will Hays of Indiana, the soon-to-be elected choice of TR as chairman of the Republican National Committee, wrote the Colonel that he "certainly did great work in Washington" and the whole trouble was that "Mr. Wilson is still trying to keep us out of war."[28] One of the first things Hays would do when elected chairman would be to announce the virtual certainty that Roosevelt would be the Republican candidate in 1920. Those TR consulted in Washington agreed to a three-pronged policy calling for the enactment of a law for permanent compulsory military training, legislation limiting other war measures to the duration of the war, and the creation of a war cabinet and a department of munitions.[29]

In the other camp, Josephus Daniels noted in his diary of January 25, "TR came to town to set up a rump gov. but failed."[30] However, that same day the Morgan partner Edward R. Stettinius, who had coordinated Allied purchasing for the firm, was made surveyor general of all army purchases, which, though not the cabinet-rank minister of munitions post the Republicans had called for, did mollify some of those who demanded a more centralized authority. Roosevelt admitted that the appointment of the "trained and capable" Stettinius represented "a certain advance." But he noted that this advance was "primarily due" to the Chamberlain committee's work and was a "striking tribute to the necessity for and the good results of that investigation." And while the appointment of Stettinius was a good thing, it did not represent "even half a step toward bringing order out of the administrative chaos at Washington." Drastic action was needed to "secure a plan providing for coordination, responsibility and efficiency, and above all, for securing the right men to administer the plan."[31]

Though not as drastic as TR wanted, in the following months several other significant changes of course were made by the administration along the lines its critics suggested. In February, at Edward M. House's urging, Wilson began weekly meetings of what came to be called the "War Cabinet," made up of those members of the larger body most directly involved with the war effort. The next month, Wilson appointed the aloof "Lone Eagle" of Wall Street, Bernard Baruch, to chair and invigorate the War Industries Board, which coordinated the national industrial effort.[32] And on the army front, Baker recalled an able officer from France, Major General Peyton March, as chief of staff in place of Tasker Bliss, who was sent to Europe as American military representative to the Supreme War Council.

The pro-Wilson papers continued their attacks on Roosevelt as heartening the Germans and being driven by his own egomania. The *Minneapolis Daily News*, for example, declared, "Like Caesar's Gaul of old, the colonel's gall is also divided into three parts—the personal pronouns *I*, *me*, and *my*."[33] TR defended his and other attacks on the administration's war effort in the *Kansas City Star*, noting that every important criticism made of "our military unpreparedness and inefficiency during the past six months and indeed the preceding three years" had been proved true, and in no case would there have been "any correction of the abuse until it was exposed." After a year at war, he went on, John J. Pershing had just written home a "scathing indictment of the military shortcomings of our higher officers abroad," which was "directly due to the character of both the civilian and the military control" that had been "exercised for the swivel chairs of the War Department during this year."[34] The critics of Pershing remarked that he gave the impression of being "alone in France," remindful of Finley Peter Dunne's famous description of TR in Cuba.[35]

In another newspaper broadside, Roosevelt declared that this was the "people's war," not the president's or congress's war. The nation was honor bound to "stand by every official that does well and against every official who fails to do well." Any other attitude was servile. Until Congress finally asserted itself with the Chamberlain and other committees, the executive branch did very badly. If Congress followed the lead given in Chamberlain's bill it would continue to do well. If it followed the lead outlined in Senator Overman's bill, it would "condone the inefficiency of the past and put a premium upon inefficiency in the future." Roosevelt exhorted the country to quit being content with "feeble mediocrity" and demand "really first-class efficiency in both preparation and performance." Though it was not agreeable to keep "pointing out our shortcomings," doing so had proved the only way of "remedying them and of securing better action in the future."[36]

Back at Sagamore Hill, Roosevelt reported to Quentin that in his four days in Washington he had been "kept on the jump, literally without a minute's intermission," seeing senators, congressmen, publicists, and army officers. He had "no time to be melancholy" but plenty of time to be "uncomfortable and indignant" over the delay and incompetence on display. He told his son that he was very busy writing and "occasionally speaking, always on behalf of the war; so long as we are still in the talky-talky stage someone has to do the talky-talky on the right side."[37] Most of those he saw in Washington, TR

told Kermit, proved "entirely congenial as to speeding up the war and putting an end if possible to the criminal delay and inefficiency" that marked
its management as far as the Wilson administration was concerned. But, he
went on, "Mother found much sadness," for their old friends (such as Henry
Adams, who would die two months later) were for the most part "dead or
else of horry age."[38]

By this time Roosevelt had developed a painful abscess on his right but-
tock, near a fistula that had remained from the South American ordeal.
The doctors called to Sagamore Hill opened the abscess, but complications
including severe earache forced him into the Roosevelt Hospital in Manhattan. On February 6 he underwent dangerous surgery for both conditions—a
"night of great suffering," Edith recorded in her diary.[39] The papers published daily bulletins on his condition, and a rumor spread that the Colonel
was dying. A representative *New York Tribune* editorial declared, "Theodore
Roosevelt—listen! You must be up and well again; we cannot have it otherwise; we could not run this world without you."[40] Called to his bedside, TR's
sister Corinne found her brother immobilized, lest any movement be fatal.
She recorded that he whispered hoarsely in her ear, "I am so glad it is not one
of my boys who is dying here, for *they* can die for their country."[41] However,
the immediate emergency passed, and ten days later while still recuperating
TR wrote to Quentin that he was "heartily ashamed of himself for being sick
at such a time" and the only feeling he had was that he would have given
anything if, "according to the custom that prevailed in the religions of two
or three thousand years ago, I could have substituted myself as a guarantee
for any one of you boys."[42]

To Kermit, Roosevelt reported that he had gone under the knife and
would be hospitalized two weeks more. He downplayed the seriousness of his
condition, telling his son that the surgery was "entirely trivial." While Roosevelt's heart thrilled with pride at the thought of the service rendered by Kermit and his brothers, he regretted that at home, a year into the war, America
had "accomplished, in a military sense, absolutely nothing." However, at
least the army in France was now reasonably well supplied—by the French.
But it was "sickening" to feel that this army including Ted and Archie might
be sacrificed without any adequate reinforcement because of the "folly and
worse than folly, of our high civilians at home, and of the fuddled elderly
fools of the regular army who were kept in high position by these same civilians." Congress, he reported, had done "infinitely better" than the president,
and the Senate investigation had "forced the worst of the swivel-chair War
Department Generals out of office." He thought there would be a slight
improvement, and in the end, though the incompetence of the administration kept the country from exerting more than a quarter of its strength, "yet
even the exertion of this quarter will accomplish a great deal."[43]

Recovering his equilibrium and strength after the surgery took several
months, and even then TR never regained the hearing in his left ear. In the
interim he reported to Ted's wife that he walked "more like a lunatic duck
than anything else."[44] It was clear to Edith that his old energy was gone,

never to return. Once back on his feet he was "immensely amused" to hear from Arthur Lee in London that the *Times* had asked his friend to update his obituary.[45]

The thousands of messages of good wishes for a speedy recovery that Roosevelt received included a cable from Britain's King George V, whom TR had met and talked with at length in 1910 at the funeral of the monarch's father Edward VII. The Colonel wrote to the king that he "felt ashamed that anyone should be concerned now with such a trivial matter" as his sickness when "we have to think of the all the dreadful suffering of all the men at the front." He hardly needed to say how immensely he admired England's "attitude and all that she has done."

The chief reason Roosevelt professed for wanting to get well was to resume his work of "endeavoring to get my country to exert her great, but lazy and unprepared, strength as speedily and effectively as possible." It was maddening to him to see Russia break and Germany "stride nearer triumph because my country failed to prepare, and failed to act decisively when the Lusitania was sunk—the moment when all our people would have responded without wavering to the call for action." There was only one thing to do, and that was to beat Germany to her knees. And if their two peoples had the "right stuff in them," this is what they would do. But if the "Lansdownes on your side of the water, and the rather more noxious representatives on this side" were "sufficiently numerous and influential," their peoples would fail. In that case they would "speedily have to sink to the position of Holland or else fight the war over again under greater disadvantages."[46]

While Roosevelt had been in the hospital, Wilson had again spoken of peace and war aims in a February 11 message to Congress in which he laid out the "Four Principles" that constituted a "minimal foundation for peace negotiations." This unilateral clarification and amplification was also a response to the reaction of Austria and Germany to the Fourteen Points speech of the previous month. A successful peace, said Wilson, would first have to be based on the "justice of particular cases and their potential for insuring a permanent settlement." Second, peoples and provinces could not be "bartered or treated as chattels." Third, the territorial settlements would have to be made to "accord with the interests of the people directly concerned, rather than to insure a successful compromise between more powerful nations." And finally, national aspirations would have to be recognized "if they did not introduce undue elements of international discord."[47] As with the Fourteen Points, Wilson had not consulted with the Allies before declaring the Four Principles, which injected self-determination into the territorial settlements and further underlined the unique course the president meant to chart for the country, alone if necessary.

On March 3, 1918, the day before Roosevelt left the hospital and managed to walk gingerly on his own to a waiting automobile, the Russian delegates signed the Treaty of Brest-Litovsk, ceding huge swathes of territory to Germany, Austria-Hungary, and Turkey. The harsh and completely unequal terms, imposed at gunpoint by the Central Powers, led TR to comment in

the *Kansas City Star* that the experience of Lenin and Trotsky in the negotiations "ought to be illuminating to our own people," who should "take warning and insist that all peace talk cease forthwith." The Germans encouraged
the Bolshevik leaders to enter negotiations, "spoke fairly to them, got them
committed to the abandonment of their allies, used them to demoralize Russia and make it impossible for her to organize effective resistance, and then
threw them over, instantly invaded their land," and now held part of Russia.
Germany was the "enemy of humanity generally" and in a "special sense"
the enemy of the United States. "Our own sons and brothers," TR went on,
were at this moment "facing death by the awful torture of poison gas," only
one of the new horrors of warfare introduced by Germany and one that "not
another civilized power would have dreamed of using." Peace on equal terms
with such a foe would mean "black shame in the present" and the "certainty
of renewed and wholesale war in the future."

Unfortunately, said Roosevelt, when Washington announced peace terms
that the pacifists and pro-Germans were able to "interpret as favorable to
their views," the Hearst papers "gleefully champion it as undoing the effect
of previous declarations that we are in this war to the finish." The country
should "quit talking peace" with a foe who, if we entered into negotiations,
would only seek to "trick us as he has already tricked the Bolsheviki." Every
"peace utterance" pleased the Germans, rendered America's allies uneasy,
and strengthened the "pacifists, pro-Germans, and the various seditious elements in our own country," while it bewildered, disheartened, and weakened
"our honest citizens."[48]

In a letter to Kermit, TR had noted that he took a "somewhat sardonic
amusement" in the "real panic" that affected a great many people who
had been "bitterly against me for the last three and a half years" and had
"denounced me beyond measure" when for a moment it looked as if "I
might not pull through." When they thought he might die, they "suddenly
had an awful feeling that I represented what down at the bottom of their
hearts they really believed to be right." Although they had followed Wilson,
they knew also, "down at the bottom of their hearts, that they did so only
because he pandered to the basest side of their natures, and gave them an
excuse for following the easy path that led away from effort and hardship
and risk and unpleasantness of every kind, and also incidentally from honor
and duty."[49]

There was indeed at this time an extraordinary outpouring of private and
public affection for TR even in settings not given to such displays, including
a performance of the Annual Review on March 22 at the Winter Garden in
New York City. A remarkable patriotic demonstration occurred at the end of
Al Jolson's comedy act, when as usual a wishing lamp was brought forward
and Jolson held it in his hands while he made a wish that "whatever it may
be will be straightway granted." That evening Jolson "made the hit of the
season" when he repeated slowly, "I wish, I wish, I wish Theodore Roosevelt
was well again." There followed "a moment of breathless pause, and then as
though that particular audience had been a powder magazine that flame had

touched the house exploded into a roar of approval that brought everyone in the great audience to their feet in as spontaneous and remarkable an outburst of enthusiasm as that blasé city has ever been treated to."[50] The nation would need all the patriotism it could muster, as another, German, powder magazine had just exploded in Europe that brought the darkest days of the war so far.

CHAPTER 12

CROWDED HOURS OF
GLORIOUS LIFE

MARCH TO JULY 1918

> I would rather have you four stand at Armageddon even than stand
> there myself. You, personally, are now in the position of the greatest
> danger; but when the trumpets sound for Armageddon only those win
> the undying honor and glory who stand where the danger is sorest.
> —TR to Theodore Roosevelt Jr., March 1918

In Flanders and France, the Allied and American forces were only too aware
that a great blow was about to be delivered by an enemy greatly strengthened by troops freed from the Russian front; the only question was where
the German onslaught would fall. Before this occurred, however, on March
12 Archie became the first of TR's sons to be bloodied in the war when he
had his left arm broken and left knee seriously injured by shrapnel bursts as
he led his platoon on a raid of the German trenches. For this action, in which
he gave several commands and stayed on his feet for some time until being
knocked down by the second wound, Archie received a Croix de Guerre
from a French general while he was on the operating table.[1]

Roosevelt, who was notified in cables from Ted and the War Department,
wrote to Archie that the family was "divided between pride and anxiety,
beloved fellow." He hoped "dearest Eleanor was with him now" and offered
any needed services he could render.

At lunch after receiving the news, TR reported to his son, Edith ordered
the opening of a bottle of Grandfather Isaac Carow's old Madeira—an
unheard of occurrence, as Archie well knew—and the company "filled the
glasses and drank them off to you." Then his mother, "her eyes shining,
her cheeks flushed, as pretty as a picture, and as spirited as any heroine of

romance, dashed her glass on the floor," declaring "that glass shall never be drunk out of again," and the rest followed suit. They now knew, he went on, "what it feels like to have a hero in the family!"[2] In a lighter mood, TR wrote to Kermit that it would have been fine to see Archie receiving his medal, and he imagined "that iron-natured young Puritan's aspect when the French general kissed him on both cheeks!"[3]

An old Rough Rider at the front, John Greenway, reported to Roosevelt about Archie that he had seen Colonel Stark, the commander of the Medical Corps, the day before and was told that the "brave kid" would be all right in four or five months. He added that he was "too delighted" the Colonel was also "mending."[4] War Secretary Newton Baker, on a tour of the front, visited Archie in the hospital, accompanied by a train of reporters. When Baker asked him what he could do for him, Archie, making sure the newsmen were listening, replied that he did not need anything but, if it was not too much trouble, would love some guns and ammunition for his men.[5] Greenway passed along to TR that Baker seemed to "think the war will shortly be over." The Colonel's old friend could not see it that way. He believed the German drive had not started, because they were waiting for dry roads and wanted to get things in the Ukraine and Romania in "safe condition" first, and he looked for their attack in the next sixty days. Greenway added that another Rough Rider there, Bill Davidson, had commented that "with Roosevelt sick—Wood wounded" and the famous ex-heavyweight champion and friend of TR John L. Sullivan dead, the country "was in a bad way."[6]

Though he continued to be denied a fighting command in France, Leonard Wood had been allowed to go to the front on an inspection tour with the other training camp commanders. There he was severely wounded when a trench mortar exploded and killed several soldiers, decapitating a French officer standing next to the general. John J. Pershing had promised Wood soon after he arrived that if he could avoid controversy during the tour he would be given an AEF command. But when Wood was lionized by the French as "America's Greatest Fighter," he was unable to keep his mouth shut, at one dinner calling Woodrow Wilson "that rabbit," and his indiscretions were reported in the foreign press. A furious Pershing reported to Army Chief of Staff Peyton March that Wood was still "the same insubordinate man he has always been" and told Newton Baker that Wood was physically unfit for command.[7]

Once he returned home, Wood further alienated the administration by writing a series of reports underlining the War Department's failures in supplying adequate arms and equipment, in particular airplanes, which the administration had promised to deliver in tens of thousands to sweep the enemy from the sky and save American lives on the ground via air power. An astounding $649 million had been committed to building an enormous air fleet, and the effort was put under the dual command of Major General George Squier and Howard Coffin, vice president of the Hudson Motor Car Company. Wood reported to Senator George Chamberlain's outraged Military Affairs Committee that, despite hundreds of millions already spent, there were one thousand AEF flyers in Europe without a single American plane. This despite claims made by George Creel's Committee on Public Information (CPI) and the War Office that several hundred aircraft had been sent and that thousands more would soon follow, an embarrassing error that had to be corrected with an admission that in fact only one had been dispatched. To derail the damaging scandal, Wilson made a rare wartime bipartisan gesture and appointed Charles Evans Hughes as a special prosecutor to look into the matter.[8]

Wood visited Roosevelt at Oyster Bay and told him that what he had seen in three months at the front bore out everything the Colonel had been preaching, except that he had underrated the AEF's needs. It would many months before the Unites States Army would be a "ponderable military factor" in France.[9] After the visit, TR wrote Wood that he was making good use of the reports he had delivered and that none of "our people in the field" had rendered as much service to America as had the general by his testimony before the Senate committee. The reports, the Colonel went on, were as "masterly" as anything of the kind he had seen. They were "*the* documents of the war."[10] Wood also reported to TR that Ted's battalion had earned a reputation as the best in the AEF, a view supported by British General Tom Bridges. Roosevelt wrote to Ted that he would "rather have you four stand at Armageddon even than stand there myself. You, personally, are now in the position of the greatest danger; but when the trumpets sound for Armageddon only those win the undying honor and glory who stand where the danger is sorest."[11]

Armageddon appeared at hand when the long-expected enemy attack finally came. On March 21, 1918, the German army, reinforced by hundreds of thousands of men moved from the Russian front, began a massive assault (codenamed "Michael") on the Allied trench lines—only the first in a series of five major drives over the next four months.[12] This final roll of the dice was meant to end the war in France before the gathering American force made victory impossible. The German government also had to take into account the domestic unrest widely reported in the press among a population dead tired of the sacrifices and burdens of war. Roosevelt had noted this the previous month in a letter to Kermit's wife, Belle, telling her that he took a "grim satisfaction" in seeing that the Germans, who had used the Bolsheviks for their own purposes, now had an "incipient Bolshevik movement of their own" that was causing trouble. He hoped this would interfere with their "Great Drive."[13]

The German attack concentrated on the British Fifth Army, at the point where the British and French sectors joined each other. British casualties in the first few days of this nearly successful attempt to split the two armies were reported to be 150,000. German and British losses the first day alone were 78,000, the highest for any single day in the war. Soon the war of motion, gone since the end of 1914, which the cavalry generals in charge had hoped to rekindle for years with futile attempts at a "breakthrough," returned with a vengeance. The London *Daily Mail* called it the "Greatest Battle of All," which would decide whether Britons would be "Free Men or Slaves."[14] Pershing recalled that he spoke to Lord Northcliffe in London on March 24 about the German advance and found him "almost unable to speak of it, so many of his friends had lost relatives."[15] The day after Pershing saw Northcliffe, the general offered to Philippe Pétain and the French the services of the American forces in the dire emergency, while making no such offer to Sir Douglas Haig and the British. Consequently, American divisions were moved into quiet sectors of the French line, freeing experienced troops for battle.[16]

While these startling developments unfolded in Europe, TR, still recovering from his surgery, was resting at Sagamore Hill. He wrote to a recuperating Archie that it appeared the "great German offensive" had begun "on an enormous scale on the British front." It was a "bitter thought" to him that it was "only our folly during the last three years, and especially during the last eighteen months, that has prevented us from having at this moment in France a couple of million fighting troops, fully equipped with guns, airplanes and everything else," in which case there could be "no German offensive, no hideous loss of life, and peace on our own terms."[17]

In the *Kansas City Star*, Roosevelt blamed the "delay and incompetence of the American Government" and the "shameful betrayal" of the Bolsheviks for giving the Germans a "free hand for their drive against the British army." Three years after the *Lusitania* was sunk and a year since Congress declared war, America was in the "ignoble position" of being "merely an onlooker." This was due to the "folly and the procrastination of our Government and its inveterate tendency to substitute rhetoric for action."

The American army was smaller than the Belgian army and was not holding more of the line than "little Portugal," which had joined the Allies in March 1916. The army in the field of the richest nation, and one of the most populous on Earth, had no airplanes or field artillery, and few machine guns except those supplied by the French. Even the uniforms of the troops were mainly supplied by the British, now engaged in the present terrible battle. In view of the fact that their fleet had protected the United States for three-and-a-half years, declared TR, "let the American people now demand that the Government recognize the need of instant and efficient action." And let the American government, which has "delayed until the Allies have been brought to the brink of destruction," quit "flirting with the Bolshevists at home and abroad." Let it declare war on Turkey at once and "stop boasting about the future and begin to act in the present." Let it act at once "lest the chance for action pass completely by."[18]

By this time Roosevelt had recovered enough (in his opinion if not that of his doctors) from his surgeries to travel to Portland, Maine, to give what he described as an "important" speech on March 28 before the Maine Republican State Convention.[19] On the way he and Edith stopped at Boston, where Archie's wife, Grace, was spending the winter with her parents, and there they met their newest grandchild, Archibald Jr., whom his father in France had never seen and whose birth he had first read of in the Paris *Herald*. The Colonel reported to Archie, now in Blake's Hospital in Paris where he would spend four months, that his "wee son" was "very sturdy and smiles continually" and "certainly does look like you."[20] The Portland address, titled "Speed Up the War and Take Thought for After the War," was meant to set the keynote for the 1918 congressional elections and would also foreshadow the prospective 1920 platform.

The speech first praised congressional Republicans for their nonpartisan support of the war while condemning the Democratic administration for its sluggishness and worse. "We are pledged to the hilt as a nation," TR declared, "to put this war through without flinching until we win the peace of overwhelming victory." America was now bound to remember that "fine phrases," that "bold and lofty declarations of purpose," were valuable only as they were "turned into brave deeds by men who are both strong and true." Consequently, Roosevelt called for a declaration of war on Bulgaria and Turkey. "Unless we war on Turkey precisely as we war on Germany," he went on, "we show that we are insincere when we say that we wish to make the world safe for democracy." The war would be won by "brains and steel not kid gloves and fine phrases."

After the war was won, the country should steer between both reaction and radicalism and individualism and collectivism. For farmers, TR wanted national measures to decrease farm tenancy, increase public irrigation projects, and encourage cooperatives. Corporations, in his long-held view, should be controlled but not destroyed. Government should help, not hamper, business, and he called for partnership between management and labor. To recast the social order and protect the interests of working men, the Colonel proposed national old age, sickness, and employment insurance; public housing projects; and a postwar eight-hour day.[21] These specific proposals encapsulated much of TR's and his party's platform for that year's elections.[22]

In the Portland speech and in *The Foes of Our Own Household*, TR wrote to William Allen White, he was trying to carry out the same purpose: to make the Republicans the party of "sane, constructive radicalism, just as it was under Lincoln." If it was not, he went on, then of course he "had no place in it." If the "Romanovs of our social and industrial world" were kept at the "head of our government," said Roosevelt, the result would be Bolshevism, and Bolshevism meant "disaster to liberty writ large across the face of this continent." He believed the book and speech represented the general direction the party must move in, but of course this could not be accepted if the party was to be one merely of criticism, delay, and reaction. They could be accepted if the party was prepared for a "liberal, constructive platform" that would seem "reasonably satisfactory to conscientious, practical and courageous men" who intended to go "unswervingly and steadily forward" and yet not to rush "headlong like a frightened hog into whatever radicalism seems at the moment to be favored by the masses of voters." Further, TR did not think he overstated the matter when he said that the Maine Progressives felt that his speech and its reception "amounted to the acceptance by the Republicans of Maine, of the Progressive Platform of 1912 developed and brought up to date."[23]

Others, particularly Democrats and those who believed that in wartime the president and administration must be supported at all costs, were less receptive. The Delaware House of Representatives, for only one example, came within one vote of passing a resolution demanding that the Justice Department proceed against TR because the Maine speech had "severely criticized the conduct of our National Government." In response the Colonel defied anyone to point out a statement in the speech that was not true or patriotic. He noted that the Senate Judiciary Committee had just recommended the passage of a sedition law in which there was a provision, "among many excellent propositions to put down disloyalty," that would make using "contemptuous or slurring language about the President" punishable by fine and imprisonment. Such a law, in Roosevelt's view, would be "sheer treason to the United States." It was a proposal to make Americans "subjects instead of citizens." He believed the law would be unconstitutional and planned to give the government the opportunity to test this, for he vowed in the future to continue to speak as needed "truthfully of the President in praise or in blame exactly as I have done in the past." He was an American and a free man and his loyalty was to the United States. Therefore it was due to the "President, the Senators, the Congressmen, and all other public servants only and to the degree in which they loyally and efficiently serve the United States."[24]

Figure 11. Quentin Roosevelt at French flight school, 1918
Theodore Roosevelt Collection, Harvard College Library

The announcement that Pershing's forces in France had been put at the "absolute disposal" of the Allies in the terrible battle led Roosevelt to declare that all who were "proud of the great name of America" would "humbly and reverently thank Heaven" that their army at the front was not to "remain in the position of an onlooker." He went on that the "wanton and cruel" long-range bombardment of Paris, which had just killed scores of women and children in a church, yet again proved that German barbarity was "as deliberate and as infamous now as at the beginning of the war." In this battle the Allies were fighting for humanity and civilization, as well as fighting the battle of the United States. Any man in America, he continued, "who at this time directly or indirectly" expressed approval or sympathy with Germany should be "arrested and either shot, hung, or imprisoned for life, according to the gravity of his offense." TR thanked "Heaven that our sons and brothers" were now to "stand at Armageddon," and to these men all Americans were forever indebted. It was a "terrible thing that our loved ones should face the great danger, but it would be a far more terrible thing if, whatever the danger, they were not treading the hard path of duty and honor."[25]

The youngest of TR's loved ones in the war, Quentin, continued to be frustrated with his duties well behind the lines at Issoudun, while his brother Archie was wounded and Ted served in the trenches. Quentin described the flood-prone airfield there as a "god-forsaken hole," where he found that the primitive Curtiss Jenny he had learned to fly at Mineola in New York had almost nothing in common with the French Nieuports, the still-outmoded aircraft sold to the newly arrived Americans while the French took to the skies in more advanced Spads. If their engines did not catch fire or stall, Quentin soon learned at first hand, the Nieuports had a bad habit of losing their wing fabric in dives.[26] A week after the German push began, he wrote to his fiancée Flora from the French school for aerial gunnery at Lac de Cazaux, where he was at last finishing his training, everyone was thinking "offensive," and he wondered if the people in America cared or realized how much depended on the drive's success or failure. The Germans, Quentin noted, were certainly lucky with the weather. Now that they had made their first big drive, the perfect weather had ended and the Allies would have to make their counter-attack, as it seemed they had all their pushes, in the rain. He also wished they had a few of the phantom "ten thousand" planes promised by the Wilson administration to help with the work.[27]

From Washington, George Lockwood, editor of the *National Republican Weekly*, sent TR a warning that the Senate Judiciary Committee had just reported out an amendment of the Espionage Act that would make criticism of Wilson sedition. Under this bill, Lockwood went on, "You probably would have been jailed many times in the last six months" for "slurring" and "contemptuous" language. The editor asked Roosevelt to use his influence against the measure.[28] TR had written a month before to Henry Stimson, training with the British in France, that at home there had been "literally outrageous work done by using the power of the Attorney General and the Postmaster General to interfere primarily with honest and truthful criticism of public officials who have been inefficient, instead of using the great power of the government to attack the powerful pro-German offenders, of the type of the Hearst and La Follette papers."[29] TR's old political enemy William Randolph Hearst was "an element of special danger" in New York, and the Colonel advised Will Hays, the Republican National Committee chairman, that the Vigilantes were "anxious to do volunteer work" against that "unhung traitor Hearst" and "for us," although the writers usually kept clear of "partisan politics."[30]

Roosevelt was only the most prominent in a host of Americans who despised Hearst and his papers and magazines, which had in patriotic self-defense begun prominently displaying the Stars and Stripes on all their front pages, as well as on their newsboys and agents. Some of these came under attack, and their publications were burned while Hearst's effigy was committed to bonfires in more than one city. He became undoubtedly the most detested public figure in the country. The *New York Tribune* began a weekly series (later bound in a pamphlet) titled *Coiled in the Flag—Hears-s-s-s-t*, comparing him to a snake, quoting his editorials for their "pro-Germanism" and accusing him of "sowing distrust of the Allies." Contrary to TR's accusations, the attorney general did look for sedition in the pages of the Hearst press, and the Department of Justice put him under surveillance with an undercover agent in his house working as a butler. Hearst fought back with advertisements in other papers trumpeting, "WHAT THE HEARST PAPERS HAVE DONE TO WIN THE WAR." At the same time, the Hearst papers took up an anti-German stridency not seen before, pledging until peace came to "forever crush the Teuton menace." There was also a newfound support of Wilson and the administration that had been missing previously and that the Colonel did not fail to criticize.[31]

The government had already moved against the *Metropolitan* when the New York postmaster notified its ownership that the March issue would be banned from the mails under the Espionage Act. The paper was sanctioned on account of an article by William Hard that took the administration to task for landing marines in Santo Domingo and for the secrecy in which the affair was cloaked. TR noted in a letter on the matter to Senator Miles Poindexter that Hard's work in the *New Republic*, which supported the administration, was not banned. And when the *Metropolitan* asked whether the action had been taken under the orders of the postmaster general or what steps would be taken to remedy the damage done to the reputation of the monthly, it received no answer except that the article in question had been reported as a "traitorous effusion." Finally, on March 11, the New York postmaster reversed his actions but made no apology or explanation. At the same time, advertisers in the *Metropolitan* began receiving letters suggesting they withdraw their support of the magazine, and at least one agent of the Justice Department made a personal visit along the same lines.[32]

The *Metropolitan*, its editor H. J. Whigham told TR, was "more or less under fire," and the news that his secretary Miss Stricker was moving out to another office might make it look like he was deserting the ship or that he "disapproves of the methods" of the magazine. Consequently, Whigham asked if she could postpone her departure for another month or so. Naturally Whigham did not want any of this to get out in the press.[33] Minnesota Senator (and future secretary of state) Frank Kellogg wrote to TR that he thought the "proceedings" against the *Metropolitan* were "outrageous," but when Wilson kept around such men as George Creel, "constantly preaching unpreparedness," it was "not at all surprising." Kellogg wanted Roosevelt to know that he was against the pending amended espionage bill but believed it would not "prohibit any legitimate criticism."[34] This is exactly what TR did believe: that Creel and Postmaster Albert S. Burleson, along with the Justice Department, were conspiring to protect the administration from the revelations of their opponents. "You have doubtless seen the attack by the Administration on the *Metropolitan* because of Hard's article," he wrote Julian Street. The situation, the Colonel went on, was growing "intolerable," and he rather thought he would "force the fighting. I would like to have the scoundrels dare to attack me!"[35]

On April 9, with their first drive stalled, the Germans launched a second major attack (codenamed "Georgette") at the British line from Givenchy to Ypres, in the end coming within 27 miles of the sea at Dunkirk.[36] In Britain the dire military straits had cast a pall over the nation and its leaders. The House of Commons was in "utmost gloom." One of the MPs, Northcliffe's brother Cecil Harmsworth, recorded in his diary that there was "not merely anxiety" but "stupefication and bewilderment at the hurried and confused retreat of our glorious army—just as if they were so many Italians or Rumanians."[37] The gravity of the situation was underlined by Sir Douglas Haig's "Special Order of the Day" of April 11, 1918: "Three weeks ago to-day the enemy began his terrific attacks on us on a fifty mile front. His objects are to separate us from the French, to take the Channel Ports and to destroy the British Army . . . With our backs to the wall and believing in the justice of our cause, each one of us must fight on to the end. The safety of our homes and the Freedom of mankind alike depend upon the conduct of each one of us at this critical moment."[38]

Borrowing Haig's exhortation to his troops for a *Kansas City Star* editorial, "Freedom Stands with Her Back to the Wall," Roosevelt once again blamed the Wilson administration for the small number of ill-supplied American troops on hand in France to help Britain and France in the emergency. Consequently, "if in this mighty battle our allies win," it would be "due to no real aid of ours," and if they "should fail, black infamy would be our portion because of the delay and the folly and the weakness and the cold, time-serving timidity of our Government, to which this failure would be primarily due." Even now, if those responsible "repented the cruel wrong they have done this nation and mankind, we could afford to wrap their past folly and evil doing in the kindly mantle of oblivion." But instead they boasted of their foolishness and excused and justified it, while they announced that they "feel pride and delight in contemplating it." The trumpets of the Lord had sounded for Armageddon, but "our rulers were supple and adroit" and not "mighty of soul." They had shown that they would not lead us and would "stand in front only if we force them forward."[39] In the crisis, with public feeling in Kansas City running strongly against criticism of the administration, the *Star* decided this article was too extreme to publish locally, but it did send it to two other papers at TR's request.[40]

In a *Metropolitan* article, "Lincoln and Free Speech," the Colonel noted that Lincoln also had to deal with critics of the "stand by the President" type and cited chapter and verse of Abraham Lincoln's repeated abuse of James K. Polk as a dishonest bungler during the Mexican War. To one critic, Lincoln answered that the "only alternative is to tell the truth or to lie" and he would not "skulk" on such a question. As in the present day, Roosevelt went on, Lincoln protested against permitting Polk to "take the whole of legislation into his hands." To Polk's "servile party supporters," Lincoln made a "distinction which also readily applies"—the distinction between the cause of the president and the cause of the county—which Polk's supporters could not perceive. "To you," said Lincoln, "the President and the country seem to be all one." But his party saw the distinction "clear enough." This, declared Roosevelt, "was the crux of the matter then and is the crux of the matter now." Patriotism, he argued, meant to stand by the country, not the president or any other public official "save exactly to the degree in which he himself stand by the country."[41]

Leonard Wood was among the many who sent TR congratulations on "Lincoln and Free Speech." It was, the general wrote, "what the people need to hear. Democracy smothering criticism" was "democracy dying." Wood also told the Colonel that in the face of a public outcry and questions from David Lloyd George as to why Wood was "buried, and at the same time being wounded," Newton Baker had made a statement that Wood would be given an "important command," but he did not believe the war secretary had the "slightest idea of doing anything more." Wood was also mystified by the recent call up of only 150,000 men, "child's play," when it should have been 1,500,000. "Don't they realize the great campaign is on?"[42] Roosevelt would have said no. He wrote to Lord Bryce that until January Wilson had never intended that the American army "should fight at all." He had first hoped the British and French would "win the war for him" and then that the Russian Bolshevists would disrupt Germany. The president was "only now reluctantly abandoning his hope for a war without bloodshed," and he still wished at times for a "peace without victory." The failure to use Wood was due to Wilson's "steady and inflexible purpose to carry this war out on the narrowest political grounds." Wood fought hard for preparedness, and this Wilson would never forgive.[43]

The German advances made it vital that American reinforcements be pressed into battle with the British and French. In the emergency, Pershing agreed to lend men to the cause, but only until the end of April. Lloyd George cabled Ambassador Lord Reading in Washington: "It rests with America to win or lose the decisive battle of the war . . . the President must overrule at once the narrow obstinacy which would put obstacles in the way of using American infantry in the only way in which it can be used to save the situation."[44] For Wilson there were also political implications to consider. "Outside of the general gravity of the situation," Edward M. House wrote to the president, he had "still further anxiety because of the effect which a grave disaster in France would have on your administration." If the German offensive failed, "no one could lift a voice of criticism," but if it succeeded, there would be "no end to the denunciations from such as Roosevelt, Wood and their kind." Pershing's feeling that an American army under his command should be established and made as formidable as possible was understandable, but the thing to be done now was to stop the Germans, and to do that "we must put in every man available."[45] Intervention from Washington with Pershing gained continued American troop support.

Meanwhile in Mesopotamia, having seen significant action in command of a light armored motor battery unit with the British, Kermit wired his father of his eagerness, after the spring fighting season was over, to join his brothers in the great battle on the Western Front.[46] The British, from his commanding general to the War Office, signed off on this plan, and TR did his part by writing to US Army Chief of Staff Peyton March, who agreed that Kermit could join the AEF with the rank of captain. Pleased that it appeared his son would soon be in the American army, the Colonel reported to Kermit's wife Belle on April 21 that he had told March that after his experience in Mesopotamia Kermit was best fitted for machine-gun work, and the transfer appeared "as good as made." But, he added, "there's many a slip twixt the cup and lip."[47] TR also confided to Belle about his dodgy equilibrium after the ear surgery that he was still "apt to be dizzy" if he turned suddenly around, but he thought he would be able to join Edith for a ride in a week or two.[48] This would take place, he told Kermit, on a "clergy-man horse of the safest type." He could now go about and see the wildflowers and planned soon to take Edith out "in the little rowboat."[49]

From Washington, Hiram Johnson sent TR a copy of the amended espionage bill, which had been stripped of the provision to which the Colonel had objected that made slurring the president sedition. Nevertheless, Johnson feared that Wilson planned an "absolutist state." He also complained of his frustration with the many members of the Senate who for two months denounced the Overman Bill, which granted Wilson unprecedented powers to coordinate government agencies in wartime, and then voted for it.[50] The day after Johnson wrote his letter, Roosevelt struck a blow of his own in a *Kansas City Star* editorial, "Sedition, a Free Press, and Personal Rule," which addressed both the Overman and the sedition bills. The espionage legislation now pending should "deal drastically with sedition" while also guaranteeing the right of the press and the people to "speak the truth freely of all their public servants, including the President." Sedition, TR went on, was a form of treason and an offense against the country, not the president. And so far the administration had been "gravely remiss" in dealing with such acts for which the punishments should be severe. On the other hand, free speech, said Roosevelt, whether exercised individually or through a free press, was a "necessity" in any country where the people were themselves free.

Congress, said TR, should not abrogate its own power and should define how the president was to reorganize the government. It should also say how large the army should be and not leave the decision to the "amiable Secretary of War, who has for two years shown such inefficiency." Congress should declare for an army of five million and inform the secretary it will "give him more the minute he asks for more." Roosevelt agreed with Congress granting the executive "the amplest powers to act" and to "hold him to stern accountability for failure to so act." But Congress itself should do the actual lawmaking and clearly define the "lines and limits of action." It should also "retain and use the fullest powers of investigation into and supervision over such action."

Over the past year, Roosevelt continued, the administration had "shown itself anxious to punish" the newspapers that, while they upheld the war, had told the truth about the government's failure to conduct the war efficiently. At the same time the administration had failed to move against "various powerful newspapers which opposed the war or attacked our allies or directly or indirectly aided Germany against this country," because these papers "upheld the administration and defended its inefficiency." Therefore no additional power should be given to the administration to deal with papers that criticized it. Further, TR called for Congress to "more closely scrutinize" the way in which Postmaster General Burleson and the attorney general, as the agents of Wilson, had "already exercised discrimination between the papers they prosecuted and the papers they failed to prosecute."[51]

In reply to this indictment, Burleson issued an official Post Office statement dated May 8 inviting Roosevelt to demonstrate the "truth or falsity" of his charges by naming the journals that had "upheld the war but which had told the truth about the administration's failure to conduct the war efficiently" and had been "punished" by his department. He equally invited TR to name the papers or magazines, "powerful or otherwise," that had "opposed the war and attacked our allies or directly or indirectly aided Germany against this country" in such manner as to violate the law and that had not been "proceeded against by this department." Failure on the part of the Colonel to respond, Burleson concluded, was to "admit his inability to do so."[52] Two days later Roosevelt released a "preliminary" reply to Burleson that listed the *Metropolitan, Collier's Weekly*, and the *New York Tribune* as victims of official "unfair discrimination" carried out by George Creel. And in addition he recounted the Post Office and Justice Department's moves against the *Metropolitan* and its advertisers two months before. All these publications, TR declared, had "consistently upheld the war, but have also told that small portion of the truth which it was absolutely necessary to tell about the administration's failure to conduct the war efficiently."

On the other hand, the Colonel went on, the "prime example of failure of the administration to proceed against really hostile and damaging utterances" was the failure to "deal with Mr. Hearst's papers as it has dealt with certain other papers." Hearst was a very wealthy man who owned a dozen newspapers and half a dozen more magazines published across the nation. At the very beginning of the war, the administration moved against the populist Tom Watson's publication in Georgia, which had done "nothing that was anything like as dangerous to this country and our allies, and as helpful to Germany, as Mr. Hearst has done." Quoting as evidence several anti-Allies and antiwar editorials from Hearst's *New York American* going back to the sinking of the *Lusitania* and forward to the previous November, the Colonel declared that it was "absolutely impossible to reconcile" the government's actions against Watson's paper with its "failure to proceed against Mr. Heart's papers on any theory that justice was to be done alike to the strong and to the weak." The government had other notice of Hearst's hostility to the Allies in the fact that they barred him from the use of their cable service, and only through the "good offices of this Government" had this privilege been recently restored.

As a final bit of evidence, the Colonel offered the tribute of the former German correspondent of the *Koeinische Zeitung* for Hearst and his editor-in-chief Arthur Brisbane as being "auxiliaries of valued influence" to Germany, especially through the editorials of the Hearst papers. The Colonel commended this to Burleson, and Josephus Daniels, on account of their recent effusive telegrams of congratulations to Brisbane, "Hearst's alter ego," on taking the editorial chair at the Chicago *Evening Journal*. In TR's view, the quotations presented deprived "Mr. Burleson and the Administration of which he is a part of any shred of justification in this matter," and he had a good deal more to say that would be in a letter he promised to deliver shortly to the Senate.[53]

It was not surprising to Burleson that the Colonel was "dissatisfied with his first attempt to support the truthfulness of his charges" and promised another effort, since he had failed to back up his charges and only obscured the issues at hand. He suggested that it might be helpful in this second attempt if the Colonel did not "obscure the issue by dragging in any more irrelevant and extraneous matter," and he awaited TR's "final effort to prove his accusations against me."[54] A week later, the postmaster general issued another statement that pointed out that his department had not acted against either *Collier's Weekly* or the *New York Tribune*. Further, the aborted attempt to ban the March *Metropolitan* from the mails had in the end not stopped any copies from being mailed and in fact the publicity had increased circulation. Moving to TR's indictment of the Hearst press and the Wilson administration's supposed complicity with it, Burleson pointed out that all but two of the Hearst articles quoted by Roosevelt had been published before the Espionage Act was passed. And no articles since, by Hearst or TR, had in Burleson's view "warranted action by the Post Office under the Espionage Act." The government, Burleson revealed, in fact received more complaints from the public that the Colonel's articles were in violation of the Espionage Act than those of Hearst. And finally, he knew no one in the administration who had aided Hearst to recover the use of the Allied cable services.[55]

In the meantime, Congress made explicit the implicit powers in the Espionage Act by passing an amended version as a new Sedition Act, which substantially increased the administration's war powers. This made illegal "uttering, printing, writing or publishing any disloyal, profane, scurrilous, or abusive language intended to cause contempt, scorn, contumely or disrepute as regards the form of government of the United States, or the Constitution, or the flag, or the uniform of the Army or Navy, or any language intended to incite resistance to the United States or to promote the cause of its enemies; urging any curtailment of production of anything necessary to the prosecution of the war with intent to hinder its prosecution; advocating, teaching, defending or suggesting the doing of any of these acts; and words or acts supporting or favoring the cause of any country at war with the United states, or opposing the cause of the United States therein." The penalty was a $10,000 fine, or not more than twenty years in prison, or both. The Sedition Act also gave the postmaster general the power to refuse to deliver mail to individuals or businesses that employed the mails to break the statute. Any such mail was returned to the sender stamped with the damning message: "Mail to this address undeliverable under the Espionage Act."[56]

Roosevelt had charged that over the previous year the actions of the Post Office, largely through Burleson, had already rendered it a "matter of some danger for any man, and especially newspaper men, to speak the truth, if that truth be unpleasant to the governmental authorities in Washington." Now it would be even more dangerous, as the administration certainly had the means to implement the "firm hand of stern repression" that Wilson had asked for if it chose to do so. And after a few months of Burleson's "capricious censorship," which Wilson refused to curb, even the press allies of the administration were alarmed. The *New York World* charged that the "bureaucrats of the Post-Office Department" seemed determined to "set up an intellectual reign of terror in the United States." Fortunately for TR and his allies at least, it would be in the main a terror carried out against socialists and other radicals, which, as Creel later pointed out, in fact silenced some voices that might have supported Wilson's brand of peace.[57]

On the political front, that May, Roosevelt's official return to the Republican fold was marked by two public events. First, a "delighted" TR was invited back into good standing and asked to retake his place in the councils of the New York Republican Club, where his portrait, consigned to storage in the basement since 1912, was rehung in a place of honor. Whatever his "divagations in 1912," declared the *New York Times*, Roosevelt was "too potent, too engaging a figure, despite his little eccentricities, exuberance and violence, to be left out of the Republican gallery." The Republican civil war was "over. The Restoration is come."[58] The Colonel made his official return to the club by giving a typically rousing speech at a dinner given in honor of the youthful and energetic new party chairman, 38-year-old Will Hays of Indiana.[59] The second public event came at the Blackstone Hotel in Chicago on May 26 when TR and William Howard Taft made a show of shaking hands and talking for half an hour, to the cheers of those in the dining room with them.

Roosevelt later told reporters that he was glad he and Taft had resumed their "relations on the old basis, for we are in entire agreement on all the vital questions concerned with winning the war by striking down Germany and putting down every form of treason here at home, and of insisting upon an absolutely unified and nationalized American citizenship."[60]

The day after the Taft dinner, Roosevelt gave three addresses at Des Moines, where beside the usual demands for speeding up the war and universal military training, he called for English as the sole language for schools, newspapers, and "other usages" in the country. TR applauded the recent proclamation by Iowa's governor that English be the only medium of instruction in the state. "This is a nation," he shouted, "not a polyglot boarding house." There was no room for any "fifty-fifty American." There could be "only one loyalty—to the Stars and Stripes: one nationality the America and therefore only one language—the English language." About the war, he went on, "We have put our hands to the plow and we will never turn back until we have driven the furrow up to Berlin."[61]

Roosevelt wrote to Archie that it was very hard to know "just the right note to strike" in his addresses, for he did not want to seem to "assail the administration too much." And yet it did "worse than no good to acquiesce" in the silly bragging and complacency in what the country had done, so he generally spoke with great frankness about the breakdowns and delays and failures and did not speak of the administration at all. But now and then he dropped "my somewhat thin mask" and lunged straight. And since the administration was afraid of him, they did "endeavor to hurry up the troops, to hurry the building of ships, guns and planes, and to make ready for reasonably serious effort," just in order to neutralize what he said. So his "constant pounding" did, in a roundabout fashion, "produce some small results—better than nothing."[62]

While TR spoke in Des Moines, on May 27 Woodrow Wilson addressed a joint session of Congress in an effort to break the impasse over stalled tax legislation. A pending bill called for $7 billion in new revenue, something members of Congress in an election year, war or no war, were loath to support. However, Wilson's clarion call to the legislators to do their fiscal duty at the "very peak and crisis" of the war thrilled public opinion so much that Congress was left with little choice but to fall in line with the new taxes on luxuries and excess profits requested by the administration. And in famous words that would come back to haunt him, in his speech Wilson assured the assembled members that "politics is adjourned" and the 1918 elections would go to those giving the least thought of winning votes. In reality, he certainly believed no such thing and had no such intention.[63]

America's "one grand duty," TR declared at Milwaukee two days later, was to "put the war through—to a knock-out." This war, he went on, was going to be "settled by the fighting Americans, who will take the burden off the shoulders of our allies."[64] These last words were prophetic, as that same day the Germans launched their third 1918 offensive (codenamed "Blücher-Yorck"), this time against the French lines, along the Aisne River.[65] By May

31 the German army again reached the Marne and threatened Paris as it had in 1914, and alarm spread across the Allied armies. Contingency plans were made to evacuate the BEF if necessary, and when Pershing dined with Ferdinand Foch, the newly created overall Allied commander, he recorded that "it would be difficult to imagine a more depressed group of officers."[66]

But a new and transformative factor, the AEF, was in place in 1918, and on May 31 the American Third Division helped the French stop the German advance along the Marne at Château-Thierry. In the next days a flood of American troops, including Major Theodore Roosevelt Jr., arrived at the front to reinforce the retreating French. Here the AEF gained a taste of serious fighting, first on the Marne and in later heavy action retaking Belleau Wood, sustaining nearly 10,000 casualties. For several days in early June the Americans held the German advance on Paris and allowed the Allied lines time to stabilize. At Cantigny, in what has been called the "first American battle" of World War I, AEF forces withstood seven German attacks over three days and suffered 200 killed and the same number incapacitated by gas.

Among the gas victims was Ted, who though blind for three days refused to give up his command. For his role at Cantigny, Ted was cited for "high courage and leadership" and received both the American Silver Star and the Croix de Guerre.[67] As soon as his battalion was relieved, he commandeered a car and sped to Paris in his tattered uniform to see Eleanor. While there, he and Quentin visited brother Archie in hospital, the first time the three had been together for a year. Meanwhile, Pershing shifted American troops from the British front to Champagne to support the hard-pressed French. These men joined American forces already on hand and gained valuable battlefield experience, which made possible that summer the creation of the First American Army.[68] Once again the German army had been stopped, and it was never so dangerous again.[69]

By this time, Kermit, now a captain of artillery in the AEF, was making his way, despite numerous obstacles, to join his brothers in Europe. First, he was waylaid in Egypt by enemy U-boat action and then in Rome by a nasty bout of malaria. But before leaving Mesopotamia, Kermit had garnered his own military decoration for single-handedly taking prisoner a group of armed Turks hiding in a house, wielding only his British officer's swagger stick as a weapon.[70] Back at Oyster Bay, TR wrote to his son that he was "proud as a peacock" that he had won the British Military Cross.[71] The Colonel happily reported these developments to Henry Stimson, by this time a staff officer with the Three-Hundred-and-Fifth Regiment near Bordeaux. He also told Stimson that on the Midwest trip he found no question but that the "feeling of our people is steadily hardening against Germany and in favor of the war." He was as well received in Wisconsin as anywhere, and it was interesting to be "cheered to the echo" in Milwaukee when he insisted that there should be no language except English used in the schools and that within a "reasonable time" all newspapers should be published in English. But the people did not yet appreciate the "magnitude of the pest" that might develop on the country because of the "dreadful breakdown of Russia" and the menace this implied to the whole world. TR went on that at present his own "fretting over the refusal to use me" had been "completely swallowed up in my bitter indignation over the wrong done in refusing to use General Wood," which no language was strong enough to condemn.[72]

Leonard Wood had been on his way to embark for France with the division he had trained when he received orders to give up his command and proceed to San Francisco to take over the Western Department. The general instead traveled to Washington, where on May 27 he had another interview with Newton Baker to state his case, as the most senior major general of the army, to be given a command in France, or even Italy. In interviews with Baker and Wilson, both men claimed only to be following Pershing's wishes in the matter. Apparently Wood shared the conversations with others, which gave the war secretary the opportunity to write him that this seemed "a significant instance of the indirect and insubordinate disposition on your part which I told you in our interview, made it difficult to combine you with an organization of which you are not the head with any expectation of harmonious cooperation."[73] In the end the public outcry finally led to Wood's return to Camp Funston, where he could at least train the new Tenth Division.

Wood wrote to TR from the camp that the reports being given out that he was satisfied with his "important mission here" were "*wholly* untrue." He had done all a soldier could do to "protest against this gross injustice" and hoped that the "official and finally the public sense of fair play" still might force a change. Pershing, he went on, was "not holding up in France," and if Pershing told the truth, he had "acted like a cad" in not working on Wood's behalf after all he had done to further Pershing's career.[74] Roosevelt wrote more charitably (and wrongly) of Pershing to Wood that he believed that political pressure had decided the AEF commander's actions in the matter and that Wilson and Baker had used him "merely as a shield's tool." It was only their desire not to "offend the country too deeply" that allowed Wood to return to Camp Funston. All this TR found "fairly stunning," and he told Wood that he had never known "such complete hypocrisy."[75] The Colonel received many letters complaining of the shelving of Wood, but on the other hand it was seen by not a few others as a good election issue. Trapped in Kansas, Wood spent quite a bit of time that fall supporting Republican candidates, while the city of Salina organized a Wood for President Club—an action that the general did not find unpleasing.

Meanwhile, in Washington, Taft had accepted Wilson's invitation to serve as cochair with the labor lawyer Frank Walsh of the National War Labor Board. Called the "Supreme Court of Labor Relations," it brought together management and union representatives to coordinate wartime labor policies.[76] But two hot and frustrating months serving as cochair led Taft to reassess his previously charitable view of the Wilson administration and its war efforts and to come round to a conception in accord with that of his restored friend Theodore. Taft sent TR a long letter indicting the Wilson administration, including accompanying documents to back up his charges of inefficiency and lack of resolve, cooperation, and coordination in the capital.[77]

Roosevelt responded that the "literally astounding" material Taft had sent illuminated the president's character "as few things could. What a dreadful creature he is!" Fortunately for the war effort, as Taft had pointed out, in public matters Wilson had not the "slightest firmness in sticking to any conviction"; therefore if only public opinion could be kept "sufficiently solid," they could count on his "sticking to the war." But the trouble was that in this "really evil crisis" the country needed a "leader not a weathercock."[78]

On the battlefront, the German army once again attacked, on June 9 opening its fourth great push (codenamed "Gneisenau") and coming within forty miles of Paris. The next day's *Daily Mail* editorial, "The Battle for Paris: Mr. Clemenceau's Heroic Lead," recounted the struggle, while the newspaper planned for evacuation. One of its staff reported to Northcliffe that it was "not believed here that Paris will fall; but it is anticipated the Boche will endeavour to get near enough the next time to bring the city under a naval gun bombardment and treat it like Rheims and Amiens. In such an event there would be a great exodus. Already 1,600,000 have gone."[79] These did not include Georges Clemenceau, who declared that he would never abandon the capital to the enemy and announced, "I will fight in front of Paris, I will fight in Paris, I will fight behind Paris."[80] As in 1914, but this time with fresh American reinforcements, the Allies stiffened before Paris and began to drive back the enemy the next month. However, German artillery, including the famous long-range cannon "Big Bertha," had already got near enough to lob shells into the French capital, killing many civilians and adding another "German Horror" to the by-now long list of atrocities, which TR pointed out in the *Kansas City Star*.[81]

After a few days of rest, Roosevelt left Sagamore Hill again to speak for the Liberty Loan at St. Louis and Indianapolis. With Paris and perhaps winning the war in jeopardy, his rhetoric took an even more strident and unforgiving tone toward the administration, traitors, and the enemy alike. At St. Louis on June 10, the Colonel added to his standard patriotic address a tribute to Leonard Wood. If the United States had followed the advice of the general, he said, there would have been "2,000,000 men prepared and under arms when war was declared." Russia would "never have been broken," and peace would have been declared "within ninety days" after America entered the war. Regarding proved traitors, the Colonel declared that all in the country should be "interred" not "interned." Mercy to traitors was "cruelty to loyal men," and weakness in dealing with them was "disloyalty to our men at the front."[82] The next day at Indianapolis, after watching a parade of 40,000 school children, the Colonel spoke in the same vein at the Coliseum, where he quieted the cries of "Roosevelt in 1920." Eschewing politics, he declared the occasion "nothing but an American meeting at which we are discussing Americanism and all it means, preparedness and putting the war over."[83]

TR's criticisms were answered at the state Democratic Convention in Indianapolis a week later using his owns words. Booming Wilson for a third term, the chairman of the convention, former Indiana Governor Samuel Ralston, quoted Roosevelt from the 1898 New York gubernatorial race after the Spanish American War. Speaking in support of William McKinley and the national Republican ticket, TR had declared, "Your votes this year will be viewed by the nations of Europe for one standpoint only." A refusal to "sustain the President this year" would be read as a "refusal to sustain the war, and to sustain the efforts of our peace commission to secure the fruits of the war." Such a refusal might well bring a "rupture on the peace negotiations" and would give "heart to our defeated antagonists." So, Ralston asked, how would the defeat of the Democrats in the coming fall elections be interpreted? "We fathers and mothers of the boys over there," he went on, could not afford to see "Woodrow Wilson's party defeated in the next election."[84]

Vice President Thomas Marshall also joined the fray at Indianapolis, but in a more jocular fashion, describing new Republican Chairman Will Hays as a "young Lochinvar" who "ambled out of the West upon the G. O. P—grand old palfrey—and with force of arms seized the Lady Theodora and carried her off to that medieval castle called the Republican headquarters where he introduced her as Republican vestal virgin." Continuing with his fable, Marshall went on that the Lady Theodora, being left at home, "concluded to take a hand in the war by writing letters in derogation and in criticism of its management to a newspaper," the *Kansas City Star*, which had published seditious documents. Some men, said Marshall, would object that if the Lady Theodora "is the Republican Party" and was going to fight this way in the columns of a newspaper, "notwithstanding her great desire to take charge of everything," they were "going to insist that she shall not be permitted to do so" earlier than inauguration day, March 4, 1921, "and not then, if God and the right prevail."[85]

After once again returning to Oyster Bay for a few days, on June 16 Roosevelt traveled to Hartford Connecticut, where he and his devil-fishing companion Russell Coles were among those who received honorary degrees at Trinity College. In his graduation address to 5,000 under the campus elms, TR declared that the war had "just begun" and Americans should not "deceive themselves with the notion that they had done their duty." He went on that the censorship, "unpleasant as it has been at times," should be extended to put a stop to "grandiloquent statements" of what Americans were going to do in the war. A prime example of this was the administration failure to supply the 20,000 airplanes promised by that spring. Consequently, many American troops in the trenches had no air cover. Not using Ted's name, Roosevelt revealed that he had received a letter that in a "certain sector" the American officers "fired back futilely with their revolvers" after being strafed with machine guns by the enemy. The American boast about 20,000 planes, said TR, "took in the Germans, but unlike our own people they built airplanes to meet it." When peace came, Roosevelt wanted a peace "given by us on our own terms." He would not negotiate with Germany but with Belgium, Serbia, Romania, France, and England. Let the peace be, he went on, one that guaranteed against the recurrence of the "hideous disaster these nations have been forced to undergo."[86]

To get into combat, Quentin had been petitioning the French to join their Air Corps, but in the end he was ordered out from Issoudun to an "entirely American outfit," the First Pursuit Group of the Ninety-Fifth Aero Squadron, known as the "Kicking Mule" squadron. Within a week Quentin was going out on patrol, he wrote his fiancée Flora, hunting for "brother Boche."[87] A "thrilled" TR wrote to Quentin of his "joy for you" and that his "pride in you drowns my anxiety." He had hoped Flora would be allowed to travel to France so that she and Quentin could be married and he, like his three brothers, have his "white hour" with the woman he loved before going into combat. But the War Office turned down the request, apparently because her brother Sonny had completed his own flight training and was scheduled to go overseas. It was "very hard," the Colonel told Quentin, that Flora could not come to him, and he could not help feeling that "a little more resolution" on the part of her influential family would have done it.[88]

Despite his assurances to Quentin about his anxiety for his and his brothers' safety, Roosevelt told a visitor to Sagamore Hill that he often woke in the middle of night wondering if the boys were "all right and thinking how I could tell their mother if anything happened."[89] TR wrote to Archie's wife Grace that now Quentin would be "where he may pay with his body for his heart's desire."[90] Ethel's little son Richard was staying with his grandparents, and TR wrote to Quentin that when an airplane flew overhead while the boy was riding his tricycle on the piazza, with a "smile of delight" Richard exclaimed, "I think that's Uncle Quentin!" The countryside, Roosevelt's letter concluded, was at its "very loveliest"; it was the "high tide of the year."[91] It was a high tide, physically and emotionally, for the Colonel as well.

CHAPTER 13

A NOBLE LIFE
GLORIOUSLY ENDED

JULY TO AUGUST 1918

Only those are fit to live who do not fear to die; and none are fit to die who have shrunk from the joy of life and the duty of life. Both life and death are parts of the same Great Adventure . . . No nation can be great unless its sons and daughters have in them the quality to rise level to the needs of heroic days . . . honor, highest honor to those who fearlessly face death for a good cause; no life is so honorable or so fruitful as such a death.

—TR, *The Great Adventure*

In July 1918, Quentin Roosevelt's pursuit squadron was tasked with engaging and destroying the enemy planes that had been strafing American troops with impunity and also with escorting reconnaissance flights over the lines. During these missions he often had trouble with the balky engine of his Nieuport and fell behind the formation. On July 6, during one of these episodes, he confided to Flora that he was "scared blue" when a "shadow came across his plane" from a German craft that had come up behind and above him, so close that he could see the "red stripes around his fuselage." Though in an overwhelming position of advantage to down Quentin, the German pilot miraculously did not attack and went back to his formation.[1] When the tables were turned five days later, Quentin showed no such mercy. He wrote in "Great Excitement" to his fiancée that he believed he had at last "got a Boche yesterday." He had been out on a patrol of 15 planes but got separated from them and then came upon 3 planes he thought were American but that on closer inspection turned out to be a German formation that did not notice him. Although "scared perfectly green," he decided to "take a crack" at the end man. There was as yet no confirmation, as he had been engaged by his target's compatriots and was unable to follow his adversary down.[2]

Word of Quentin's accomplishment traveled fast. The same day, July 10, Quentin's mother recorded in her diary that the Associated Press had "called up with the news."[3] Two days later the newspapers carried confirmed reports from France that Quentin had posted his first aerial victory, downing a German plane over Château-Thierry. The New York *Sun* praised him for single-handedly attacking three enemy planes and "shooting one of them down."[4] Theodore and Edith were "immensely excited" over the news, which they got just as TR was going into New York to act as a pall bearer for John Purroy Mitchel. The former mayor had been killed a week before in a flight-training accident at an airfield in Louisiana. Whatever now befell Quentin, TR wrote his daughter Ethel, he had had "his day of honor and triumph." Poor unfortunate Mitchel, he went on, had neither, as he died before he was able to get to the front and "feel the thrill generous souls ought to feel when they have won the honorable renown of doing their duty with exceptional courage and efficiency."[5]

Roosevelt exalted to Ted, who had ridden Quentin hard for his previous lack of action, that the "last of lion's brood has been bloodied."[6] The day after Quentin's victory, Archie reported to Flora Whitney from his hospital bed in Paris that her fiancé "blew in here yesterday."[7] After surprising Archie with strawberries and Normandy cream, Quentin and Ted's wife Eleanor dined at Ciro's to celebrate the victory. The next morning, July 13, he rode his motorcycle back to his unit. Quentin looked well, Archie told Flora, but he could not help but worry because, like everyone else in the American army, Quentin had to take "castoff machines from the Allies and they have added dangers."[8] Now that he was in combat, Quentin had taken to writing Flora almost daily, and she was only too well aware of the tremendous risks he took every time he flew a mission. He had confided to her that he had "doped it out" with his old friend and flying compatriot Hamilton Coolidge to look out for each other's things if one of them was killed and to send them home to the family. "Not that I ever think he will have to," Quentin added, "for I love you too much not to come back, my dearest."[9]

Letters and cables of congratulations on Quentin's achievement, on top of that of his brothers, poured into Oyster Bay. The writer Mary Roberts Rinehart sent TR a representative note: "Heavens! How proud you must be these days!"[10] Albert Beveridge, who had visited Sagamore Hill shortly before this, wrote that the news about Quentin was "glorious." The former senator had also read Roosevelt's last two *Metropolitan* pieces, which he called "sound, strong and timely, both of them."[11] In his July article the Colonel had declared that Woodrow Wilson's "cult of internationalism" was the cult of a "doctrine of fatal sterility." It had been "much in vogue" at the beginning of the war among the "professional intellectuals" and "inevitably emasculates its sincere votaries." In his view there was "no limit to the greatness of the future before America," but it could be realized "only if we are

Americans, if we are nationalists, with all the fervor of our hearts and all the wisdom of our brains."[12]

Beveridge agreed, writing TR, "Nationalism! In this sign we conquer." In his opinion Roosevelt was doing "the best and biggest work of your life thus far." Beveridge thanked God that Wilson had "hoisted the motley flag of internationalism," for that made it the issue of the 1918 election campaign. Against the president's "mongrel and promiscuous internationalism," the Republicans offered "Straight Americanism, unadulterated," which contained both "sense and sentiment," appealed to the "mind and the heart" of the people, and was a winning platform. TR, he went on, had become the "voice of America," while Wilson was trying to be the voice of world. A brotherhood of nations sounded well, "only one doesn't care to have brothers 'wished on' him." What "rot" it all was to Beveridge, "how juvenile and childish."[13]

Another visitor to Sagamore Hill early that July of 1918, Edgar Lee Masters, hauntingly painted a very human Roosevelt in verse:

> He's dressed in canvas khaki, flannel shirt,
> Laced boots for farming, chopping trees, perhaps;
> A stocky frame, curtains of skin on cheeks,
> Drained slightly of their fat; gash in the neck,
> Where pus was emptied lately; one eye dim,
> And growing dimmer; almost blind in that,
> And when he walks he rolls a little like
> A man whose youth is fading, like a cart
> That rolls when springs are old. He is a moose,
> Scarred, battered from the hunters, thickets, stones;
> Some finest tips of antlers broken off;
> And eyes where images of ancient things
> Flit back and forth across them, keeping still
> A certain slumberous indifference,
> Or wisdom it may be.[14]

At the 1918 Bastille Day celebration at Philadelphia, the Republican lawyer George Wharton Pepper read a message from Roosevelt that praised France as the "keystone of the arch of resistance to the weight of German brutality." For this France had suffered terribly, and after the war not only must Germany make good her losses but France must be "guaranteed against the repetition of the wrongdoing." The only way to do this, and to avoid a "German peace," was to insist on the restoration of Alsace and Lorraine and thereby return France to her pre-1870 boundaries. Since Woodrow Wilson had also now committed to this, for once TR stood "unequivocally with the President." When the peace negotiations came, Roosevelt's letter went on, America must also insist on justice for "every nationality oppressed by Austria, Turkey or Bulgaria," whether in Asia Minor, the Balkans or Austria-Hungary. At the same time, Germany must be prevented from exploiting the gains made at the expense of Russia, Belgium should be "amply indemnified," and Japan and Britain allowed to keep the colonies they had won from the enemy.[15]

That same day in the skies over France, Quentin was shot down behind the German lines. For several days his fate was unknown, and it was hoped he had landed safely and only been captured. John J. Pershing sent a cablegram that he regretted that Quentin had been reported missing. He had gone out on July 14 with a patrol of 12 planes protecting a photographic section and had encountered an enemy force. A member of the squadron reported seeing one of the American planes pull out of the combat and into the clouds, and the French had reported a descending plane. Pershing expressed his hope that Quentin may have landed safely and would send any further information as soon as it was received.[16] As it turned out, however, Quentin was dead: shot twice in the head before his plane crashed into a field near the village of Chaméry.

On July 17, Roosevelt received the official news that his son had been killed in the action three days before and buried by the enemy with full military honors, including a thousand German soldiers, as the son of a former president. The Colonel gave the reporters at Sagamore Hill, who had alerted him that something was afoot several days before, a one sentence statement: "Quentin's mother and I are very glad that he got to the front and had a chance to render some service to his country, and show the stuff that was in him before his fate befell him."[17] Phil Thompson, the Associated Press reporter standing vigil at Sagamore Hill, recorded that on the afternoon that the official news came, while TR "exorcised his grief by waging war on his mail," Edith came out of the house, red-eyed but bearing herself with dignity, and, referring to her husband, told Thompson, "We must do everything we can to help him. The burden must not rest entirely on his shoulders."[18]

On Sunday July 21, Roosevelt wrote to Kermit that they had heard the first rumors of Quentin's fate that Tuesday, but not until the previous day (when they received a telegram of confirmation and condolence from the White House) were they absolutely sure of his death. There was not much to say. It was dreadful that the young should die, but no man could have "died in finer or more gallant fashion; our pride equals our sorrow." Ethel and Alice had come to Sagamore Hill, as had "poor heart-broken Flora." It was "hard for the women who weep—and harder for those who weep but little—when word comes that henceforth they are to walk in the shadow." Mother, he went on, had been "wonderful as always in a great crisis. She has the hero's soul."[19] To Archie in similar vein TR wrote that Quentin had fallen "as the heroes of old died, as brave and fearless men must die when a great cause calls." And if America did not "contain such men it would not be our country." He bitterly mourned that Quentin had not been able to marry as had Archie and leave behind his own children, but the "children's children of his brothers and of Ethel will speak of him with pride as long as our blood flows in the veins of man or woman."

Roosevelt was also bitter that Quentin and many thousands like him will have "paid with their blood for the sins of the pacifists and sharp political demagogues and dull military pedants and tape-enmeshed bureaucrats." However, he went on, Quentin's gallant death had "thrilled the country: for some reason it seemed to bring the war home to multitudes of people" who had previously viewed the war "like a movie show." The word had also just come that Ted had a bullet through his leg, and the Colonel concluded his letter, "Heavens—my sons have stood at the forefront of the battle. My pride in all of you surpasses words."[20] Ted, shot through the left kneecap, after triage on the battlefield made his way to Paris, where he surprised Eleanor at the house on the rue de Villejuste. Luckily, Richard Derby happened to be on hand and forced Ted to the hospital, where he was operated on in time to save his leg, although he never regained feeling in his left heel.[21]

Once the official news of Quentin's fate became public, a river of letters, telegrams, and poems of sympathy and tribute flowed into Oyster Bay. Will Taft commiserated with his friends Theodore and Edith by telegram that they had "given of your heart's blood for your country." Quentin's was a "noble life gloriously ended," and he and his wife's sympathy for them was deepened when they remembered that Quentin and their son Charlie, also serving in France, were "boys together" in Washington and "babes of the same year."[22] In a handwritten note of sympathy to TR and "Dear Mrs. Roosevelt," Leonard Wood confided that he could not say how deeply grieved he was to hear of the death of their "gallant boy" in action with the enemy. But he was sure it was the death Quentin "would have chosen when the time came, that of a soldier in action. We give all we can give—rest his gallant soul in peace."[23]

From France another old friend, Henry Stimson, sent his deepest sympathies. Stimson, whose artillery battery had just fired their first shots in a barrage the night before, well knew how strong were the bonds of affection that tied Roosevelt's family together and "how heavy the blow will fall on you." But in his personal sorrow TR could take at least some satisfaction that, "very largely because of the example and leadership in civic duty which you have set for us," thousands of men were "over here trying to do our share."[24] Many other condolences also arrived from Europe, including a particularly poignant letter from Gladys Selous, the widow of TR's friend Sir Frederick, killed himself in the fighting in British East Africa the previous year. From Heatherside—her Surrey house, which Theodore and Edith had visited in 1910—Mrs. Selous sent her "most sincere & heartfelt sympathy" to them for the loss of Quentin. She knew how her husband would have grieved for them. Mrs. Selous could fully enter their feelings as she had lost her own boy in a "terrible accident" that January while he flew over the German lines. It was a "glorious ending for these splendid, gallant lads, fighting for their countries." Their courage and spirit was remarkable, but the "blank left for the parents, nothing can fill and time only soften the blow."[25]

Of all the messages he received from rulers of nations and leaders of people, Roosevelt valued most that of Georges Clemenceau, for whom he had a "peculiar admiration" and felt had played a "greater part than any man not a soldier, and a greater part than any soldier, except one or two," in the war. It was a very sad thing, he replied to Clemenceau, to see the young die when

Figure 12. "The Difference between Democracy and Autocracy," *Chicago Sunday Tribune*, August 4, 1918

Theodore Roosevelt Collection, Harvard College Library

the old who were doing nothing, as he was doing, were left alive. Because of this, he went on, it was "very bitter to me that I was not allowed to face the danger with my sons." But whatever may be their fate, TR was "glad and proud that my sons have done their part in this mighty war against despotism and barbarism." He thanked heaven that it had begun to look as if at last Germany "had spent her strength," and he thanked heaven also that "we now have at least a few hundred thousand Americans to fight beside the French."[26]

A week before TR wrote this letter, 300,000 American troops had joined the Aisne-Marne offensive, playing a major role in the first Allied advance of 1918 and what would prove the military turning point in the war on the Western Front.

After the Allies took the ground near Chaméry on which Quentin had fallen, his grave became a place of pilgrimage for American and French soldiers. General Robert Bullard, who had been a commander at Cantigny and whom Pershing made head of the Second United States Army, had his headquarters nearby. Bullard recalled that, whether early or late, he never failed to see a "continuous stream of men" passing the grave. So great was the "fame of a name" that even in the "midst of war and continued danger, men did not fail to pay their respect to it."[27] And on the German side, Quentin's death must also have had an effect on morale by making apparent the differing sacrifices made by the son of an American president in comparison with the safe, behind-the-lines duties assigned the sons of the Kaiser.

The army offered to have Quentin's body brought home, but Roosevelt believed soldiers should be buried where they fell. He and Edith received a description of Quentin's grave written by a comrade in arms, Joe Chapple. To get to the site from the village, the party walked across a large open field of still "bleeding ground" and found the spot where Quentin fell and was buried by the Germans. The grave, which overlooked a landscape remindful of the plains of Dakota, was enclosed and decorated by the blue cross of the Germans "between the crosses erected by the Americans, with the simple plate and the more elaborated headmark by the French," who also left a wreath. Cypress trees had been planted on the four corners. As Chapple leaned over the fence, he saw "among the withered flowers, blossoms, faded, a little blue violet peeping up towards the sky overhead, the most fitting emblem of his tragic fall, from the blue skies overhead to a glory as true blue as the flag he served."[28] Major General W. C. Kerry, the director of military aeronautics, informed TR that the air field at Mineola where Quentin trained had been named "Roosevelt Field" to "commemorate his giving his life for his country. We honor him, and you Sir, his father."[29] And a resident of the Pennsylvania village formerly called Bismarck wrote to TR that its name had been changed to Quentin "in honor of your son who had the privilege of giving the last measure of devotion to his country."[30]

Despite Quentin's death, Roosevelt insisted on carrying out the commitment he had made to join Taft and speak at the July 18 Republican gathering at Saratoga Springs, which that day's *New York Tribune* hailed as a challenge to the notion that "partisanship is tabu in time of war." When he approached the podium at Saratoga Springs, Roosevelt was greeted with such a roar of applause that after many minutes he had to raise his hand and plead with the audience to cease. At first he appeared ashen with grief and lacked his old vigor, but soon he warmed as he began by reciting his standard patriotic themes of Americanism and putting the war through. But his address, as in the March speech in Maine, concentrated on present necessities and future possibilities, laying out a "win-the-war" platform meant to elect a Republican Congress. Halfway through, TR looked up from his typescript and appealed directly to the men and women in the audience:

> Surely in this great crisis where we are making sacrifices and making ready for sacrifices on a scale never before known, surely, when we are demanding such fealty and idealism on the part of the young men sent abroad to die, surely we have the right to ask and expect an equal idealism in life from the men and women who stay at home. Our young men have gone to the other side, very many of them to give up in their joyous prime all the glory and all the beauty of life to pay the greatest price of death in battle for a lofty ideal. Now, when they are doing that, cannot we men and women at home make up our minds to try and insist on a loftier idealism here at home?[31]

This appearance so galvanized the partisan audience that the Colonel's friends once again urged him to run for governor of New York. However, after conferring with Will Hays and others, he decided against such a bid. He wrote to Taft that he hated not to do as he and other friends wanted, but Hays agreed with him that "under existing conditions" it was not wise. He simply did not think he could make himself go into a contest over local issues. TR told his friend Will that his heart was "wrapped up in my boys at the front," and he was not thinking in terms of New York conditions.[32] In a July 22 statement published in the *New York Times*, Roosevelt declared that for the past four years his "whole being" had been "absorbed in the tremendous problems, national and international, created by the war." He could not "turn from them with any heart to deal with any other subjects."[33] At the same time, TR confided to his sister Corinne that he only had "one fight left in me, and I think I should reserve my strength in case I am needed in 1920."[34]

On July 25, Theodore and Edith departed for Islesboro, Maine, for two weeks in relative seclusion with Ethel and her small children, Richard and Edie. Roosevelt confided to Kermit from Ethel's modest summer rental house at Dark Harbor that he was glad he got Edith away from Sagamore Hill, for she saw Quentin in every room. He hoped Archie would be sent home to recover from his wounds, as it would comfort her. Quentin's death, he reported, had had a "most extraordinary effect on this nation." It had served as a text for the newspapers across the land and had visualized the war, whereas before it had seemed "misty and unreal." Quentin had now taken his place with "young Shaw and young Lowell" of the Civil War in the pantheon of American heroes. "All four of you," TR went on, "now typify to our people just exactly what I am most proud to have you typify. My pride in you dims my sorrow and my anxiety."[35]

Their little grandson's devotion to Edith, Theodore wrote to his sister Corinne from Islesboro, had done "whatever could be done to ease the dull, steady, aching of her heart" over Quentin. Corinne's son Stewart had died in an accident nine years before, and TR told his sister that when the young died "at the crest of life, in their golden morning," the degrees of difference were merely "degrees in bitterness." Yet for the living there was "nothing more foolish and cowardly than to be beaten down by sorrow which nothing we can do will change." But he nevertheless dreaded the day that Edith received the letters still to come that Quentin had written "before his death—the letters from her dead boy." Corinne and others had suggested that Quentin's letters home should be published, but TR thought them, though very dear, "only such letters as many, many other gallant, clever, manly and gentle boys wrote home," just as their loss was "merely like countless other such losses." It was to Quentin's own family, and to his fiancée Flora Whitney, who visited them at Islesboro, that the "tragedy and heroism" stood by themselves.[36]

When Theodore and Edith returned to Sagamore Hill on August 10, they found waiting the last letters from Quentin that TR had dreaded. These, he reported to Kermit's wife, Belle, reflected Quentin proud and happy at last to be at the fighting front, yet "singularly modest, with all his pride, and his pleasure at showing his metal." He was in a wonderful company of men, flying their "swift battle planes," all bound together in the close ties of men who knew that most were to die and who faced their fate "high of heart and with a gallant defiance." Quentin had written that he would "not for any consideration have been anywhere else." Two days before he was killed, he was with Ted's wife, Eleanor, in Paris, and she was "so proud of him, and took him round as the young hero." So Quentin had his "crowded hour of glorious life." But Roosevelt did not pretend to Belle that it was "not very dreadful that his young life, of such promise, should be darkened at dawn." And for Edith and Flora the pain was great, and it was a real comfort when they returned home to find Alice waiting for them.[37] As for himself, some portion of the light had gone out of TR's life, never to return—replaced, as Edith wrote to Kermit, with "sad thoughts of what Quentin would have counted for in the future."[38]

Roosevelt had not mentioned his own suffering in his letter to Belle, but he did reveal a glimpse of its depth in reply to a message of condolence from Edith Wharton. TR wrote his friend that it was "no use of my writing of Quentin; for I should break down if I tried." His death was heartbreaking, but it would have been "far worse if he had lived at the cost of the slightest failure to perform his duty."[39] And the Colonel would take the same attitude toward what he believed was his own duty to the nation in the months ahead that remained to him. Taft wrote truly to his friend that he knew that "such blows" as Quentin's death "and their anxiety over the wounding of Theodore" would only lead him to "tighten the fastenings of your armor for the fight that we shall have to make to keep up the fighting of this war to the finish."[40] Quentin's death in a second-rate French airplane redoubled Roosevelt's bitterness at the failure of the Wilson administration to prepare and to supply America's fighting men with everything they needed to win the war. No matter the cost to himself physically, he was determined to do all he could to take the political direction of the war, and of the peace, out of the hands of Woodrow Wilson.

CHAPTER 14

PEACE WITH VICTORY

AUGUST TO NOVEMBER 1918

> When the war first broke out I did not think the Kaiser was really to blame. I thought he was simply a tool . . . The last fortnight has shown that he was not even a valorous barbarian—he was unwilling to pay with his body when his hopes were wrecked. Think of the Kaiser and his six sons saving their own worthless carcasses at the end, leaving their women, like their honor, behind them. If ever there was a case where on the last day of the fighting the leaders should have died, this was the case.
> —TR to Arthur Lee, November 19, 1918

That summer on the Western Front the German army's last glimmer of hope for a military victory was extinguished when their fifth and final 1918 drive (codenamed "Marneschütz-Reims") failed as all the others had.[1] German morale waned, while the Allies, heartened by a million fresh American troops and unified under the command of Field Marshal Ferdinand Foch, counterattacked and caught the enemy off guard to conclude the Second Battle of the Marne, again keeping the foe from Paris. On August 8, 1918, which General Erich Ludendorff dubbed the "Black Day of the German Army," the British began a new Somme offensive and made major gains.[2] Later that month, British and Empire troops that had been practically surrounded for three bloody years at the Ypres salient took the offensive and also pushed the enemy back.

American soldiers played a part, with more than 100,000 on the Somme and 50,000 at Ypres, and again showed their raw courage. Roosevelt heartily congratulated John J. Pershing for the "admirable work our army under you has done! And what wonderful soldiers our men make!" Pershing and those under him, TR went on, had "written your names forever on the highest honor roll of our nation."[3] However, even those closest to battlefield developments predicted the war would last well into 1919 or longer, with the Germans entrenched on a shorter line in fierce defense of their own soil. Allied planning and strategy were made on that basis, despite ongoing rumors of peace.

About settling the terms, TR wrote to Lord Bryce that he did not think there would be "need of so much wisdom as firmness." The peace terms in principle he had been preaching were simple enough. To begin with, England and Japan must keep the German colonies they had won. In Europe, France must get back Alsace and Lorraine and Belgium must be restored and indemnified. Further, *Italia irredenta* down to Istria must go to Italy, Romanian Hungary go to Hungary, and Czecho-Slovak, Polish, and Yugoslav commonwealths created as independent states. The Turk should be driven from Europe, and Albania and Armenia made independent under the protection of the Allies. Elsewhere in the old Ottoman Empire, the Jews should be given Palestine, the Syrian Christians protected, and the Arabs made independent. In Russia, the broken-up nationalities should be made commonwealths free from German domination. Also the Poles, Slavs of Siberia, and Danes of North Schleswig should all be "freed from the German yoke."[4]

Meanwhile, William Howard Taft sent another report on the administration's incompetence from Washington, where he continued to serve as joint chairman of the National War Labor Board. He was sorry to tell TR that "watchful waiting" had once again become the policy of the Wilson administration. In what was supposed to be "a campaign to bring Germany to her knees," the president did "nothing of his own leadership," nor did Newton Baker, "except what circumstance known to the public" forced on them. At the same time Woodrow Wilson made "brave speeches" at Baltimore and to the Red Cross, Taft confided that the president gave an off-the-record talk to foreign editors in which he said that he looked forward to making a reasonable peace with the present government of Germany. This showed that Wilson remained "of the same mind" as when he talked to Lawrence Lowell and Taft four months before concerning the plans of the League to Enforce Peace.[5]

By this time the only real point of difference between Taft and Roosevelt was the former's continued support of the league, which, since the United States joined the war, had become more and more TR-like in calling for the defeat of Germany. To remedy their remaining differences, Roosevelt wrote Taft that he thought he had "found a *modus vivendi!*" The Colonel would back the league idea "as an addition to but not a substitute for, our preparing our own strength for our own defense." He sent Taft his August 4 *Kansas City Star* article on these lines, "Sound Nationalism and Sound Internationalism." Taft in turn agreed to support universal training and service, as practiced in Switzerland and Australia, as an addition to and not a substitution for a League of Nations.[6]

In his *Star* article TR also trumpeted the "glorious victory" of the Allies, who with the help of "hard-fighting" American forces had triumphed in the Second Battle of the Marne before Paris. At the same time, the Colonel feared that the failure of German arms could mean a renewed "peace offensive" in which the enemy would "seek to cover their retention of some of their ill-gotten substantial gains by nominal and theoretical support of some glittering proposal about a league of nations to end all war." He warned against the "internationalists" who would "bid us promise to abandon the idea of keeping America permanently ready to defend her right by her strength" and to trust instead to written agreements by which all nations form a league and agree to disarm and to treat one another, large or small, "on an exact equality." Nationalists such as Roosevelt answered that they were ready to join any league to enforce peace that offered a likelihood of limiting future wars, but only on condition that "we do not promise what will not or ought not to be performed, or be guilty of proclaiming a sham." In addition TR would not "surrender our right and duty to prepare our own strength for our own defense."

Further, for it not to be "utterly impotent," any such league must include the nine nations that had the greatest military power, including Germany, Austria, Turkey, and Russia. But the Central Powers had shown in the last four years that "no written or other promise of the most binding kind has even the slightest effect upon their actions," and Russia, under the Bolsheviks, had been guilty of the "grossest possible betrayal of her allies and of the small kindred Slavonic peoples and of world democracy." Consequently, none of the four power's signatures would be worth the paper on which it was written. This meant that the creation of a league for the future would be simply "a pledge by the present Allies to make their alliance perpetual and all go to war again whenever one is attacked." In TR's view this might be necessary, but it did not imply future disarmament as called for in the Fourteen Points.

Additionally, for the United States "to come into court with clean hands," she must not pledge herself without reservation to "self-determination" for all peoples while behaving as she was toward Haiti and Santo Domingo. It was not possible for TR to say whether American actions toward these nations had been right or wrong, because the administration, "with its usual horror of publicity" and its "inveterate predilection for secret and furtive diplomacy," had kept most of the facts hidden, unlike in the case of the Panamanian revolution during his administration when all the details were laid "without reservation" before Congress. In any event, America's continuing occupations of Santo Domingo and Haiti made it "hypocritical for us to lay down any universal rules about self-determination for all nations." Americans, in TR's view, should "put our trust neither in rhetoric nor hypocrisy," be "honest with ourselves," and "trust for our salvation to a sound and intense American nationalism." Above all, he concluded, let us treat any sort of international agreement or covenant "as a mere addition to, and never as a substitute for, the preparation in advance of our own armed power." And in the present crisis, since no one could tell how long the war would go on, Roosevelt called for four million American fighting men to be ready for the "battle front next spring."[7]

In the Senate on August 23, Henry Cabot Lodge followed TR's line with a demand for unconditional surrender from Germany before any peace was made. He then outlined a 10-point program in place of Wilson's 14 that made no mention of freedom of the seas, reduction of armaments, lowering economic barriers, or a League of Nations. It was a plan to return to the pre-1914 status quo with Germany eliminated and the Allies enriched by the spoils of war. Pleased by his performance and the attention his speech attracted, Lodge reported to the Colonel that his plan would "make good standing ground for the Republican party."[8] Roosevelt praised Lodge's "noble speech," declaring in the *Kansas City Star* that only a "great statesman" such as the senator possessed the "courage, the knowledge, and the power of expression" to set forth in convincing fashion the detailed statement of the objects that must be attained if the war was to be "crowned by a peace wholly worth the terrible cost of life and happiness." And it was men in the Congress such as Lodge, not Wilson, that had in fact "adjourned politics" in the tradition of Clay, Webster, and Calhoun.[9]

TR and Edith spent several days in the last week of August in Illinois as the guests of Republican Governor Frank Lowden. Edith traveled with him now, the Colonel confided to Kermit, because after Quentin's death it was "very hard for her to be left alone" at Sagamore Hill.[10] The highlight of the trip came at Springfield on August 26 in a speech to 100,000 at the Illinois State Fair on the occasion of the state's centennial celebration. The two great needs of the moment, TR declared, were to "insist upon thorough-going and absolute Americanism" and to speed up the war. It was also necessary for the country to prepare for the tasks that were to come after the war: first, ensuring that never again would "war find us helpless," and second, "preparing for the social and industrial problem which this earth-shaking conflict of giants will leave in its ruinous wake."

This could all be accomplished, Roosevelt went on, if Americans took pride in their national past and future. "We are not internationalists," he said, "We are American nationalists." The country intended to do justice to all other nations, but in the previous four years the "professional internationalists like the professional pacifists" had played the game of "brutal German autocracy." He warned his audience to beware of German propaganda in the peace negotiations, wherein the internationalists would "prance in the foreground and furnish the rhetoric," and to remember that the country's strength rested on its armed forces and not on a utopian League of Nations or any other mechanism to do away with war.[11]

The *New York World* responded to "Mr. Roosevelt's Gospel of Reaction" that there was "no salvation in the old formula of preparedness." This was now "pre-eminently a war to end wars," and a League of Nations was "the only way out of the Golgotha of militarism." It was not a proposal to be "sneered at or dismissed as Utopian." It was instead today the "one ray of hope of a civilization weltering in blood and agony."[12]

Soon after they returned from the Illinois trip, and as Roosevelt had hoped, Archie returned home to rehabilitate his paralyzed left arm, for which he received treatments at a New York hospital. Having one of her boys home, TR wrote to Kermit, proved a great comfort to "darling mother's wounded heart." Archie, he went on, was "broken-winged, but his soul as high as ever, never did four falcons fly with such daring speed at such formidable quarry."[13] In fact, though he may have hidden it from a father who did not want to see, Archie returned a changed man. As countless other combat veterans, he had difficulties adjusting to civilian life, which in his case included trouble bonding with the infant son he now met for the first time as a stranger.

The Colonel reported to Arthur Lee that the surgeons held out hopes Archie might recover in time to return to Europe for the spring fighting. Ted, they had heard, was still on crutches but aimed to get back into the fray soon, while Kermit, "swelling with wrath," rather than being assigned to machine-gun duty as they had hoped had been sent to the Artillery School at Saumur for three months. The Colonel was very proud of the way the American troops had fought and the fact that they were a "real factor in the war at a very critical period." He wished he could see Lee and "talk over the things necessary to do now to win the war and to crown it with a peace which the Allies dictate, and the tremendous problems which we shall have to face after the war." About Quentin, Roosevelt told his English friend, there was "nothing to be said." It was very dreadful that he should have been killed, but it would have been worse had he not gone.[14]

After Quentin's death, TR and Edith began to hold Saturday afternoon entertainments at Oyster Bay for soldiers from nearby camps. The Colonel's naturalist friend William Beebe, who had himself seen some flying at the front, was on hand early that September when twenty men from Camp Mills, Mineola, visited Sagamore Hill. He recorded that when they departed, after tea and a tour of TR's trophies, few of the machine gunners were "dry-eyed and they roared out a good-bye, and snapped into salute as they stood in the lorry." While the two men walked in the surrounding woods, Roosevelt pointed out several magnificent tulip trees, and Beebe commented that it was "better for any race to die out big & fine like a tulip tree than to peter out like some Indian pipe or a lichen." TR agreed that he would "rather have been the last sabre-toothed Tiger than some measly little Montmartre-mouse opossum." And, he added soon after, "how much finer for Quentin to have died with two bullets through his brain than in a mere flying accident."[15]

That month on the battlefield in France, 550,000 American and 110,000 French soldiers advanced on the St. Mihiel salient, capturing 16,000 Germans and 443 artillery pieces. This was the opening gambit of the newly created American First Army, which in late September began, again in cooperation with the French, the Meuse-Argonne offensive that would last until the end of the war. More than a million AEF troops undertook the bloodiest and largest American engagement since the Civil War, suffering 120,000 dead and wounded—American blood paid for the blunders at home that failed to deliver needed artillery, shells, and airplanes that almost certainly would have cleared the way and saved thousands of casualties.[16]

Mid-September peace feelers from Austria-Hungary met a cold response in the American press, which in the heated wartime mood followed TR's lead and called for unconditional surrender and pilloried the *New York Times* when it became the first and only major daily to back the acceptance of terms.[17] Roosevelt wrote of the prospects of peace to Arthur Lee, who had resigned his post as British director-general of food production in a row with David Lloyd George over his authority. Nevertheless, for his service to the nation, he had been created Viscount Lee of Fareham, which TR called "a bully title." The Colonel told Lee that it would be a "crime" if Great Britain was not allowed to keep the German colonies she had captured. And "to propose to have the natives settle the matter by vote would be worthy of Bedlam were it not so transparently dishonest." Roosevelt also wished that their friend Sir Edward Grey would not continue to "bleat with feeble amiability about securing universal peace through a League of Nations." Not only did this distract attention from the "prime duty" of winning the war, but it also played right into the hands of the pro-Germans and pacifists who were only waiting for the chance to "clamor that the slaughter must stop, that no nation must be punished, and all future wars prevented by a League—of which Germany, Austria, Turkey and Russia would be four of the guarantors!"[18]

Still at Camp Funston, Leonard Wood could not understand the present German withdrawal, which took a heavy Allied toll. He wrote TR that in his opinion the enemy had not had serious enough losses to in any way "affect their general military power." Instead, as did many others, Wood believed they had "something important up their sleeve" and there was "something coming later." Nevertheless, he hoped things would "so shape themselves so that when the great settlement after the war" was made the Colonel might be able to represent the country. He realized that under present circumstances this would be difficult but still thought it "absolutely vital." This would be the greatest service Roosevelt could render, "unless the people again should have the good sense to bring you to the presidency."[19]

Among those who had also proposed that TR be given a place at the peace conference was Charles Grasty, the war correspondent of the *New York Times.* Roosevelt commented that he knew nothing of Grasty, but he did know the administration and couldn't believe that Wilson was "anything but angered by the proposal if he saw it." In his view there was not one chance in a million that Wilson would include him in the peace talks.[20] In fact, the odds were even longer than that. In the ongoing discussion about the composition of the American Peace Commission for the conference, Wilson, who named himself head, had already dismissed Roosevelt and Taft as possible Republican members.[21] Colonel Edward M. House, who would be joined by Democrats Robert Lansing and General Tasker Bliss as members, thought Elihu Root would be the best man. But in the end the sole Republican chosen was the retired diplomat Henry White, who, although a friend of TR, as Wilson well knew was hardly a party stalwart. This led to the commission being referred to as "four Wilsons and one White."[22]

Roosevelt continued as honorary president of the American Defense Society, which kept up its propaganda in a series of pamphlets, producing more than thirty during the war. One of Wilson's correspondents, Tariff Commissioner William Kent, forwarded an ADS publication that called for the Allies to keep up the blockade until achieving total victory in the war, while adding that the organization also stood for a postwar "eternal boycott" of German goods. "Such stuff," Kent told Wilson, was "not only vile from the standpoint of common humanity" but also "inherent sedition as interfering with matters of life and death in our own country." If the Germans believed they were to be "starved and oppressed throughout the centuries," they would, at a time when they were crumbling, find a "new resistance—that of a rat in a corner." Consequently, American boys might be killed in "unnecessary fighting due to just such utterances." Kent knew the president had "consistently refrained from talking back at the irrepressible Roosevelt," and he was not advocating Wilson's "paying personal heed to this infamous interference with statecraft," but he believed that "somehow or other it should be brought home to these people" that they were "overstepping the bounds of private opinion" and "interfering in the war, and should be subject to treatment in accordance with their deserts."[23]

The Fourth Liberty Loan drive began on September 18 and ran for the next three weeks, during which the political parties more or less agreed to minimize partisan campaign activities and devote their energies to raising money for the war. But this uneasy truce was soon broken. Roosevelt condemned William Gibbs McAdoo and Wilson for hitting below the belt after Democratic workers at Liberty Loan rallies handed out circulars with the message, "Don't spoil all now by letting the election go against the government. Vote with President Wilson for the Democratic ticket and hasten the end of the war."[24] Wilson redefined and defended his peace position at a September 27 Liberty Loan rally at the Metropolitan Opera House in New York, where Republican Governor Charles S. Whitman presided. To great applause, the president told his audience that there would be "no bargain or compromise" peace with the Central Powers. But, to ensure the sanctity of future international agreements, a league of nations must be an essential part of any final peace. In this speech Wilson added "Five Particulars" that the league would enforce, including a ban on alliances furthering special interests, selfish economic combinations, and secret treaties.[25] Concerning the territorial settlement, he declared that no special interests should be recognized, only what was common to all. It should be a peace of the peoples, not just their rulers.[26]

Roosevelt responded to Wilson while on a 12-day speaking tour to Nebraska and Montana on behalf of the Fourth Liberty Loan. Before he departed, TR had written to Kermit that he had come to loathe public speaking, but some, such as in support of the Liberty Loans, was necessary. The "incessant fluid rhetoric" of Wilson had made him feel as if "silence and damn little of that" ought to be the motto of all Americans who were not in the fighting. But he felt duty bound to preach "uncompromising doctrine" about the terms of peace and the "wild plans" about disarmament under a "League of Nations" idea, otherwise the "foolish sentimentalists would at the end of the war deliver us over, bound hand and foot, either to the sinister autocracy of Germany or the sinister anarchists" such as the Bolsheviks of Russia.[27] At Baltimore, the first stop on his tour, in addition to booming the Liberty loan, TR also advocated registration of men and women for industrial training in peacetime.[28]

While Roosevelt was out on his tour, Bulgaria signed the Salonika Armistice and became the first of the Central Powers to leave the war.[29] Taft commented on the "glorious news" from both the Balkans and France that he thought the Bulgarian collapse refuted the narrow "western frontism" of the generals and showed the "wisdom of our sending one hundred thousand men to Vladivostok." Germany's hold on Russia, Taft believed, was "now the only weak place in the armor of the Allies," and if the administration would move with "anything like proper speed, that defect might be repaired." Washington, he reported, had become a "dreadful place now." It was crowded with "bustling people making one another uncomfortable, each seeking that 'something.'"[30]

The final stop of the Liberty Loan tour, at Billings, Montana, on October 5, allowed TR to revisit his ranching past. Over a long and representative day, he praised patriotism to massed schoolchildren, supported the suffrage cause before an assembly of women, and greeted many old friends and neighbors from 35 years before. These included Sheriff Jack Hawkins, under whom Roosevelt had served as a deputy. In his main address, to 7,500 in the city's new auditorium, the Colonel spoke as usual of Americanism, loyalty, and the vigilance required to meet the twin dangers of anarchy and tyranny.[31] TR reported to Kermit that in Montana his old ranch friends "turned up as usual." He went on that it was "really rather touching to see how eagerly they came to greet me, to live again the times of long ago" with the certainty that they were the "sharers of any fame and distinction which I may at the moment have." Everywhere on the tour he found the "war spirit aroused and resolute"; everywhere there was "immense enthusiasm" when he insisted that America must accept no terms save Germany's unconditional surrender.[32]

The deteriorating conditions in Germany led the head of the new government, Prince Max of Baden, who had been told by his military commander Ludendorff to make the best peace he could, to ask Woodrow Wilson for an armistice "for the purpose of taking up negotiations" for a peace based on the Fourteen Points and Wilson's "subsequent pronouncements," particularly the address of September 27.[33] A formal note to this effect was presented, via the Swiss, to Wilson on October 7, 1918, the same day Austria-Hungary also asked for negotiations. The president responded to the German note the next day in what Robert Lansing called "a query not a reply." Wilson did not agree to an armistice but held out the prospect of further discussions and posed several questions. Did the German government fully accept the Fourteen and other points, and would the peace conference merely discuss their implementation? Was the chancellor speaking for his people or merely the leaders who had been heretofore conducting German policy? Further, a necessary condition of an armistice would be German withdrawal from all occupied areas.[34] At the same time the Allied prime ministers, with whom Wilson did not consult about the German offer and who had not agreed to the Fourteen Points as a basis for negotiations, met in Paris to consider their own response to this development.[35]

Most of the press, in America and Europe, dismissed the German proposal as an obvious sham to gain time for the German army to regroup. Absolute surrender, the *Baltimore Sun* demanded in a representative article, was the "sine qua non for peace."[36] In London, the *Daily Mail* labeled the German request for an armistice "not peace but trickery" and printed a warning to the Allies (attributed to a German in Switzerland): "They will cheat you yet, those junkers! Having won half the world by bloody murder, they are going to win the other half with tears in their eyes, crying for mercy."[37] A week later the paper speculatively described "The Great War of 1938," which occurred only because the Allies had not "seen the thing through" in 1918.[38]

In the Senate debate of October 8, which universally denounced the German proposal, Henry Cabot Lodge and Miles Poindexter of Washington agreed that it was not too strong a statement to say that an armistice now would be tantamount to the loss of the war.[39] As it fell out, the negotiations between Wilson and the Germans would go back and forth for a month before the final armistice was signed, in part because on October 10 a German submarine sank the Irish mail packet streamer RMS *Leinster*, killing hundreds of crew and passengers, including many women and children. That day Roosevelt released a statement in the *New York Times* that Wilson should not have begun to negotiate until the war was won and Germany had surrendered unconditionally. TR also instructed Will Hays that the Republican response to the armistice negotiations should "emphatically state that the offer of the President in starting negotiations with Germany, was stopped only by the vigorous Senate protests of men like Lodge and Poindexter," who had been the "staunchest upholders of the war." Further, it was "our war" and it was "our business to send Republicans to Congress now, to avert the danger of any improper yielding by the Democrats, Administration and Party, in this war." More men were needed in Washington like Lodge and Poindexter, who would "back up every measure to speed up the war" and would "set their faces like flint against any improper yielding of our position."[40]

In the October 12 *Kansas City Star*, Roosevelt noted the "greedy eagerness" with which the Central Powers had accepted Wilson's Fourteen Points. He hoped that when the time came for discussing peace proposals, "we shall ourselves repudiate" some of them and insist on having all of them put into "plain and straightforward language before we assent to any of them." For example, the Colonel wanted to know exactly what was meant by freedom of the seas and freedom of commercial intercourse. Also, what was meant by "abolishing secret diplomacy?" He heartily agreed with the idea if it meant the administration would renounce the "system of secret and furtive diplomacy" that it now carried out in Mexico, Haiti, and Santo Domingo. But he did not see why the government needed an "international mandate" before it told "our people the truth in these matters." The administration also needed to explain to the American people why it kept secret for two years the "full knowledge it had of Germany's conduct and attitude towards us" as set out in Ambassador James Gerard's recent book *My Four Years in Germany*, which warned that Americans understood neither the magnitude nor the importance of the war and that the military and naval power of Germany remained unbroken. The country, said TR, had never seen such secret diplomacy as that carried out in the last five years.

Finally, if a league of nations meant that Germany, Austria, Turkey, and Russia "as presently constituted" would "have the say-so about America's future destiny, we ought to be against it." Roosevelt preferred the de facto league made up of the United States and the Allies to which the country already belonged. In his view, America's war aim ought to be the unconditional surrender of Germany and her vassals, and the country should not consider any peace proposal "until this war aim has been accomplished by the victorious arms of our allies and ourselves." He reminded his readers that the Senate shared with the president the right to make treaties and that the people were the "ultimate arbiters" and their will should be followed.[41]

The Colonel repeated these points the same day in a speech at Oyster Bay for the Liberty Loan and over the following days in New York in talks to the Council of Jewish Women at Temple Emanu-El on Fifth Avenue and the Liederkranz Association at their hall, where he denounced the Kaiser, "preached the straightest American doctrine," and was "wildly applauded."[42] Wilson, TR wrote to Kermit the next day, had made his "800th volte face" when, after having announced with "dramatic emphasis" there would be no peace negotiations, he began negotiating. And as Wilson invariably turned "somersaults on every question of policy," as he was both an "untrustworthy friend and an irresolute foe," and his objectives were "wholly personal," TR could not begin to guess what "this may portend."[43]

The president was unsure himself how to proceed, and he and House conferred over the response to Germany's second note sent on October 12, which accepted the Fourteen Points and Wilson's other pronouncements without reservation and shrewdly asked if the Allies also accepted them. The peace conference, said the note, would only be to "agree upon practical details of the application of these terms." Germany agreed to evacuate Allied territory, and Prince Max suggested an Allied and German "mixed commission" meet to plan this. He also declared that he spoke for the German government and people.[44] House argued that if Germany was beaten, she would accept any terms, and if she was not beaten, "we did not wish to make terms with her." At the same time, neither man wanted to make a "vengeful peace" or have the Allied armies "ravage Germany" as she had ravaged the countries she had invaded. Wilson was "especially insistent that no stain of this sort should rest upon allied arms." House thought the president "very fine in this feeling" and was sorry he was "hampered by the Allies and the vociferous cry in this country." It was difficult to do the "right thing in the right way with people like Roosevelt, Lodge, Poindexter and others clamoring for the undesirable and impossible."[45]

As Wilson realized, however, TR and Lodge were far from alone in their demand for unconditional surrender, and on October 15 he dispatched a stiff reply to the German note. In light of the *Leinster* sinking, there would be no armistice so long as Germany continued unrestricted submarine warfare, and the president wanted proof that the present government spoke for the German people. Further, the conditions of the armistice would be left to the military advisors of the Allied and Associated Powers so as to provide "absolutely satisfactory safeguards and guarantees of the maintenance of the present military supremacy of the armies of the United States and of the Allies in the field." Wilson also noted that the United States had entered the war to "destroy arbitrary power" and asked for assurances of this, a not-so-veiled demand for the abdication of Wilhelm II.[46]

This note, unlike the first, was well received in Europe and America. The *Daily Mail* wholeheartedly endorsed what it called the "unconditional surrender" reply by Wilson to the German entreaties.[47] The president, Roosevelt confided to Kermit, had "received a lesson." Two weeks before Wilson had believed he could "step in as a Peace-God," make a negotiated peace with the Central Powers, and be "humbly followed by the allies and slavishly adored by our own people." But his first note to Germany had produced "such an outburst of protest here at home that he promptly turned a somersault" and was now "rigidly for real victory." Germany, TR went on, was being "thrust out" of France and Belgium, but her armies remained unbroken and her new positions would be formidable. He hoped Germany would soon capitulate, but he thought it would be as "unwise to count on this" as it was that Wilson would not "ease up in his preparations."[48]

While the peace negotiations continued, on October 17 Roosevelt gave a speech for the Liberty Loan at Providence, Rhode Island, and then traveled by speedboat with Governor Robert Beeckman to the Newport Naval Training Station. He told the men of the naval brigade that "in this war he did not want a decision by points." He wanted a knockout, and he would discuss terms with the Kaiser "only to the extent of telling him what the terms were" and having him say, "Yes, sir." The only city that was "worthy and entirely appropriate" for this postwar "discussion" was Berlin. As he did not want to be unreasonable, TR would settle for Cologne or one of the other Rhine cities, but Berlin would be his first choice.[49] This visit gave the Colonel the opportunity to report to Ted that Grace Vanderbilt had "convulsed Newport by announcing that as the wife of a Brigadier General she was entitled to take precedence of everybody except to the Governor." When he was appealed to for a ruling, TR explained that the situation was "gravely complicated by her also being the mother of an enlisted man, a chauffeur," and that he thought the "only solution was for her to sit in the Governor's lap during the early courses of dinner, but as the mother of a chauffeur, to eat her desert in the kitchen."[50]

On October 20, Prince Max replied to Wilson's second note that German submarines would no longer sink passenger ships. But the German note maintained that the armistice must preserve the present balance between the two armies and trusted that the president would approve of "no demand which would be irreconcilable with the honor of the German people and with opening a way to peace with justice." In answer to Wilson's comments about "arbitrary power," the note restated the previous reply that the government represented the Reichstag. Four days later the president responded that because Germany had accepted the Fourteen Points, their spokesmen represented a majority on the Reichstag, and they promised to cease inhumane practices in war, he would take up the matter of the armistice with the Allies. And if their governments were "disposed to effect peace upon the terms and principles indicated," their military advisors, along with those of the United States, would be asked to draw up armistice terms that would leave the Germans unable to renew hostilities and leave the Allied and Associated governments with "unrestricted power" to enforce the peace. These military safeguards were necessary, Wilson went on, because the German government was still unreformed with the old leaders and emperor still in control. Four days later, the Germans responded that they awaited Allied proposals for an armistice.[51]

Roosevelt responded by sending his Senate allies, Lodge, Poindexter, and Hiram Johnson, a telegram printed in the newspapers. TR declared that he hoped that their body, which was part of the treaty-making process in the United States, would take "affirmative action against a negotiated peace with Germany" and in favor of unconditional surrender. He also "earnestly hoped" that, on behalf of the American people, the Senate would "declare against the adoption in their entirety" of Wilson's Fourteen Points "as offering a basis for peace satisfactory to the United States." The only peace offer that should be considered from Germany would be an "offer to accept such terms as the Allies without our aid have imposed on Bulgaria." The country also ought to declare war on Turkey "without an hour's delay." Not doing so had caused the talk about "making the world safe for democracy" look unpleasantly like "mere insincere rhetoric." While the Turk was in Europe and "permitted to tyrannize over the subject peoples," the world was thoroughly "unsafe for democracy." Let us, Roosevelt went on, "dictate the peace by the hammering guns and not chat about peace to the accompaniment of the clicking of typewriters."

Further, TR believed "we should find out what the President means by continually referring to this country merely as an associate," instead of an ally of the nations with whose troops American soldiers were "actually brigaded in battle." If by this he meant that America was "something less than an ally" of France, England, Italy, Belgium, and Serbia, then he meant that America was "something less than an enemy" of Germany and Austria. "We ought to make it clear to the world," he went on, "that we are neither an untrustworthy friend nor an irresolute foe." Let the country show that it did not desire to "pose as an umpire between our faithful and loyal friends and our treacherous and brutal enemies" but was the "staunch ally of our friends and the staunch foe of our enemies." Only when the German people repudiated the Hohenzollerns would it be time to "discriminate between them and their masters."[52]

Roosevelt repeated many of these arguments in an October 26 *Kansas City Star* editorial endorsement of an unconditional surrender policy. He added that "sensible men and women do not negotiate with an outlaw . . . or ask for a peace with him on terms of equality if he will give up his booty." To the contrary, they expected the law to "take him by force and to have him tried and punished" and this was the way Germany should be treated. He admitted that it was a "sad and dreadful thing" to face months of additional bloodletting, but it would be a much worse thing to "quit now and the children now growing up obliged to do the job all over again, with ten times as much bloodshed and suffering, when their turn comes." The surest way to ensure a lasting peace was to overthrow the "Prussianized Germany of the Hohenzollerns as Napoleon was overthrown."[53] That day, as Germany continued to fall apart, Ludendorff was forced to resign as first quartermaster general, leaving Paul von Hindenburg alone in command of the retreating German army. And in Paris, Colonel House arrived to attend the meeting of the Supreme War Council that would hash out the terms of the armistice, while at home the people of the United States went to the polls in the 1918 congressional elections.

Even though Wilson had declared "politics is adjourned" on May 27, that fall he faced the very real electoral prospect of losing the slight Democratic majority of three in the House and even perhaps a safer majority of ten in the Senate. Consequently, and against the advice of his cabinet, Wilson decided to make a partisan appeal for a Democratic Congress to support his policies. The opposition party, charged Wilson in a statement broadcast in the press on October 25, had at "almost every turn since we entered the war" sought to "take the choice of policy and the conduct of the war out of my hands" and put it under the control of "other instrumentalities of their own choosing." This was not the time for either "divided counsel or divided leadership." Therefore, if the country had approved of his leadership and wished him to "continue to be your unembarrassed spokesman in affairs at home and abroad," Wilson earnestly begged that voters would "express yourself unmistakably" by returning a Democratic House and Senate.[54] Today such a statement would be politics as usual, but in 1918, in wartime, this about-face was widely considered, in both parties, to be at the least bad form and an outright insult to Republicans who, while they criticized, had supported the war effort more than Wilson's own party and whose votes had been vital to pass much of the administration's war agenda.

On his sixtieth birthday two days later, TR reported to Kermit that Wilson had come out with a "frank appeal for Democratic success" to give him a free hand in the peace negotiation. In Roosevelt's view, the president wanted "any kind of peace which he can persuade people to accept as satisfactory, wholly without regard to its ultimate effect on our country or on the world," and he had no idea how successful Wilson would be. He told Kermit that he was glad to be sixty, as it somehow gave him the right to be "titularly as old as I feel." He only hoped that when his son reached the same age he would have "as much happiness to look back upon" as he did and would be "as proud of his sons and daughters" as he was of his.[55] The Colonel, suffering from crippling attacks of rheumatism, undoubtedly was feeling his age, and he signed a letter of thanks to his sister Corinne for her birthday greeting, "Ever Yours, Methusaleh's understudy."[56] He also told his sister that, whatever came, he had "kept the promise that I made to myself when I was twenty-one . . . that I would work *up to the hilt* until I was sixty, and I have done it."[57]

In light of Wilson's partisan call for a Democratic Congress to support him, TR threw away the speech he planned to deliver October 28 to Republicans at Carnegie Hall and instead replied to the president's appeal with a "detailed denunciation" of Wilson, his conduct in the war, and his peace proposals. "This meeting," the Colonel began, was held under "peculiar circumstances." If the president was "right in the appeal he has just made to the voters then you and I," declared Roosevelt, "have no right to vote in this election or to discuss public questions while the war lasts." If Wilson's appeal was justified, then "only that faction of the Democratic Party which accepts towards the President the rubber-stamp attitude of complete servility is entitled to control Congress." And no man who was a Republican or put "loyalty to the people ahead of loyalty to the servant of the people" was to have a vote in "determining the great questions ever brought before this nation." In Wilson's "extraordinary" election appeal, which repudiated and reversed his previous announcement that "politics is adjourned," the president did not ask for loyalty to the nation, but only support for himself.

Roosevelt was glad that Wilson had taken off his mask by now declaring that this was a party war and that the Republicans, although he admitted they had been "unquestionably pro-war," were to be excluded from any share in controlling the war or the peace. Wilson did not ask for the defeat of the antiwar Democrats, who made up half the party. To the contrary, he supported such men if they were "anti-war but pro-Administration." The Colonel asked the nation to consider that it was the Republican Party that had almost to a man supported the declaration of war, the draft measure, sending an army overseas, and every demand for money whether by taxation or loan. On almost every issue the Republicans had supported the war and the speeding of it, and yet the president now made a partisan appeal in favor of the Democrats who "opposed the war measures and against the Republicans who supported them."

Wilson declared that this was "no time for divided counsels." To Roosevelt it was "mere insolence" for the servant of the people to say that he would not counsel with other servants of the people when they have elected them for the "express purpose" of giving him counsel. He went on that the world would now be better off by "hundreds of thousands of fearless lives and many billions of treasure if Mr. Wilson had been willing to supplement his own self-sufficient ignorance by the counsel of those who would gladly have counseled him wisely but who would not creep into his presence as slaves."[58] Alice, who had read the speech page by page as TR crafted it at Sagamore Hill, recalled the "extraordinary enthusiasm" that night at Carnegie hall and that it was a "joy to hear Father say in public all that Mr. Wilson's reconvening of politics made it possible to say." The opportunity had been given and was "swiftly taken to clear the atmosphere for the voter to see straight" at the election a week later.[59]

On October 31 Roosevelt and Taft issued a joint counterappeal for a Republican Congress to assure the unconditional surrender of Germany, the participation of the Senate in the peace making, minimal disturbance in reconverting the economy to peacetime, and a careful accounting of the Democratic stewardship over wartime expenditures.[60] Among those converted by the joint appeal was Harvard Professor Albert Bushnell Hart, who confessed to TR that when Wilson's election appeal came out, he was "at first inclined to think that there would be more concentration and directness of policy if he had a party majority behind him." Since the start of the war, Hart had "stood by the president in the sense of backing his war policy and his peace propositions," but TR's speech and his joint statement with Taft "settled the matter" in his mind.

The professor admitted he did not completely agree with Roosevelt's criticism of Wilson's peace terms, "but you succeeded in fixing the attention of the country on the proposition that this is a national war, in which the members of both parties participated," and that the president was, to use the vernacular, "trying to 'hog the war.'" He noted that Roosevelt had changed his opinion of Taft and perhaps in time would do the same for Wilson. Hart, who was editing a collection of Wilson's speeches, agreed with TR that Wilson "says more than he does," but what stuck in Hart's crop was Wilson's "insensate adherence to second rate men: a secretary of state who gets his dispatches from the presidential typewriter; a secretary of war whose department seems to get on best when he is overseas; a secretary of the treasury who has assumed the management of all the railways and been a conspicuous failure." Finally, it made Hart "hot under the collar that in this great crisis of the world's history, the United States of America should have no civil representative in Europe." Woodrow Wilson had one in Colonel House, "responsible to him only as a friend!"[61]

Roosevelt, who had been remarkably silent on the unofficial peace peregrinations of House over the previous years, agreed. He noted in the *Kansas City Star* that "Mr. House of Texas" had been sent abroad on a diplomatic mission, in the company of Frank Cobb, editor of the *New York World*, which had "recently been busy in denouncing as foolish the demand made by many Americans for unconditional surrender by Germany." House, TR went on, was not in the public service of the nation, but in the "private service of Mr. Wilson." The envoy was usually called Colonel House, and in the "semiofficial biography, published in an ardently admiring New York paper," it was explained that the Texan had once been appointed colonel on a governor's staff but disliked "military ostentation" so much he gave his uniform "to a negro servant to wear on social occasions." This attitude of respect for the uniform apparently made the president feel that House was "peculiarly fit to negotiate on behalf of our fighting men abroad for whom the uniform is sacred." Roosevelt did not doubt that House and Cobb possessed "charming social attributes and much private worth," but as they were sent over on a diplomatic mission "presumably vitally affecting the whole country," he asked why their instructions and purpose were "shrouded in profound mystery." It seemed permissible to ask the president why in this particular instance diplomacy was not proceeding "frankly in the public view," as the first of his Fourteen Points mandated.[62]

The Colonel's unceasing attacks on Wilson lead the *Nation* to ask in an article, "Why is Roosevelt Unjailed?" The journal asked what would have happened to any other "humble citizen" that had attracted a crowd in the street and then denounced the president by saying, as TR had, that "in the cloak rooms of Congress it is a bitter jest to speak of the President thus: 'Here's to our Czar, last in war, first toward peace, long may he waver.'" The *Nation* was inclined to believe that if any other soapbox orator had used those words he would have been given twenty years in jail for "interfering with the draft."[63]

When Turkey followed Bulgaria and left the war at the end of October, Roosevelt commented that the United States had no share in the honor of what had been done, because Wilson, instead of aiding our allies, had "preserved the same cold neutrality between the Armenians and their Turkish butchers that he formerly did between the Belgians and their German oppressors." Since the country had taken no hand in freeing Palestine, Syria, and Armenia, it was the British and French who would determine the fate of Turkey. Roosevelt earnestly hoped that the Turk would be expelled from Europe and Armenia made independent, but he lamented that "we have lost the right to insist on these points." The United States was contributing to the great contest on the Western Front, and Wilson might still serve as a "channel of communications," but it would be General Foch who would be the real master of the situation. The "men with the guns and not the men with fountain pens" would "dictate the terms."[64] The day the Turks left the war, Foch wrote to Pershing, who wanted to fight on to Berlin if necessary to defeat the enemy completely, that the punitive armistice conditions he was preparing "might not bear the name of unconditional surrender," but they would be "approximate to that."[65]

The "men with the guns" at the front now included Kermit, who two days after his father's birthday finished with Artillery School in time to see action with the AEF's First Division in the last weeks of the Meuse-Argonne fighting. He joined his brother Ted, who had been promoted lieutenant colonel, TR's rank in Cuba. Still limping from his leg wound, Ted had been sidelined to Langres as an instructor in the Army Line School, but he managed to finesse himself back into the command of his old regiment, the Twenty-Sixth, and thereby became the first reserve officer to command a regular army regiment in action during the chaotic last weeks of the war.[66] Roosevelt, glad to hear that Kermit had finally got to the front, warned him that Wilson had opened peace negotiations, "doubling and turning like a rabbit." Unquestionably the surrender of Turkey and Bulgaria, and the breakup of Austria-Hungary, had made Germany "eagerly wish peace and feel they confront a more serious situation." There were also strong peace parties in "warweary England, France and Italy," and if they could reach an agreement for an armistice, peace might come at any time.

Of course, TR told his son, he would accept no terms "until our armies had actually marched onto German soil" and reached Cologne at least. But Wilson's "one thought" was to "sit at the head of the peace table." However, TR went on, "we have won; Germany is defeated."

Meanwhile, he had had to take a part in the election campaign. Republicans feared the good news from the battle fronts would aid the Democrats and there might not be "much hope of winning, but *somebody* has to stand up to Wilson, and if nobody else does it I must."[67] TR wrote to Kermit's wife, Belle, that "evidently all the combatants" were "heartily sick of the war, and the head of the only nation that is eager to go on is himself more eager for peace than anyone else." Therefore he would not be surprised if "peace came at any moment now."[68] The same day Roosevelt wrote this letter, November 3, the envoys of Austria-Hungary signed the Villa Giusta Armistice and left the war.[69]

In the last few days before the 1918 election, while the Colonel rested at Oyster Bay, Democratic appeals made the choice a very clear one—between Wilson and Roosevelt. One such national advertisement asked voters to remember that when they went to the polls they would not be voting for Republicans or Democrats "as individuals but for the leaders who would control them when they go to Congress." The appeal asked, "Whose leadership do you prefer? That of Senator Lodge, Senator Penrose and Colonel Roosevelt, who would dominate a Republican majority and block the President, or the leadership of Woodrow Wilson?" The Republican leaders were on record as against Wilson's 14 war aims, which had been "applauded by public opinion throughout the world, and constitute the basis of an enduring peace." With Roosevelt "denouncing the whole basis of these peace terms and Senator Lodge rejecting all the fundamentals," what could the country expect the Republicans to do with the peace treaty if they came to control the congressional committees? This was the issue that was now "squarely before the country." The people had to decide whether they would "follow President Wilson or Colonel Roosevelt"—whether they wanted a peace of "liberalism and justice" or a peace of "imperialism, standpatism, and militarism" that left "all the old causes of war exactly where they were before we undertook to root out militarism and the rule of force and war itself."[70] The *New York Times* called the election "momentous and epochal beyond any fight for the control of Congress . . . since the Civil War."[71]

On Election Day, November 5, the Colonel disobeyed doctor's orders and, despite a foot so swollen he could not wear a shoe, hobbled out to vote for a Republican Congress. The country followed his lead, rejecting Wilson's partisan call for a Democratic victory and giving the Republicans a major-ity of 44 in the House and 1 in the Senate. Most significant for the future, the victory meant that Henry Cabot Lodge would be both majority leader and chairman of the Senate Foreign Relations Committee that would con-sider any peace treaty signed by Wilson. From Oyster Bay, Roosevelt com-mented that the result of the election was "really extraordinary," given that the "entire Pro-German and pacifist vote was behind the Wilson Democratic ticket" and that the "enormous war powers of the Administration have such adroit and unscrupulous partisanship." However, TR viewed the result as "much more a victory for straight Americanism than for Republicanism," as many Democrats had also voted for "genuine democracy here at home, and of the aroused purpose to stand beside our allies and against Germany to the end."[72] For the Republicans it represented "not so much a victory as an opportunity." The party, which had won as the opponents of Kaiser-ism and Bolshevism, now intended to "shape our internal policy for the real substantial benefit of the average man," to help tenant farmers, small busi-ness, and labor.[73]

Though Roosevelt failed publicly to admit them, as always there were other election issues that cost the Democrats. In the West, price controls on wheat, while Southern cotton was not controlled, lost the administra-tion many agrarian votes. TR's friend Gifford Pinchot helped start an orga-nization in Washington, the Federal Board of Farm Organizations, to take advantage of this "price-fixing" and to bring farm votes to the Republican Party. In all Democrats lost 21 seats in the farm belt. Another problem for the Democrats nationally was the women's suffrage issue, which Wilson came round to supporting but for which his party, and particularly the Southern wing, did not have the same enthusiasm. Also, turnout was held down by the influenza pandemic, which in the end killed 500,000 Americans. And finally, had the Armistice with Germany come a week earlier, who knows what effect the euphoria of victory might have had on voters.

In Roosevelt's view, the electoral result was also a victory for uncondi-tional surrender, and it served "notice on Germany" that Foch would dictate the terms of the armistice and that the terms of peace would be "deter-mined by all the Allies representing the free and democratic world, acting together against Kaiserism in the first place, and against all tyranny, whether of the Hohenzollerns or the Bolsheviks."[74] The Colonel was correct that it was Foch and the generals in Europe who hammered out the punitive terms of the armistice that ended the conflict, disarmed the enemy, and ensured that Germany would fight no more. Many of the war aims of the Allies were already included in these terms, and TR could declare with some truth that peace came, "not on Mr. Wilson's fourteen points, but on General Foch's twenty-odd points," which had "all the directness, the straightforwardness, and the unequivocal clearness" that the Fourteen Points "strikingly lacked."[75]

After the election results were in, an avalanche of congratulatory messages hit Oyster Bay. Frank Munsey sent TR a telegram: "I cannot let this day pass without warmly congratulating you as the foremost figure in all that America stands for and votes for when aroused."[76] Charles M. Thomas, associate editor of the *Washington Eagle*, gushed to "My Dear Colonel," "You can trust the American people to do the right thing at the right time . . . To you, by your fearless, lucid exposure of the weaknesses and fallacies of the administration, is due the moral awakening which resulted in the great victory which I know you must be enjoying today." He asked Roosevelt to "please keep your health and store your ammunition for 1920." The editor hoped TR could "make the party leaders see the moral aspects of the reconstruction program," for he felt that "only on that basis can you lead them in your own highest manner when they make you the standard bearer in the next national campaign."[77]

A 96-year-old Civil War veteran from Nebraska sent Roosevelt congratulations on the "wonderful victory, and a much needed rebuke to one man power." In his opinion, "never in history" had the country "needed a statesman at the head of affairs as we need him now." Some people could teach school, but it took "men to run a government like the good old U. S. A." The old vet went on that he wanted to live long enough "to cast another vote for Theodore Roosevelt to fill the place that has been vacant since the war began." He added a postscript that on the road to mail his letter "the word came Kiser [sic] Bill heard the success of the Republicans and signed surrender terms."[78] The Kaiser had not surrendered, but the announcement of his abdication on November 9 opened the way for the signing of an armistice. Wilhelm and his sons soon after went into exile in Holland.

The signing of the Armistice with Germany on November 11, 1918, prompted another deluge of joyous messages. "On this, the most wonderful day in history of the world," a Denver supporter wrote, "I want to thank you for the splendid part you took in the recent campaign, the result of which was the election of a Republican 'unconditional surrender' congress." His correspondent could not "but believe that Germany had taken into account this condition." At the least, the prospect of the new Congress had "given no comfort to the enemy, the President notwithstanding."[79] TR's biographer Charles Washburn wrote from France, "Now that we have a peace *with* victory, we will never forget those who paid the awful price that made it possible. I shall linger at Quentin's grave today in the company with thousands of my countrymen—Der Tag—and what a day it is."[80] That day an American soldier wrote that he was sending Roosevelt a piece of Quentin's plane taken from the "mashed up" wreckage in France. He told the Colonel that he had camped near the site without knowing its significance until he saw the parade of French troops who stopped to pay their respects at "Winton's" grave.[81] Two months later, Quentin's father would be at rest in a grave of his own.

Epilogue

November 1918 to January 1919

Theodore Roosevelt is dead, and I have lost a friend . . . something vital has gone. Something fine. Something that seemed as though it could not die. Fearless, reckless, boyish Theodore Roosevelt has joined the army at last.[1]

—Mary Roberts Rinehart

The day the Armistice was signed with Germany and the guns silenced, the Colonel was admitted to Roosevelt Hospital in Manhattan. He had been suffering from a collection of chronic illnesses for some time, but he insisted on soldiering on until after the election. A flare up of his gout forced him into bed, and further complications including inflammatory rheumatism sent him to the hospital, where he stayed until Christmas. The public was told he was suffering an attack of sciatica. The end of the war and the vindication of Roosevelt's criticisms implicit in the election defeat of Woodrow Wilson and the Democrats had not softened his loathing for the man. He told one of the doctors that he would like to be "left alone in this room with our great and good president for about fifteen minutes, and then I would be cheerfully hung."[2]

The Colonel's illness prompted another flurry of letters from friends and admirers. E. A. Van Valkenberg, himself laid up with sciatica, commiserated with the Colonel. The editor went on, "How jubilant you must feel today. Without you as the way-shower and the nation's soul-stirrer this country would have dawdled along until too late to hurl its decisive military weight upon the Hun at the last battle of the Marne." He earnestly hoped that TR would soon "again be in the best of health." It seemed to him that the country had "never needed you so much as right now." The problems that loomed were "almost appalling."[3] The war correspondent Harry Walker wrote that he was "pained beyond measure to hear of your indisposition." For months he had been stopping and talking to soldiers about TR. Just now he had met one with his leg shot off, and he reported, "They love you." Walker went on that in two years the soldiers "will boss the country and it is your duty to tell them how. You always did your duty so hurry and get well."[4]

From his hospital bed, Roosevelt continued to criticize Wilson and his Fourteen Points, especially the fourth, which called for "adequate guarantees given and taken that national armaments will be reduced to the lowest point consistent with domestic safety." TR wrote to the president of the University of Wisconsin, Charles Van Hise, that he would "never consent to substitute anything for our own forehanded preparedness for our own self-defense." In his view, which he also declared publicly in the *Kansas City Star*, America's land forces should be based on universal military service on the Swiss model, with nine months of training for all young men between the ages of 19 and 23. This would be the "best kind of universal education, not only in self-defense but in citizenship." Such an army would not be an offensive weapon, but it would be "the most powerful possible deterrent to war."[5] In the same vein, TR told Lord Bryce that he was not willing to play the part that "even Aesop held up to derision" when he wrote how the wolves and the sheep agreed to disarm and how the sheep as a guarantee of good faith sent away the watchdogs and were then "forthwith eaten by the wolves."[6]

On the seas, with the exception of England, Roosevelt would not be willing that "any outside power should surpass our navy."[7] The Colonel told another correspondent, who had asked for his support of the American branch of the English-Speaking Union, that though he did not wish to put his name on any new organization, he would do all he could to strengthen American relations with Great Britain and the self-governing Empire of Canada, Australia, and New Zealand. In regard to all these, he would be for "any alliance and agree to arbitrate every question of any kind," accepting in advance the theory that under no condition was there any possibility of war with them. On the other hand, he went on, the present "hysterical British praise of Wilson" made him "rather contemptuous of them."[8]

Roosevelt commented to one such Englishman, Bryce, who he thought had been guilty of overpraising Wilson throughout the war, that there were certain points on which he used to think he was out of sympathy with his own country, and he had come to the conclusion that he was just as out of sympathy on those points with the majority of Englishmen. For example, they did not seem to be "horrified or revolted by hypocrisy" such as Wilson's call for "self-determination" and kept portions of their consciences in "separate watertight compartments." In one they stowed all the phrases about "absolute self-determination for all peoples" and in another the "actual facts about the treatment of those peoples," which, more or less justly, were "in the event found unfit for self-determination." They loved the fine language, though they knew it could not be translated into fact, and so applauded "hypocritical promises and cynical repudiation of the promises." To propose in any real sense to give "African savages" more than a consultative and subordinate share in their own affairs was at present "simply silly." Yet there were many people including Wilson and David Lloyd George who liked to "use language which means this or nothing." In the same way, at the moment the United States had deprived and was depriving Haiti and Santo Domingo of self-determination. It had "destroyed democracy in these two little festering black republics" and was ruling them by marines, but no one could find "a published word by the President even relating to what has been done." Was the peace conference going to "solemnly listen to chatter about impossible promises for self-determination for everybody in the future" and not ask for some rule that made the "hypocrisies about such cases as Haiti and Santo Domingo a little less blatant than at present?"[9]

On what would have been Quentin's twenty-first birthday, November 19, an introspective Roosevelt wrote to another old British friend with whom he was in more accord, Arthur Lee. "Well, we have seen the mighty days and you, at least, have done your full share in them." They had lived through the "most tremendous tragedy in the history of civilization" and should be "sternly thankful that the tragedy ended with a grim appropriateness, too often lacking," in which the people responsible had "come down in the crash." The last two weeks had shown that the Kaiser was "not even a valorous barbarian—he was unwilling to pay with his body when his hopes were wrecked." Instead, at the end he and his six sons saved their "own worthless carcasses," leaving their women, "like their honor, behind them." If ever there was a case "where on the last day of the fighting the leaders should have died, this was the case."[10]

The war, otherwise, Roosevelt wrote to Rudyard Kipling, ended "very satisfactorily," and he had the intense, and of course "purely personal, interest" that his other two sons would now come back to him. Archie, as Kipling knew, was already at home and might be permanently crippled, but it would not interfere with his work. Ted, he went on, had "moved Heaven and earth to get to the front and to get Kermit to the front." And just weeks before the end they went back to the First Division, Ted as lieutenant colonel commanding his regiment, and Kermit as a captain of artillery. Neither was hurt in the final Argonne fight, and they were now "marching their men through Germany toward the Rhine." Roosevelt did not know if the censor would allow it, but he was sending Kipling a copy of his new book, *The Great Adventure*, dedicated to "ALL WHO IN THIS WAR HAVE PAID WITH THEIR BODIES FOR THEIR SOULS' DESIRE." The first chapter, he told his friend, was "written with Quentin vividly before me, and your son, and Selous's son," and many others.[11]

After Wilson announced that he would break precedent and go in person to Paris to join Georges Clemenceau and Lloyd George at the peace conference table, Roosevelt declared in the *Metropolitan* that no "public end of any kind" would be served by the president going to Paris with "Mr. Creel, Mr. House, and his other personal friends." TR reminded his readers that in the election that he had just lost, Wilson had "abandoned the position of President of the whole people" and appealed to the people as a "party dictator." In any other "free country in the world today," this defeat would have forced Wilson to resign and be "a private citizen like the rest of us." Therefore, in the Colonel's view, "our allies and our enemies, and Mr. Wilson himself," should all understand that he had "no authority whatever to speak for the American people at this moment." His Fourteen Points and four supplementary points and his five complementary points had "ceased to have any shadow of right to be accepted as expressive of the will of the American people." It was the newly elected Congress that came far nearer to having that right.

Roosevelt went on that if the president acted in good faith to the American people, he would not claim to speak for them, but there was not the "slightest indication" that he intended to "so act." In fact, his purpose was clearly shown by sending over Creel and 16 Committee on Public Information (CPI) employees, who were announced as "the United States official press mission to the Peace Conference" and whose task would be to "interpret the work of the Peace Conference by keeping up world-wide propaganda to disseminate American accomplishments and American ideals." Further, Postmaster Albert S. Burleson seized the cables after the war was over, when there could be "no possible object except to control the news in the interest of President Wilson," as Creel and Burleson had been doing for some time. These actions could have no other "real purpose than to make the news sent out from the Peace Conference, both to ourselves, to our allies, and our enemies, what they desire to have told from their own standpoint and nothing more."[12]

On December 2, Wilson delivered a perfunctory annual message to Congress in which, Roosevelt charged, the president had failed to give the "slightest explanation" of his views on the peace or why he planned to attend the conference himself. Wilson had not allowed the American people to pass judgment on his proposals, which he had never "defined or clarified." The Fourteen Points, TR went on, had been accepted "enthusiastically" by the enemy, but not by the Allies or the people of the United States, who if they had expressed an opinion at all had rejected them at the November elections. It was true that "certain individuals" in America, including Wilson and William Randolph Hearst, "along with a number of German sympathizers, pacifists and international socialists," advocated the president's plan. The "simple truth" was that some of the points were "thoroughly mischievous under any interpretation" and that most of the others were so "vague and ambiguous" that it was nonsense to do anything with them until they had been "defined and made definite."

Roosevelt also hoped that, as Wilson was going to Paris, he would not act as an umpire between the enemy and the Allies but "loyally as one of the Allies," who had suffered more and rendered more service than had the United States. It was the British navy and the French, British, and Italian armies that had done the most to "bring about the downfall of Germany, and therefore the safety of the United States," and it was "our business" to stand by them. America should "instantly concede" that the British Empire needed the greatest navy in the world, and the United States should have the second largest. Further, "freedom of the seas" was a phrase that might mean "anything or nothing," and if it was to be interpreted as did Germany, it was "thoroughly mischievous." France needed greater military strength than did

America, but the country should still have all young men trained at arms along the lines of the Swiss system.[13]

Two days after addressing Congress, Wilson sailed for France on the SS *George Washington*, an interned German ocean liner that had been converted into an army transport. In an interview given before he departed, Wilson commented that he was surprised at TR's statement in the morning papers that England had virtually "won the war and should have everything she wants." The president did not believe that "our boys who fought over there will be inclined to feel just that way about it." They had won the war at Château-Thierry. "A single half hour's delay there in our coming up that day would have made a vast difference," and the Allies, said Wilson, admitted this fact. He went on that militarism was "equally as dangerous when applied to sea forces as to land forces." The idea that the British and American navies should become the "sea patrol of the world" was only a "new kind of militaristic propaganda." No one or two powers should be supreme. The whole world, he went on, "must be in on all measures designed to end wars for all time." And if England refused to reduce naval armaments, the United States should "show her how to build a navy."[14]

Building a "spite navy," as Wilson threatened, which the country did not need, was in TR's view the worst thing the United States could do. He also pointed out the "very extraordinary conflict" between one of Wilson's Fourteen Points that called for "practically complete disarmament" and at the same moment "demanding we should build the biggest navy in the world." Either one course or the other "must necessarily be improper." Unlike the scattered British Empire, the US domains were "pretty much in a ring fence," and the country ought not to "undertake the task of policing Europe, Asia and Northern Africa." America's navy was needed to guard the "Monroe Doctrine or any attempt by Europe or Asia to police America." Only if Britain abolished her navy would it be necessary for America to build one larger than called for at present.[15]

In the postwar period, as before and during the conflict, Roosevelt continued to correspond directly with the leaders of Europe, now as the voice of the American opposition party. In letters to Lloyd George and Arthur Balfour, who would second the prime minister at the Paris Peace Conference, TR announced that neither he nor his party believed in Wilson's interpretation of "Freedom of the Seas," which would become an immediate bone of contention for the British at the peace conference. The Royal Navy, Roosevelt continued, because of the needs of the Empire, should be the most powerful in the world, and the Republicans had no intention of rivaling it any more than they planned to rival the French army. But they also believed that the United States must have a first-class navy and "some policy for a people's army," trained on the lines of Switzerland.[16]

At the same time, the Colonel advised Clemenceau that he did not view Wilson's Fourteen Points as a satisfactory program for peace for the "excellent reason" that they could be interpreted in so many ways as to make it possible to "accept them in a sense that would be purely to the interest of Germany."

The Republican Party, of which he was one of the leaders, would have a majority in the next Congress and stood for "absolute loyalty to France and England in the peace negotiations." While they would "gladly welcome any feasible scheme for a League of Nations," they preferred that it began with their present allies and be only an addition to, and not a substitute for, the "preparedness of our own strength for our own defense." The United States had no intention of rivaling France's military preparations or the strength of the British fleet, because they recognized that France and Britain must prepare in a way unnecessary for America. Above all, TR and the Republicans believed that at the peace conference the United States should act, "not as an umpire between our allies and our enemies, but as one of the allies bound to come to an agreement with them, and then to impose this common agreement upon our vanquished enemies."[17]

After Wilson sailed for Europe, Pennsylvania Senator Philander Knox, who had been TR's attorney general and William Howard Taft's secretary of state, introduced a resolution that asked for the separation of the League of Nations from the broader peace terms and called for the earliest possible formal conclusion of the war. This embarrassed Wilson and those who supported the league idea, including Taft, and was tabled. Roosevelt on the other hand "heartily endorsed" Knox's action and wrote him that a league might do a little good, but the "more pompous" it was and the more it pretended to do, the less it would "really accomplish." The talk had for TR a "grimly humorous suggestion" of the only slightly more ethereal Holy Alliance of a century before at the Congress of Vienna, which also had as "its main purpose the perpetual maintenance of peace," with Czar Alexander as the Wilson of the time.[18]

In his message to Congress, Wilson had once again asked the Senate to ratify the treaty with Colombia negotiated by William Jennings Bryan in 1914, which paid an indemnity and apologized for taking Panama. Knox and a number of Republicans had, for a variety of reasons including pending oil concessions, come to support a settlement. Roosevelt told the senator that he wished his conscience had not forced him to taken an attitude "universally accepted as backing President Wilson in a purely malevolent attempt to blacken the Administration of which you were part." Since Wilson had appeared before Congress in person, if there was "any disposition to put that Treaty through," TR wished he could come before the committee in person at the same time as the president, who could ask any questions he would like. At the same time, Roosevelt would in return like to ask Wilson a number of questions about Haiti and Santo Domingo. This, he told Knox, would "give the committee an entertaining morning!"[19]

On December 15, Henry Cabot Lodge called at the hospital to talk of Wilson's League of Nations and of the speech he would soon after give in the Senate attacking it. At the same time rheumatism racked Roosevelt's arm so hard that it had to be bound and put in a splint. The pain was such that at times TR was unable to have visitors, and narcotics became necessary. On one of the Colonel's better days, William Allen White brought the news that Leonard Wood, who had gotten a taste of politics when he used his popularity as a brave soldier wronged to support Republicans in Kansas, was considering entering the 1920 presidential contest. This prompted Roosevelt to tell White that he would probably "have to get in this thing in June." For an hour, White recalled, the two talked of "all sorts of schemes, devices, platform plank plans," not for political advancement, but for "social betterment." These included old-age pensions, child-labor measures, a nonpartisan tariff commission with powers, a universal eight-hour day, "a thousand chimera, visions, utopian wish-structures for industrial and economic justice."[20]

When the doctors told the Colonel there was not much more they could do for him and that he might be in a wheeled chair for the rest of his life, TR responded with characteristic vigor, "All Right! I can work and live that way too."[21] Consequently, after almost seven weeks spent in hospital, Roosevelt's rheumatic specialist, Dr. John H. Richards, discharged him in time to go home for Christmas dinner. The Colonel was still weak from fever and anemia, and an ear infection made his balance unsure as he left the hospital. But when a doctor tried to take his arm Roosevelt shook him off, telling him "I am not sick" and that the sight of him needing help would give the wrong impression. He then braced himself and walked through the press contingent to his car. Arriving at Sagamore Hill, TR continued the charade, telling his neighbors gathered outside, "I'm feeling Bully, and I was treated well at the hospital. The sciatica got the best of me for a time, but I'm alright."[22]

The family waiting for Theodore and Edith at the big house included Alice, Archie, Ethel, and her little daughter Edie, who Roosevelt described as running around "exactly as if she was a small mechanical toy." But he tired easily and was unable to play with his granddaughter more than a short time before he had to rest.[23] With his father ill, Archie had taken his place at that year's Cove School Christmas Tree event. The Colonel reported to Kermit that his brother had done remarkably well making his speech as Santa at their old school. The landscape, he went on, looked beautiful, "even in its sad, frozen winter" state. He told his son that his medical conditions meant a "long period of getting better." He was still a cripple, unable to do anything but hobble a few yards, but "very happy—for all of you have made me so proud, and you will now be coming home in safety; and in a couple of months I think I shall be moving round again." He hoped they all would be returning reasonably soon, "unless Wilson goes into something which he hopes will be for his own selfish advantage, but which for the army would be dreary quixotism."[24] In response to those who once again dredged up TR's 1914 articles offering loyal support to Wilson early in the world crisis, Roosevelt released a statement that the "only error I committed in connection with the war was the support I thus gave President Wilson for the first sixty days." No one now had any business to quote these without also stating the fact that he was, "at the outset of the war," endeavoring to support the president, but as soon as he became convinced Wilson was wrong, TR took the position that he held for the next four years and that "I today hold."[25]

Ted's wife Eleanor had already returned from France, and she told Roosevelt that his eldest son had always "worried for fear he would not be worthy of you." TR replied, "Worthy of me? Darling, I'm so very proud of him." Ted had won "high honor not only for his children but, like the Chinese, he has ennobled his ancestors." His father walked with his head higher because of him. Roosevelt had always taken pride that he had fought in the war with Spain, and he "did my best to get into this one. But my war was a bow-and-arrow affair compared to Ted's, and no one knows this better than I do."[26] In the following days TR rested on the library sofa while he read and dictated letters, including one to Ted, whom he hoped to see home as soon as possible. He told his son that he did not "believe in our undertaking a general and indefinite policing of European squabbles."[27]

The anticipated return of the troops served up a final occasion for Roosevelt to be involved, if peripherally, in a controversy with Hearst, after Mayor Hylan of New York made the newspaper magnate chairman of a committee to welcome the soldiers home. This drew a firestorm of outraged editorials and a public airing of the findings of the government investigations into Hearst. These revelations included Hearst's opposition to sending the troops abroad in the first place, his agreement at the time with George Sylvester Viereck's contention that the Zimmerman Telegram had been a "brazen forgery," his orders to his editors to use "little flags" on his newspapers to convey a tone of patriotism, and his prewar printing of the pro-German dispatches of the journalist William Bayard Hale, who turned out to be in the pay of the Kaiser. When Hylan and Hearst both refused to back down, a rival committee to greet the soldiers was formed with TR at its head.[28] It was an honor and duty he would not live to fulfill.

After renewed severe pain beginning on New Year's Day, 1919, Roosevelt spent most of his time upstairs, on a sofa in the old nursery, the warmest room in the house. Ethel recorded in her diary, "Father very miserable—it's terrible to see him suffer so."[29] On January 5, he seemed to rebound and worked 11 hours principally correcting the proofs of a *Metropolitan* article and an editorial for the *Kansas City Star*. A naturalist to the last, one of the final letters TR dictated was a complimentary message to William Beebe on a long book he had written about pheasants.[30] That night, on January 6, 1919, Roosevelt died of a coronary occlusion. His last words, to his former valet James Amos, who had been called back to service at Sagamore Hill from his job with a detective agency in New York, were, "James, will you please put out the light?"[31] Edgar Lee Masters, who had not seen the Colonel again after his visit to Sagamore Hill just days before Quentin's death, wrote,

> One thing was fitting—dying in your sleep—
> A touch of Nature, Colonel, who you loved
> And were beloved of Nature, felt her hand
> Upon your brow at last to give to you
> A bit of sleep, perhaps,

Rest and Rejuvenation, you will wake
To newer labors, fresher victories . . .[32]

Archie took charge of the funeral arrangements and wired his brothers, at Coblenz with the First Division, "The Old Lion is Dead."

The news of TR's death reached London the same day. Ruth Lee recorded in her diary that Arthur came to her late that afternoon and said: "A terrible thing has happened; Theodore is dead." It was a blow for both of them, but especially for Arthur, who, Ruth wrote, "loved him better than any human being in the world except me." The most touching Roosevelt valedictory for Arthur and Ruth was a poem by Helen Gray Cone that they saved:

How shall we say "God rest him!"
Of him who loved not rest
But the pathless plunge in the forest
And the pauseless quest,
And the call of the billowing mountains
Crest upon crest?

Hope, rather, God will give him
His spirit's need—
Rapture of ceaseless motion
That is rest indeed,
As the cataract sleeps in the cliff-side
White with speed.

So shall his soul go ranging
Forever swift and wide,
With a strong man's rejoicing
As he loved to ride;
But all our days are poorer
For the part of him that died.[33]

The other two Englishmen to whom Roosevelt felt closest, Kipling and Sir Henry Rider Haggard, were also hard hit. As a tribute Kipling wrote the poem "Great-Heart," which was published in newspapers across the world. In TR, Haggard declared in a letter to the *Times* of London, the world had lost a "great and good man" and one of its "purest and most intrepid spirits." He sent the paper a letter from the Colonel dated a month before his death in which Roosevelt doubted he would "ever again go back into public place," as he had had to "go into too much and too bitter truth telling" in the previous years. Like Haggard, he was "not at all sure about the future." TR hoped Germany would "suffer a change of heart," but he was "anything but certain" and did not put "much faith in the League of Nations, or any corresponding universal cure-all." Kipling wrote to Haggard that he was "awfully heavy-hearted about Roosevelt," who was "the best friend we had there and I can't see who takes his place."[34]

From round the world messages of condolence and sympathy for Edith and her family flooded into Oyster Bay. Georges Clemenceau sent his "profound regret" at the news. France, he went on, had lost "an excellent friend." Always animated by "generous ardor," her husband had shown his sympathy for France "on every occasion" and "been proud to give his sons to the Allied cause and thus to contribute to the triumph of right."[35] Will Taft wrote Edith that his "heart goes out to you and yours in your great sorrow." The county could "ill afford in this critical period of history to lose one who has done and could in the next decade have done so much for it and humanity." The United States had lost a "great patriotic American, a great world figure, the most commanding figure in our public life since Lincoln."[36]

Woodrow Wilson cabled, "Please accept my heartfelt sympathy in the death of your distinguished husband, the news of which has shocked me very much." The president had received the news while in the railroad station at Modena, Italy, en route back to Paris from Rome. Reporters on the platform watched his face as he read the message, and after shock came a smile of "transcendent triumph." With his chief rival now gone, Wilson was sure that after he imposed his peace on Europe he could return home and do the same in the United States.[37] Shortly after this, in Paris, David Lloyd George, who with Clemenceau would do all he could to block Wilson's plan, recalled that after he offered condolences on TR's death, he was "aghast at the outburst of acrid detestation which flowed from Wilson's lips."[38]

A month after his friend Theodore's death, Arthur Lee helped to arrange an unprecedented London memorial service in Westminster Abbey, timed to coincide with others held across the English-speaking world. Never before had there been such a service in the abbey "for any individual, either British or foreign," not actually buried there. Archdeacon William Hartley Carnegie delivered the sermon, in which he noted that the tribute shown at Westminster, "the shrine of the Anglo-Saxon race," proved the high place Roosevelt "held in the hearts of the British people." The archdeacon recounted TR's support of Britain "on the side of the right" from the invasion of Belgium. Since then, to win the war, the Colonel had literally "spent himself" and "sacrificed his life," but before he died he "realized his allotted task was completed." Lee arranged for his friend's favorite hymn, "How Firm a Foundation," to be sung, followed by the "Battle Hymn of the Republic" and "God Save the King." Finally, as the archdeacon and other clergy left the Abbey in procession, "the western sun poured through the windows," and the organ "burst forth" with "The Star Spangled Banner."[39]

* * *

What to say in summation of Theodore Roosevelt's part in the Great War? His preparedness crusade, for that is what it truly was to him, certainly pushed the nation (and the politically astute Woodrow Wilson) to a course of army and navy preparedness that would not otherwise have been followed. By 1917 at least the "preconditions" for a full-scale war effort had been created, without which, in the words of one chronicler, "it would have been psychologically as well as physically impossible for us to go in, when we did, as deeply as we did."[40] However, as the Colonel shouted at the time, these measures were still inadequate and were so proved once the United States associated itself with the Allied side in the war against Germany. Roosevelt's loud and persistent demand to lead volunteers to France motivated the Wilson administration (and its military advisors), sooner rather than later, to send troops to Europe and to turn to conscription to build the mass army needed for the cause.

Near the end of its laudatory editorial appraisal of TR's life and many distinguished achievements, the *New York Times* found "not less notable" his "more recent service in arousing the American people to a true conception of the moral issues of the great war and to their need of preparing for their part." The paper pointed to the series of "extraordinary speeches" that Roosevelt delivered in the early summer of 1916, which "resounded through the land like an alarm bell in the night." These awoke the people from that "selfish and comfortable indifference which the far-sighted among us had deplored." The pacifist spirit was dominant in many states, and the people had listened to those who preached against "militarism." But the change came soon and "candid men" recognized "Mr. Roosevelt's great part in bringing it about." After America joined the war, TR continued to criticize the administration, but in doing so, declared the paper, he "nobly served it as he served the American people" by continuing to reveal the country's continued unreadiness for tasks that finally America "performed with such glorious distinction to the victorious end of the war."[41]

In settling the peace, Henry Cabot Lodge would take up the fight for TR against the Versailles Treaty with Germany and the League of Nations, the internationalism of which the Colonel railed against in his last contribution to the *Kansas City Star*, published posthumously on January 13, 1919. America, he preached, should not become an international "Meddlesome Matty." The country did not want to take on the responsibility of sending its "gallant young men to die in obscure fights in the Balkans" or in a "war we do not approve of." Moreover, America did not intend to give up the Monroe Doctrine. Let "civilized Europe and Asia" introduce police systems for the "weak and disorderly countries at their thresholds." The United States would treat Mexico as "our Balkan peninsula" and refuse to allow other powers to interfere on this continent. Its people had no desire to fight abroad except "for a very great cause."

The United States never joined Wilson's league, nor did the Senate ratify the German treaty. The war would be officially declared over by Joint Resolution of Congress in the next—Republican—administration, which also agreed to pay Colombia the $25,000,000 "blackmail"—but without an apology. Loyal to the end, Hiram Johnson refused to support the treaty. In the debate, the senator declared that he yielded "to no man in the affection" for TR while he was living or in reverence now that he was dead. He had followed Theodore Roosevelt in fair weather and foul, whether Republican or

Progressive, and was "always glad to follow him." The Panama Canal, John-son went on, was a "world monument to the greatest man of this generation" and to American genius, enterprise, and statesmanship. He declined to "write upon that great monument the dishonor of my country and the infamy of my people."[42]

On the political front, with TR gone, wily little Will Hays organized War-ren G. Harding's victorious 1920 presidential campaign. In memorial of the Colonel, Hays wrote that he was "for peace when peace was right, but if to win right for right's sake war was necessary, then he was for war or what-ever else was needed, and there he was the severest partisan."[43] TR's death ensured that the Republicans after 1920 became the conservative party they remain, shorn of their progressive brethren, many of whom would be helpful to another—Democratic—Roosevelt in the White House and would enact in his New Deal—much of the program "Uncle Ted" had in his prospective 1920 platform. In foreign affairs, the Harding administration offered the world Wilsonian disarmament in lieu of US membership in the League of Nations, while at home whatever slim chance there might have been for post-war preparedness or universal service on Rooseveltian lines was extinguished by his absence.

Finally, what of TR's personal and political vendetta against Woodrow Wilson, in pursuit of which, more than one observer has charged, he crossed the line into mania? Was the Colonel truly driven at least temporarily mad by jealousy that he was not in the White House to steer the United States into war sooner? Was the realization that his own 1912 Progressive campaign for the presidency had put the cowardly and idealistic Wilson in power too much for him? In fact, as has been shown in the preceding chapters, TR's differences with Wilson began before the war and were mainly in foreign policy. Well before August 1914, he was already infuriated by the administra-tion's "cooling off" treaties, its peripatetic course in Mexico, and what the Colonel considered its base submission to Colombia concerning the Panama Canal affair. And when the European war did not end in the three months widely predicted, Roosevelt broke with the vast majority of Americans who supported what he saw as Wilson's spiritless and pacific neutrality. The cold-blooded atrocities carried out against Belgium by Germany made the righ-teousness of the Allied cause blazingly apparent—to TR at least. As he well knew, The Hague Conventions signed by the United States did not obli-gate her to military action in defense of Belgium, but the refusal of Wilson and Bryan even to send a note condemning Germany and reminding her of her own treaty obligations was to the Colonel thoroughly dishonorable. And worse, their inaction dragged the honor of the United States through the mud as well.

Roosevelt the realist knew, as should have Woodrow Wilson the historian, that if the war continued, the United States would inexorably be drawn in one way or another, as she had before into every lengthy European great power conflict. After the sinking of the *Lusitania*, even Wilson's confidant Edward M. House believed the entry of the United States would save lives and secure America's place in the postwar peace process. But in the face of Wilson's "Too Proud to Fight" declaration, preparedness became the Colonel's crusade, damning the political consequences for himself or the Progressive Party, which he thought less and less viable after the 1914 election debacle. This campaign took him into a political wilderness of unpopularity such as he had never experienced, but he pressed on, believing that the people of the United States must have their eyes opened. And over time more and more Americans, finally even including Woodrow Wilson, at last began to awake to the dangers.

Unfortunately for him, Roosevelt's political stock had not risen enough by June 1916 to gain the Republican nomination, and a viable alternative arose for the party leaders in the blank slate that was Charles Evans Hughes. The bitterness of TR's speeches in the campaign came because of his continued detestation of Wilson and the prospect of his guiding the country's fate for four more years but also because he was forced to promote a man he knew would not be his equal if elected. As many of his supporters pointed out, the defeat of Hughes gave Roosevelt an inside position for the 1920 nomination, but he did not want to look that far ahead while the world war raged on, five months after the 1916 election with America as a participant, if a limited one. This simply proved to Roosevelt that he had been right all along, and he continued unable to support Wilson, even with the nation at war. Once in the fight, the rhetorical transformation of the administration, led by the propaganda of the CPI, was breathtaking and made the anti-German and antihyphenate statements TR had been condemned for before 1917 look almost moderate in comparison.

Though he took it hard, Wilson's refusal to allow Roosevelt a gallant death on the Western Front was ameliorated to a certain extent by his sons' service in the fighting. And their being in harm's way only made TR more vocal than ever in pointing out the many failures to properly supply the American troops in the field. As Roosevelt endlessly declaimed, much more could and should have been done after April 1917, and the cost was, at a minimum, thousands of lives that might have been spared on all sides, not least in an American Expeditionary Force tragically short of modern planes, artillery, and machine guns in its fight with the German foe. One authority on Wilson in the war has described the president and Newton Baker as "ignoramuses" when it came to the nation's wartime supply problems. With no business experience, "They thought that because they could write requisitions and make speeches, were clever at posing in uniform or presenting themselves before Congress, they could manage industrial mobilization by, so to speak, the seat of their pants." By some sort of "legerdemain, which they did not bother to investigate, the necessary ships and military hardware would come out of the large end of the American industry's cornucopia."[44]

Gravely ill when the war ended, Roosevelt took limited solace in the victory. The death of Quentin, which killed the boy in him, and the prospect of a Wilsonian peace made the outlook bleak. Only his own death less than two months after the Armistice ended the struggle with Wilson, who was fated soon to lose both his battle for the peace in Paris and the fight at home over the treaty in a Senate led by Henry Cabot Lodge, who perhaps most shared Roosevelt's loathing of the president. In a Senate tribute the same day as the service in Westminster Abbey, Lodge pointed out that the importance of TR's work in stirring the soul and rousing the spirit of the American people "was proven by the confession of his country's enemies, for when he died the only discordant note, the only harsh words, came from the German press. Germany knew whose voice it was that had more powerfully than any other called America to the battle on behalf of freedom and civilization."[45]

NOTES

PREFACE

1. "Introduction," in John Milton Cooper Jr., ed., *Reconsidering Woodrow Wilson: Progressivism, Internationalism, War, and Peace* (Baltimore: Johns Hopkins University Press, 2008), 13.

PROLOGUE

1. Roosevelt to Lodge, May 5, 1910, in Elting Morison, ed., *The Letters of Theodore Roosevelt*, 8 vols. (Cambridge: Harvard University Press, 1954), 7: 81 (Hereafter *TRL*).
2. David Patterson, *Towards a Warless World: The Travail of the American Peace Movement 1887–1914* (London: Routledge, 1976), 35, 146.
3. For a more detailed look at TR's 1910 peace mission, see J. Lee Thompson, *Theodore Roosevelt Abroad: Nature, Empire, and the Journey of an American President* (New York: Palgrave Macmillan, 2010).
4. Carnegie to Tower, January 23, 1907, in Burton J. Hendrick, *The Life of Andrew Carnegie*, 2 vols. (New York: Doubleday, Doran, 1932), 2: 311. For TR and the 1907 conference, see Calvin DeArmond Davis, *The United States and the Second Hague Peace Conference: American Diplomacy and International Organization 1899–1914* (Durham, NC: Duke University Press, 1975).
5. Theodore Roosevelt, *African and European Addresses* (New York: Charles Scribner's Sons, 1910), 78–83.
6. For comment on the Willy-Teddy relationship that includes the 1910 trip, see Ragnhild Fiebig-von Hase, "The Uses of 'Friendship': The 'Personal Regime' of Wilhelm II and Theodore Roosevelt, 1901–1909," in Annika Mombauer and Wilhelm Diest, eds., *The Kaiser: New Research on Wilhelm II's Role in Imperial Germany* (Cambridge: Cambridge University Press, 2003), 143–75.
7. For the Kaiser, see Lamar Cecil, *Wilhelm II*, 2 vols. (Chapel Hill: University of North Carolina Press, 1989).
8. Raimund Lammersdorf, "The Advantages of Cooperation: German-American Friendship as a Fundamental Principle of German *Weltpolitik* and Theodore Roosevelt's Big Stick Diplomacy," in Hans-Jürgen Schröder, ed., *Confrontation and Cooperation: Germany and the United States in the Era of World War I, 1900–1924* (Oxford: Berg, 1993), 89.
9. Viscount Lee of Fareham, *"A Good Innings and a Great Partnership: Being the Life Story of Arthur and Ruth Lee,"* 3 vols. (Privately Printed, 1939), 1: 418.

10. Lawrence F. Abbott, *Impressions of Theodore Roosevelt* (Garden City, NY: Doubleday, Page, 1919), 248–51.

11. Henry Pringle, *Theodore Roosevelt: A Biography* (New York: Harcourt, Brace and World, 1931), 365.

12. TR to George Otto Trevelyan, October 1, 1911, Series 3A, Reel 369, Theodore Roosevelt Papers, Library of Congress (Hereafter TRP).

13. Ibid.

14. Ibid.

15. Ibid.

16. Ibid; For an analysis of the prewar US-German rivalry largely consonant with TR's view, see Ragnhild Feibeg-von Hase, "The United States and Germany in the World Arena, 1900–1917," in Schröder, *Confrontation and Cooperation*.

17. Archibald Butt, *Taft and Roosevelt: The Intimate Letters of Archie Butt Military Aide,* 2 vols. (Garden City, NY: Doubleday, Doran, 1930), 1: 348.

18. *Daily News,* May 13, 1910.

19. Carnegie to TR, May 13, 1910, Series 1, Reel 91, TRP.

20. Carnegie to TR, May 14, 1910, Series 1, Reel 91, TRP.

CHAPTER 1

1. For this see Joseph Ornig, *My Last Chance to Be a Boy: Theodore Roosevelt's South American Expedition of 1913–1914* (New York: Stackpole Books, 1994); and Candace Millard, *River of Doubt: Theodore Roosevelt's Darkest Journey* (New York: Doubleday, 2005).

2. Edith's biographer, Sylvia Jukes Morris, speculates that Edith was also suffering the effects of menopause. *Edith Kermit Roosevelt: Portrait of a First Lady* (New York: Coward, McCann and Geoghegan, 1980), 403.

3. Morris, *Edith Kermit Roosevelt*, 403–4.

4. Only one separate study of TR in the war has been published: Hermann Hagedorn's *The Bugle That Woke America: The Saga of Theodore Roosevelt's Last Battle for His Country* (New York: John Day, 1940). Some recent works have touched on the subject in volumes on TR's postpresidential career, including notably Patricia O'Toole, *When Trumpets Call: Theodore Roosevelt after the White House* (New York: Simon and Schuster, 2005); and Edmund Morris, *Colonel Roosevelt* (New York: Random House, 2010).

5. For this see William Tilchin, *Theodore Roosevelt and the British Empire* (New York: St. Martin's Press, 1997); and David H. Burton, "Theodore Roosevelt and the 'Special Relationship' with Britain," *History Today* 23, no. 8 (1973): 527–35.

6. Only three years before the US war with Spain, during the 1895–96 Venezuela crisis with British Guiana, TR had called for war with Britain, despite the disparity in naval power. He confided to one of his imperialist brethren, Henry Cabot Lodge, "Let the fight come if it must; I don't care whether our seacoast cities are bombarded or not; we would take Canada." Tilchin, *Roosevelt and the British Empire*, 17.

7. Ibid., 17–19.

8. For a life in which these similarities are well noted, see John Milton Cooper Jr., *Walter Hines Page: The Southerner as American 1855–1918* (Chapel Hill: University of North Carolina Press, 1977).

9. Viscount Lee of Fareham, *"A Good Innings and a Great Partnership: Being the Life Story of Arthur and Ruth Lee,"* 3 vols. (Privately Printed, 1939), 1: 523.

10. Quoted in Michael and Eleanor Brock, eds., *H. H. Asquith: Letters to Venetia Stanley* (Oxford: Oxford University Press, 1982), 87 and note 4.

11. Lee of Fareham, *"A Good Innings,"* 1: 525–26. For the two preeminent Unionists, see R. J. Q. Adams, *Bonar Law* (London: John Murray, 1999) and *Balfour: The Last Grandee* (London: John Murray, 2007).

12. Lee of Fareham, *"A Good Innings,"* 1: 524–25.

13. Ibid., 525.

14. Ornig, *My Last Chance to Be a Boy,* 214–15.

15. For views of both the compulsory service issue and the role of Lord Roberts, see R. J. Q. Adams and Philip P. Poirier, *The Conscription Controversy in Great Britain, 1900–1918* (Columbus: Ohio State University Press, 1987); R. J. Q. Adams, "Field-Marshall Earl Roberts: Army and Empire," in J. A. Thompson and Arthur Mejia, eds., *Edwardian Conservatism: Five Studies in Adaptation* (London: Croom Helm, 1988); and David James, *Lord Roberts* (London: Collins, 1954).

16. Lee of Fareham, *"A Good Innings,"* 1: 525–26.

17. For this see Godfrey Hodgson, *Woodrow Wilson's Right Hand: The Life of Colonel Edward M. House* (New Haven: Yale University Press, 2006), 97–101. For Grey and House, see Joyce Grigsby Williams, *Colonel House and Sir Edward Grey: A Study in Anglo-American Diplomacy* (Lanham, MD: University Press of America, 1984). House and Grey had first met the year before when the Colonel was in London to facilitate an Anglo-American understanding over Mexico.

18. June 1, 1914 entry, House Diary, in Charles Seymour, ed. *The Intimate Diaries of Colonel House, Volume I: Behind the Political Curtain* (London: Ernest Been, 1926), 261–62.

19. For this see Larry L. Fabian, *Andrew Carnegie's Peace Endowment: The Tycoon, The President, and Their Bargain of 1910* (Washington, DC: Carnegie Endowment for Peace, 1985).

20. Peter Krass, *Carnegie* (Hoboken, NJ: John Wiley and Sons, 2002), 514.

21. Lee of Fareham, *"A Good Innings,"* 1: 525–26.

22. June 8, 1914 entry, House Diary, in Seymour, *Intimate Diaries of Colonel House,* 1: 265.

23. For Edith, see Morris, *Edith Kermit Roosevelt;* and Tom Lansford, *A "Bully" First Lady: Edith Kermit Roosevelt* (Huntington, NY: Nova History Publications, 2001).

24. For TR's older sibling, see Lilian Rixley, *Bamie: Theodore Roosevelt's Remarkable Sister* (New York: David McKay, 1963).

25. Quoted in David H. Burton, "Theodore Roosevelt and His English Correspondents: A Special Relationship of Friends," *Transactions of the American Philosophical Society,* New Series, Volume 63, Part 2 (Philadelphia, 1973), 9. For Spring Rice, see David H. Burton, *Cecil Spring Rice: A Diplomat's Life* (Madison, NJ; Fairleigh Dickinson University Press, 1990).

26. For Ted, and his brothers, in the war, see H. Paul Jeffers, *Theodore Roosevelt Jr.: The Life of a War Hero* (Novato, CA: Presidio Press, 2002); and Edward J. Renehan Jr., *The Lion's Pride: Theodore Roosevelt and His Family in Peace and War* (New York: Oxford University Press, 1998).

27. TR to George Otto Trevelyan, October 1, 1911, Series 3A, Reel 369, Theodore Roosevelt Papers, Library of Congress (Hereafter TRP).

28. TR to Lee, June 29, 1914, in Elting Morison, ed., *The Letters of Theodore Roosevelt*, 8 vols. (Cambridge: Harvard University Press, 1954), 7: 769 (Hereafter *TRL*).

29. John A. Gable, *The Bull Moose Years: Theodore Roosevelt and the Progressive Party* (Port Washington, NY: Kennikat Press, 1978), 182.

30. For Perkins see John A. Garraty, *Right-Hand Man: The Life of George Perkins* (New York: Harper and Brothers, 1957).

31. July 22, 1914, in Gable, *Bull Moose Years*, 211–14.

32. Quoted in Morris, *Colonel Roosevelt*, 358.

33. Michael Kazin, *A Godly Hero: A Life of William Jennings Bryan* (New York: Alfred A. Knopf, 2006), 220.

34. TR to Lodge, September 9, 1913, in *TRL*, 7: 747. Wilson declared the policy of "watchful waiting" for Mexico on August 27, 1913, before a joint session of Congress.

35. For TR and the canal, see Richard Collin, *Theodore Roosevelt's Caribbean: The Panama Canal, the Monroe Doctrine and the Latin American Context* (Baton Rouge: Louisiana State University Press, 1990). For more recent and general works on the canal, see Noel Maurer and Carlos Yu, *The Big Ditch: How America Took, Ran, and Ultimately Gave Away the Panama Canal* (Princeton: Princeton University Press, 2011); and Julie Greene, *The Canal Builders* (New York: Penguin Press, 2009).

36. Quoted in *TRL*, 7: 774, n. 1.

37. *New York World*, June 25, 1914, quoted in Arthur Link, ed., *The Papers of Woodrow Wilson* (Princeton; Princeton University Press, 1979), 30: 209 (Hereafter *PWW*).

38. Lee to TR, July 21, 1914, Series 1, Reel 188, TRP.

39. *Daily Mail*, July 23, 24, 1914.

CHAPTER 2

1. O'Laughlin to TR, August 3, 1914, Reel 189, Series 1, Theodore Roosevelt Papers, Library of Congress (Hereafter TRP). The 79-year-old Carnegie was at one of his retreats in Scotland when hostilities broke out. He bemoaned that fact that men were again "slaying each other like wild beasts" and added his voice to those who urged Wilson to intervene. The war, his age, and illnesses combined to make Carnegie a semi-invalid for the rest of his life. Patricia O'Toole, *When Trumpets Call: Theodore Roosevelt after the White House* (New York: Simon and Schuster, 2005), 261.

2. TR to Lee, August 1, 1914, in Elting Morison, ed., *The Letters of Theodore Roosevelt*, 8 vols. (Cambridge: Harvard University Press, 1954), 7: 790–91 (Hereafter *TRL*).

3. Cameron Hazlehurst, *Politicians at War July 1914 to May 1915: A Prologue to the Triumph of Lloyd George* (London: Jonathan Cape, 1971), 25–31.

4. L. C. F. Turner, *Origins of the First World War* (New York: W. W. Norton, 1970), 114. The Kaiser took England's action as a personal insult, writing his cousin King George V, who he believed had promised him his country would not intervene, "This was the thanks for Waterloo" (where the Prussian army

had saved the day for the British). Wilhelm returned the honorary insignia of a British field marshal and admiral of the fleet he had been given, while the British Crown soon revoked his Garter Knighthood. Lamar Cecil, *Wilhelm II*, 2 vols. (Chapel Hill: University of North Carolina Press, 1989), 240–49; Robert B. Asprey, *The German High Command at War: Hindenburg and Ludendorff Conduct World War I* (New York: William Morrow, 1991), 49.

5. For Wilson in the period of neutrality, see Robert W. Tucker, *Woodrow Wilson and the Great War: Reconsidering America's Neutrality 1914–1917* (Charlottesville: University of Virginia Press, 2007); and Patrick Devlin, *Too Proud to Fight: Woodrow Wilson's Neutrality* (New York: Oxford University Press, 1975). For the following period, see Robert H. Ferrell, *Woodrow Wilson & World War I, 1917–1921* (New York: Harper and Row, 1985). For a recent and notable life, see John Milton Cooper Jr., *Woodrow Wilson: A Biography* (New York: Alfred A. Knopf, 2009). For seminal comparisons of the two men, see Cooper's *The Warrior and the Priest: Woodrow Wilson and Theodore Roosevelt* (Cambridge, MA: Belknap Press, 1983); and Robert Endicott Osgood, *Ideals and Self-Interest in America's Foreign Relations: The Great Transformation of the Twentieth Century* (Chicago: University of Chicago Press, 1953). For a recent modification of Osgood's idealist/realist comparison in foreign affairs, see Greg Russell, "Theodore Roosevelt, Geopolitics, and Cosmopolitan Ideals," *Review of International Studies* 32 (2006): 541–59.

6. Viscount Grey of Fallodon, *Twenty-Five Years, 1892–1916*, 2 vols. (New York: Frederick A. Stokes, 1925), 2: 20.

7. Philip Magnus, *Kitchener: Portrait of an Imperialist* (London: John Murray, 1959), 278–79, 282. For Kitchener's plans for a "nation in arms," see David French, *British Economic and Strategic Planning 1905–1915* (London: Allen and Unwin, 1982), 51–70, 124–35; David French, *British Strategy and War Aims 1914–1916* (London: Allen and Unwin, 1986), 25.

8. Magnus, *Kitchener*, 288.

9. Ibid., 279–81. French had made his reputation as a cavalry officer in the Boer War. For more on his career, see Richard Holmes, *The Little Field-Marshall Sir John French* (London: Jonathan Cape, 1981).

10. David Stevenson, *Cataclysm: The First World War as Political Tragedy* (New York: Basic Books, 2004), 40.

11. J. M. Bourne, *Britain and the Great War 1914–1918* (London: Edward Arnold, 1989), 18–19.

12. Holmes, *The Little Field-Marshall*, 219–20.

13. Lee to TR, August 13, 1914, Reel 189, Series 1, TRP; Viscount Lee of Fareham, *"A Good Innings and a Great Partnership: Being the Life Story of Arthur and Ruth Lee,"* 3 vols. (Privately Printed, 1939), 1: 586. The Kaiser commented about Italy's course, and the failure of Rumania also to join the fight as he had hoped, that Germany's allies were "falling away from us like rotten apples!" Cecil, *Wilhelm II*, 2: 209.

14. Abbott to TR, August 5, 1914, Reel 189, Series 1, TRP.

15. This began in 1913, while Spring Rice was ill, when Sir William Tyrell dealt with the administration. In 1916 Sir Horace Plunkett played the same role and in 1917 Sir William Wiseman with Wilson's surrogate Colonel House. David H. Burton, *Cecil Spring Rice: A Diplomat's Life* (London: Fairleigh Dickinson Press, 1990), 149.

16. Spring Rice to Grey, August 25, 1914, quoted in Stephen Gwynn, ed., *The Letters and Friendships of Sir Cecil Spring Rice: A Record*, 2 vols. (Boston: Houghton Mifflin, 1929), 2: 218–19.

17. Gwynn, *Spring Rice*, 2: 219.

18. Cooper, *Wilson*, 263.

19. House to Wilson, August 22, 1914, quoted in David Lloyd George, *War Memoirs*, 2 vols. (London: Odhams Press, 1939), 2: 395.

20. For the German ambassador, see Reinhard Doerries, *Imperial Challenge: Ambassador Count Bernstorff and German-American Relations, 1908–1917* (Chapel Hill: University of North Carolina Press, 1989). For broader US relations with Germany, see Ragnhild Fiebig-von Hase, "The United States and Germany in the World Arena, 1900–1917," in Hans-Jürgen Schröder, ed., *Confrontation and Cooperation: Germany and the United States in the Era of World War I, 1900–1924* (Oxford: Berg, 1993), 33–68.

21. Reinhard Doerries, "Promoting Kaiser and Reich: Imperial German Propaganda in the United States during World War I," in Schröder, *Confrontation and Cooperation*, 156. British propaganda in World War I, particularly in America, has received attention from several scholars. For an overview of this topic, see M. L. Sanders and Philip M. Taylor, *British Propaganda during the First World War* (London: Constable, 1982). For a work that considers many of the personalities involved, see Gary S. Messinger, *British Propaganda and the State in the First World War* (Manchester: Manchester University Press, 1992). Other, less recent works still of value include H. C. Peterson, *Propaganda for War: The Campaign against American Neutrality* (Norman: University of Oklahoma Press, 1939); and James Duane Squires, *British Propaganda at Home and in the United States* (Cambridge: Harvard University Press, 1935).

22. For the German propaganda campaign, see Stewart Halsey Ross, *Propaganda for War: How the United States Was Conditioned to Fight the Great War of 1914–1918* (London: McFarland, 1996); and Reinhard Doerries, "Promoting Kaiser and Reich: Imperial German Propaganda in the United States during World War I," in Schröder, *Confrontation and Cooperation*, 135–65. For Bernstorff and the American press, see Kevin J. O'Keefe, *A Thousand Deadlines: The New York Press and American Neutrality, 1914–1917* (The Hague: Martinus Nijhoff, 1972).

23. *The History of The Times, Volume IV*, 2 parts (London: The Times, 1952), pt. 1, 220. For the press lord in the war, see J. Lee Thompson, *Politicians, the Press and Propaganda: Lord Northcliffe and the Great War, 1914–1919* (London: Associated University Presses, 1999).

24. Viereck to TR, August 5, 1914, Reel 189, Series 1, TRP. For a still useful look at the German-American Alliance, see Clifton J. Child, *The German-Americans in Politics* (Madison: University of Wisconsin Press, 1939).

25. See *Boston Herald*, August 5, 1914.

26. This was the note struck by Wilhelm in a speech to rally the nation before the Reichstag in the first days of the war in which he declared that Germany, "With a clear conscience and with clean hands" took up arms "in self-defense that has been forced upon us." He also famously told the Reichstag, "I no longer acknowledge parties; I know only Germans." Asprey, *German High Command*, 48; Cecil, *Wilhelm II*, 209.

27. TR to Münsterberg, August 8, 1914, in *TRL*, 7: 794–96.

28. Kazin, *Godly Hero*, 235.

29. Ruhl J. Bartlett, *The League to Enforce Peace* (Chapel Hill: University of North Carolina Press, 1944), 22; Lodge to TR, January 20, 1915, in Henry Cabot Lodge and Charles F. Redmond, eds., *Selections from the Correspondence of Theodore Roosevelt and Henry Cabot Lodge*, 2 vols. (New York: Charles Scribner's Sons, 1925), 2: 453. For a comparison of TR and Lodge's view of diplomacy, see William C. Widenor, *Henry Cabot Lodge and the Search for an American Foreign Policy* (Berkeley: University of California Press, 1980).

30. Isaac Russell, a newsman who had covered Wilson since 1912, later put down the failure to have any sort of celebration to the president's "fear of big men and an utter inability to cooperate with them." He was therefore "entirely prepared for the shabby treatment" of TR and George Goethals, the man on the ground who had engineered the canal's completion. "No ceremony, no show, no letting Goethals stand expansively forth as a fruitful servant of the Nation." Russell to TR, December 16, 1916, Reel 218, Series 1, TRP.

31. Noel Maurer and Carlos Yu, *The Big Ditch: How America Took, Ran, and Ultimately Gave Away the Panama Canal* (Princeton: Princeton University Press, 2011), 98.

32. Ibid., 167–68.

33. TR to Lee, August 22, 1914, in *TRL*, 7: 809–12.

34. TR to Eleanor Alexander Roosevelt, March 20, 1917, in *TRL*, 8: 1165.

35. TR to Arthur Lee, November 19, 1918, in *TRL*, 8: 1396–97.

36. Spring Rice to TR, September 10, 1914, CASR 9/1, Spring Rice Papers, Churchill College, Cambridge.

37. David Stevenson, *French War Aims Against Germany, 1914–1919* (Oxford: Clarendon Press, 1982), 12–13; and Stevenson, *Cataclysm*, 77.

38. Richard H. Collin, "Theodore Roosevelt's Visit to New Orleans and the Progressive Campaign of 1914," *Louisiana History* 12, no. 1 (Winter 1971): 11–15.

39. For a more detailed view of the 1914 campaign, see John A. Gable, *The Bull Moose Years: Theodore Roosevelt and the Progressive Party* (Port Washington, NY: Kennikat Press, 1978), 207–28.

40. Spring Rice to TR, September 10, 1914, CASR 9/1, Spring Rice Papers, Churchill College, Cambridge.

41. Grey to TR, September 10, 1914, in Grey of Fallodon, *Twenty-Five Years*, 2: 143–44.

42. *Daily Mail*, August 12, 17, 1914.

43. *Daily Mail*, August 28, 1914.

44. James Read, *Atrocity Propaganda 1914–1919* (New Haven: Arno Press, 1941), 56. For a recent reappraisal of the whole atrocity issue that gives more credence to the claims, see John Horne and Alan Kramer, *German Atrocities, 1914: A History of Denial* (New Haven: Yale University Press, 2001).

45. O'Keefe, *Thousand Deadlines*, 28.

46. Kipling to TR, September 15, 1914, Series 1, Reel 190, TRP. Also quoted in Russell Buchanan, "Theodore Roosevelt and American Neutrality, 1914–1917," *American Historical Review* 43 (July 1938): 778–79.

47. Quoted in Hermann Hagedorn's *The Bugle That Woke America: The Saga of Theodore Roosevelt's Last Battle for His Country* (New York: John Day, 1940), 15.

48. Page to House, September 22, 1914, in Charles Seymour, ed., *The Intimate Diaries of Colonel House, Volume I: Behind the Political Curtain* (London: Ernest Been, 1926), 340.

49. Theodore Roosevelt, "The World War: Its Tragedies and Its Lessons," *The Outlook*, September 23, 1914, 169–178. For a recent view of TR and the idea of a league of nations, see Stephen Wertheim, "The League That Wasn't: American Designs for a Legalist-Sanctionist League of Nations and the Intellectual Origins of International Organization, 1914–1920," *Diplomatic History* 35, no. 5 (November 2011): 797–836.

50. TR to Grey, October 3, 1914, in Grey of Fallodon, *Twenty-Five Years*, 2: 144–45.

51. Grey to TR, Oct 20, 1914, Series 1, Reel 192, TRP; TR to Grey, November 11, 1914, in Grey of Fallodon, *Twenty-Five Years*, 2: 145–46.

52. *New York Times*, September 28, 1914.

53. TR to Kipling, October 3, 1914, in *TRL*, 8: 830, n. 2.

54. TR to Kipling, November 4, 1914, in *TRL*, 8: 830.

55. The French also published a 1915 official report, *Les Atrocities Allemandes en France*, a copy of which is in Series 1, Reel 169, TRP.

56. *New York Times*, September 27, 1914.

57. *Daily Mail*, September 28, 1914.

58. Quoted in the *New York Times*, October 5, 1914.

59. Quoted in the *New York Times*, October 2, 1914.

60. TR to Spring Rice, October 3, 1914, in *TRL*, 8: 821–22. The Hague Conventions did not obligate the United States, as TR must have known, to defend Belgium militarily, but they did assert the integrity of neutral states and declare their territory inviolable, while forbidding belligerents to move armies or armaments through them. Calvin DeArmond Davis, *The United States and the Second Hague Peace Conference: American Diplomacy and International Organization 1899–1914* (Durham, NC: Duke University Press, 1975), 211–12.

61. TR to Sara Roosevelt, October 2, 1914, in *TRL*, 8: 821. For a recent life of FDR, see H. W. Brands, *Traitor to His Class: The Privileged Life and Radical Presidency of Franklin Delano Roosevelt* (New York: Random House, 2008).

62. Alice later wondered if FDR would have "emerged politically if my father had lived and had another term." Michael Teague, *Mrs. L: Conversations with Alice Roosevelt Longworth* (Garden City, NY: Doubleday, 1981), 156, 159.

63. For this subject, see James L. Golden, "FDR's Use of the Symbol of TR in the Formation of His Political Persona and Philosophy," in Natalie Naylor, Douglas Brinkley, and John Allen Gable, eds., *Theodore Roosevelt: Many-Sided American* (Interlaken, NY: Heart of Lakes, 1992). For another view of the commonalities between the two men, see J. Simon Rofe and John M. Thompson, "'Internationalists in Isolationist Times'—Theodore Roosevelt and Franklin Roosevelt and a Rooseveltian Maxim," *Journal of Transatlantic Studies* 9, no. 1 (March 2011): 46–62.

64. J. Simon Rofe, "Under the Influence of Mahan: Theodore and Franklin Roosevelt and Their Understanding of American National Interest," *Diplomacy and Statecraft* 19, no. 2 (2008): 736.

65. John Gable in a letter to James Golden, cited in Cooper, *Warrior and Priest*, 593, n. 30; Edward J. Renehan Jr., *The Lion's Pride: Theodore Roosevelt and His Family in Peace and War* (New York: Oxford University Press, 1998), 89.

66. Cooper, *Warrior and Priest*, 348.

67. Gable, *Bull Moose Years*, 220.

68. Kazin, *Godly Hero*, 232.

69. For Gompers in these years, see Frank L. Grubbs, *Samuel Gompers and the Great War: Protecting Labor's Standards* (Wake Forest, NC: Meridional, 1982).

70. Gable, *Bull Moose Years*, 222–23.

71. John Patrick Finnegan, *Against the Specter of the Dragon: The Campaign for American Preparedness, 1914–1917* (London: Greenwood Press, 1974), 24–27.

72. Alice Roosevelt Longworth, *Crowded Hours: Reminiscences of Alice Roosevelt Longworth* (London: Charles Scribner's Sons, 1934), 239.

73. Widenor, *Lodge and Foreign Policy*, 200; Finnegan, *Against the Specter of a Dragon*, 24–27.

74. For relations between the two men, see Kenneth S. Davis, "No Talent for Subordination: FDR and Josephus Daniels," in Edward J. Marolda, ed., *FDR and the U. S. Navy* (New York: St. Martin's Press, 1998): 1–11. When FDR was first appointed assistant secretary in 1913, Daniels mistakenly referred to him as Frederick D. Roosevelt. He was more prescient when he remarked in his diary the same day that FDR's "distinguished cousin TR went from that place to the presidency. May history repeat itself?" May 15, 1913 entry, in E. David Cronon, ed., *The Cabinet Diaries of Josephus Daniels 1913–1921* (Lincoln: University of Nebraska Press, 1963), 10.

75. *New York Times*, October 31, 1914. For comment on Germany's plans, see Reinhard Doerries, "The Politics of Irresponsibility: Imperial Germany's Defiance of United States Neutrality during World War I," in Hans Trefousse, ed., *Germany and America: Essays on Problems of International Relations and Immigration* (New York: Brooklyn College Press, 1980).

76. Captain B. H. Liddell Hart, *The Real War 1914–1918* (Boston: Little, Brown, 1964), 68–70. The press was not allowed to report fully about this episode for several months.

77. Stevenson, *Cataclysm*, 75–76.

78. David Stevenson, *With Our Backs to the Wall: Victory and Defeat in 1918* (Cambridge, MA: Belknap Press, 2011), 7–9.

79. Cecil, *Wilhelm II*, 2: 233.

80. TR to Kipling, November 4, 1914, in *TRL*, 8: 829.

81. Ethel Roosevelt Derby to Edith Roosevelt, October 10, 1914, Derby Papers, Theodore Roosevelt Collection, Harvard University (Hereafter TRC).

82. TR to Ethel Roosevelt Derby, October 5, 1914, MS Am 1834, TRC.

83. The attacks began on October 13, 1914, in the *Morning Post* and were soon picked up by other papers. Martin Gilbert, *Winston S. Churchill, Volume 3: The Challenge of War, 1914–1916*, 2 parts (Boston: Houghton Mifflin, 1971), pt. 1, 193–94.

84. He led a volunteer force across the channel, which suffered heavy casualties. Further, the foray was blamed (because it gave false hope) for delaying and therefore making more costly the retreat of the Belgian army.

85. *New York Times*, November 6, 1914.

86. TR to Kermit Roosevelt, November 11, 1914, MS Am 1541, TRC.

87. Gable, *Bull Moose Years*, 224.

88. Quoted in Gable, *Bull Moose Years*, 226.

89. TR to Belle Willard Roosevelt, November 7, 1914, MS Am 1454.46, TRC.

90. For Croly, see David W. Levy, *Herbert Croly of the New Republic: The Life and Thought of an American Progressive* (Princeton, NJ: Princeton University

Press, 1985). For Lippmann, see Larry L. Adams, *Walter Lippmann* (Boston: Twayne, 1977).

91. Quoted in *New York Times*, November 5, 1914.

92. Oscar King Davis, *Released for Publication: Some Inside Political History of Theodore Roosevelt and His Times 1898–1918* (Boston: Houghton Mifflin, 1925), 442–43.

93. Lodge to TR, December 7, 1914, Series 1, Reel 195, TRP; TR to Lodge, December 8, 1914, in *TRL*, 8: 861–63.

CHAPTER 3

1. TR to Ethel Roosevelt Derby, November 4, 1914, MS Am 1834, Theodore Roosevelt Collection, Harvard University (Hereafter TRC).

2. *New York Times*, November 6, 1914.

3. Cited in Alan Price, *The End of the Age of Innocence: Edith Wharton and the First World War* (New York: St. Martin's Press, 1996), 35.

4. Kevin J. O'Keefe, *A Thousand Deadlines: The New York Press and American Neutrality, 1914–1917* (The Hague: Martinus Nijhoff, 1972), 65.

5. TR to Sanger, November 23, 1914, Theodore Roosevelt Papers, Library of Congress (Hereafter TRP); quoted in Elting Morison, ed., *The Letters of Theodore Roosevelt*, 8 vols. (Cambridge: Harvard University Press, 1954), 8: 851, n. 1 (Hereafter *TRL*).

6. For TR's sons in the war, see Edward J. Renehan Jr., *The Lion's Pride: Theodore Roosevelt and His Family in Peace and War* (New York: Oxford University Press, 1998). For Archie in particular, see David M. Esposito, "Archibald Bulloch Roosevelt, 1894–1979," in Natalie Naylor, Douglas Brinkley, and John Allen Gable, eds., *Theodore Roosevelt: Many-Sided American* (Interlaken, NY: Heart of Lakes, 1992), 107–18.

7. TR to Archibald Roosevelt, December 2, 1914, in *TRL*, 8: 851–52.

8. Renehan, *Lion's Pride*, 116.

9. For the league, and for the preparedness movement, see John Patrick Finnegan, *Against the Specter of a Dragon: The Campaign for American Preparedness, 1914–1917* (London: Greenwood Press, 1974); and Robert D. Ward, "The Origin and Activities of the National Security League, 1914–1919," *Mississippi Valley Historical Review* 47 (June 1960): 51–65.

10. For Wood, see Jack McCallum, *Leonard Wood: Rough Rider, Surgeon, Architect of American Imperialism* (New York: New York University Press, 2006); and Jack C. Lane, *Armed Progressive: General Leonard Wood* (London: Presidio Press, 1978).

11. Wood to TR, December 30, 1914, Reel 196, Series 1, TRP.

12. McCallum, *Leonard Wood*, 262.

13. For Mahan and TR (and FDR), see J. Simon Rofe, "Under the Influence of Mahan: Theodore and Franklin Roosevelt and Their Understanding of American National Interest," *Diplomacy and Statecraft* 19, no. 2 (2008): 732–45.

14. Renehan, *Lion's Pride*, 62.

15. TR to Ellen Mahan, December 5, 1914, in *TRL*, 8: 861. For TR's public obituary of Mahan, see the January 13, 1915 *Outlook*.

16. O'Keefe, *Thousand Deadlines*, 61.

17. *The Sun*, December 23, 1914, in O'Keefe, *Thousand Deadlines*, 73.

18. *Daily Mail*, December 18, 1914.

19. TR to Mrs. Ralph Sanger, December 22, 1914, in *TRL*, 8: 867–68. Twenty years before, in the April 1894 *Forum*, TR had declared that there was no room in "any healthy American community for a German-American vote or an Irish-American vote, and it is contemptible demagogy to put planks into any party platform with the purpose of catching such a vote. We do not have any room for people who do not act and vote simply as Americans, and nothing else." Frederick Luebke, *Bonds of Loyalty: German-Americans and World War I* (De Kalb: Northern Illinois University Press, 1974), 68–69.

20. Clifton J. Child, *The German-Americans in Politics* (Madison: University of Wisconsin Press, 1939), 114.

21. December 8, 1914 Annual Address, quoted in John Garry Clifford, *The Citizen Soldiers: The Plattsburg Training Camp Movement, 1913–1917* (Lexington: University of Kentucky Press, 1972), 42.

22. "Utopia or Hell," *The Independent*, January 4, 1915.

23. Quoted in Clifford, *Citizen Soldiers*, 42–43.

24. Lodge to TR, December 11, 1914, in Henry Cabot Lodge and Charles F. Redmond, eds., *Selections from the Correspondence of Theodore Roosevelt and Henry Cabot Lodge*, 2 vols. (New York: Charles Scribner's Sons, 1925), 2: 450.

25. Henry Breckenridge Diary, February 4, 1916, quoted in Clifford, *Citizen Soldiers*, 47.

26. TR to Lodge, December 8, 1914, in *TRL*, 8: 861–63.

27. TR to Kermit Roosevelt, December 28, 1914, MS Am 1541, TRC.

28. Ibid.

29. For the company in the war, see Roberta A. Dayer, "Strange Bedfellows: J. P. Morgan & Co., Whitehall and the Wilson Administration During World War I," *Business History Review* 18, no. 2 (1976): 127–51.

30. Kathleen Burk, *Britain, America and the Sinews of War 1914–1918* (Boston: Allen and Unwin, 1985), 7.

31. For this and a still valuable view of Hearst in the war, see W. A. Swanberg, *Citizen Hearst: A Biography of William Randolph Hearst* (New York: Charles Scribner's Sons, 1961).

32. David French, *British Strategy and War Aims 1914–1916* (London: Allen and Unwin, 1986), 25.

33. Marion Siney, *The Allied Blockade of Germany 1914–1916* (Ann Arbor: University of Michigan, 1957), 12.

34. Ibid., 22–23.

35. O'Keefe, *Thousand Deadlines*, 48.

36. Armin Rappaport, *The British Press and Wilsonian Neutrality* (Stanford: Stanford University, 1951), 27.

37. TR to Theodore Roosevelt Jr., January 25, 1915, in Renehan, *Lion's Pride*, 94.

38. For Reed in the war, see Frederick C. Giffin, *Six Who Protested: Radical Opposition to the First World War* (Port Washington, NY: Kennikat Press, 1977).

39. Quoted in Lawrence O. Ealy, *Yanqui Politics and the Isthmian Canal* (University Park: Pennsylvania State University Press, 1971), 76.

40. Ealy, *Yanqui Politics and the Isthmian Canal*, 77.

41. Putnam to TR, December 30, 1914, Reel 196, Series 1, TRP.

42. Quoted in Alan Price, *The End of the Age of Innocence: Edith Wharton and the First World War* (New York: St. Martin's Press, 1996), 44.

43. Mrs. Winthrop Chanler, *Autumn in the Valley* (Boston: Little, Brown, 1936), 110.

44. Price, *End of the Age of Innocence*, 180.

45. Hermione Lee, *Edith Wharton* (New York: Alfred A. Knopf, 2007), 459.

46. February 10, 1915 statement, in Charles Seymour, ed., *The Intimate Diaries of Colonel House, Volume I: Behind the Political Curtain* (London: Ernest Been, 1926), 373.

47. February 5, 1915 entry, House Diary, in Seymour, *Intimate Papers of Colonel House*, 1: 367.

48. For the ship purchase controversy and the wartime shipping question in general, see William J. Williams, *The Wilson Administration and the Shipbuilding Crisis of 1917: Steel Ships and Wooden Ships* (Lewiston, NY: Edwin Mellen Press, 1992).

49. TR to Spring Rice, February 5, 1915, Reel 416, Series 4A, TRP.

50. O'Keefe, *Thousand Deadlines*, 54. The *Dacia* incident also led Germany to decide not to sell the ships, since they feared they would only be seized and used in trade against her. Williams, *Shipbuilding Crisis*, 34.

51. Lodge to TR, February 17, 1915, Reel 198, Series 1, TRP.

52. Lodge to TR, February 19, 1915, Reel 198, Series 1, TRP.

53. Lodge to TR, March 1, 1915, in William C. Widenor, *Henry Cabot Lodge and the Search for an American Foreign Policy* (Berkeley: University of California Press, 1980), 208.

54. For one example, see *Milwaukee Journal*, March 29, 1915.

55. April 13, 1915, in Arthur Link, ed., *The Papers of Woodrow Wilson* (Princeton; Princeton University Press, 1979), 50: 715–17.

56. *New York Times*, February 12, 1915.

57. *New York Times*, March 1, 1915.

58. TR to Hausmann, February 22, 1915, quoted in *New York Times*, March 1, 1915.

59. *New York Times*, February 12, 1915.

60. Garrison to Wood, March 11, 1915, quoted in *New York Times*, March 12, 1915.

61. Quoted in Clifford, *Citizen Soldiers*, 51.

62. Bullock to TR, March 15, 1915, Series 1, Reel 199, TRP.

63. Patrick Devlin, *Too Proud to Fight: Woodrow Wilson's Neutrality* (New York: Oxford University Press, 1975), 203; *New York Evening Post*, March 3, 1915, in O'Keefe, *Thousand Deadlines*, 85.

64. Siney, *Allied Blockade of Germany*, 66–67.

65. Godfrey Hodgson, *Woodrow Wilson's Right Hand: The Life of Colonel Edward M. House* (New Haven: Yale University Press, 2006), 108.

66. France was also content with the benevolent neutrality of the United States and feared American entry on the side of the Allies would harm its interests. There was also a lack of confidence in the European capitals that House could deliver the agreements he offered. TR's friend Jusserand was among those who warned of this. David Stevenson, *French War Aims Against Germany, 1914 –1919* (Oxford: Clarendon Press, 1982), 14–15.

67. David Stevenson, *Cataclysm: The First World War as Political Tragedy* (New York: Basic Books, 2004), 106–7, 111–12.

68. Renehan, *Lion's Pride*, 97.

69. Lee to TR, March 21, 1915, Series 1, Reel 199, TRP. Norman Angell's antiwar book, *The Great Illusion* (originally published in 1909 as *Europe's Optical Illusion*), attacked the notion that any nation could profit from war in the twentieth century; it completely underestimated the power of nationalism and the state of international rivalries. Carnegie, besides funding his Endowment for Peace, was also the president of the New York Peace Society and supported Wilsonian neutrality. Patterson, *Towards a Warless World*, 203–4, 246–47.

70. Theodore Roosevelt, "The Need of Preparedness," *Metropolitan Magazine*, April 1915.

71. Jusserand to TR, March 26, 1915, Reel 200, Series 1, TRP.

72. Stephen Gwynn, ed., *The Letters and Friendships of Sir Cecil Spring Rice: A Record*, 2 vols. (Boston: Houghton Mifflin, 1929), 2: 287.

73. Lee to TR, March 21, 1915, Series 1, Reel 199, TRP.

74. Churchill proposed a joint action with Greece even before Turkey entered the war. For Churchill and the Dardanelles, see Martin Gilbert, *Winston S. Churchill: The Challenge of War 1914–1916*, 2 vols. (Boston: Houghton Mifflin, 1971).

75. Lee to TR, March 21, 1915, Series 1, Reel 199, TRP.

76. Philip Magnus, *Kitchener: Portrait of an Imperialist* (London: John Murray, 1959), 310. For Kitchener's strategic considerations of Russia and the Dardanelles operation, see Keith Neilson, *Strategy and Supply: The Anglo-Russian Alliance, 1914–17* (London: Unwin, 1984), 61–77.

77. Lee to TR, March 21, 1915, Series 1, Reel 199, TRP.

78. Jan Cohn, *Improbable Fiction: The Life of Mary Roberts Rinehart* (Pittsburgh: University of Pittsburgh Press, 1980), 81–82.

79. Mary Roberts Rinehart, *My Story* (New York: Farrar and Rinehart, 1931), 198.

80. George Miller to TR, April 2, 1915, Reel 200, Series 1, TRP.

81. For Addams, see Allen F. Davis, *American Heroine: The Life and Legend of Jane Addams* (New York: Oxford University Press, 1973); and Jean Bethke Elshtain, *Jane Addams and the Dream of American Democracy* (New York: Basic Books, 2002).

82. TR to Spring Rice, May 1, 1915, Reel 416, Series 4A, TRP.

83. TR to Winston Churchill, August 4, 1915; TR to Henry Green, July 2, 1915, in *TRL*, 8: 959. In the following months, TR referred to Addams as "poor bleeding Jane," a "Bull Mouse," and "one of the shrieking sisterhood." Davis, *American Heroine*, 223.

84. *New York Times*, April 16, 1915.

85. *Harper's Weekly*, July 3, 1915.

86. TR to William Rainsford, July 10, 1915, in *TRL*, 8: 948.

87. TR to Belle Willard Roosevelt, April 15, 1915, MS Am 1454.46, TRC.

88. Wood to TR, April 17, 1915, Reel 200, Series 1, TRP.

89. Blackton to TR, April 5, 1915, Reel 200, Series 1, TRP.

90. Michael T. Isenberg, *War on Film: The American Cinema and World War I, 1914–1941* (London: Associated University Press, 1981), 102.

91. John A. Gable, *The Bull Moose Years: Theodore Roosevelt and the Progressive Party* (Port Washington, NY: Kennikat Press, 1978), 199.

92. For an analysis of the trial, see John Robert Greene, "Theodore Roosevelt and the Barnes Libel Case: A Reappraisal," *Presidential Studies Quarterly* 19, no. 1 (Winter 1989): 95–105.

93. Gable, *Bull Moose Years*, 233.

94. After the ingrate Hughes claimed not to remember the episode TR wanted him to recount in court, the Colonel told a friend, "Mr. Hughes is grateful to nobody but Almighty God, and I am not sure he is overgrateful to him." Quoted in Patricia O'Toole, *When Trumpets Call: Theodore Roosevelt after the White House* (New York: Simon and Schuster, 2005), 293.

95. James L. Golden, "FDR's Use of the Symbol of TR in the Formation of His Political Persona and Philosophy," in Natalie Naylor, Douglas Brinkley, and John Allen Gable, eds., *Theodore Roosevelt: Many-Sided American* (Interlaken, NY: Heart of Lakes, 1992), 581, 584.

96. Letter to O'Laughlin, March 25, 1915, Reel 358, Series 2, TRP.

97. *New York Times*, May 5, 1915. The *Gulflight* was not sunk, but its captain died of a heart attack and two sailors who jumped overboard drowned. Attacks on American ships in the war zone had begun in March, when the freighter *William P. Frye* was sunk by a German cruiser. On March 28, the British liner *Falaba* was torpedoed at the cost of one hundred lives, one of them American. Bryan, who believed Americans should be warned off belligerent vessels, opposed raising the matter with Germany, and in April there were no further incidents.

98. TR to O'Laughlin, May 6, 1915, in *TRL*, 8: 921–22.

CHAPTER 4

1. For a recent overview, see Diana Preston, *Lusitania: An Epic Tragedy* (New York: Walker, 2002). The dead included New York County Progressive Chairman Lindon Bates, among others TR knew.

2. *The World*, May 8, 1915, *New York Times*, May 8, 1915, in Kevin J. O'Keefe, *A Thousand Deadlines: The New York Press and American Neutrality, 1914–1917* (The Hague: Martinus Nijhoff, 1972), 91.

3. May 8, 1915, in O'Keefe, *Thousand Deadlines*, 93.

4. Edward J. Renehan Jr., *The Lion's Pride: Theodore Roosevelt and His Family in Peace and War* (New York: Oxford University Press, 1998), 100.

5. "Comments on the Sinking of the Lusitania," in Viscount Lee of Fareham, *"A Good Innings and a Great Partnership: Being the Life Story of Arthur and Ruth Lee,"* 3 vols. (Privately Printed, 1939), 3: 1000–1001; Renehan, *Lion's Pride*, 100–101.

6. O'Laughlin to TR, May 8, 1915, Reel 200, Series 1, Theodore Roosevelt Papers, Library of Congress (Hereafter TRP).

7. Only six of the one thousand editors who telegraphed their opinions to New York newspapers reportedly called for intervention. John Milton Cooper Jr., *The Vanity of Power: American Isolationism and the First World War 1914–1917* (Westport, CT: Greenwood, 1969), 34.

8. Preston, *Lusitania*, 333–34; O'Keefe, *Thousand Deadlines*, 98.

9. May 9, 1915, in Charles Seymour, ed., *The Intimate Diaries of Colonel House, Volume I: Behind the Political Curtain* (London: Ernest Been, 1926), 437.

10. Armin Rappaport, *The British Press and Wilsonian Neutrality* (Stanford: Stanford University, 1951), 34–36.

11. TR to Lee, June 17, 1915, in Elting Morison, ed., *The Letters of Theodore Roosevelt*, 8 vols. (Cambridge: Harvard University Press, 1954), 8: 937–39 (Hereafter *TRL*).

12. "Comments on the Sinking of the Lusitania," in Lord Lee of Fareham, *"A Good Innings,"* 3: 1000–1001.

13. O'Laughlin to TR, May 12, 1915, Reel 200, Series 1, TRP.

14. Belasco to TR, May 12, 1915, Reel 200, Series 1, TRP.

15. Trevelyan to TR, May 13, 1915, Reel 200, Series 1, TRP.

16. Rider Haggard to TR, May 11, 1915, Reel 200, Series 1, TRP. The writer also shared an account of the death in battle of his nephew, Mark Haggard, which he described as "a remarkable instance of berserker courage in a modern."

17. Gerald Monsman, *H. Rider Haggard and the Imperial Frontier* (Greensboro, NC: ELT Press, 2006), 233.

18. Ruth Lee to TR, May 12, 1915, Reel 200, Series 1, TRP.

19. Philip Magnus, *Kitchener: Portrait of an Imperialist* (London: John Murray, 1959), 335.

20. Richard Holmes, *The Little Field-Marshall Sir John French* (London: Jonathan Cape, 1981), 287–88; Magnus, *Kitchener*, 336.

21. For the munitions details in brief, see Peter Fraser, "The British Shells Scandal of 1915," *Journal of Canadian History* 18 (1983): 69–86.

22. *Times*, May 14, 1915. Repington had previously pointed out the artillery ammunition problem on April 27.

23. The historian John Grigg found "credible" Repington's claim to this in *The First World War 1914–1918*, 2 vols. (Boston: Houghton Mifflin, 1920), 1: 39. Grigg, *Lloyd George: From Peace to War, 1912–1916* (Berkeley: University of California Press, 1985), 248.

24. For a detailed view of the political developments surrounding the formation of the new government, see Cameron Hazlehurst, *Politicians at War July 1914 to May 1915: A Prologue to the Triumph of Lloyd George* (London: Jonathan Cape, 1971).

25. TR to Lloyd George, June 1, 1915, in *TRL*, 8: 926.

26. Balfour to TR, June 15, 1915, Reel 201, Series 1, TRP. In November, Churchill resigned from the cabinet and became a battalion commander on the Western Front.

27. Preston, *Lusitania*, 333–34; O'Keefe, *Thousand Deadlines*, 98.

28. Preston, *Lusitania*, 335–39.

29. TR to Anna Roosevelt Cowles, May 14, 1915, MS Am 1834, Theodore Roosevelt Collection, Harvard University (Hereafter TRC).

30. *Metropolitan*, June 1915.

31. TR to Kermit Roosevelt, May 27, 1915, MS Am 1541, TRC.

32. Germany immediately broke relations, but Italy did not declare war on the other Triple Alliance signatory until August 28, 1916.

33. TR to Lee, June 17, 1915, in *TRL*, 8: 937–39.

34. John Robert Greene, "Theodore Roosevelt and the Barnes Libel Case: A Reappraisal," *Presidential Studies Quarterly* 19, no. 1 (Winter 1989): 103.

35. John A. Gable, *The Bull Moose Years: Theodore Roosevelt and the Progressive Party* (Port Washington, NY: Kennikat Press, 1978), 233. Though he won the suit, TR claimed in a letter to Raymond Robins that it would still cost him between $30,000 and $40,000 in legal fees. *TRL*, 8: 935.

36. Taft to Helen H. Taft, April 10, 1915, quoted in G. E. Mowry, *Roosevelt and the Progressive Movement* (New York: Hill and Wang, 2000), 327.

37. Mabie to TR, May 28, 1915, Reel 200, Series 1, TRP.

38. Wood to TR, May 27, 1915, Reel 200, Series 1, TRP.

39. Wood to TR, May 27, 1915, Reel 200, Series 1, TRP.

40. Blackton to TR, June 1, 1915, Reel 201, Series 1, TRP.

41. Lodge to TR, July 15, 1915, Reel 201, Series 1, TRP.

42. R. N. Moffat to TR, January 1, 1916, Reel 204, Series 1, TRP.

43. Julian Street, *The Most Interesting American* (New York: Century, 1915), 28.

44. For Sprinkle, see Douglas Brinkley, *The Wilderness Warrior: Theodore Roosevelt and the Crusade for America* (New York: HarperCollins, 2009), 571–72.

45. Theodore Roosevelt, *A Book Lover's Holiday in the Open,* in *The Works of Theodore Roosevelt, National Edition* (New York: Charles Scribner's Sons, 1926), 3: 360–63.

46. Preston, *Lusitania*, 341–42.

47. Michael Kazin, *A Godly Hero: A Life of William Jennings Bryan* (New York: Alfred A. Knopf, 2006), 240.

48. W. A. Swanberg, *Citizen Hearst: A Biography of William Randolph Hearst* (New York: Charles Scribner's Sons, 1961), 299.

49. TR to Lee, June 17, 1915, in *TRL*, 8: 937–39.

50. TR to Hart, June 1, 1915, in *TRL*, 8: 927.

51. For the league, see Ruhl F. Bartlett, *The League to Enforce Peace* (Chapel Hill: University of North Carolina Press, 1944). For a briefer and more recent view of the league, see Stephen Wertheim, "The League That Wasn't: American Designs for a Legalist-Sanctionist League of Nations and the Intellectual Origins of International Organization, 1914–1920," *Diplomatic History* 35, no. 5 (November 2011): 797–836.

52. Quoted in Bartlett, *League to Enforce Peace*, 26.

53. For this see Larry L. Fabian, *Andrew Carnegie's Peace Endowment: The Tycoon, the President, and Their Bargain of 1910* (Washington, DC: Carnegie Endowment for Peace, 1985).

54. Quoted in Seymour, *Intimate Papers of Colonel House*, 1: 443.

55. Bartlett, *League to Enforce Peace*, 41. For the platform of the league, see 40–41.

56. Short to TR, July 27, 1915, Reel 201, Series 1, TRP.

57. Quoted in Wertheim, "The League That Wasn't," 811.

58. TR to Lee, June 17, 1915, in *TRL*, 8: 937–39.

59. Cooper, *Vanity of Power*, 55–58.

60. "Peace Insurance by Preparedness against War," August 1915 *Metropolitan*, quoted in Cooper, *Vanity of Power*, 60.

61. Quoted in Cooper, *Vanity of Power*, 146.

62. *New York Times*, July 12, 1915.

63. *New York Times*, July 20, 1915, quoted in Mowry, *Roosevelt and the Progressive Movement*.

64. Julie Greene, *The Canal Builders* (New York: Penguin Press, 2009), 357. For the background of the exposition, see Robert Rydell, *All the World's a Fair: Visions of Empire at American International Expositions, 1876–1916* (Chicago: University of Chicago Press, 1984). For pictorial histories, see William Lipsky, *San Francisco's Panama-Pacific International Exposition* (Charleston, SC: Arcadia, 2005); and Donna Ewald and Peter Clute, *San Francisco Invites the World* (San Francisco: Chronicle, 1991).

65. *New York Times*, July 22, 1915.

66. For the competition between San Francisco and San Diego over their expositions, see Rydell, *All the World's a Fair*.

67. TR to Lee, August 6, 1915, in *TRL*, 8: 960.

68. *New York Times,* July 28, 1915.
69. TR to Lee, August 6, 1915, in *TRL,* 8: 960.
70. *New York Times,* July 27, 1915.
71. Quoted in Cooper, *Vanity of Power,* 104.
72. For Mitchel, see Edwin R. Lewinson, *John Purroy Mitchel: The Boy Mayor of New York* (New York: Astra, 1965).
73. Blackton to TR, August 3, 1915, Reel 201, Series 1, TRP.
74. Michael T. Isenberg, *War on Film: The American Cinema and World War I, 1914–1941* (London: Associated University Press, 1981), 102–3.
75. Craig Campbell, *Reel America and World War I* (McFarland: London, 1985), 39; Isenberg, *War on Film,* 102–3.
76. Munsterberg to TR, October 29, 1915, Reel 202, Series 1, TRP.
77. Lodge to TR, August 5, 1915, Reel 201, Series 1, TRP.
78. TR to Lodge, August 7, 1915, in Henry Cabot Lodge and Charles F. Redmond, eds., *Selections from the Correspondence of Theodore Roosevelt and Henry Cabot Lodge,* 2 vols. (New York: Charles Scribner's Sons, 1925), 2: 462.
79. For the movement, see John Garry Clifford, *The Citizen Soldiers: The Plattsburg Training Camp Movement, 1913–1920* (Lexington: University of Kentucky Press, 1972); and Ralph Barton Perry, *The Plattsburg Movement: A Chapter of America's Participation in the World War* (New York: E. P. Dutton, 1921). Perry, a professor of philosophy at Harvard, was one of the attendees at Plattsburg. For Ted, and his brothers, in the war, see H. Paul Jeffers, *Theodore Roosevelt Jr.: The Life of a War Hero* (Novato, CA: Presidio Press, 2002); and Edward J. Renehan Jr., *The Lion's Pride: Theodore Roosevelt and His Family in Peace and War* (New York: Oxford University Press, 1998).
80. Wood to TR, August 14, 1915, Reel 201, Series 1, TRP.
81. Wilson to Wood, August 16, 1915, Reel 201, Series 1, TRP.
82. Wilson to Galt, August 15, 1915, in Arthur Link, ed., *The Papers of Woodrow Wilson* (Princeton; Princeton University Press, 1979), 34: 209 (Hereafter *PWW*).
83. Malone to Wilson, August 5, 1915, quoted in Clifford, *Citizen Soldiers,* 81–82.
84. TR to Kermit Roosevelt, July 10, 1915, MS Am 1541, TRC.
85. Richard Derby to Ethel Roosevelt Derby, August 12, 1915, Derby Papers, TRC.
86. *New York Times,* August 22, 1915.
87. *New York Times,* August 24, 1915.
88. For the text of von Bernstorff's statement and Lansing's reply, see the *New York Times,* September 2, 1915.
89. Devlin, *Too Proud to Fight,* 336.
90. Renehan, *Lion's Pride,* 111.
91. *New York Times,* August 26, 1915.
92. Quoted in Clifford, *Citizen Soldiers,* 85.
93. *New York Times,* August 26, 1915.
94. Ibid.
95. *New York Times,* August 27, 1915.
96. Galt to Wilson, August 26, 1915, in *PWW,* 34: 337.
97. Wilson to Galt, August 28, 1915, in *PWW,* 34: 353.
98. Quoted in Jack McCallum, *Leonard Wood: Rough Rider, Surgeon, Architect of American Imperialism* (New York: New York University Press, 2006), 264.
99. Street, *The Most Interesting American,* 7, 13–15, 18–19, 22–23, 32–33.

100. Hamilton to TR, July 2, 1915, Reel 201, Series 1, TRP. For Hamilton's rec-ollections of the campaign, see his *Gallipoli Diary*, 2 vols. (London: Edward Arnold, 1920).

101. For the roles of Hamilton and Murdoch in the Gallipoli affair, see Alan Moore-head, *Gallipoli* (New York: Dutton, 1956); Ian B. M. Hamilton, *The Happy Warrior: A Life of General Sir Ian Hamilton* (London: Cassell, 1966); and Desmond Zwar, *In Search of Keith Murdoch* (Melbourne: Macmillan, 1980).

102. An original report, addressed to Asquith, had been seized at Marseilles by Brit-ish representatives warned by Hamilton. Murdoch then simply wrote another, and equally hostile, 8,000-word report on his own. This was the document he gave to Northcliffe and others. Moorehead, *Gallipoli*, 308–9. A copy is in the Northcliffe Add. Mss. at the British Library and is largely reproduced in Zwar, *In Search of Keith Murdoch*.

103. *Daily Mail*, December 21, 1915.

CHAPTER 5

1. Theodore Roosevelt, *A Book Lover's Holiday in the Open*, in *The Works of Theo-dore Roosevelt, National Edition* (New York: Charles Scribner's Sons, 1926), 3: 378–400.

2. Holbrook Bonney to TR, October 30, 1915, Reel 202, Series 1, Theodore Roosevelt Papers, Library of Congress, (Hereafter TRP).

3. *Metropolitan*, October 1915.

4. Lodge to TR, September 25, 1915, in Henry Cabot Lodge and Charles F. Red-mond, eds., *Selections from the Correspondence of Theodore Roosevelt and Henry Cabot Lodge*, 2 vols. (New York: Charles Scribner's Sons, 1925), 2: 463.

5. *New York Times*, October 13, 1915.

6. TR to Kermit Roosevelt, October 15, 1915, MS Am 1541, Theodore Roos-evelt Collection, Harvard University (Hereafter TRC).

7. *Metropolitan*, January 1916, 66.

8. *New York Times*, November 28, 1915.

9. *Metropolitan*, January 1916, 13.

10. All quoted in John A. Thompson, *Reformers and War: American Progressive Publicists and the First World War* (Cambridge: Cambridge University Press, 2003), 148–49.

11. Ibid., 131.

12. Kevin J. O'Keefe, *A Thousand Deadlines: The New York Press and American Neutrality, 1914–1917* (The Hague: Martinus Nijhoff, 1972), 115.

13. Wharton to TR, October 19, 1915, Derby Papers, TRC.

14. "International Duty and Hyphenated Americanism," *Metropolitan*, November 1915, quoted in *New York Times*, October 23, 1915.

15. Strachey to TR, October 26, 1915, Reel 202, Series 1, TRP.

16. *New York Times*, November 19, 1915.

17. John Garry Clifford, *The Citizen Soldiers: The Plattsburg Training Camp Move-ment, 1913–1920* (Lexington: University of Kentucky Press, 1972), 123.

18. Ibid. For Goldman in the period, see Frederick C. Giffin, *Six Who Protested: Radical Opposition to the First World War* (Port Washington, NY: Kennikat Press, 1977).

19. *New York Times*, November 12, 1915.

20. TR to Kermit Roosevelt, November 2, 1915, MS Am 1541, TRC.

21. TR to John Carter Rose, November 12, 1915, in Elting Morison, ed., *The Letters of Theodore Roosevelt*, 8 vols. (Cambridge: Harvard University Press, 1954), 8: 978–79 (Hereafter *TRL*).

22. *New York Times*, November 10, 1915.

23. *New York Times*, November 11, 1915.

24. *New York Times*, December 14, 1915.

25. For this see Maceo Crenshaw Dailey Jr., "An Uneasy Alliance: Theodore Roosevelt and Emmett Jay Scott, 1900–1919," in Natalie Naylor, Douglas Brinkley, and John Allen Gable, eds., *Theodore Roosevelt: Many-Sided American* (Interlaken, NY: Heart of Lakes, 1992), 471–84.

26. *New York Times*, December 13, 1915.

27. Shaw to TR, November 10, 1915, Reel 202, Series 1, TRP.

28. TR to George Moseley, November 17, 1915, in *TRL*, 8: 979.

29. *New York Times*, November 19, 1915.

30. Steven Watts, *The People's Tycoon: Henry Ford and the American Century* (Random House: New York, 2006), 230.

31. O'Keefe, *Thousand Deadlines*, 110–11. For this subject, see Barbara Kraft, *The Peace Ship: Henry Ford's Pacifist Adventure in the First World War* (Macmillan: New York, 1978); and Burnet Hershey, *The Odyssey of Henry Ford and the Great Peace Ship* (New York: Tappinger, 1967).

32. TR to Henry Reuterdahl, November 30, 1915, in *TRL*, 8: 993.

33. *New York Times*, December 3, 1915.

34. O'Keefe, *Thousand Deadlines*, 111.

35. Michael T. Isenberg, *War on Film: The American Cinema and World War I, 1914–1941* (London: Associated University Press, 1981), 100.

36. *New York Times*, December 8, 1915; G. E. Mowry, *Roosevelt and the Progressive Movement* (New York: Hill and Wang, 2000), 317–18.

37. *New York Times*, December 8, 1915.

38. Lane to John Wigmore, December 8, 1915, in Anne W. Lane and Louise Herrick Hall, eds., *The Letters of Franklin K. Lane: Personal and Political* (Boston: Houghton Mifflin, 1922), 188. For Lane, see Keith W. Olson, *Biography of a Progressive: Franklin K. Lane, 1864–1921* (Westport, CT: Greenwood Press, 1979).

39. TR to Lodge, December 7, 1915, in *TRL*, 8:995.

40. Mowry, *Roosevelt and the Progressive Movement*, 329.

41. Lodge to TR, December 2, 1915, in William C. Widenor, *Henry Cabot Lodge and the Search for an American Foreign Policy* (Berkeley: University of California Press, 1980), 198.

42. Phyllis Lee Levin, *Edith and Woodrow: The Wilson White House* (New York: Scribner, 2001), 131.

43. Devlin, *Too Proud to Fight*, 364.

44. TR to Charles Bull, February 4, 1916, in *TRL*, 8: 1014. Roosevelt had remarried himself two years after the death of his first wife, Alice Lee, and at least for a time he felt tremendous guilt over his "inconstancy." Michael Teague, *Mrs. L: Conversations with Alice Roosevelt Longworth* (Garden City, NY: Doubleday, 1981), 5.

45. *Metropolitan*, January 1916.

46. *New York Times*, January 14, 1916.

47. John Milton Cooper Jr., *Walter Hines Page: The Southerner as American 1855 –1918* (Chapel Hill: University of North Carolina Press, 1977), 325.

48. For this see Robert D. Ward, "The Origin and Activities of the National Security League, 1914–1919," *Mississippi Valley Historical Review* 47 (June 1960): 55.

49. ADS Resolution adopted January 5, 1916, Reel 208, Series 1, TRP.

50. Barbara J. Steinson, *American Women's Activism in World War I* (New York: Garland, 1982), 211–12.

51. *New York Times*, January 21, 1916.

52. For Fiske's recollection of the war years, see his *From Midshipman to Rear-Admiral* (New York: Century, 1919).

53. Quoted in O'Keefe, *Thousand Deadlines*, 133.

54. TR to John Graves, February 9, 1916, in *TRL*, 8: 1021.

55. *Evening Post*, March 8, 1916, in O'Keefe, *Thousand Deadlines*, 131.

56. Spring Rice to TR, February 12, 1916, in Stephen Gwynn, ed., *The Letters and Friendships of Sir Cecil Spring Rice: A Record*, 2 vols. (Boston: Houghton Mifflin, 1929), 2, 311.

57. November 28, 1915 entry, House Diary, quoted in W. B. Fowler, *British-American Relations, 1917–1918: The Role of Sir William Wiseman* (Princeton: Princeton University Press, 1969), 10.

58. Kathleen, Lady Scott, *Self-Portrait of an Artist: From the Diaries and Memoirs of Lady Kennet* (London: John Murray, 1949), 135–36.

59. For the memorandum, see Joyce Grigsby Williams, *Colonel House and Sir Edward Grey: A Study in Anglo-American Diplomacy* (Lanham, MD: University Press of America, 1984), 73–118.

60. Godfrey Hodgson, *Woodrow Wilson's Right Hand: The Life of Colonel Edward M. House* (New Haven: Yale University Press, 2006), 119–21.

61. Diana Preston, *Lusitania: An Epic Tragedy* (New York: Walker, 2002), 360.

62. Robert H. Ferrell, *Woodrow Wilson & World War I, 1917–1921* (New York: Harper and Row, 1985), 15.

63. For Baker in the period, see Daniel R. Beaver, *Newton D. Baker and the American War Effort 1917–1919* (Lincoln: Nebraska University Press, 1966).

64. Ferrell, *Woodrow Wilson & World War I*, 24.

65. TR to Anna Roosevelt Cowles, January 27, 1916, in *TRL*, 8: 1007.

66. *New York Times*, February 12, 1916.

67. Ibid.

68. TR to Kermit Roosevelt, January 19, 1916, MS Am 1541, TRC.

69. Undated Publicity Sheet, Series 1, TRP.

70. *New York Times*, February 19, 25, 26, March 4, 8, 1916.

71. For the two, see Carol Gould, "William Beebe and Theodore Roosevelt," *The Princeton University Library Chronicle*, 65, no. 2 (March 2004): 265–81.

72. William Beebe, "The Naturalist and Book-Lover: An Appreciation," in *The Works of Theodore Roosevelt, National Edition* (New York: Charles Scribner's Sons, 1926), 3: 179.

73. TR to Kermit Roosevelt, February 24, 1916, MS Am 1541, TRC.

74. February 25, 1916 entry, Edith Kermit Roosevelt Diary, Derby Papers, TRC.

75. *New York Times*, March 13, 1916.

76. Henry Stoddard to TR, April 19, 1916, Reel 208, Series 1, TRP.

CHAPTER 6

1. For Stoddard's sometimes questionable recollection of events, see his *As I Knew Them: Presidents and Politics from Grant to Coolidge*, 2 vols. (New York: Harper and Brothers, 1927), 2: 429–31.

2. *New York Times*, March 13 1916. The March 9, 1916, statement is also reproduced in Elting Morison, ed., *The Letters of Theodore Roosevelt*, 8 vols. (Cambridge: Harvard University Press, 1954), 8: 1024–25, n. 1 (Hereafter *TRL*).

3. *New York Times*, March 25, 1916.

4. *New York Times*, March 31, 1916.

5. William C. Widenor, *Henry Cabot Lodge and the Search for an American Foreign Policy* (Berkeley: University of California Press, 1980), 239.

6. Philip C. Jessup, *Elihu Root*, 2 vols. (New York: Dodd, Mead, 1938), 2: 344–45.

7. *New York Times*, April 2, 1916.

8. *New York Times*, April 1, 1916.

9. Jessup, *Root*, 2: 346–48.

10. *New York Times*, April 6, 1916.

11. *New York Times*, April 7, 1916.

12. *New York Times*, April 8, 1916.

13. Pershing to TR, May 24 15, 1916, Reel 210, Series 1, Theodore Roosevelt Papers, Library of Congress (Hereafter TRP).

14. TR to Pershing, June 6, 1916, in *TRL*, 8: 1050–51.

15. *New York Times*, April 14, 1916.

16. TR to Strachey, October 25, 1906, quoted in David Nasaw, *The Chief: The Life of William Randolph Hearst* (Boston: Houghton Mifflin, 2000), 210.

17. TR to Hearst, April 15, 1916, Reel 416, Series 4A, TRP.

18. Quoted in Nasaw, *Chief*, 249–50.

19. *Papers Relating to the Foreign Relations of the United States, 1916* (Washington, DC: Government Printing Office, 1925), 232–34.

20. *New York Times*, April 18, 1916.

21. *New York Times*, April 20, 1916.

22. *New York Times*, May 11, 1916.

23. Other members of the league included Mrs. Jacob Riis, Miss Anne Morgan, Mrs. Leigh Hunt, Mrs. William G. Willcox, and Dr. Katharine Bement Davis, a nationally prominent penologist.

24. *New York Times*, April 29, 1916.

25. *New York Times*, April 30, 1916.

26. For this issue, see L. Margaret Barnett, *British Food Policy during the First World War* (London: George Allen and Unwin, 1985).

27. C. Paul Vincent, *The Politics of Hunger: The Allied Blockade of Germany, 1915 –1919* (Athens: Ohio University Press, 1985), 10.

28. *Daily Mail*, May 26, 1916.

29. TR to Lee, February 18, 1916, in *TRL*, 8: 1022–23.

30. TR to Lee, June 7, 1916, in *TRL*, 8: 1054.

31. Lee to TR, July 26, 1916, Reel 212, Series 1, TRP.

32. "Nobody for Hughes—But the People," *North American Review* 203 (May 1915): 641–57. TR later claimed that, before this article was published, he and Harvey met at lunch, and the editor spoke of Hughes with contempt while talking of supporting Roosevelt. His terms, however, that TR drop his advocacy

of universal training and service, were unacceptable. TR to Hiram Johnson, February 17, 1917, in *TRL*, 8: 1155.

33. "A Talk with the President," May 12, 1916, in Arthur Link, ed., *The Papers of Woodrow Wilson* (Princeton; Princeton University Press, 1979), 37: 37–38 (Hereafter *PWW*).

34. Quoted in Jack McCallum, *Leonard Wood: Rough Rider, Surgeon, Architect of American Imperialism* (New York: New York University Press, 2006), 267.

35. *New York Times*, May 14, 1916.

36. Wood to TR, April 15, 1916, Reel 208, Series 1, TRP.

37. TR to Ford, February 9, 1916, in *TRL*, 8: 1022. Among other things, at the beginning of 1914 in his automobile plants Ford had put in place an eight-hour day with a $5.00 daily minimum wage.

38. *New York Times*, May 20, 1916.

39. G. E. Mowry, *Roosevelt and the Progressive Movement* (New York: Hill and Wang, 2000), 336.

40. *New York Times*, May 21, 1916.

41. Joyce Grigsby Williams, *Colonel House and Sir Edward Grey: A Study in Anglo-American Diplomacy* (Lanham, MD: University Press of America, 1984), 107–8.

42. Ibid., 108.

43. TR to Lee, June 7, 1916, in *TRL*, 8: 1054.

44. *New York Times*, May 28, 1916.

45. *New York Times*, May 30, 1916.

46. *New York Times*, May 31, 1916.

47. *New York Times*, May 31, 1916.

48. *New York Times*, June 1, 1916.

49. David Stevenson, *Cataclysm: The First World War as Political Tragedy* (New York: Basic Books, 2004), 207–8.

50. TR to Bryce, June 19, 1916, in *TRL*, 8: 1065–66.

51. Allen to TR, May 23, 1916, Series I, Reel 210, TRP.

52. A. J. P. Taylor, *English History 1914–1945* (London: Oxford University Press, 1965), 58.

53. *New York Times*, June 7, 1916.

54. TR to Lee, June 7, 1916, in *TRL*, 8: 1052–56.

55. Mowry, *Roosevelt and the Progressive Movement*, 135.

56. *New York Times*, June 1, 1916.

57. John A. Gable, *The Bull Moose Years: Theodore Roosevelt and the Progressive Party* (Port Washington, NY: Kennikat Press, 1978), 243.

58. TR to Lee, June 7, 1916, in *TRL*, 8: 1052–56.

59. Quoted in Edmund Morris, *Colonel Roosevelt* (New York: Random House, 2010), 457.

60. Julian Street, "The Convention and the Colonel," *Collier's Weekly*, July 1, 1916, 26.

61. W. A. Swanberg, *Citizen Hearst: A Biography of William Randolph Hearst* (New York: Charles Scribner's Sons, 1961), 300.

62. Ben Proctor, *William Randolph Hearst: Final Edition, 1911–1951* (Oxford: Oxford University Press, 2007), 50.

63. Undated Statement, in *TRL*, 8: 1063.

64. Gable, *Bull Moose Years*, 247–48.

65. John A. Thompson, *Reformers and War: American Progressive Publicists and the First World War* (Cambridge: Cambridge University Press, 2003), 113.

66. TR to Progressive National Committee, June 22, 1916, in *TRL*, 8: 1069–71.

67. *New York Times*, June 27, 1916.

68. Huey Chalmers to TR, June 24, 1916, Reel 212, Series 1, TRP.

69. TR to William Wadsworth, June 23, 1916, in *TRL*, 8: 1078.

70. Hughes to TR, June 26, 1916, Reel 212, Series 1, TRP.

71. Hughes to TR, June 26, 1916, Reel 212, Series 1, TRP.

72. Hughes to TR, July 10, 1916, Reel 212, Series 1, TRP.

73. TR to Lodge, July 3, 1916, in *TRL*, 8: 1086–87.

74. Lee to TR, July 26, 1916, Reel 212, Series 1, TRP.

CHAPTER 7

1. *New York Times*, July 5, 1916.

2. TR to Street, July 3, 1916, in Elting Morison, ed., *The Letters of Theodore Roosevelt*, 8 vols. (Cambridge: Harvard University Press, 1954), 8: 1085–86 (Hereafter *TRL*).

3. Bullock to TR, July 1, 1916, Reel 212, Series 1, Theodore Roosevelt Papers, Library of Congress (Hereafter TRP).

4. For example, see *New York Times*, July 10, 11, 1916; the June papers had carried many such articles.

5. TR to Baker, July 6, 1916, Reel 416, Series 4A, TRP.

6. *New York Times*, June 1, 1916.

7. TR to Street, July 3, 1916, in *TRL*, 8: 1085–86.

8. Lodge to TR, July 15, 1916, Reel 212, Series 1, TRP.

9. *New York Times*, July 3, 1916; Heney to Wilson, July 1, 1916, in Arthur Link, ed., *The Papers of Woodrow Wilson* (Princeton; Princeton University Press, 1979), 37: 338–42 (Hereafter *PWW*).

10. *New York Times*, June 28, 1916. In fact, a week before the election, 11 of the 19 members of the platform committee of the 1912 Progressive National Convention issued a statement supporting Wilson. Meyer Nathan, "Theodore Roosevelt and the 1916 Election," *The Rocky Mountain Social Science Journal* 5, no. 2 (October 1968): 69.

11. John Garry Clifford, *The Citizen Soldiers: The Plattsburg Training Camp Movement, 1913–1920* (Lexington: University of Kentucky Press, 1972), 149; Jack McCallum, *Leonard Wood: Rough Rider, Surgeon, Architect of American Imperialism* (New York: New York University Press, 2006), 266.

12. *New York Times*, September 1, 1916.

13. TR to Anna Roosevelt Cowles, July 23, 1916, in *TRL*, 8: 1094.

14. TR to Bass, July 28, 1916, in *TRL*: 8, 1096.

15. *New York Times*, September 15, 1916.

16. For Lloyd George's strained relations with the military, see David Woodward, *Lloyd George and the Generals* (London: Associated University Presses, 1983).

17. Lee to TR, July 26, 1916, Reel 212, Series 1, TRP.

18. Spring Rice to TR, July 15, 1916, CASR 9/1, Spring Rice Papers, Churchill College, Cambridge.

19. TR to Spring Rice, July 16, 1916, Reel 416, Series 4A, TRP.

20. Morton Cohen, ed., *Rudyard Kipling and Rider Haggard: The Record of a Friendship* (London: Hutchinson, 1965), 90–91.

21. TR to Bass, July 28, 1916, in *TRL*, 8: 1095.

22. *New York Times*, August 1, 1916. For this incident and other German sabotage, see Captain Henry Landau, *The Enemy Within: The Inside Story of German Sabotage in America* (New York: G. P. Putnam's Sons, 1937).

23. *New York Times*, July 13, August 9, 1916.

24. Nevertheless, German Americans did vote more Republican than the rest of the population. Frederick Luebke, *Bonds of Loyalty: German-Americans and World War I* (De Kalb: Northern Illinois University Press, 1974), 176–77, 190.

25. Clifton J. Child, *The German-Americans in Politics* (Madison: University of Wisconsin Press, 1939), 117, 133.

26. TR to Hughes, August 11, 1916; TR to William Willcox, August 21, 1916, in *TRL*, 8: 1098–99.

27. As Willcox suggested, TR substituted "professional German-Americans" for the "German American Alliance," which had come out publicly against TR and Wilson. TR to Hughes, August 28, 1916, in *TRL*, 8: 1110.

28. "Duty First," speech at Lewiston Maine, August 31, 1916, in Theodore Roosevelt, *Americanism and Preparedness: Speeches July 1916 to November 1916* (New York: General Books, 2010), 1–16.

29. *New York Times*, September 1, 1916.

30. *New York Times*, September 2, 1916.

31. *New York Times*, September 9, 1916.

32. Devlin, *Too Proud to Fight*, 531.

33. O'Leary to Wilson, September 29, 1916, in Jeremiah A. O'Leary, *My Political Trial and Experiences* (New York: Jefferson, 1919), 45–46; Kevin J. O'Keefe, *A Thousand Deadlines: The New York Press and American Neutrality, 1914–1917* (The Hague: Martinus Nijhoff, 1972), 153; Stewart Halsey Ross, *Propaganda for War: How the United States Was Conditioned to Fight the Great War of 1914–1918* (London: McFarland, 1996), 118.

34. Wilson to O'Leary, September 29, 1916, in *PWW*, 38: 286.

35. In Germany, Wilhelm certainly feared the worst and consequently agreed to appoint the duo of Hindenburg and Ludendorff to supreme command. Their predecessor, Erich von Falkenhayn, warned him, "If your Majesty takes Hindenburg and Ludendorff, then your Majesty will cease to be Kaiser." And afterwards Wilhelm, as his biographer Lamar Cecil has noted, "no longer played even the already nominal role he had previously." *Wilhelm II*, 2 vols. (Chapel Hill: University of North Carolina Press, 1989), 2: 237–38.

36. *New York Times*, September 29, 1916.

37. See Robert Lansing to Wilson, September 30, 1916, in *PWW*, 38: 313.

38. *New York Times*, September 23, 1916. Other prolabor legislation passed as the election loomed included the Kerm-McGillicuddy Workers Compensation Act and the Keating-Owen Child labor Act.

39. September 29, 1916, in *PWW*, 50: 751.

40. "Words and Deeds," speech at Battle Creek, Michigan, September 30, 1916, in Roosevelt, *Americanism and Preparedness*, 16–35; and *New York Times*, October 1, 1916.

41. *New York Times*, October 3, 1916.

42. TR's father was one of the founder members of the club, which sponsored a black regiment in the Civil War and would later sponsor another, "Harlem's

Hellfighters," in the Great War. TR had been a member since 1884, but he
had been black-balled in his first attempt to join, largely because his mother's
family members were prominent Confederates and she was a supporter of the
South. He had been persona non grata since 1912, and his portrait had been
consigned to the basement.

43. *New York Times*, September 23, 1916.

44. *New York Times*, October 4, 1916.

45. *New York Times*, October 8, 1916.

46. *New York Times*, October 9, 1916.

47. *New York Times*, October 11, 1916.

48. *New York Times*, October 15, 1916.

49. "The Square Deal in Industry," speech at Wilkes Barre, Pennsylvania, October
14, 1916, in Roosevelt, *Americanism and Preparedness*, 35–46.

50. *New York Times*, October 22, 1916; Corinne Roosevelt Robinson, *My Brother
Theodore Roosevelt* (New York: Charles Scribner's Sons, 1921), 313.

51. Untitled speech at Denver, Colorado, October 24, 1916, in Roosevelt, *Americanism and Preparedness*, 59–69.

52. TR to Alvin Hert, October 26, 1916, in *TRL*, 8: 1121.

53. October 27, 1916, quoted in Child, *German-Americans in Politics*, 150. This
mirrors the views of Ambassador von Bernstorff.

54. Untitled speech at Chicago, Illinois, October 26, 1916, in Roosevelt, *Americanism and Preparedness*, 69–77.

55. Robinson, *My Brother Theodore*, 314.

56. Oscar King Davis, *Released for Publication: Some Inside Political History of Theodore Roosevelt and His Times 1898–1918* (Boston: Houghton Mifflin, 1925),
450–54.

57. *New York Times*, October 28, 1916.

58. Edward Fuller to Strachey, November 2, 1916, STR/26/3/1j, Strachey
Papers, Parliamentary Archives.

59. *New York Times*, November 4, 1916.

60. "The Soul of the Nation," speech at Cooper Union, New York, November 3,
1916, in Roosevelt, *Americanism and Preparedness*, 77–84.

61. Lodge to TR, March 6, 1917, Reel 224, Series 1, TRP.

62. O'Keefe, *Thousand Deadlines*, 148.

63. Ray Stannard Baker, *Woodrow Wilson: Life and Letters*, 8 vols. (New York:
Greenwood Press, 1968), 6: 296, n. 1.

64. The normally Republican Ohio went narrowly to Wilson, some say because
of the solid support of the Scripps newspaper chain. See Dale E. Zacher, *The
Scripps Newspapers Go to War* (Urbana: University of Illinois Press, 2008). For
an analysis that gives TR credit for keeping Wilson from an even more impressive victory, see John Milton Cooper Jr., "If TR Had Gone Down with the
Titanic: A Look at His Last Decade," in Natalie Naylor, Douglas Brinkley, and
John Allen Gable, eds., *Theodore Roosevelt: Many-Sided American* (Interlaken,
NY: Heart of Lakes, 1992), 507–8.

65. Davis, *Released for Publication*, 454.

66. Quoted in Nathan, "Theodore Roosevelt and the 1916 Election," 74–75.

67. Though the German-American Alliance pledged itself to Hughes and voted
Republican, many of its members stayed at home. And once the country
entered the war four months later, its membership and viability as an organization went into rapid decline. Child, *German-Americans in Politics*, 166.

68. *New York Times*, November 11, 1916. Some people at the time and later accused Roosevelt of consciously scuttling Hughes with his rabid rhetoric to ensure his own nomination in 1920. But even such a critic (at the time) as Taft exonerated TR from this charge. Taft wrote that he did not believe Roosevelt "intentionally defeated Hughes," but it was "a matter of temperament with him" that he could not "shape his arguments to the needs of the campaign, but must gratify his personal desire to say the things that hurt our cause." Nathan, "Theodore Roosevelt and the 1916 Campaign," 73.

69. "The Election," *Metropolitan*, January 1917, quoted in *New York Times*, December 1, 1916.

70. TR to Quentin Roosevelt, November 7, 1916, MS Am 1834, TRP.

71. TR to Wheeler, November 29, 1916, in *TRL*, 8: 1127.

72. TR to White, January 1, 1917, in *TRL*, 8: 1135–37.

73. Rankin to TR, January 30, 1917, Reel 221, Series 1, TRP. For a recent view of Rankin, see James Lopach and Jean Luckowski, *Jeannette Rankin: A Political Woman* (Boulder: University Press of Colorado, 2005).

74. *New York Times*, January 11, 1917.

Chapter 8

1. Rucker to TR, December 10, 1916, Reel 254, Series 1, Theodore Roosevelt Papers, Library of Congress (Hereafter TRP).

2. *Weekly Dispatch*, December 10, 1916.

3. For the president and Liberal party, see Laurence W. Martin, *Peace without Victory: Woodrow Wilson and the British Liberals* (New Haven: Yale University Press, 1958).

4. House to Wilson, December 3, 1916, in Arthur Link, ed., *The Papers of Woodrow Wilson* (Princeton; Princeton University Press, 1979), 40: 133 (Hereafter *PWW*).

5. Joyce Grigsby Williams, *Colonel House and Sir Edward Grey: A Study in Anglo-American Diplomacy* (Lanham, MD: University Press of America, 1984), 111.

6. *New York Times*, January 4, 1917.

7. Lodge to TR, December 21, 1916, Reel 217, Series 1, TRP.

8. Page to Lansing, December 22, 1916, in *PWW*, 40: 319.

9. Godfrey Hodgson, *Woodrow Wilson's Right Hand: The Life of Colonel Edward M. House* (New Haven: Yale University Press, 2006), 132.

10. *Papers Relating to the Foreign Relations of the United States, 1916* (Washington: Government Printing Office, 1925), 101–2, quoted in Kevin J. O'Keefe, *A Thousand Deadlines: The New York Press and American Neutrality, 1914–1917* (The Hague: Martinus Nijhoff, 1972), 158–59.

11. O'Laughlin to TR, December 22, 1916, Reel 218, Series 1, TRP.

12. O'Keefe, *Thousand Deadlines*, 160.

13. Wilson to Lansing, December 21, 1916, quoted in John Milton Cooper Jr., *The Vanity of Power: American Isolationism and the First World War 1914–1917* (Westport, CT: Greenwood, 1969), 134.

14. O'Laughlin to TR, December 22, 1916, Reel 218, Series 1, TRP.

15. Seward W. Livermore, *Politics Is Adjourned: Woodrow Wilson and the War Congress, 1916–1918* (Middletown, CT: Wesleyan University Press, 1966), 11.

16. TR to Strachey, January 1, 1917, in Elting Morison, ed., *The Letters of Theodore Roosevelt*, 8 vols. (Cambridge: Harvard University Press, 1954), 8: 1139 (Hereafter *TRL*).

17. *St Louis Republic*, December 23, 1916.

18. TR to Lee, November 11, 1916, F/1/2/4, Lloyd George Papers, Parliamentary Archive.

19. Wheeler to TR, December 4, 1916, Reel 217, Series 1, TRP.

20. Thomas Ewing to TR, December 6, 1916, Reel 217, Series 1, TRP.

21. *New York Times*, January 4, 1917.

22. Quoted in *New York Times*, January 3, 1917.

23. Quoted in Ruhl F. Bartlett, *The League to Enforce Peace* (Chapel Hill: University of North Carolina Press, 1944), 77.

24. *New York Times*, January 3, 1917.

25. *New York Times*, February 11, 1917.

26. For Selous and TR, see J. Lee Thompson, *Theodore Roosevelt Abroad: Nature, Empire, and the Journey of an American President* (New York: Palgrave Macmillan, 2010).

27. *New York Times*, January 7, 1917.

28. *Outlook*, March 7, 1917, 410–11.

29. David W. Levy, *Herbert Croly of the New Republic: The Life and Thought of an American Progressive* (Princeton, NJ: Princeton University Press, 1985), 231.

30. Martin, *Peace without Victory*, 124–25.

31. *New York Times*, January 23, 1917.

32. *Chicago Tribune*, January 29, 1917.

33. McCormick to TR, January 31, 1917, Reel 221, Series 1, TRP.

34. Quoted in O'Keefe, *Thousand Deadlines*, 165. After seeing Wilson at Shadow Lawn in October, von Bernstorff had assured the press that there would be "no violation of German pledges about submarine warfare. The German Government has promised and the German Government always keeps its promises, everywhere." Quoted in *TRL*, 8: 1139, n. 2.

35. Roberta A. Dayer, "Strange Bedfellows: J. P. Morgan & Co., Whitehall and the Wilson Administration During World War I," *Business History Review* 18, no. 2 (1976): 133.

36. TR to Baker, February 2, 1917; Baker to TR, February 3, 1917, in *TRL*, 8: 1149–50.

37. Devlin, *Too Proud to Fight*, 638.

38. *New York Times*, February 4, 1917.

39. Baker to TR, February 9, 1917, in *TRL*, 8: 1151, n. 1.

40. TR to Lodge, February 12, 1917, in Henry Cabot Lodge and Charles F. Redmond, eds., *Selections from the Correspondence of Theodore Roosevelt and Henry Cabot Lodge*, 2 vols. (New York: Charles Scribner's Sons, 1925), 2: 495.

41. TR to White, February 17, 1917, in *TRL*, 8: 1152–53.

42. TR to Jusserand, February 16, 1917, in *TRL*, 8: 1152.

43. Wood to TR, February 5, 1917, Reel 221, Series 1, TRP.

44. *New York Times*, February 18, 1917.

45. TR to Johnson, February 17, 1917, in *TRL*, 8: 1153–54. For a recent view of La Follette, see Nancy C. Unger, *Fighting Bob La Follette: The Righteous Reformer* (Chapel Hill: University of North Carolina Press, 2000).

46. *New York Times*, March 5, 1917.

47. TR to O'Laughlin, March 8, 1917, in *TRL*, 8: 1161.

48. O'Keefe, *Thousand Deadlines*, 172–75.

49. TR to Kermit Roosevelt, March 1, 1917, MS Am 1541.1, Theodore Roosevelt Collection, Harvard University (Hereafter TRC).

50. Herrick to TR, March 5, 1917, Reel 224, Series 1, TRP. Wilson took the oath privately on Sunday, March 4.

51. Letter to editor dated March 7, 1917, *Baltimore Sun*.

52. TR to Lodge, February 28, 1917, in Lodge, *Correspondence*, 2: 498.

53. Barbara J. Steinson, *American Women's Activism in World War I* (New York: Garland, 1982), 231.

54. *New York Times*, March 5, 1917.

55. *New York Times*, March 6, 1917.

56. *New York Times*, March 16, 1917.

57. TR to Lodge, March 13, 1917, in *TRL*, 8: 1162.

58. Lodge to TR, March 6, 1917, Reel 224, Series 1, TRP.

59. TR to Lodge, March 13, 1917, in Lodge, *Correspondence*, 2: 503.

60. "Liberal Russia," *Metropolitan*, June 1917.

61. Robert B. Bruce, *A Fraternity of Arms: America and France in the Great War* (Laramie: University Press of Kansas, 2003), 71; David French, *The Strategy of the Lloyd George Coalition 1916–1918* (Oxford: Oxford University Press, 1995), 53–55.

62. *New York Times*, March 20, 1917.

63. TR to Baker, March 19, 1917, in *TRL*, 8: 1164.

64. Baker to TR, March 20, 1917, in *TRL*, 8: 1164, n. 2.

65. TR to Baker, March 23, 1917, in *TRL*, 8: 1166.

66. Baker to TR, March 26, 1917, in *TRL*, 8: 1166, n. 1.

67. Wilson to Baker, March 27, 1917, in *PWW*, 41: 478.

68. TR to Lodge, March 22, 1917, in *TRL*, 8: 1165–66.

69. Philip C. Jessup, *Elihu Root*, 2 vols. (New York: Dodd, Mead, 1938), 2: 327.

70. *New York Times*, March 25, 1917.

71. *New York Times*, March 26, 1917.

72. *New York Times*, April 4, 1917.

73. *New York Times*, April 2, 1917.

74. House to Wilson, March 30, 1917, in *PWW*, 41: 501–2.

75. For this see Daniel R. Beaver, *Newton D. Baker and the American War Effort 1917–1919* (Lincoln: Nebraska University Press, 1966), 28–30.

76. John Patrick Finnegan, *Against the Specter of a Dragon: The Campaign for American Preparedness, 1914–1917* (London: Greenwood Press, 1974), 188.

77. *New York Times*, April 4, 1917.

78. John Milton Cooper Jr., *Woodrow Wilson: A Biography* (New York: Alfred A. Knopf, 2009), 384.

79. Grey to TR, April 4, 1917, Reel 227, Series 1, TRP.

80. Roosevelt to Lee, April 8, 1917, in Viscount Lee of Fareham, *"A Good Innings and a Great Partnership: Being the Life Story of Arthur and Ruth Lee,"* 3 vols. (Privately Printed, 1939), 2: 1008.

81. *New York Times*, April 4, 1917.

CHAPTER 9

1. David French, *The Strategy of the Lloyd George Coalition 1916–1918* (Oxford: Oxford University Press, 1995), 60–61.

2. Seward W. Livermore, *Politics Is Adjourned: Woodrow Wilson and the War Congress, 1916–1918* (Middleton, CT: Wesleyan University Press, 1966), 17.

3. TR to O'Lauglin, April 13, 1917, MS Am 1454.26, Theodore Roosevelt Collection, Harvard University (Hereafter TRC).

4. Thomas Brahany Diary, April 10, 1917, in Arthur Link, ed., *The Papers of Woodrow Wilson* (Princeton; Princeton University Press, 1979), 42: 31–32 (Hereafter *PWW*). In a 1919 conversation with the Liberal British journalist A. G. Gardiner during the peace conference, Wilson claimed that in this White House interview he was amazed that TR "wanted to go in command of the First Army, just as a spectacular feat to put himself before the public." Wilson frankly did not think him qualified, "but he wanted to take along a certain number of officers who would advise him and cover up his mistakes!" These were the "best men in the army" and "invaluable for building up the new Army." Wilson added that if he had published the conversation, Roosevelt would simply have denied it, as he did with press stories he had warned reporters he would disavow if published. Edith Benham Diary, January 21, 1919, in *PWW*, 54: 198.

5. House to Wilson, April 10, 1917, in *PWW*, 42: 29.

6. TR to Chamberlain, April 12, 1917, in Elting Morison, ed., *The Letters of Theodore Roosevelt*, 8 vols. (Cambridge: Harvard University Press, 1954), 8: 1170–71 (Hereafter *TRL*). This recitation of their conversation was also reprinted in the April 14, 1917 *New York Times*. In Washington, TR also met with General Joseph Kuhn, president of the War College, and Daniel Willard, Howard Coffin, and Julius Rosenwald, all members of the Council of National Defense. *New York Times*, April 11, 12, 1917.

7. Spring Rice to TR, April 19, 1917, CASR 9/1, Spring Rice Papers, Churchill College Archive, Cambridge.

8. Baker to TR, April 13, 1917, in *PWW*, 42: 56–57.

9. Quentin to Flora Whitney, n.d., Flora Whitney Miller Papers, TRC; TR to Kermit, May 31, 1917, MS Am 1541.1, TRC.

10. For a recent look at the American air forces in the war, see Bert Frandsen, *Hat in the Ring: The Birth of American Air Power in the Great War* (Washington: Smithsonian Books, 2003).

11. TR to Spring Rice, April 16, 1917, Reel 416, Series 4A, Theodore Roosevelt Papers, Library of Congress (Hereafter TRP).

12. Copy of April 28, 1917 statement, Series 1, Reel 230, TRP. For Johnson's statement, also see Corinne Roosevelt Robinson, *My Brother Theodore Roosevelt* (New York: Charles Scribner's Sons, 1921), 328–29.

13. Quoted in A. Lincoln, "My Dear Senator: Letters between Theodore Roosevelt and Hiram Johnson in 1917," *California Historical Society Quarterly* 42, no. 3 (1963): 228.

14. *New York Times*, April 24, 1917.

15. *New York Times*, April 26, 1917.

16. *New York World*, April 29, 1917.

17. Livermore, *Politics Is Adjourned*, 27.

18. Harding to TR, April 30, 1917, Series 1, Reel 230, TRP.

19. Lodge to TR, April 30, 1917, Series 1, Reel 230, TRP.

20. Johnson to TR, May 1, 1917, Series 1, Reel 230, TRP.

21. Longworth to TR, n.d., Series 1, Reel 230, TRP.

22. H. W. Brands, *Traitor to His Class: The Privileged Life and Radical Presidency of Franklin Delano Roosevelt* (New York: Random House, 2008), 105.

23. Daniel R. Beaver, *Newton D. Baker and the American War Effort 1917–1919* (Lincoln: Nebraska University Press, 1966), 43.

24. Wood to TR, May 15, 1917, Series 1, Reel 213, TRP.

25. TR to John Parker, April 10, 1917, in *TRL*, 8: 1169.

26. Baker to TR, May 5, 1917, in *TRL*, 8: 1183–84, n. 3.

27. Alvin Johnson, *Pioneer's Progress: An Autobiography* (New York: Viking Press, 1952), 253.

28. For these and others, see Series 1, Reels 230, 238, TRP.

29. Undated magazine advertisement, Series 1, Reel 230, TRP.

30. Craig Campbell, *Reel America and World War I* (London: McFarland, 1985), 54–55.

31. Colonel W. G. Lyddon, *British War Missions to the United States 1914–1918* (London: Oxford University Press, 1938), 18.

32. *New York Times*, May 2, 1917.

33. Alice Roosevelt Longworth, *Crowded Hours: Reminiscences of Alice Roosevelt Longworth* (London: Charles Scribner's Sons, 1934), 249.

34. H. Paul Jeffers, *Theodore Roosevelt Jr.: The Life of a War Hero* (Novato, CA: Presidio Press, 2002), 87. Joffre was skilled at telling his listeners what they wanted to hear, as this was not exactly the message transmitted to Wilson and others. Patricia O'Toole, *When Trumpets Call: Theodore Roosevelt after the White House* (New York: Simon and Schuster, 2005), 318–19.

35. Robert B. Bruce, *A Fraternity of Arms: America and France in the Great War* (Laramie: University Press of Kansas, 2003), xv, xvi, 37–47.

36. TR to Anna Roosevelt Cowles, May 17, 1917, in *TRL*, 8: 1192.

37. *New York Times*, May 16, 1917.

38. *New York Times*, May 17, 1917.

39. For a recent view of the AEF, see Mark Grotelueschen, *The AEF Way of War: The American Army and Combat in World War I* (New York: Cambridge University Press, 2007).

40. Pershing to TR, May 22, 1917, Series 1, Reel 234, TRP.

41. TR to Pershing, May 20, 1917, in *TRL*, 8: 1192–93.

42. For the fight in Congress, see Livermore, *Politics Is Adjourned*, 15–31. For a persuasive argument that TR's call for a command in Europe was decisive in Wilson's conversion to supporting conscription, see John Whitelaw Chambers II, "Decision for the Draft," *OAH Magazine of History,* October 2002.

43. Wilson to TR, May 19, 1917, Series 1, Reel 234, TRP.

44. May 18, 1917 statement in *PWW*, 42: 324–26.

45. O'Laughlin to TR, May 19, 1917, Series 1, Reel 234, TRP.

46. *New York Times*, May 21, 1917.

47. TR to Kermit Roosevelt, June 18, 1917, Kermit Roosevelt Papers, quoted in Joseph Ornig, *My Last Chance to Be a Boy: Theodore Roosevelt's South American Expedition of 1913–1914* (New York: Stackpole Books, 1994), 219.

48. TR to White, May 5, 1917, quoted in Livermore, *Politics Is Adjourned*, 30.

49. White to TR, May 19, 1917, Series 1, Reel 234, TRP.

50. Harbord to TR, May 22, 1917, Series 1, Reel 234, TRP. For Harbord's recollection of this incident and his view of the war, see his *The American Army in France 1917–1919* (Boston: Little, Brown, 1936).

51. *New York Times*, May 28, 1917.

52. TR to Clemenceau, June 6, 1917, in *TRL*, 8: 1200–1201.

53. Beaver, *Newton D. Baker*, 44–46.

54. For this see David Esposito, "Woodrow Wilson and the Origins of the AEF," *Presidential Studies Quarterly* 19, no. 1 (Winter 1989): 127–40.

55. For the CPI, see Stephen Vaughn, *Holding Fast the Inner Lines: Democracy, Nationalism and the Committee on Public Information* (Chapel Hill: University of North Carolina Press, 1980).

56. For a brief view of this subject, see Jörg Nagler, "Pandora's Box: Propaganda and War Hysteria in the United States during World War I," in Hugh Cecil and Peter Liddle, eds., *Facing Armageddon: The First World War Experienced* (London: Leo Cooper, 1996).

57. Paul L. Murphy, *World War I and the Origin of Civil Liberties in the United States* (New York: W. W. Norton, 1979), 74–77.

58. Livermore, *Politics Is Adjourned*, 33.

59. Quoted in Geoffrey R. Stone, "Mr. Wilson's First Amendment," in John Milton Cooper, ed., *Reconsidering Woodrow Wilson: Progressivism, Internationalism, and Peace* (Washington: Woodrow Wilson Center Press, 2008), 194.

60. Murphy, *World War I and the Origin of Civil Liberties*, 79–80, 98–99; David M. Kennedy, *Over Here: The First World War and American Society* (Oxford: Oxford University Press, 1980), 75.

61. Harry N. Scheiber, *The Wilson Administration and Civil Liberties, 1917–1921* (Ithaca, NY: Cornell University Press, 1960), 22.

62. Rider Haggard to TR, April 28, 1917, Series 1, Reel 230, TRP.

63. For this cooperation, see Michael Simpson, ed., *Anglo-American Naval Relations 1917–1919* (Aldershot: Scolar Press, 1991).

64. David Stevenson, *Cataclysm: The First World War as Political Tragedy* (New York: Basic Books, 2004), 266.

65. Sims to TR, May 29, 1917, Series 3A, Reel 392, TRP. For Sims's naval recollections, see *The Victory at Sea* (Garden City, NY: Doubleday, Page, 1921).

66. Thomas Fleming, *The Illusion of Victory: America in World War I* (New York: Basic Books, 2003), 145.

67. Jusserand to TR, June 22, 1917, Series 1, Reel 238, TRP.

68. Lee to TR, July 25, 1917, Series 1, Reel 241, TRP.

69. Kipling to TR, August 5, 1917, Series 1, Reel 242, TRP.

70. TR to Kermit Roosevelt, May 26, 1917, MS Am 1541.1, TRC.

71. TR to Spring Rice, June 19, 1917, Reel 416, Series 4A, TRP. For TR's letter to Lee, see *TRL*, 8: 1201–3. For the June 20, 1917 letters to Lloyd George and Grey, see MS Am 1541.1, TRC.

72. Mrs. Theodore Roosevelt Jr., *Day Before Yesterday: The Reminiscences of Mrs. Theodore Roosevelt, Jr.* (New York: Doubleday, 1959), 74. For Northcliffe's role as head of the British War Mission, see J. Lee Thompson, *Politicians, the Press, and Propaganda: Lord Northcliffe and the Great War* (London: Associated University Press, 1999), 148–69.

73. Thompson, *Politicians, the Press, and Propaganda*, 149.

74. The insider Lord Beaverbrook's account in *Men and Power 1917–1918* (London: Collins, 1956), 63–64, emphasizes that Lloyd George was considering

bringing Winston Churchill back into the government, a move he believed Northcliffe would bitterly oppose.

75. Longworth, *Crowded Hours*, 253–54. Northcliffe also added his voice to the many who urged TR to tour the front, telling him that it was Lloyd George's constant visits that gave him "his hold over the British people." TR replied that, unlike himself, the Welshman had the power to act, while he could do nothing. "They would give me a great reception and I might buck them up for about one day and a half," he said, but then "they would want to know how soon we were going to have a million men at the front," and about that he would not lie. He would simply be "most damnably in the way." Hermann Hagedorn, *The Bugle That Woke America: The Saga of Theodore Roosevelt's Last Battle for His Country* (New York: John Day, 1940), 147–48.

76. TR to Kermit Roosevelt, July 3, 1917, MS Am 1541.1, TRC.

77. TR to Wood, June 22, 1917, in *TRL*, 8: 1203.

78. Balfour to House, June 28, 1917, Series I, Box 10, House Papers, Sterling Library, Yale University.

79. Northcliffe cabled Balfour concerning this breach of diplomatic etiquette. Northcliffe to Balfour, June 29, 1917, FO 800/209, Public Record Office.

80. William G. McAdoo, *Crowded Years* (Boston: Houghton Mifflin, 1931), 400.

81. Northcliffe to Lady Northcliffe, July 1, 1917, Northcliffe Papers, Harmsworth Archive.

82. Wilson to House, July 21, 1917, quoted in David F. Trask, *The United States in the Supreme War Council: American War Aims and Inter-Allied Strategy, 1917–1918* (Middleton, CT: Wesleyan University Press, 1961), 7–8. In *Over Here: The First World War and American Society* (Oxford: Oxford University Press, 1980), David M. Kennedy argues that Wilson in fact failed to use this economic weapon effectively.

83. McCoy to TR, July 3, 1917, Series 1, Reel 239, TRP.

84. *New York Times*, July 5, 1917.

85. Bruce, *A Fraternity of Arms*, 92–94.

86. *New York Times*, July 6, 1917. One intrepid French tank commander, Lieutenant Begarie, also named his armored behemoth after "Teddy" and sent Roosevelt a series of photographs of the machine overcoming various terrain and obstacles. Series 1, Reel 239, TRP.

87. Mann to TR, July 4, 1917, Series 1, Reel 239, TRP.

88. The spread leaves out cousin Philip, soon an operations officer in the Air Corps.

89. Mrs. Theodore Roosevelt Jr., *Day Before Yesterday*, 76–77.

90. TR to Theodore Roosevelt Jr., July 8, 1917, in *TRL*, 8: 1208.

91. Jeffers, *Theodore Roosevelt Jr.*, 91–92; Edward J. Renehan Jr., *The Lion's Pride: Theodore Roosevelt and His Family in Peace and War* (New York: Oxford University Press, 1998), 136–37.

92. TR to Archibald Roosevelt, July 8, 1917, MS Am 1541.5, TRC.

93. Lee to TR, July 25, 1917, Series 1, Reel 241, TRP.

94. Ruth Lee to Edith Roosevelt, August 16, 1917, Derby Papers, TRC.

95. Robert H. Ferrell, *Woodrow Wilson & World War I, 1917–1921* (New York: Harper and Row, 1985), 111.

96. Fleming, *Illusion of Victory*, 146.

97. Quentin Roosevelt to Flora Whitney, n.d., Flora Whitney Miller Papers, TRC.

98. Jusserand to TR, July 26, 1917, Series 1, Reel 241, TRP.

99. Hagedorn, *Bugle That Woke America*, 141.

100. Street to TR, July 28, 1917, Series 1, Reel 241, TRP.

CHAPTER 10

1. "Correspondence of Theodore Roosevelt and the Secretary of War," *Metropolitan*, August, 1917.

2. TR to Lee, August 17, 1917, in Elting Morison, ed., *The Letters of Theodore Roosevelt*, 8 vols. (Cambridge: Harvard University Press, 1954), 8: 1224–25 (Hereafter *TRL*).

3. W. A. Swanberg, *Citizen Hearst: A Biography of William Randolph Hearst* (New York: Charles Scribner's Sons, 1961), 306.

4. "The Peace of Victory For Which We Strive," *Metropolitan*, July 1917.

5. August 21, 1917 entry, in E. David Cronon, ed., *The Cabinet Diaries of Josephus Daniels 1913–1921* (Lincoln: University of Nebraska Press, 1963), 194.

6. TR to Archibald Roosevelt, October 7, 1917, MS Am 1541.5, Theodore Roosevelt Collection, Harvard University (Hereafter TRC).

7. David Stevenson, *With Our Backs to the Wall: Victory and Defeat in 1918* (Cambridge, MA: Belknap Press, 2011), 25.

8. *New York Times*, September 9, 1917.

9. Eleanor Alexander Roosevelt to Ethel Roosevelt Derby, September 1, 1917, Derby Papers, TRC.

10. TR to Theodore Roosevelt Jr., September 1, 1917, in *TRL*, 8: 1230.

11. TR to Archibald Roosevelt Jr., September 1, 1917, MS Am 1541.5, TRC.

12. September 8, 1917, in Edward J. Renehan Jr., *The Lion's Pride: Theodore Roosevelt and His Family in Peace and War* (New York: Oxford University Press, 1998), 160.

13. TR to Quentin Roosevelt, September 1, 1917, MS Am 1834, TRC.

14. *New York Times*, September 14, 1917.

15. TR to Theodore Roosevelt Jr., September 13, 1917, in *TRL*, 8: 1240.

16. TR to Quentin Roosevelt, September 17, 1917, MS Am 1834, TRC.

17. For the manuscript of the appeal, see MS Am 1454.17, TRC.

18. *New York Times*, August 18, September 21, 1917.

19. As printed on Vigilante letterhead in Herman Hagedorn to TR, December 7, 1917, Reel 254, Series 1, Theodore Roosevelt Papers, Library of Congress (Hereafter TRP).

20. Transcript of speech dated September 12, 1917, Regent Theater, Pittsburg, signed A. E. Anderson, Series 1, Reel 246, TRP. TR also used this disease metaphor in *The Foes of Our Own Household*, declaring that "Kultur" could be translated as culture "only in a pathological sense." German "Kultur" was "precisely analogous to a 'culture' of cholera germs." Quoted in Paul Finkelman, "The War on German Language and Culture, 1917–1925," in Hans-Jürgen Schröder, ed., *Confrontation and Cooperation: Germany and the United States in the Era of World War I, 1900–1924* (Oxford: Berg, 1993), 182.

21. TR to Kermit, September 16, 1917, MS Am 1541.1, TRC.

22. *New York Times*, September 21, 1917.

23. TR to Archibald Roosevelt, September 28, 1917, MS Am 1541.4, TRC.

24. *New York Times*, September 25, 1917.

25. Nancy C. Unger, *Fighting Bob La Follette: The Righteous Reformer* (Chapel Hill: University of North Carolina Press, 2000), 254. The Associated Press account sent out further stirred anti–La Follette feeling by quoting him as saying the United States had "no grievance against Germany," when in fact he had declared that the country had suffered serious grievances. Eight months later it admitted the error. Robert L. Morlan, *Political Prairie Fire: The Nonpartisan League, 1915–1922* (Minneapolis: University of Minnesota Press, 1955), 144.

26. *New York Times*, September 29, 1917.

27. TR to Kermit Roosevelt, October 20, 1917, MS Am 1541.1, TRC.

28. Chicago *Tribune*, September 27, 1917, in Daniel R. Beaver, *Newton D. Baker and the American War Effort 1917–1919* (Lincoln: Nebraska University Press, 1966), 88.

29. TR to Archibald Roosevelt, September 28, 1917, MS Am 1541.4, TRC.

30. TR to Munsey, October 4, 1917, in *TRL*, 8: 1243–44.

31. Ibid.

32. "Sam Weller and Mr. Snodgrass," October 2, 1917, in Theodore Roosevelt, *Roosevelt in the Kansas City Star: War-Time Editorials by Theodore Roosevelt* (Boston: Houghton Mifflin, 1921), 9.

33. Ralph Stout, "Introduction," in Roosevelt, *Roosevelt in the Kansas City Star*, xxxiv–xxxv.

34. "Why Cry Over Spilt Milk," October 28, 1917, in Roosevelt, *Roosevelt in the Kansas City Star*, 36–38.

35. Quoted in Seward W. Livermore, *Politics Is Adjourned: Woodrow Wilson and the War Congress, 1916–1918* (Middleton, CT: Wesleyan University Press, 1966), 64.

36. October 5, 1917 entry, in Cronon, ed., *Daniels Diaries*, 216.

37. Stout, "Introduction," in Roosevelt, *Roosevelt in the Kansas City Star*, xli.

38. "Dr. Fitzsimmons's Death," September 17, 1917, in Roosevelt, *Roosevelt in the Kansas City Star*, 1–2.

39. Quoted in Lilian Rixley, *Bamie: Theodore Roosevelt's Remarkable Sister* (New York: David McKay, 1963), 289.

40. TR to Eleanor Alexander Roosevelt, October 20, 1917, in *TRL*, 8: 1245–46.

41. TR to Kermit Roosevelt, October 17, 1917, MS Am 1541.1, TRC.

42. *New York Times*, October 22, 23, 27, 1917.

43. Sylvia Jukes Morris, *Edith Kermit Roosevelt: Portrait of a First Lady* (New York: Coward, McCann and Geoghegan, 1980), 416–17.

44. Robert B. Bruce, *A Fraternity of Arms: America and France in the Great War* (Laramie: University Press of Kansas, 2003), 140–41.

45. "We Are in This War to the Finish," November 2, 1917, in Roosevelt, *Roosevelt in the Kansas City Star*, 43–44.

46. Kipling to TR, November 12, 1917, Reel 252, Series 1, TRP.

47. Dixon to TR, November 17, 1917, Reel 252, Series 1, TRP.

48. "A Difficult Question to Answer," October 18, 1917, in Roosevelt, *Roosevelt in the Kansas City Star*, 23–25.

49. Frank Owen, *Tempestuous Journey: Lloyd George, His Life and Times* (New York: McGraw-Hill, 1954), 430–32.

50. For the American role, see David F. Trask, *The United States in the Supreme War Council: American War Aims and Inter-Allied Strategy, 1917–1918* (Middleton, CT: Wesleyan University Press, 1961).

51. TR to Kermit Roosevelt, November 9, 1917, MS Am 1541.1, TRC.

52. TR to Quentin Roosevelt, November 9, 1917, MS Am 1834, TRC.

53. TR to Bryce, November 26, 1917, in *TRL*, 8: 1252–54. "My war aim," Clemenceau told the chamber of deputies, "is to win." David Stevenson, *French War Aims Against Germany, 1914–1919* (Oxford: Clarendon Press, 1982), 95.

54. Arthur Brisbane to Northcliffe, November 19, 1917, FO 395/86, Public Record Office.

55. Northcliffe to TR, January 11, 1918, Reel 259, Series 1, TRP.

56. *New York World*, November 18, 1917.

57. *New York World*, November 18, 1917, in Livermore, *Politics Is Adjourned*, 64.

58. House Diary, November 16, 1917, Series II, Diary 12, House Papers, Sterling Library, Yale University.

59. Elting E. Morison, *Turmoil and Tradition: A Study of the Life and Times of Henry L. Stimson* (Boston: Houghton Mifflin, 1960), 230–31.

60. *New York Times*, November 19, 1917.

61. TR to Kermit Roosevelt, November 21, 1917, MS Am 1541.1, TRC.

62. Alice Roosevelt Longworth, *Crowded Hours: Reminiscences of Alice Roosevelt Longworth* (London: Charles Scribner's Sons, 1934), 263.

63. TR to Quentin Roosevelt, December 7, 1917, MS Am 1834, TRC.

64. *New York Times*, December 30, 1917.

65. *New York Times*, November 27, 1917.

66. Flora Whitney to Quentin Roosevelt, n.d., Derby Papers, TRC.

67. TR to Theodore Roosevelt Jr., November 29, 1917, in *TRL*, 8: 1256–57. For Kermit's theater, see Charles Townshend, *Desert Hell: The British Invasion of Mesopotamia* (Cambridge: Harvard University Press, 2011); and David R. Woodward, *Hell in the Holy Land: World War I in the Middle East* (Lexington: University of Kentucky Press, 2006).

68. Kermit Roosevelt to Ethel Roosevelt Derby, November 17, 1917, Derby Papers, TRC.

69. TR to Kermit Roosevelt, November 29, 1917, in *TRL*, 8: 1257–58.

70. For the controversy about the use of American troops and American-Allied cooperation in general, see David F. Trask, *The AEF and Coalition Warmaking, 1917–1918* (Lawrence: University Press of Kansas, 1993); and David R. Woodward, *Trial by Friendship: Anglo-American Relations 1917–1918* (Lexington: University of Kentucky Press, 1993).

71. Laurence W. Martin, *Peace without Victory: Woodrow Wilson and the British Liberals* (New Haven: Yale University Press, 1958), 153.

72. House Diary, December 11, 1917, Series II, Diary 12, House Papers, Sterling Library, Yale University.

73. Lansdowne had put a similar proposal before the British cabinet a year earlier and first submitted his letter to the *Times*, but the editor Geoffrey Dawson refused to print it, fearing it would damage the effectiveness of the first meeting of the Supreme War Council. For Dawson's account, see John Evelyn Wrench, *Geoffrey Dawson and Our Times* (London: John Murray, 1955), 156–57.

74. Owen, *Tempestuous Journey*, 441–42.

75. Livermore, *Politics Is Adjourned*, 65.

76. "The Lansdowne Letter," December 2, 1917, in Roosevelt, *Roosevelt in the Kansas City Star*, 60–62.

77. "Being Brayed in a Mortar," December 18, 1917, in Roosevelt, *Roosevelt in the Kansas City Star*, 68–69. Baker had also expressed his "delight" in the "happy confusion" of a nation unaccustomed to think in military terms. Hermann

Hagedorn, *The Bugle That Woke America: The Saga of Theodore Roosevelt's Last Battle for His Country* (New York: John Day, 1940), 143.

78. Livermore, *Politics Is Adjourned*, 66–67.

79. "The President's Message," December 5, 1917, in Roosevelt, *Roosevelt in the Kansas City Star*, 62–64.

80. "Four Bites of a Cherry," December 7, 1917, in Roosevelt, *Roosevelt in the Kansas City Star*, 64–66.

81. TR to Kermit Roosevelt, December 10, 1917, MS Am 1541.1, TRC.

82. TR to Belle Willard Roosevelt, MS Am 1454.46, TRC.

83. Stout to TR, December 15, 1917, Reel 255, Series 1, TRP.

84. "Being Brayed in a Mortar," December 18, 1917, in Roosevelt, *Roosevelt in the Kansas City Star*, 69–71.

85. Brisbane to Wilson, December 18, 1917, in Arthur Link, ed., *The Papers of Woodrow Wilson* (Princeton; Princeton University Press, 1979), 45: 320–21 (Hereafter *PWW*). A Senate investigation the following year revealed that German-American brewers had "loaned" Brisbane $375,000 to purchase the paper without any sort of signed agreement. Swanberg, *Citizen Hearst*, 318–19.

86. Wilson to Tumulty, c. December 18, 1917, in *PWW*, 45: 320.

87. TR to Archibald Roosevelt, January 20, 1918, MS Am 1541.7, TRC.

88. *New York Times*, December 21, 1917.

89. TR to Quentin Roosevelt, December 24, 1917, MS Am 1834, TRC.

90. For her work in the war, see Mrs. Theodore Roosevelt Jr., *Day Before Yesterday: The Reminiscences of Mrs. Theodore Roosevelt, Jr.* (New York: Doubleday, 1959).

91. For this see Carol R. Byerly, *Fever of War: The Influenza Epidemic in the U. S. Army during World War I* (New York: New York University Press, 2005).

92. TR to Quentin Roosevelt, January 18, 1918, MS Am 1834, TRC.

CHAPTER 11

1. TR to Spring Rice, January 2, 1918, Reel 416, Series 4A, Theodore Roosevelt Papers, Library of Congress (Hereafter TRP).

2. Alice Roosevelt Longworth, *Crowded Hours: Reminiscences of Alice Roosevelt Longworth* (London: Charles Scribner's Sons, 1934), 267.

3. David H. Burton, *Cecil Spring Rice: A Diplomat's Life* (London: Fairleigh Dickinson Press, 1990), 205.

4. TR to Lady Spring Rice, March 10, 1918, CASR 10/7, Spring Rice Papers, Churchill College Archive, Cambridge.

5. *New York Times*, January 17, 1918.

6. Perdicaris to TR, January 1, 1918, Series 1, Reel 258, TRP.

7. David Stevenson, *With Our Backs to the Wall: Victory and Defeat in 1918* (Cambridge, MA: Belknap Press, 2011), 25; Keith Neilson, *Strategy and Supply: The Anglo-Russian Alliance, 1914–1917* (London: George Allen and Unwin, 1984), 296.

8. For a detailed and still useful look at the Brest-Litovsk negotiations and settlements, see John W. Wheeler-Bennett, *Brest-Litovsk: The Forgotten Peace, March 1918* (New York: Macmillan, 1956).

9. John Milton Cooper Jr., *Woodrow Wilson: A Biography* (New York: Alfred A. Knopf, 2009), 422–23.

10. Edward J. Renehan Jr., *The Lion's Pride: Theodore Roosevelt and His Family in Peace and War* (New York: Oxford University Press, 1998), 171–72.

11. Edward B. Parsons, "Some International Implications of the 1918 Roosevelt-Lodge Campaign Against Wilson and a Democratic Congress," *Presidential Studies Quarterly* 19, no. 1 (Winter 1989), 142.

12. *New York Times*, January 20, 1918.

13. TR to Kermit Roosevelt, January 20, 1918, MS Am 1541.1, Theodore Roosevelt Collection, Harvard University (Hereafter TRC).

14. TR to Archibald Roosevelt, January 5, 1918, MS Am 1541.7, TRC.

15. *New York Times*, January 20, 1918, quoted in Elting Morison, ed., *The Letters of Theodore Roosevelt*, 8 vols. (Cambridge: Harvard University Press, 1954), 8: 1274, n. 4 (Hereafter *TRL*); and Arthur Link, ed., *The Papers of Woodrow Wilson* (Princeton; Princeton University Press, 1979), 46: 49, n. 1 (Hereafter *PWW*).

16. Quoted in Daniel R. Beaver, *Newton D. Baker and the American War Effort 1917–1919* (Lincoln: Nebraska University Press, 1966), 97.

17. January 22, 23, 1918 entries, in E. David Cronon, ed., *The Cabinet Diaries of Josephus Daniels 1913–1921* (Lincoln: University of Nebraska Press, 1963), 270–71.

18. Press Release, January 21, 1918, in *PWW*, 46: 55–56.

19. *New York Times*, January 22, 1918.

20. *New York Times*, January 23, 1918.

21. A. Lincoln, "My Friend and Champion: Letters between Theodore Roosevelt and Hiram Johnson in 1918," *California Historical Society Quarterly* 48, no. 1 (1969): 21.

22. Carol R. Byerly, *Fever of War: The Influenza Epidemic in the U. S. Army during World War I* (New York: New York University Press, 2005), 58.

23. Alice Longworth, *Crowded Hours*, 268–69; *Cleveland Plain Dealer*, January 23, 1918, quoted in Seward W. Livermore, *Politics Is Adjourned: Woodrow Wilson and the War Congress, 1916–1918* (Middleton, CT: Wesleyan University Press, 1966), 266, n. 7.

24. *Washington Times*, January 24, 1918, quoted in *PWW*, 46: 102, n. 1.

25. Wilson to Brisbane, January 26, 1918, in *PWW*, 46: 102.

26. *New York Times*, January 25, 1918. TR also received an invitation to speak at a Gridiron Club dinner in Washington. This club, made up of the Washington newspaper bureau chiefs, had two rules for its dinners: "Ladies are always present" (they never were present; this meant no bad language) and "No reporters present" (of course they were all newsmen; this meant all remarks were off the record).

27. TR to White, April 4, 1918, in *TRL*, 8: 1305–7.

28. Hays to TR, January 29, 1918, Reel 262, Series 1, TRP.

29. *New York Times*, January 24, 1918.

30. January 25, 1918 entry, in Cronon, *Daniels Diaries*, 272. A war cabinet bill never came to a vote.

31. "Justification of Constructive Criticism," January 28, 1918, in Theodore Roosevelt, *Roosevelt in the Kansas City Star: War-Time Editorials by Theodore Roosevelt* (Boston: Houghton Mifflin, 1921), 93–95.

32. For an incisive view of Baruch, see David M. Kennedy, *Over Here: The First World War and American Society* (Oxford: Oxford University Press, 1980), 129–30.

33. Patricia O'Toole, *When Trumpets Call: Theodore Roosevelt after the White House* (New York: Simon and Schuster, 2005), 325.

34. "Let Uncle Sam Get into the Game," February 5, 1918, in Roosevelt, *Roosevelt in the Kansas City Star*, 102.

35. Robert H. Ferrell, *Woodrow Wilson & World War I, 1917–1921* (New York: Harper and Row, 1985), 48.

36. "The People's War," February 26, 1918, in Roosevelt, *Roosevelt in the Kansas City Star*, 105–9.

37. TR to Quentin Roosevelt, January 27, 1918, in *TRL*, 8: 1276–77.

38. TR to Kermit Roosevelt, January 27, 1918, MS Am 1541.1, TRC.

39. February 2–8, 1918 entries, Edith Kermit Roosevelt Diary, Derby Papers, TRC.

40. Once it was announced he was on the way to recovery, a February 14, 1917 *New York Times* editorial proclaimed that TR had been a "great figure in our national history; he is an inspiring force, a compelling force. The value of his service to the people of the United States during the last three years in arousing them to a sense of the national peril and of their duty is beyond all estimate."

41. Corinne Roosevelt Robinson, *My Brother Theodore Roosevelt* (New York: Charles Scribner's Sons, 1921), 337–38.

42. TR to Quentin Roosevelt, February 16, 1918, Derby Papers, TRC.

43. TR to Kermit Roosevelt, February 18, 1918, in *TRL*, 8: 1285–86.

44. Renehan, *Lion's Pride*, 174.

45. TR to Lee, April 12, 1918, in Viscount Lee of Fareham, *"A Good Innings and a Great Partnership: Being the Life Story of Arthur and Ruth Lee,"* 3 vols. (Privately Printed, 1939), 2: 1011.

46. TR to George V, March 12, 1918, in *TRL*, 8: 1299–1300.

47. David F. Trask, *The United States in the Supreme War Council: American War Aims and Inter-Allied Strategy, 1917–1918* (Middleton, CT: Wesleyan University Press, 1961), 51.

48. "Quit Talking Peace," March 5, 1918, in Roosevelt, *Roosevelt in the Kansas City Star*, 111–13.

49. TR to Kermit Roosevelt, February 18, 1918, in *TRL*, 8: 1285–86.

50. *San Francisco Argonaut*, March 30, 1918.

CHAPTER 12

1. Richard Derby to TR, March 13, 1918, Derby Papers, Theodore Roosevelt Collection, Harvard University (Hereafter TRC). TR wrote to Georges Clemenceau that he was prouder of Archie's Croix de Guerre than he was of being president. H. Paul Jeffers, *Theodore Roosevelt Jr.: The Life of a War Hero* (Novato, CA: Presidio Press, 2002), 98.

2. TR to Archibald Roosevelt, March 13, 1918, MS Am 1541.7, TRC. In another letter four days later, TR commented to Archie, "Well, I guess Peter Dunne [of Mr. Dooley fame] was right when he said that my sons would put <u>my</u> name on the map!" March 17, 1918, MS Am 1541.7, TRC.

3. TR to Kermit, March 17, 1918, MS Am 1541.1, TRC.

4. Greenway to TR, March 19, 1918, Reel 269, Series 1, Theodore Roosevelt Papers, Library of Congress (Hereafter TRP).

5. Edward J. Renehan Jr., *The Lion's Pride: Theodore Roosevelt and His Family in Peace and War* (New York: Oxford University Press, 1998), 193.

6. Greenway to TR, March 19, 1918, Reel 269, Series 1, TRP. TR's old friend Sullivan had died the month before just as the Colonel entered the hospital, and TR consequently was unable to be pall bearer at the funeral. *New York Times*, February 5, 1918.

7. Robert B. Bruce, *A Fraternity of Arms: America and France in the Great War* (Laramie: University Press of Kansas, 2003), 155–56. Besides his recent wounds, Wood continued to suffer the effects of a freak accident from his days as commander in Cuba, when a hanging lamp fell on his head.

8. For the airplane scandal, see Seward W. Livermore, *Politics Is Adjourned: Woodrow Wilson and the War Congress, 1916–1918* (Middleton, CT: Wesleyan University Press, 1966), 125–30. Also see Wilson to Creel, March 30, 1918, in Arthur Link, ed., *The Papers of Woodrow Wilson* (Princeton; Princeton University Press, 1979), 47: 207 (Hereafter *PWW*).

9. TR to Kermit Roosevelt, March 24, 1918, MS Am 1541.1, TRC.

10. TR to Wood, April 16, 1918, in Elting Morison, ed., *The Letters of Theodore Roosevelt*, 8 vols. (Cambridge: Harvard University Press, 1954), 8: 1309 (Hereafter *TRL*).

11. Jeffers, *Theodore Roosevelt Jr.*, 101–2.

12. For "Michael," see David Stevenson, *With Our Backs to the Wall: Victory and Defeat in 1918* (Cambridge, MA: Belknap Press, 2011), 53–68.

13. TR to Belle Willard Roosevelt, February 24, 1918, MS Am 1454.46, TRC.

14. *Daily Mail*, March 23, 1918.

15. John J. Pershing, *My Experiences in the War* (New York: Frederick Stokes, 1931), 1: 356.

16. Bruce, *A Fraternity of Arms*, 191–92.

17. TR to Archibald Roosevelt, March 24, 1918, MS Am 1541.7, TRC.

18. "The Fruits of Our Delay," March 26, 1918, in Theodore Roosevelt, *Roosevelt in the Kansas City Star: War-Time Editorials by Theodore Roosevelt* (Boston: Houghton Mifflin, 1921), 120–22.

19. TR to Kermit Roosevelt, March 11, 1918; TR to Stimson, March 12, 1918, in *TRL*, 8: 1297, 1298.

20. March 31, 1918, in Renehan, *Lion's Pride*, 178.

21. *New York Times*, March 29, 1918. This is also reproduced in William Griffith, ed., *The Roosevelt Policy: Speeches, Letters, and Magazine Articles Dealing with the War, Before and After, and Other Vital Topics* (Honolulu: University Press of the Pacific, 2001), 906–38.

22. *TRL*, 8: 1294, n. 2.

23. TR to White, April 4, 1918, in *TRL*, 8: 1305–7.

24. "Citizens or Subjects?," April 6, 1918, in Roosevelt, *Roosevelt in the Kansas City Star*, 129–32.

25. "Thank Heaven!," April 2, 1918, in Roosevelt, *Roosevelt in the Kansas City Star*, 128–29.

26. Thomas Fleming, *The Illusion of Victory: America in World War I* (New York: Basic Books, 2003), 202.

27. Quentin Roosevelt to Flora Whitney, March 30, 1918, Flora Whitney Miller Papers, TRC.

28. Lockwood to TR, April 3, 1918, Reel 270, Series 1, TRP.

29. TR to Stimson, March 12, 1918, in *TRL*, 8: 1299.

30. TR to Hays, March 26, 1918, in *TRL*, 8: 1305.

31. W. A. Swanberg, *Citizen Hearst: A Biography of William Randolph Hearst* (New York: Charles Scribner's Sons, 1961), 312–13.

32. TR to Poindexter, May 22, 1918, in *TRL*, 8: 1322–23.

33. Whigham to TR, March 21, 1918, Reel 269, Series 1, TRP.

34. Kellogg to TR, April 16, 1918, Reel 272, Series 1, TRP.

35. Hermann Hagedorn, *The Bugle That Woke America: The Saga of Theodore Roosevelt's Last Battle for His Country* (New York: John Day, 1940), 175.

36. For "Georgette," see Stevenson, *With Our Backs to the Wall*, 68–78.

37. Reginald Pound and Geoffrey Harmsworth, *Northcliffe* (London: Cassell, 1959), 630.

38. Stevenson, *With Our Backs to the Wall*, 73.

39. April 20, 1918, in Roosevelt, *Roosevelt in the Kansas City Star*, 140–42. Newton Baker had expressed his "delight" in the "happy confusion" of a nation unaccustomed to think in military terms. Hagedorn, *Bugle That Woke America*, 143.

40. Roosevelt acquiesced in this decision due to local conditions. Ralph Stout, "Introduction," in Roosevelt, *Roosevelt in the Kansas City Star*, xxxix–xl.

41. *Metropolitan*, May 1918.

42. Wood to TR, April 18, 1918, Reel 272, Series 1, TRP.

43. TR to Bryce, May 2, 1918, in *TRL*, 8: 1313–14.

44. Lloyd George to Reading, April 18, 1918, quoted in Frank Owen, *Tempestuous Journey: Lloyd George, His Life and Times* (New York: McGraw-Hill, 1954), 476.

45. House to Wilson, April 9, 1918, in *PWW*, 47: 302–3.

46. The two had been corresponding about this for several months. For Kermit's recollections of war with the British and the AEF, see his *War in the Garden of Eden* (New York: Charles Scribner's Sons, 1919).

47. TR to Belle Willard Roosevelt, April 21, 1918, MS Am 1454.46, TRC.

48. TR to Belle Willard Roosevelt, April 21, 1918, MS Am 1454.46, TRC.

49. TR to Kermit Roosevelt, May 19, 1918, MS Am 1541.1, TRC.

50. Johnson to TR, May 6, 1918, Reel 275, Series 1, TRP.

51. *Kansas City Star*, May 7, 1918.

52. *New York Times*, May 9, 1918.

53. *New York Times*, May 11, 1918.

54. *New York Times*, May 12, 1918.

55. *New York Times*, May 20, 1918.

56. Harry N. Scheiber, *The Wilson Administration and Civil Liberties, 1917–1921* (Ithaca, NY: Cornell University Press, 1960), 22–25.

57. Scheiber, *Wilson and Civil Liberties*, 27–30, 40. Oswald Garrison Villard made a similar charge at the time, writing that if Wilson lost "his great fight for humanity, it will be because he was deliberately silent when freedom of speech and the right of conscience were struck down in America." David M. Kennedy, *Over Here: The First World War and American Society* (Oxford: Oxford University Press, 1980), 89.

58. *New York Times*, May 23, 24, 1918.

59. *New York Times*, June 6, 1918.

60. *New York Times*, June 11, 1918.

61. *New York Times*, May 28, 1918.

62. TR to Archibald Roosevelt, May 23, 1918, MS Am 1541.7, TRC.

63. Livermore, *Politics Is Adjourned*, 135.

64. *New York Times*, May 30, 1918.

65. For this see Stevenson, *With Our Backs to the Wall*, 78–88.

66. Ibid., 85.

67. Jeffers, *Theodore Roosevelt Jr.*, 103–4.

68. Daniel R. Beaver, *Newton D. Baker and the American War Effort 1917–1919* (Lincoln: Nebraska University Press, 1966), 147–48.

69. Stevenson, *With Our Backs to the Wall*, 88.

70. For a brief account of this, see his *War in the Garden of Eden*, 122–24.

71. TR to Kermit Roosevelt, June 2, 1918, MS Am 1541.1, TRC.

72. TR to Stimson, June 5, 1918, in *TRL*, 8: 1337–38.

73. Baker to Wood, June 5, 1918, Reel 279, Series 1, TRP.

74. Wood to TR, June 6, 1918, Reel 279, Series 1, TRP.

75. TR to Wood, July 10, 1918, in *TRL*, 8: 1347–48.

76. John Milton Cooper Jr., *Woodrow Wilson: A Biography* (New York: Alfred A. Knopf, 2009), 430.

77. TR to Stimson, June 5, 1918, in *TRL*, 8: 1337.

78. TR to Taft, June 5, 1918, in *TRL*, 8: 1336–37.

79. George Curnock to Northcliffe, June 14, 1918, Northcliffe Add. Mss., 62205, British Library.

80. Bruce, *A Fraternity of Arms*, 204–6.

81. "The German Horror," May 2, 1918, in Roosevelt, *Roosevelt in the Kansas City Star*, 145–47.

82. *New York Times*, June 11, 1918.

83. *New York Times*, June 12, 1918.

84. *New York Times*, June 20, 1918.

85. Ibid.

86. *New York Times*, June 17, 1918.

87. Quentin Roosevelt to Flora Whitney, June 18, 23, 1918, Flora Whitney Miller Papers, TRC.

88. TR to Quentin Roosevelt, June 19, 1918, MS Am 1541.4, TRC.

89. Quoted in Jeffers, *Theodore Roosevelt Jr.*, 100.

90. TR to Grace Lockwood Roosevelt, June 19, 1918, MS Am 1541.7, TRC.

91. TR to Quentin Roosevelt, June 19, 1918, MS Am 1541.4, TRC.

Chapter 13

1. Quentin Roosevelt to Flora Whitney, July 6, 1918, Flora Whitney Miller Papers, Theodore Roosevelt Collection, Harvard University (Hereafter TRC).

2. Quentin Roosevelt to Flora Whitney, July 11, 1918, Flora Whitney Miller Papers, TRC.

3. Edith Carow Roosevelt Diary, Derby Papers, TRC.

4. Quoted in Marc Wortman, *The Millionaires' Unit: The Aristocratic Flyboys Who Fought the Great War and Invented American Airpower* (New York: Public Affairs, 2006), 218.

5. TR to Ethel Roosevelt Derby, July 12, 1918, in Elting Morison, ed., *The Letters of Theodore Roosevelt*, 8 vols. (Cambridge: Harvard University Press, 1954), 8: 1351 (Hereafter *TRL*).

6. Quoted in H. Paul Jeffers, *Theodore Roosevelt Jr.: The Life of a War Hero* (Novato, CA: Presidio Press, 2002), 105.

7. Thomas Fleming, *The Illusion of Victory: America in World War I* (New York: Basic Books, 2003), 234.

8. Ibid., 234.

9. Patricia O'Toole, *When Trumpets Call: Theodore Roosevelt after the White House* (New York: Simon and Schuster, 2005), 386.

10. Rinehart to TR, July 12, 1918, Reel 284, Series 1, Theodore Roosevelt Papers, Library of Congress (Hereafter TRP).

11. Beveridge to TR, July 15, 1918, Reel 284, Series 1, TRP.

12. "Don't Spread Patriotism Too Thin," *Metropolitan*, July 1918, quoted in *TRL*, 8: 1352, n. 1.

13. Beveridge to TR, July 15, 1918, Reel 284, Series 1, TRP.

14. "At Sagamore Hill," in Edgar Lee Masters, *Selected Poems* (New York: Macmillan, 1925), 51.

15. TR to Pepper, July 2, 1918, in *TRL*, 8: 1345–46.

16. Pershing to TR, n.d., Derby Papers, TRC.

17. *New York Times*, July 18, 1918.

18. Edward J. Renehan Jr., *The Lion's Pride: Theodore Roosevelt and His Family in Peace and War* (New York: Oxford University Press, 1998), 196.

19. TR to Kermit Roosevelt, July 21, 1918, MS Am 1541.1, TRC.

20. TR to Archibald Roosevelt, July 21, 1918, MS Am 1541.7, TRC.

21. Renehan, *Lion's Pride*, 204–5.

22. Taft to TR, July 17, 1918, Reel 284, Series 1, TRP.

23. Wood to TR, July 17, 1918, Reel 284, Series 1, TRP.

24. Stimson to TR, July 28, 1918, Reel 287, Series 1, TRP.

25. Selous to TR, July 27, 1918, Reel 287, Series 1, TRP.

26. TR to Clemenceau, July 25, 1918, in *TRL*, 8: 1354–55.

27. Robert Lee Bullard, *Personalities and Reminiscences of the War* (Garden City, NY: Doubleday, Page, 1925), 233.

28. Typed letter extract, dated December 19, 1918, Reel 258, Series 1, TRP. (This is misfiled chronologically with January 1918 material.)

29. Kerry to TR, September 30, 1918, Reel 294, Series 1.

30. A. J. Smith to TR, October 2, 1918, Reel 294, Series 1, TRP.

31. *New York Times*, July 19, 1918.

32. TR to Taft, July 25, 1918, in *TRL*, 8: 1355.

33. *New York Times*, July 23, 1918.

34. Quoted in Sylvia Jukes Morris, *Edith Kermit Roosevelt: Portrait of a First Lady* (New York: Coward, McCann and Geoghegan, 1980), 424.

35. TR to Kermit, July 28, 1918, MS Am 1541.1, TRC.

36. TR to Corinne Roosevelt Robinson, August 3, 1918, in *TRL*, 8: 1355, n. 1. As a tribute to his fallen brother, Kermit edited a volume of the letters, published as *Quentin Roosevelt: A Sketch with Letters* (New York: Charles Scribner's Sons, 1921). And in 1928, Ted dedicated his book about American military heroes, *Rank and File: True Stories of the Great War*, to Quentin.

37. TR to Belle Willard Roosevelt, August 11, 1918, MS Am 1454.46, TRC.

38. October 29, 1918, in Renehan, *Lion's Pride*, 204.

39. TR to Edith Wharton, August 15, 1918, in *TRL*, 8: 1363.

40. Taft to TR, July 27, 1918, Reel 287, Series 1, TRP.

CHAPTER 14

1. For this see David Stevenson, *With Our Backs to the Wall: Victory and Defeat in 1918* (Cambridge, MA: Belknap Press, 2011), 105–11.

2. Erich Ludendorff, *My War Memories 1914–1918*, 2 vols. (London: Collins, 1919), 2: 679.

3. TR to Pershing, August 19, 1918, in Elting Morison, ed., *The Letters of Theodore Roosevelt*, 8 vols. (Cambridge: Harvard University Press, 1954), 8: 1363 (Hereafter *TRL*).

4. TR to Bryce, August 7, 1918, in *TRL*, 8: 1358–59.

5. Taft to TR, July 27, 1918, Reel 287, Series 1, Theodore Roosevelt Papers, Library of Congress (Hereafter TRP).

6. TR to Taft, August 15, 26, 1918, in *TRL*, 8: 1362.

7. "Sound Nationalism and Sound Internationalism," August 4, 1918, in Theodore Roosevelt, *Roosevelt in the Kansas City Star: War-Time Editorials by Theodore Roosevelt* (Boston: Houghton Mifflin, 1921), 188–95.

8. Seward W. Livermore, *Politics Is Adjourned: Woodrow Wilson and the War Congress, 1916–1918* (Middleton, CT: Wesleyan University Press, 1966), 210–11.

9. "Senator Lodge's Noble Speech," September 1, 1918, in Roosevelt, *Roosevelt in the Kansas City Star*, 209–10.

10. TR to Kermit Roosevelt, August 29, 1918, MS Am 1541.1, Theodore Roosevelt Collection, Harvard University (Hereafter TRC).

11. *New York Times*, August 27, 1918.

12. *New York World*, August 28, 1918.

13. TR to Kermit Roosevelt, September 8, 1918, MS Am 1541.1, TRC.

14. TR to Lee, September 8, 1918, in *TRL*, 8: 1368–69.

15. Carol Gould, "William Beebe and Theodore Roosevelt," *The Princeton University Library Chronicle*, 65, no. 2 (March 2004): 277–78.

16. Robert H. Ferrell, *America's Deadliest Battle: Meuse-Argonne, 1918* (Lawrence: University Press of Kansas, 2007), 6–8. For another recent view of the battle, see Edward G. Lengel, *To Conquer Hell: The Meuse-Argonne, 1918* (New York: Henry Holt, 2008).

17. Livermore, *Politics Is Adjourned*, 212.

18. TR to Lee, September 8, 1918, in *TRL*, 8: 1368–69.

19. Wood to TR, September 19, 1918, Reel 292, Series 1, TRP.

20. TR to John King, September 6, 1918, in *TRL*, 8: 1367–68.

21. House Diary, August 15, 1918, in Arthur Link, ed., *The Papers of Woodrow Wilson* (Princeton; Princeton University Press, 1979), 49: 267 (Hereafter *PWW*).

22. Joyce Grigsby Williams, *Colonel House and Sir Edward Grey: A Study in Anglo-American Diplomacy* (Lanham, MD: University Press of America, 1984), 122.

23. Kent to Wilson, September 28, 1918, in *PWW*, 51: 147–48.

24. Livermore, *Politics Is Adjourned*, 185.

25. Thomas Fleming, *The Illusion of Victory: America in World War I* (New York: Basic Books, 2003), 284–85.

26. Livermore, *Politics Is Adjourned*, 213.

27. TR to Kermit Roosevelt, September 26, 1918, MS Am 1541.1, TRC.

28. *TRL*, 8: 1394, n. 2.

29. Bullitt Lowry, *Armistice 1918* (Kent, OH: Kent State University Press, 1996), 7.

30. Taft to TR, October 2, 1918, Reel 294, Series 1, TRP.

31. James F. Vivian, "Last Round-Up: Theodore Roosevelt Confronts the Non-Partisan League, October 1918," *Montana: The Magazine of Western History* 36, no. 1 (Winter 1986): 42.

32. TR to Kermit Roosevelt, October 13, 1918, MS Am 1541.1, TRC.

33. Lowry, *Armistice 1918*, 12.

34. Lowry, *Armistice 1918*, 32; David F. Trask, *The United States in the Supreme War Council: American War Aims and Inter-Allied Strategy, 1917–1918* (Middleton, CT: Wesleyan University Press, 1961), 153.

35. The Allied leaders drew up an eight-point plan that restored the prewar balance of power. Germany and Austria-Hungary on all fronts were required to withdraw their troops from all occupied territory, including Alsace-Lorraine. The final point was that submarine warfare must cease. Lowry, *Armistice 1918*, 12.

36. Fleming, *Illusion of Victory*, 288.

37. "The German Offer. What It Means," *Daily Mail*, October 7, 1918.

38. *Daily Mail*, October 14, 1918.

39. Fleming, *Illusion of Victory*, 288.

40. TR to Hays, October 16, 1918, in *TRL*, 8: 1375–76.

41. "War Aims and Peace Proposals," October 12, 1918, in Roosevelt, *Roosevelt in the Kansas City Star*, 226–29.

42. *New York Times*, October 16, 1918; TR to Kermit Roosevelt, October 20, 1918, MS Am 1541.1, TRC.

43. TR to Kermit Roosevelt, October 13, 1918, MS Am 1541.1, TRC.

44. Lowry, *Armistice 1918*, 34; Trask, *United States and the Supreme War Council*, 156.

45. House Diary, October 15, 1918, in *PWW*, 51: 340–41.

46. Lowry, *Armistice 1918*; Fleming, *Illusion of Victory*, 290.

47. *Daily Mail*, October 16, 1918.

48. TR to Kermit Roosevelt, October 20, 1918, MS Am 1541.1, TRC.

49. *New York Times*, October 18, 1918.

50. Mrs. Theodore Roosevelt Jr., *Day Before Yesterday: The Reminiscences of Mrs. Theodore Roosevelt, Jr.* (New York: Doubleday, 1959), 109.

51. Lowry, *Armistice 1918*, 37–41.

52. TR to Lodge, October 24, 1918, in *New York Times*, October 25, 1918.

53. "Unconditional Surrender," October 26, 1918, in Roosevelt, *Roosevelt in the Kansas City Star*, 239–41.

54. Livermore, *Politics Is Adjourned*, 1; Godfrey Hodgson, *Woodrow Wilson's Right Hand: The Life of Colonel Edward M. House* (New Haven: Yale University Press, 2006), 187.

55. TR to Kermit Roosevelt, October 27, 1918, MS Am 1541.1, TRC.

56. TR to Corinne Roosevelt Robinson, October 27, 1918, in *TRL*, 8: 1383.

57. Sylvia Jukes Morris, *Edith Kermit Roosevelt: Portrait of a First Lady* (New York: Coward, McCann and Geoghegan, 1980), 430.

58. *New York Times*, October 29, 1918.

59. Alice Roosevelt Longworth, *Crowded Hours: Reminiscences of Alice Roosevelt Longworth* (London: Charles Scribner's Sons, 1934), 274.

60. *New York Times*, November 1, 1918.

61. Hart to TR, November 7, 1918, Reel 300, Series 1, TRP.

62. "What Are the Fourteen Points?," October 30, 1918, in Roosevelt, *Roosevelt in the Kansas City Star*, 241–43.

63. *Nation*, November 9, 1918, in James R. Mock, *Censorship 1917* (New York: Da Capo Press, 1972), 193–94.

64. "The Turks Surrender Unconditionally," November 3, 1918, in Roosevelt, *Roosevelt in the Kansas City Star*, 251–53. For the Mudros Armistice with Turkey, see Lowry, *Armistice 1918*, 94–95.

65. Lowry, *Armistice 1918*, 99.

66. H. Paul Jeffers, *Theodore Roosevelt Jr.: The Life of a War Hero* (Novato, CA: Presidio Press, 2002), 111.

67. TR to Kermit Roosevelt, November 3, 1918, MS Am 1541.1, TRC.

68. TR to Belle Willard Roosevelt, November 3, 1918, MS Am 1454.46, TRC.

69. For this see Lowry, *Armistice 1918*, 112.

70. Enclosure in Tumulty to Wilson, November 3, 1918, in *PWW*, 51: 572–73.

71. Fleming, *Illusion of Victory*, 292.

72. *New York Times*, November 7, 1918.

73. "An American Congress," November 18, 1918, in Roosevelt, *Roosevelt in the Kansas City Star*, 265–66.

74. *New York Times*, November 7, 1918.

75. "The League of Nations," November 17, 1918, in Roosevelt, *Roosevelt in the Kansas City Star*, 261. For the development of Foch's points, see Lowry, *Armistice 1918*.

76. Munsey to TR, n.d., Reel 300, Series 1, TRP.

77. Thomas to TR, November 6, 1918, Reel 300, Series 1, TRP.

78. Philip Jenkin to TR, November 7, 1918, Reel 300, Series 1, TRP.

79. William Howland to TR, November 11, 1918, Reel 301, Series 1, TRP.

80. Washburn to TR, November 11, 1918, Reel 301, Series 1, TRP.

81. Captain Ernest Wood to TR, November 11, 1918, Reel 301, Series 1, TRP.

EPILOGUE

1. Quoted in Frederick Wood, *Roosevelt as We Knew Him* (Philadelphia: John C. Winston, 1927), 454.

2. H. Paul Jeffers, *Theodore Roosevelt Jr.: The Life of a War Hero* (Novato, CA: Presidio Press, 2002), 116.

3. Van Valkenberg to TR, November 12, 1918, Reel 301, Series 1, Theodore Roosevelt Papers, Library of Congress (Hereafter TRP).

4. Walker to TR, November 12, 1918, Reel 301, Series 1, TRP.

5. TR to Charles Van Hise, November 15, 1918, in Elting Morison, ed., *The Letters of Theodore Roosevelt*, 8 vols. (Cambridge: Harvard University Press, 1954), 8: 1393–94 (Hereafter *TRL*).

6. TR to Bryce, November 19, 1918, in *TRL*, 8: 1400.

7. TR to Charles Van Hise, November 15, 1918, in *TRL*, 8: 1393–94.

8. TR to George Haven Putnam, November 15, 1918, in *TRL*, 8: 1394–95.

9. TR to Bryce, November 19, 1918, in *TRL*, 8: 1400–401.

10. TR to Arthur Lee, November 19, 1918, in *TRL*, 8: 1396–97.

11. TR to Kipling, November 23, 1918, in *TRL*, 8: 1403–6. TR told Rider Haggard, who he knew to be a friend of Kipling, about his error of omission in a December 6 letter found in *TRL*, 8: 1414.

12. "President Wilson and the Peace Conference," November 26, 1918, in Theodore Roosevelt, *Roosevelt in the Kansas City Star: War-Time Editorials by Theodore Roosevelt* (Boston: Houghton Mifflin, 1921), 272–75.

13. *New York Times*, December 4, 1918, in Arthur Link, ed., *The Papers of Woodrow Wilson* (Princeton; Princeton University Press, 1979), 53: 315–16, n. 4 (Hereafter *PWW*).

14. Grayson Diary, December 4, 1918, in *PWW*, 53: 313–14. Whatever Wilson might have claimed, the Allies, and particularly the British, certainly did not believe that the American army had won the war, but their own efforts. For this see Mark E. Grotelueschen, "The Junior Partner: Anglo-American Military Cooperation in World War I," in Jennifer D. Keene and Michael S. Neiberg, eds. *Finding Common Ground: New Directions in First World War Studies* (Boston: Brill, 2011), 230.

15. "Let Us Have Straightforward Speaking," December 24, 1918, in Roosevelt, *Roosevelt in the Kansas City Star*, 287–89.

16. TR to Lloyd George, December 10, 1918, LG/F/94/3/81, Lloyd George Papers, Parliamentary Record Office; TR to Balfour, December 10, 1918, in *TRL*, 8: 1414–16.

17. TR to Clemenceau, December 10, 1918, Reel 398, Series 3A, TRP.

18. TR to Knox, December 6, 1918, in *TRL*, 8: 1413–14.

19. TR to Knox, December 6, 1918, in *TRL*, 8: 1413–14.

20. Undated speech to Roosevelt Memorial Association, Series E, Box 8, William Allen White Papers, Library of Congress.

21. Sylvia Jukes Morris, *Edith Kermit Roosevelt: Portrait of a First Lady* (New York: Coward, McCann and Geoghegan, 1980), 430–31.

22. *New York Times*, December 26, 1918.

23. Morris, *Edith Roosevelt*, 430–31.

24. TR to Kermit Roosevelt, December 29, 1918, MS Am 1541.1, Theodore Roosevelt Collection, Harvard University (Hereafter TRC).

25. *New York Times*, December 28, 1918.

26. Mrs. Theodore Roosevelt Jr., *Day Before Yesterday: The Reminiscences of Mrs. Theodore Roosevelt, Jr.* (New York: Doubleday, 1959), 118.

27. Morris, *Edith Roosevelt*, 430–31.

28. W. A. Swanberg, *Citizen Hearst: A Biography of William Randolph Hearst* (New York: Charles Scribner's Sons, 1961), 317–320.

29. January 1, 1919 entry, Ethel Roosevelt Derby Diary, Derby Papers, TRC.

30. *New York Times*, January 9, 1919.

31. James E. Amos, *Theodore Roosevelt: Hero to His Valet* (New York: John Day, 1927), 156.

32. "At Sagamore Hill," in Edgar Lee Masters, *Selected Poems* (New York: Macmillan, 1925), 54.

33. Viscount Lee of Fareham, *"A Good Innings and a Great Partnership: Being the Life Story of Arthur and Ruth Lee,"* 3 vols. (Privately Printed, 1939), 2: 758–59.

34. Morton Cohen, ed., *Rudyard Kipling and Rider Haggard: The Record of a Friendship* (London: Hutchinson, 1965), 108–9.

35. *New York Times*, January 9, 1919.

36. *New York Times*, January 8, 1919.

37. *New York Times*, January 8, 1919; Geoffrey Ward, *A First-Class Temperament: The Rise of Franklin Roosevelt* (New York: Harper and Row, 1989), 422. Arthur

Krock, one of the Wilson partisans among the reporters present, described his reaction more charitably as "a kind of spontaneous relaxation." *Memoirs: Sixty Years on the Firing Line* (New York: Funk and Wagnalls, 1968), 109–10.

38. David Lloyd George, *Memoirs of the Peace Conference*, 2 vols. (New Haven: Yale University Press, 1939), 1: 147.

39. Lee of Fareham, *"A Good Innings,"* 2: 759–60; *New York Times*, February 10, 1919.

40. Walter Millis, quoted in John Patrick Finnegan, *Against the Specter of a Dragon: The Campaign for American Preparedness, 1914–1917* (London: Greenwood Press, 1974), 191.

41. *New York Times*, January 7, 1919.

42. Quoted in A. Lincoln, "'My Dear Friend and Champion': Letters between Theodore Roosevelt and Hiram Johnson in 1918," *California Historical Society Quarterly* 47, no. 1 (1989): 34.

43. *New York Times*, February 8, 1919.

44. Robert H. Ferrell, *Woodrow Wilson & World War I, 1917–1921* (New York: Harper and Row, 1985), 117.

45. *New York Times*, February 10, 1919.

Selected Bibliography

Primary Sources

Manuscript Collections Consulted

Asquith Papers, Bodleian Library, Oxford University
Balfour Papers, British Library, London
Carnegie Papers, Library of Congress
Churchill Papers, Churchill College Archive, Cambridge University
Cromer Papers, National Archive and Private Collection, London
Curzon Papers, Asia, Pacific and Africa Collections, British Library, London
Derby Papers, Houghton Library, Harvard University
Flora Whitney Miller Papers, Houghton Library, Harvard University
James R. Garfield Papers, Library of Congress
Kermit Roosevelt Papers, Library of Congress
Kitchener Papers, National Archive, Kew
Lloyd George Papers, Parliamentary Record Office, London
Lord Lee of Fareham Papers, Courtauld Institute, London
Northcliffe Papers, British Library, London
O'Laughlin Papers, Library of Congress
Oscar Straus Papers, Library of Congress
Pinchot Papers, Library of Congress
Root Papers, Library of Congress
Spring Rice Papers, Churchill College Archive, Cambridge University
Strachey Papers, Parliamentary Record Office, London
Taft Papers, Library of Congress
Theodore Roosevelt Collection, Harvard University
Theodore Roosevelt Papers, Library of Congress
White Papers, Library of Congress
Wister Papers, Library of Congress

Newspapers and Periodicals

Baltimore Sun
Daily Mail (London)
Daily News (London)
Harper's Weekly
The Independent
Leslie's Illustrated Weekly

Metropolitan
Milwaukee Journal
The National Review (London)
The New York Evening Post
The New York Times
The New York Tribune
The New York World
The North American Review
Providence Journal
The San Francisco Argonaut
The Spectator (London)
The Times (London)
The Washington Post

Collections of Printed Primary Documents

Abbott, Lawrence, ed. *The Letters of Archie Butt: Personal Aide to President Roosevelt.* Garden City, NY: Doubleday, Page, 1924.

Baker, Ray Stannard. *Woodrow Wilson Life and Letters.* 6 vols. New York: Greenwood Press, 1968.

Brock, Michael and Eleanor, eds. *H. H. Asquith: Letters to Venetia Stanley.* Oxford: Oxford University Press, 1982.

Butt, Archibald. *Taft and Roosevelt: The Intimate Letters of Archie Butt, Military Aide.* 2 vols. Garden City, NY: Doubleday, Doran, 1930.

Cowles, Anna Roosevelt. *Letters from Theodore Roosevelt to Anna Roosevelt Cowles, 1870–1918.* New York: Charles Scribner's Sons, 1924.

Cronon, E. David, ed. *The Cabinet Diaries of Josephus Daniels, 1913–1921.* Lincoln: University of Nebraska Press, 1963.

Ford, Worthington Chauncey, ed. *Letters of Henry Adams.* 2 vols. Boston: Houghton Mifflin, 1930–38.

Griffith, William, ed. *The Roosevelt Policy: Speeches, Letters, and Magazine Articles Dealing with the War, Before and After, and Other Vital Topics.* Vol. 3. Honolulu: University Press of the Pacific, 2001.

Gwynn, Stephen, ed. *The Letters and Friendships of Sir Cecil Spring Rice: A Record.* 2 vols. Boston: Houghton Mifflin, 1929.

Kerr, Joan Paterson. *A Bully Father: Theodore Roosevelt's Letters to His Children.* New York: Random House, 1995.

Lane, Anne W., and Louise Herrick Hall, eds. *The Letters of Franklin K. Lane: Personal and Political.* Boston: Houghton Mifflin, 1922.

Link, Arthur, ed. *The Papers of Woodrow Wilson.* Vols. 30–54. Princeton: Princeton University Press, 1979–1986.

Lodge, Henry Cabot, and Charles F. Redmond, eds. *Selections from the Correspondence of Theodore Roosevelt and Henry Cabot Lodge.* 2 vols. New York: Charles Scribner's Sons, 1925.

Morison, Elting, ed. *The Letters of Theodore Roosevelt.* Vols. 7 and 8. Cambridge, MA: Harvard University Press, 1952 and 1954.

Papers Relating to the Foreign Relations of the United States, 1916. Washington, DC: Government Printing Office, 1925.

Roosevelt, Theodore. *African and European Addresses*. New York: Charles Scribner's Sons, 1910.

———. *A Book Lover's Holiday in the Open*, in *The Works of Theodore Roosevelt, National Edition*. Vol. 3. New York: Charles Scribner's Sons, 1926.

———. *Literary Essays*. New York: Charles Scribner's Sons, 1926.

———. *Roosevelt in the Kansas City Star: War-Time Editorials by Theodore Roosevelt*. Boston: Houghton Mifflin, 1921.

Vincent, John. *The Crawford Papers: The Journals of David Lindsay, Twenty-Seventh Earl of Crawford and Tenth Earl of Balcarres, 1871–1940 during the Years 1892 –1940*. Manchester: Manchester University Press, 1984.

Memoirs and Autobiographies

Abbott, Lawrence F. *Impressions of Theodore Roosevelt*. Garden City, NY: Doubleday, Page, 1919.

Amos, James E. *Theodore Roosevelt: Hero to His Valet*. New York: John Day, 1927.

Asquith, Herbert Henry. *Memories and Reflections, 1852–1927*. Boston: Little Brown, 1928.

Bullard, Robert Lee. *Personalities and Reminiscences of the War*. Garden City, NY: Doubleday, Page, 1925.

Chanler, Margaret Terry. *Autumn in the Valley*. Boston: Little, Brown, 1936.

Davis, Oscar King. *Released for Publication: Some Inside Political History of Theodore Roosevelt and His Times*. Boston: Houghton Mifflin, 1925.

Dawson, Francis Warington. *Opportunity and Theodore Roosevelt*. New York: Honest Truth, 1923.

Grey, Edward. *Twenty-Five Years, 1892–1916*. 2 vols. New York: Frederick A. Stokes, 1925.

Kennet, Kathleen Bruce Young. *Self-Portrait of an Artist: From the Diaries and Memoirs of Lady Kennet*. London: John Murray, 1949.

Krock, Arthur. *Memoirs: Sixty Years on the Firing Line*. New York: Funk and Wagnalls, 1968.

Lee, Arthur Hamilton. *A Good Innings and a Great Partnership: Being the Life Story of Arthur and Ruth Lee*. 3 vols. Privately Printed, 1939.

Lloyd George, David. *Memoirs of the Peace Conference*. 2 vols. New Haven: Yale University Press, 1939.

———. *War Memoirs*. 2 vols. London: Odhams Press, 1939.

Longworth, Alice Roosevelt. *Crowded Hours: Reminiscences of Alice Roosevelt Longworth*. London: Charles Scribner's Sons, 1934.

McAdoo, William G. *Crowded Years*. Boston: Houghton Mifflin, 1931.

O'Leary, Jeremiah A. *My Political Trial and Experiences*. New York: Jefferson, 1919.

Pinchot, Gifford. *Breaking New Ground*. New York: Harcourt, Brace, 1947.

Rinehart, Mary Roberts. *My Story*. New York: Farrar and Rinehart, 1931.

Robinson, Corrine Roosevelt. *My Brother Theodore Roosevelt*. New York: Charles Scribner's Sons, 1921.

Roosevelt, Eleanor Butler. *Day before Yesterday: The Reminiscences of Mrs. Theodore Roosevelt, Jr.* New York: Doubleday, 1959.

Roosevelt, Kermit. *War in the Garden of Eden*. New York: Charles Scribner's Sons, 1919.

Seymour, Charles, ed. *The Intimate Diaries of Colonel House, Volume I: Behind the Political Curtain*. London: Ernest Been, 1926.

Sullivan, Mark. *Our Times*. 6 vols. New York: Charles Scribner's Sons, 1939.

Wood, Frederick S. *Roosevelt as We Knew Him*. Philadelphia: John C. Winston, 1927.

SECONDARY WORKS

Books

Adams, Larry L. *Walter Lippmann*. Boston: Twayne, 1977.

Adams, R. J. Q. *Balfour: The Last Grandee*. London: John Murray, 2007.

———. *Bonar Law*. London: John Murray, 1999.

Asprey, Robert B. *The German High Command at War: Hindenburg and Ludendorff Conduct World War I*. New York: William Morrow, 1991.

Bartlett, Ruhl J. *The League to Enforce Peace*. Chapel Hill: University of North Carolina Press, 1944.

Beaver, Daniel R. *Newton D. Baker and the American War Effort, 1917–1919*. Lincoln: University of Nebraska Press, 1966.

Bourne, J. M. *Britain and the Great War, 1914–1918*. London: Edward Arnold, 1989.

Brands, H. W. *Traitor to His Class: The Privileged Life and Radical Presidency of Franklin Delano Roosevelt*. New York: Random House, 2008.

Brinkley, Douglas. *The Wilderness Warrior: Theodore Roosevelt and the Crusade for America*. New York: HarperCollins, 2009.

Bruce, Robert B. *A Fraternity of Arms: America and France in the Great War*. Laramie: University Press of Kansas, 2003.

Burton, David. *Cecil Spring Rice: A Diplomat's Life*. Madison, NJ: Fairleigh Dickinson University Press, 1990.

———. *Taft, Roosevelt and the Limits of Friendship*. Madison, NJ: Fairleigh Dickinson University Press, 2005.

Byerly, Carol R. *Fever of War: The Influenza Epidemic in the U.S. Army during World War I*. New York: New York University Press, 2005.

Campbell, Craig. *Reel America and World War I*. London: McFarland, 1985.

Caroli, Betty Boyd. *The Roosevelt Women*. New York: Basic Books, 1998.

Cecil, Lamar. *Wilhelm II*. 2 vols. Chapel Hill: University of North Carolina Press, 1996.

Child, Clifton J. *The German-Americans in Politics*. Madison: University of Wisconsin Press, 1939.

Clifford, John Garry. *The Citizen Soldiers: The Plattsburg Training Camp Movement, 1913–1917*. Lexington: University of Kentucky Press, 1972.

Cohen, Morton, ed. *Rudyard Kipling and Rider Haggard: The Record of a Friendship*. London: Hutchinson, 1965.

Cohn, Jan. *Improbable Fiction: The Life of Mary Roberts Rinehart*. Pittsburgh: University of Pittsburgh Press, 1980.

Collin, Richard. *Theodore Roosevelt's Caribbean: The Panama Canal, the Monroe Doctrine, and the Latin American Context*. Baton Rouge: Louisiana State University Press, 1990.

Cooper, John Milton, Jr., ed. *Reconsidering Woodrow Wilson: Progressivism, Internationalism, War, and Peace*. Baltimore: Johns Hopkins University Press, 2008.

———. *The Vanity of Power: American Isolationism and the First World War, 1914–1917*. Westport, CT: Greenwood Press, 1969.

———.*Walter Hines Page: The Southerner as American, 1855–1918.* Chapel Hill: University of North Carolina Press, 1977.

———. *The Warrior and the Priest: Woodrow Wilson and Theodore Roosevelt.* Cambridge, MA: Belknap Press, 1983.

———. *Woodrow Wilson: A Biography.* New York: Alfred A. Knopf, 2009.

Cotton, Edward H. *The Ideals of Theodore Roosevelt.* New York: D. Appleton, 1923.

Cutwright, Paul. *Theodore Roosevelt: The Making of a Conservationist.* Urbana: University of Illinois Press, 1985.

Davis, Allen F. *American Heroine: The Life and Legend of Jane Addams.* New York: Oxford University Press, 1973.

Davis, Calvin DeArmond. *The United States and the Second Hague Peace Conference: American Diplomacy and International Organization, 1899–1914.* Durham, NC: Duke University Press, 1975.

Devlin, Patrick. *Too Proud to Fight: Woodrow Wilson's Neutrality.* New York: Oxford University Press, 1975.

Doerries, Reinhard. *Imperial Challenge: Ambassador Count Bernstorff and German-American Relations, 1908–1917.* Chapel Hill: University of North Carolina Press, 1989.

Dyer, Thomas. *Theodore Roosevelt and the Idea of Race.* Baton Rouge: Louisiana State University Press, 1980.

Ealy, Lawrence O. *Yanqui Politics and the Isthmian Canal.* University Park: Pennsylvania State University Press, 1971.

Elshtain, Jean Bethke. *Jane Addams and the Dream of American Democracy.* New York: Basic Books, 2002.

Esthus, Raymond. *Theodore Roosevelt and the International Rivalries.* Waltham, MA: Ginn-Blaisdell, 1970.

Fabian, Larry L. *Andrew Carnegie's Peace Endowment: The Tycoon, the President and Their Bargain of 1910.* Washington, DC: Carnegie Endowment for Peace, 1985.

Ferrell, Robert H. *America's Deadliest Battle: Meuse-Argonne, 1918.* Lawrence: University Press of Kansas, 2007.

———. *Woodrow Wilson & World War I, 1917–1921.* New York: Harper and Row, 1985.

Finnegan, John Patrick. *Against the Specter of the Dragon: The Campaign for American Preparedness, 1914–1917.* London: Greenwood Press, 1974.

Fleming, Thomas. *The Illusion of Victory: America in World War I.* New York: Basic Books, 2003.

Frandsen, Bert. *Hat in the Ring: The Birth of American Air Power in the Great War.* Washington, DC: Smithsonian Books, 2003.

French, David. *British Economic and Strategic Planning, 1905–1915.* London: Allen and Unwin, 1982.

———. *British Strategy and War Aims, 1914–1916.* London: Allen and Unwin, 1986.

———. *The Strategy of the Lloyd George Coalition, 1916–1918.* Oxford: Oxford University Press, 1995.

Fromkin, David. *The King and the Cowboy: Theodore Roosevelt and Edward the Seventh, Secret Partners.* New York: Penguin, 2008.

Gable, John A. *The Bull Moose Years: Theodore Roosevelt and the Progressive Party.* Port Washington, NY: Kennikat Press, 1978.

Gardner, Joseph L. *Departing Glory; Theodore Roosevelt as Ex-President.* New York: Charles Scribner's Sons, 1973.

Garraty, John A. *Right-Hand Man: The Life of George Perkins.* New York: Harper and Brothers, 1957.

Giffin, Frederick C. *Six Who Protested: Radical Opposition to the First World War.* Port Washington, NY: Kennikat Press, 1977.

Gilbert, Martin. *Winston S. Churchill: The Challenge of War, 1914–1916.* 2 vols. Boston: Houghton Mifflin, 1971.

Gilmour, David. *Curzon.* London: John Murray, 1994.

———. *The Long Recessional: The Imperial Life of Rudyard Kipling.* London: John Murray, 2002.

Gould, Lewis. *Four Hats in the Ring: The 1912 Election and the Birth of Modern American Politics.* Lawrence: University Press of Kansas, 2008.

Greene, Julie. *The Canal Builders.* New York: Penguin, 2009.

Grigg, John. *Lloyd George: From Peace to War, 1912–1916.* Berkeley: University of California Press, 1985.

Grotelueschen, Mark. *The AEF Way of War: The American Army and Combat in World War I.* New York: Cambridge University Press, 2007.

Hagedorn, Hermann. *The Bugle That Woke America: The Saga of Theodore Roosevelt's Last Battle for His Country.* New York: John Day, 1940.

Hazlehurst, Cameron. *Politicians at War July 1914 to May 1915: A Prologue to the Triumph of Lloyd George.* London: Jonathan Cape, 1971.

Hendrick, Burton J. *The Life of Andrew Carnegie.* 2 vols. Garden City, NY: Doubleday, Doran, 1932.

Herwig, Holger. *Germany's Vision of Empire in Venezuela, 1871–1914.* Princeton: Princeton University Press, 1986.

Hodgson, Godfrey. *Woodrow Wilson's Right Hand: The Life of Colonel Edward M. House.* New Haven: Yale University Press, 2006.

Horne, John, and Alan Kramer. *German Atrocities, 1914: A History of Denial.* New Haven: Yale University Press, 2001.

Isenberg, Michael T. *War on Film: The American Cinema and World War I, 1914 –1941.* London: Associated University Press, 1981.

James, David. *Lord Roberts.* London: Hollis and Carter, 1956.

Jeffers, H. Paul. *Theodore Roosevelt, Jr.: The Life of a War Hero.* Novato, CA: Presidio Press, 2002.

Jessup, Philip C. *Elihu Root.* 2 vols. New York: Dodd, Mead, 1938.

Johnson, Alvin. *Pioneer's Progress: An Autobiography.* New York: Viking Press, 1952.

Judd, Denis. *Balfour and the British Empire: A Study in Imperial Evolution.* London: Macmillan, 1968.

Juergens, George. *News from the White House: The Presidential-Press Relationship in the Progressive Era.* Chicago: University of Chicago Press, 1981.

Kazin, Michael. *A Godly Hero: A Life of William Jennings Bryan.* New York: Alfred A. Knopf, 2006.

Kennedy, David M. *Over Here: The First World War and American Society.* Oxford: Oxford University Press, 1980.

Kraft, Barbara. *The Peace Ship: Henry Ford's Pacifist Adventure in the First World War.* New York: Macmillan, 1978.

Krass, Peter. *Carnegie.* Hoboken, NJ: John Wiley and Sons, 2002.

Lane, Jack C. *Armed Progressive: General Leonard Wood.* London: Presidio Press, 1978.

Lansford, Tom. *A "Bully" First Lady: Edith Kermit Roosevelt.* Huntington, NY: Nova History Publications, 2001.

Lee, Hermione. *Edith Wharton*. New York: Alfred A. Knopf, 2007.

Levin, Phyllis Lee. *Edith and Woodrow: The Wilson White House*. New York: Scribner, 2001.

Levy, David W. *Herbert Croly of the New Republic: The Life and Thought of an American Progressive*. Princeton: Princeton University Press, 1985.

Lewinson, Edwin R. *John Purroy Mitchel: The Boy Mayor of New York*. New York: Astra Books, 1965.

Livermore, Seward W. *Politics Is Adjourned: Woodrow Wilson and the War Congress, 1916–1918*. Middletown, CT: Wesleyan University Press, 1966.

Lopach, James, and Jean Luckowski. *Jeannette Rankin: A Political Woman*. Boulder: University Press of Colorado, 2005.

Lowry, Bullitt. *Armistice 1918*. Kent, OH: Kent State University Press, 1996.

Luebke, Frederick. *Bonds of Loyalty: German-Americans and World War I*. DeKalb: Northern University of Illinois Press, 1974.

Marchand, C. Roland. *The American Peace Movement and Social Reform, 1898–1918*. Princeton: Princeton University Press, 1972.

Maurer, Noel, and Carlos Yu. *The Big Ditch: How America Took, Ran, and Ultimately Gave Away the Panama Canal*. Princeton: Princeton University Press, 2011.

McCallum, Jack. *Leonard Wood: Rough Rider, Surgeon, Architect of American Imperialism*. New York: New York University Press, 2006.

Messinger, Gary S. *British Propaganda and the State in the First World War*. Manchester: Manchester University Press, 1992.

Millard, Candace. *River of Doubt: Theodore Roosevelt's Darkest Journey*. New York: Doubleday, 2005.

Miller, Char. *Gifford Pinchot and the Making of Modern Environmentalism*. Washington, DC: Island Press, 2001.

Mock, James R. *Censorship 1917*. New York: Da Capo Press, 1972.

Mombauer, Annika, and Wilhelm Diest, eds. *The Kaiser: New Research on Wilhelm II's Role in Imperial Germany*. Cambridge: Cambridge University Press, 2003.

Monsman, Gerald. *H. Rider Haggard on the Imperial Frontier*. Greensboro, NC: ELT Press, 2006.

Morison, Elting E. *Turmoil and Tradition: A Study of the Life and Times of Henry L. Stimson*. Boston: Houghton Mifflin, 1960.

Morris, Edmund. *Colonel Roosevelt*. New York: Random House, 2010.

Morris, Sylvia Jukes. *Edith Kermit Roosevelt: Portrait of a First Lady*. New York: Coward, McCann and Geoghegan, 1980.

Murphy, Paul L. *World War I and the Origin of Civil Liberties in the United States*. New York: W. W. Norton, 1979.

Naylor, Natalie, Douglas Brinkley, and John Allen Gable, eds. *Theodore Roosevelt: Many-Sided American*. Interlaken, NY: Heart of Lakes Publishing, 1992.

Nevins, Allan. *Henry White: Thirty Years of American Diplomacy*. New York: Harper and Brothers, 1930.

O'Keefe, Kevin J. *A Thousand Deadlines: The New York Press and American Neutrality, 1914–1917*. The Hague: Martinus Nijhoff, 1972.

O'Toole, Patricia. *When Trumpets Call: Theodore Roosevelt after the White House*. New York: Simon and Schuster, 2005.

Ornig, Joseph. *My Last Chance to Be a Boy: Theodore Roosevelt's South American Expedition of 1913–1914*. New York: Stackpole Books, 1994.

Osgood, Robert Endicott. *Ideals and Self-Interest in America's Foreign Relations: The Great Transformation of the Twentieth Century.* Chicago: University of Chicago Press, 1953.

Owen, Roger. *Lord Cromer: Victorian Imperialist, Edwardian Proconsul.* Oxford: Oxford University Press, 2004.

Patterson, David. *Towards a Warless World: The Travail of the American Peace Movement. 1887–1914.* London: Routledge, 1976.

Ponder, Stephen. *Managing the Press: Origins of the Media Presidency, 1897–1933.* New York: St. Martin's Press, 1998.

Preston, Diana. *Lusitania: An Epic Tragedy.* New York: Walker, 2002.

Price, Alan. *The End of the Age of Innocence: Edith Wharton and the First World War.* New York: St. Martin's Press, 1996.

Pringle, Henry. *Theodore Roosevelt: A Biography.* New York: Harcourt, Brace and World, 1931.

Proctor, Ben. *William Randolph Hearst: Final Edition, 1911–1951.* Oxford: Oxford University Press, 2007.

Rappaport, Armin. *The British Press and Wilsonian Neutrality.* Stanford, CA: Stanford University Press, 1951.

Read, James. *Atrocity Propaganda, 1914–1919.* New Haven: Yale University Press, 1941.

Reckner, James R. *Teddy Roosevelt's Great White Fleet.* Annapolis, MD: Naval Institute Press, 1988.

Renehan, Edward J. *John Burroughs: An American Naturalist.* Post Mills, VT: Chelsea Green, 1992.

———. *The Lion's Pride: Theodore Roosevelt and His Family in Peace and War.* New York: Oxford University Press, 1998.

Rose, Kenneth. *King George V.* London: Frank Cass, 1984.

Ross, Stewart Halsey. *Propaganda for War: How the United States Was Conditioned to Fight the Great War of 1914–1918.* London: McFarland, 1996.

Rydell, Robert. *All the World's a Fair: Visions of Empire at American International Expositions, 1876–1916.* Chicago: University of Chicago Press, 1984.

Sanders, M. L., and Philip M. Taylor. *British Propaganda during the First World War.* London: Constable, 1982.

Scheiber, Harry N. *The Wilson Administration and Civil Liberties, 1917–1921.* Ithaca, NY: Cornell University Press, 1960.

Schröder, Hans-Jürgen, ed. *Confrontation and Cooperation: Germany and the United States in the Era of World War I, 1900–1924.* Oxford: Berg, 1993.

Siney, Marion. *The Allied Blockade of Germany, 1914–1916.* Ann Arbor: University of Michigan Press, 1957.

Steinson, Barbara J. *American Women's Activism in World War I.* New York: Garland Publishing, 1982.

Stevenson, David. *Cataclysm: The First World War as Political Tragedy.* New York: Basic Books, 2004.

———. *French War Aims against Germany, 1914–1919.* Oxford: Clarendon Press, 1982.

———. *With Our Backs to the Wall: Victory and Defeat in 1918.* Cambridge, MA: Belknap Press, 2011.

Street, Julian. *The Most Interesting American.* New York: The Century Company, 1915.

Swanberg, W. A. *Citizen Hearst: A Biography of William Randolph Hearst.* New York: Charles Scribner's Sons, 1961.

Taylor, Stephen. *The Mighty Nimrod: A Life of Frederick Courteney Selous, African Hunter and Adventurer, 1851–1917*. London: Collins, 1989.

Teague, Michael. *Mrs. L: Conversations with Alice Roosevelt Longworth*. Garden City, NY: Doubleday, 1981.

Thompson, J. Lee. *Northcliffe: Press Baron in Politics*. London: John Murray, 2000.

———. *Politicians, the Press, and Propaganda: Lord Northcliffe and the Great War*. London: Associated University Press, 1999.

———. *Theodore Roosevelt Abroad: Nature, Empire and the Journey of an American President*. New York: Palgrave Macmillan, 2010.

Tilchin, William. *Theodore Roosevelt and the British Empire*. New York: St. Martin's Press, 1997.

Townshend, Charles. *Desert Hell: The British Invasion of Mesopotamia*. Cambridge, MA: Harvard University Press, 2011.

Trask, David F. *The AEF and Coalition Warmaking, 1917–1918*. Lawrence: University Press of Kansas, 1993.

———. *The United States in the Supreme War Council: American War Aims and Inter-Allied Strategy, 1917–1918*. Middletown, CT: Wesleyan University Press, 1961.

Trevelyan, Laura. *A Very British Family: The Trevelyans and Their World*. London: I. B. Tauris, 2006.

Tucker, Robert W. *Woodrow Wilson and the Great War: Reconsidering America's Neutrality, 1914–1917*. Charlottesville: University of Virginia Press, 2007.

Turner, L. C. F. *Origins of the First World War*. New York: W. W. Norton, 1970.

Unger, Nancy C. *Fighting Bob La Follette: The Righteous Reformer*. Chapel Hill: University of North Carolina Press, 2000.

Vaughn, Stephen. *Holding Fast the Inner Lines: Democracy, Nationalism, and the Committee on Public Information*. Chapel Hill: University of North Carolina Press, 1980.

Vincent, C. Paul. *The Politics of Hunger: The Allied Blockade of Germany, 1915–1919*. Athens: Ohio University Press, 1985.

Watts, Steven. *The People's Tycoon: Henry Ford and the American Century*. New York: Random House, 2006.

Wheeler-Bennett, John W. *Brest-Litovsk: The Forgotten Peace, March 1918*. New York: Macmillan, 1956.

Widenor, William C. *Henry Cabot Lodge and the Search for an American Foreign Policy*. Berkeley: University of California Press, 1980.

Williams, Joyce Grigsby. *Colonel House and Sir Edward Grey: A Study in Anglo-American Diplomacy*. Lanham, MD: University Press of America, 1984.

Wimmel, Kenneth. *Theodore Roosevelt and the Great White Fleet: American Sea Power Comes of Age*. Washington, DC: Brassey's, 1998.

Woodward, David R. *Trial by Friendship: Anglo-American Relations, 1917–1918*. Lexington: University of Kentucky Press, 1993.

Wortman, Marc. *The Millionaires' Unit: The Aristocratic Flyboys Who Fought the Great War and Invented American Airpower*. New York: Public Affairs, 2006.

Articles and Book Chapters

Buchanan, Russell. "Theodore Roosevelt and American Neutrality, 1914–1917." *American Historical Review* 43 (July 1938).

Burroughs, John. "Theodore Roosevelt." *Natural History* 19, no. 1 (January 1919).

Burton, David H. "Theodore Roosevelt and His English Correspondents: A Special Relationship of Friends." *Transactions of the American Philosophical Society, n.s.* 63, pt. 2 (1973).

Chambers, John Whitelaw, II. "Decision for the Draft." *OAH Magazine of History* 17, no. 1 (October 2002).

Collin, Richard H. "Theodore Roosevelt's Visit to New Orleans and the Progressive Campaign of 1914." *Louisiana History* 12, no. 1 (Winter 1971).

Davis, Kenneth S. "No Talent for Subordination: FDR and Josephus Daniels." In Edward J. Marolda, ed., *FDR and the U.S. Navy*. New York: St. Martin's Press, 1998.

Dayer, Roberta A. "Strange Bedfellows: J. P. Morgan & Co., Whitehall and the Wilson Administration during World War I." *Business History Review* 18, no. 2 (1976).

Doerries, Reinhard. "The Politics of Irresponsibility: Imperial Germany's Defiance of United States Neutrality during World War I." In Hans Trefousse, ed., *Germany and America: Essays on Problems of International Relations and Immigration*. New York: Brooklyn College Press, 1980.

Esposito, David M. "Archibald Bulloch Roosevelt, 1894–1979." In Natalie Naylor, Douglas Brinkley, and John Allen Gable, eds., *Theodore Roosevelt: Many-Sided American*. Interlaken, NY: Heart of Lakes Publishing, 1992.

———. "Woodrow Wilson and the Origins of the AEF." *Presidential Studies Quarterly* 19, no. 1 (Winter 1989).

Fiebig-von Hase, Ragnhild. "The Uses of 'Friendship': The 'Personal Regime' of Wilhelm II and Theodore Roosevelt, 1901–1909." In Annika Mombauer and Wilhelm Diest, eds., *The Kaiser: New Research on Wilhelm II's Role in Imperial Germany*. Cambridge: Cambridge University Press, 2003.

Golden, James L. "FDR's Use of the Symbol of TR in the Formation of His Political Persona and Philosophy." In Natalie Naylor, Douglas Brinkley, and John Allen Gable, eds., *Theodore Roosevelt: Many-Sided American*. Interlaken, NY: Heart of Lakes Publishing, 1992.

Gould, Carol. "William Beebe and Theodore Roosevelt." *The Princeton University Library Chronicle* 65, no. 2 (March 2004).

Greene, John Robert. "Theodore Roosevelt and the Barnes Libel Case: A Reappraisal." *Presidential Studies Quarterly* 19, no. 1 (Winter 1989).

Grotelueschen, Mark E. "The Junior Partner: Anglo-American Military Cooperation in World War I." In Jennifer D. Keene and Michael S. Neiberg, eds., *Finding Common Ground: New Directions in First World War Studies*. Boston: Brill, 2011.

Lincoln, A. "My Dear Senator: Letters between Theodore Roosevelt and Hiram Johnson in 1917." *California Historical Society Quarterly* 42, no. 3 (1963).

———. "My Friend and Champion: Letters between Theodore Roosevelt and Hiram Johnson in 1918." *California Historical Society Quarterly* 48, no. 1 (1969).

Meyer, Nathan. "Theodore Roosevelt and the 1916 Election." *The Rocky Mountain Social Science Journal* 5, no. 2 (October 1968).

Miller, Char. "Keeper of His Conscience? Pinchot, Roosevelt, and the Politics of Conservation." In Natalie Naylor, Douglas Brinkley, and John Allen Gable, eds., *Theodore Roosevelt: Many-Sided American*. Interlaken, NY Heart of Lakes Publishing, 1992.

Nagler, Jörg. "Pandora's Box: Propaganda and War Hysteria in the United States during World War I." In Hugh Cecil and Peter Liddle, eds., *Facing Armageddon: The First World War Experienced*. London: Leo Cooper, 1996.

Parsons, Edward B. "Some International Implications of the 1918 Roosevelt-Lodge Campaign against Wilson and a Democratic Congress." *Presidential Studies Quarterly* 19, no. 1 (Winter 1989).

Ricard, Serge. "The Anglo-German Intervention in Venezuela and Theodore Roosevelt's Ultimatum to the Kaiser: Taking a Fresh Look at an Old Enigma." In Serge Ricard and Hélène Cristol, eds., *Anglo-Saxonism in U.S. Foreign Policy: The Diplomacy of Imperialism, 1899–1919.* Aix-en-Provence, France: Publications de l'Université de Provence, 1991.

———. "Foreign Policy Making in the White House: Rooseveltian-Style Personal Diplomacy." In William Tilchin and Charles E. Neu, eds., *Artists of Power: Theodore Roosevelt, Woodrow Wilson, and Their Enduring Impact on U.S. Foreign Policy.* London: Praeger, 2006.

Rofe, J. Simon. "Under the Influence of Mahan: Theodore and Franklin Roosevelt and Their Understanding of American National Interest." *Diplomacy and Statecraft* 19, no. 2 (2008).

Rofe, J. Simon, and John M. Thompson. "'Internationalists in Isolationist Times'— Theodore Roosevelt and Franklin Roosevelt and a Rooseveltian Maxim." *Journal of Transatlantic Studies* 9, no. 1 (March 2011).

Russell, Greg. "Theodore Roosevelt, Geopolitics, and Cosmopolitan Ideals." *Review of International Studies* 32 (2006).

Testi, Arnaldo. "The Gender of Reform Politics: Theodore Roosevelt and the Culture of Masculinity." *The Journal of American History* 81, no. 4 (March 1995).

Wallace, David. "Sagamore Hill: An Interior History." In Natalie Naylor, Douglas Brinkley, and John Allen Gable, eds., *Theodore Roosevelt: Many-Sided American.* Interlaken, NY: Heart of Lakes Publishing, 1992.

Wertheim, Stephen. "The League That Wasn't: American Designs for a Legalist-Sanctionist League of Nations and the Intellectual Origins of International Organization, 1914–1920." *Diplomatic History* 35, no. 5 (November 2011).

INDEX

Printed in the United States of America